An Early History of the Economic Institutions of Europe

An Early History of the Economic Institutions of Europe

by Frederick L. Nussbaum

BeardBooks
Washington, DC

ISBN 1-58798-112-2

Reprinted 2002 by Beard Books, Washington, D.C.

Printed in the United States of America

ECONOMIC EUROPE
1000 A.D.

The area of substantially common economic institutions out of which modern European economic institutions grew

Arab- Byzantine culture (maximum development)

To

THE MEMORY OF

MY FATHER

FREDERICK NUSSBAUM

† 1925

and

MY SISTER

CLARA LOUISE NUSSBAUM

† 1909

PREFACE

I HAVE sought in these pages to appropriate for the purposes of American readers and students the main lines of the synthesis of the economic history of Europe embodied in *Der Moderne Kapitalismus* of Werner Sombart.* Although I have taken with both hands from Professor Sombart's monumental accumulations, in justice to him it must be stated that I have not pretended to limit myself to his materials or to his formulation. The sin of omission, on the other hand, is implicit in my task and apparent on every page.

Sombart's synthesis has a peculiar value for present-day American readers and students. Forced to recognize the involvement of the United States with the European world, they must also recognize that the political units of Europe are not mutually independent and self-determining in the economic sense, as they claim to be in the political sense; that fundamental institutional changes operate across and frequently in disregard of political boundaries. In this book, special pains have been taken to retain and even to emphasize the generalized *gesamtwirtschaftliche* character of Sombart's work. A constant effort has been made to avoid substituting political or technical history for the record of the evolution of the modes and the institutions of economic action, of the ways of getting and spending. Consequently it has been necessary to avoid as much as possible the prevalent fallacy of political history, the constant use of terms with variant content, by the regular and persistent practice of definition. It is hoped that nevertheless the form thus defined in each part and each chapter also *moves* and

* *Der moderne Kapitalismus. Historisch-systematishe Darstellung des gesamteuropaischen Wirtschaftsleben von seinen Anfangen bis zum Gegenwart.* 3 vols. in 6 parts. Munich and Leipzig, 1916–1927.

thus is material for history as well as for theory. No attempt has been made to substitute a survey of recent and present-day conditions for the true function of historical study, the realization of past experience in terms corresponding to our realization of the present.

The manuscript of the book has been read at various stages by a number of economists and economic historians with varying reactions according to their schools of thought, but always with helpful criticism of the very greatest value in a venture of such wide range and complicated character. To Professor Frank H. Knight, Professor Max Handmann, Dr. Witt Bowden, Professor E. P. Cheyney, Professor A. P. Watts and Professor J. D. Magee, I wish to express here my grateful appreciation of their constructive assistance. To Professor Sombart and to his publishers, the firm of Duncker & Humblot, I am deeply grateful for their generous permission to make unrestricted use of the materials of *Der Moderne Kapitalismus.*

To Professor Sombart, I feel a gratitude that goes beyond any sense of personal favor, the gratitude of a remote disciple for the intellectual consequences of a long study of his work, which have permeated my whole outlook on history. My original intention was to extend this preface to include an analytical appreciation of the significance of *Der Moderne Kapitalismus* for the historiography of our day. That venture, however, has grown under my hands beyond the decent limits of a preface and must await another occasion. Meanwhile Professor Talcott Parsons, in his substantial article on Capitalism in Recent German Literature: Sombart and Weber,* has remedied the lack of an intelligent formulation in English of the significance of Sombart's work from the economic point of view.

Whatever is good in this book, to paraphrase Sombart's own expression about his relation to Marx, is not only due to the spirit of *Der Moderne Kapitalismus* but is taken from it. I cannot pre-

* Journal of Political Economy, volumes 36, 37.

tend to have concentrated in this limited space all that is valuable and important in its more than three thousand pages. My purpose will be attained if, in its degree, this summary serves as does the original to open new and significant paths of thought for its readers and especially if it serves to open the path to the work of Sombart himself.

FREDERICK L. NUSSBAUM

Laramie, Wyoming,
January 31, 1933.

TABLE OF CONTENTS

Part III. Early Capitalism

Part IV. Capitalism Dominant

ILLUSTRATIONS, MAPS AND CHARTS

INTRODUCTION

THE PROBLEM OF EUROPEAN ECONOMIC HISTORY

THE PROBLEM OF EUROPEAN ECONOMIC HISTORY

The Problem of History

History is the imaginative reconstruction of past experience upon the basis of vestigial evidence. The creative character of this act of reconstruction imposes upon the historian a problem of abstraction, of defining the entity with which he proposes to deal. Even the biographer, although he can be sure that he has to do with what was once a specimen of the genus *man,* with all or most of the generic characteristics, has to create his character. If he undertakes to write political history, his task is only more complex. Without the assurance of biological identity, he has the problem of establishing the characters and features of the political organism of the time and place, the aggregate of forms through which people of that time and place acted politically. More important still, it is necessary to present that aggregate as having evolved and evolving, undergoing, like biological organisms, growth and decay. This problem is often ignored. For example, it is quite common to see statements that the English state or the French state was encroached upon by the church or by the feudal nobles, as though the state at that time had all the functions and rights that a fully developed modern state has; whereas the fact is that the state as we now conceive it was only just beginning its development and was already encroaching upon the historically established functions of the church and the feudal nobility, and was destined as it grew to absorb practically all of them. The same problem imposes itself on the historian of religion, of art, or of any other phase of human experience.

The Problem of Economic History

The same burden of defining his problem devolves upon the economic historian, even, one may say, in aggravated form. Adjectives, as compared with substantives, have a certain vague indefiniteness. Hence the use of the adjectival expression, "economic history," has given economic historians more than ordinary opportunity to vary in their conceptions of what should be talked about under that category, and, indeed, in what they do talk about. One point of agreement always occurs: man, like all animals, must seek sustenance. Unfortunately, this point of agreement, since it is equally true of the first man and of the last, has no history. Unlike the beasts, however, man's pursuit of sustenance has been, above all, a social fact. He has lived by exchange of goods and by cooperation in their production. It has been a political fact. Men have been compelled to labor for other men. Property is in all economic societies defined by political power; so also are the conditions under which labor is performed. It has been a fact of technique. Man is conspicuously and uniquely a tool-using animal. Over all but about the last one-hundredth of his existence, the tools he left behind him are all that we know of his economic life. It has been a fact of quantity. The amount of goods accumulated and consumed by societies and individuals has varied greatly from time to time. All of these phases of economic life have had historical character, that is to say, evolved in time and space through the familiar cycle of all human and earthly things; birth, growth, maturity, decay and disappearance.

Corresponding to these phases of economic life, several different approaches to the problem of its history have been used in distinguished and significant ways. It was the impressive advance of technique that served as the starting point of Porter's *Progress of the Nation* (1836) and Samuel Smiles's *Lives of the Engineers* (3 vols., 1861–1862). This sort of economic historiography culminated in Arnold Toynbee's *Lectures on the Industrial Revolution*

(1884), which definitely contributed that somewhat fallacious expression to the language.

What we may call the political history of economic life—that is to say, the attitudes and actions of political powers in regard to it—has been the stuff and substance of another important series of works, among which the most important are Bishop Cunningham's *Growth of English Industry and Commerce* (6th ed., 2 vols. in 3, 1915–1921); Levasseur's *Histoire des classes ouvrières et de l'industrie en France avant 1789* (2d ed., 2 vols., 1900–1901), *Histoire des classes ouvrières et de l'industrie en France depuis 1798 à 1870* (2d ed., 1903–1904), and *Histoire du commerce de la France* (2 vols., 1911–1912); and Von Inama-Sternegg's *Deutsche Wirtschaftsgeschichte* (3 vols. in 4, 1879–1901). These works of the last half of the nineteenth century, formulated before the development of the present-day sociological point of view, deal principally with the legal regulation of economic life and the formulation and realization of economic, especially commercial policy by the political powers of the respective states. Without depreciating their importance, it may be said that they are histories of law rather than of economic life.

As a sociological fact, economic life has been portrayed by the sociologists themselves in what they call history, but what it would be more appropriate to call retrospective sociology. One of the most brilliant examples of that category is the *General Economic History* of the great German sociologist, Max Weber (Eng. trans., 1927). In the same category, Karl Bücher's *Entstehung der Volkswirtschaft* (1893 and later editions; translated into English as *Industrial Evolution,* 1897), established the concept of successive stages through which economic life developed. Bücher's "stages" are no longer accepted as he formulated them, but his fundamental idea has had fruitful application in the work of other men, as for example in the *Introduction to Economic History* of Norman S. B. Gras. Strictly speaking, the objective of these writers is not history at all, not the reconstruction of past experience, as it happened, so much as scientific generalization from the elements common to the similar experiences of different peoples.

The evolution of historical and of economic thought, however, permits, if it does not dictate another method. For several decades, historians have been approaching the conception of world-history as a succession of cultures, each with its distinct characters, aims, and values evolving as a distinct entity in time and space. Economists, on their part, have similarly been approaching the concept of economic activity as a set of institutions, evolving as a part of the culture in correspondence with it. From this point of view, economic history is the history of institutions, the social ways of getting and spending, as they evolved in one or several cultures. Such economic history includes technique and legislation as subordinate features of its central problem. It differs from the methods of the retrospective sociologists in that its aim is purely historical, that is to say, the portrayal of a unique evolution rather than the deduction of generalizations from similarities among the several evolutions. Such history, of course, must be genetic. The culture as a whole and the economic institutions in particular are conceived in terms of life and growth, maturity, decay, and disappearance. An essential part of the problem of such history is the changing psychological attitude with which men in the given culture have approached the question of sustenance and profit. Economic life is conceived as a unit among the functions of the organic group in which the men of the culture have developed. Such in brief summary is the method of Professor Werner Sombart in *Der moderne Kapitalismus* (3 vols. in 6, 1916–1927) and of this book, which is largely derived from his work.

The Problem of the Economic History of Europe

As a geographical concept, Europe is a continent, or more accurately, a peninsula of the Eurasian continent extending from the Urals to the Arctic, the Atlantic, and the Mediterranean. As a world-historical concept, it is a social dynamic entity only imperfectly coinciding with the geographical concept. This social entity undoubtedly originated within that peninsula, but by no possible interpretation has it been coincident with it. If a line be drawn from the Adriatic to the mouth of the Elbe with another to cut off the Italian peninsula and most of the Spanish peninsula, a fairly accurate picture of the area in which this beginning social organism appeared will be had. On the other hand, its evolution has carried it far beyond these original bounds, far beyond the bounds of the peninsula as a whole, and indeed to the uttermost bounds of the earth. Australians and Americans are not less identical with the society which produced them for living far from the ancient homes of their culture and of their ancestors. The economic organs of European culture have been especially effective in extending their domination, even into areas where other organs have been quite unable to penetrate, where, more concretely, European political control, religious influence, aesthetic or ethical standards have not gone. From our point of view, then, the Europe whose economic aspect we have to study is more limited in its beginnings than geographical Europe and is world-wide in its ultimate developments.

It is implicit in what has been said that our problem is not to be the cumulative combination of histories of the several states of Europe. The state and capitalism, as complementary aspects of European civilization, have been of the very greatest importance to each other, as we shall see more particularly. But we are not concerned with the economic aspect of the state; our concern with the state is rather with the political aspect of capitalism.[1]

[1] Under the influence of Sombart, we shall habitually refer to the evolving economic society of Europe as "capitalism." The expression will be more specifically defined at a later point. (See p. 61.) Here it is only necessary to say that the connotation intended is not that this society alone used "capital," nor even that the presence of larger amounts of capital in connection with economic activities is its most significant feature. From the standpoint of economic science, capital is always present in any economic activity, and modern economic society differs from earlier societies in that respect only in degree and not in kind.

The Place of European Economic Culture in World History

If European economic society is limited in space, it is also limited in time. Its world-historical relationship and its inheritance or lack of inheritance from other cultures need also to be considered.

Part of the problem suggested by this title will occupy our attention throughout this study, that is to say, the place in world history of European economic society as it was evolving. It is necessary here, however, before entering upon the story of that long and amazing development, to attempt some statement of the general relationship of the economic life of the Europe which we have defined as a social dynamic entity to those which preceded it, immediately and remotely.

This economic Europe was coterminous and briefly contemporary with what may be called the Byzantine-Arab culture. The political form of this culture was dual, as was also its religious form—Christian and Mohammedan, the Eastern Empire and Islam. Conceiving it as a world-historical unity, it extends in time back to the date when the Western barbarism of Rome, mighty in arms, fell under the spell of the renascent cultural force of the peoples whom it had conquered. That is not a period to which a date can be assigned, but we can mark the emergence of the general fact by certain symptoms. One of the clearest is the establishment of the Empire. If it was not until 212 A.D. that Caracalla extended Roman citizenship over the whole empire, if it was not until 285 that Diocletian established the Oriental forms of absolutism to correspond to the substance, if it was not until 325 that Constantine established the New Rome (Constantinople) on the Bosporus, it was implicit in the situation of 52 B.C. that Rome's conquests in the Mediterranean world were too strong, economically and culturally, to be merely her possessions. Eastern religion had long troubled the city by its curious insistence on transcendental experience. Mithraism and Christianity, both Eastern religions, were to conquer the whole Roman world before an internecine duel left one of them supreme and exclusive. Roman youth went to Athens, to Smyrna, and to Alexandria for education. Oriental teachers found their most profitable fields of activity in the West.

When Constantine moved the capital to his new city, he was only recognizing what had long been the fact, that the available sources of power were no longer in the West, but were in the area that, with proper vagueness, we call the eastern Mediterranean.

This Byzantine culture, then, in its economic aspect was geographically coincident with the eastern Mediterranean area. The centers around which Justinian organized his government—and his commercial policy—were Byzantium, Smyrna, Beirut, Antioch, Alexandria. In his governmental activity is reflected vigorous economic life that has no relation whatever to the miseries and terrors of the final decay of the properly Roman culture of the West.

Sancta Sophia, the great church with which he embellished his capital, is the sign of a society that was capable of an enormous surplus production. The codification of the Roman law is the manifestation of a society that had large complexities with which to deal. The aspirations of Justinian for direct contact with China and with India reflect an economic organization that was capable of desiring and of paying for the precious wares of those exotic areas. The introduction of the silkworm illustrates a spirit of enterprise for which there is no exact parallel in the West until the days of Louis XIV. When Rome had declined again to a mere group of villages huddled among the seven hills and the ancient monuments of a departed grandeur, Constantinople had a million inhabitants, who, we may believe, did not live by taking in each other's washing.

This culture, as we have remarked, had a dual political and

religious character. Between 630 and 875 the Arabs established Mohammedan religious and political empire from the East Indies along the southern Mediterranean coast and up to the Pyrenees. The economic interrelations between the two were so close that in our perspective they may be regarded as one. Between the two there were close commercial and financial dealings. Each had a highly developed form of industrial association, the gild, much more thoroughly controlled, however, by government, than the corresponding institution which we shall observe at a later time in Western Europe. Both were marked by a highly developed technique that was a source of amazement to the few Western travelers who saw it before 1000. Both had long-distance commerce, the lines of which extended from China and the East Indies to the raw material areas of Russia, northern Germany, to Italy and Gaul. Both had, apparently, large and adequate supplies of the precious metals. The Arabs reopened the neglected silver mines of Spain. The Greek bezant was the standard coin of the whole Mediterranean world. In the eleventh century, just before the Crusades, the annual revenue of the Byzantine government was almost half a billion dollars.

By that time both were in decline and liable, as declining cultures seem to be, to barbarian invasion. From the East came the Turks, and from the West the Crusaders. The Byzantine outposts in the West, Venice, Amalfi, Genoa, began to turn their faces to the West and to serve the Westerners as they had served the East. It is not our concern here to tell the story of Byzantine and Arab decay, but elsewhere we shall see how between 1095 and 1453 the areas of this older civilization served for the development of the first European colonial empires.

Roman economic organization was displaced in the East by the superior Byzantine-Arab culture; in the West, it merely declined to the vanishing point without having to face the competition of any equivalent organization.

The Europe with which we are concerned was for a significant period linked with this Eastern culture. While Rome was still economically an outpost of the Greek culture, it had conquered Spain, Gaul, and Britain; and these countries within the empire and the Germanic borderlands across the Rhine and the Danube, that is, outside the empire, functioned as colonial areas for the industrially and commercially advanced East. They were sources of raw materials and noncompetitive markets.

The immediate effect of Roman conquest on Gaul was an increase in prosperity that manifested itself in a very considerable increase in population. Urban centers especially became numerous. Industry was well organized in *collegia,* or gilds, and developed especially a capacity for mass production of cheap tunics and cheap pottery. Agriculture was improved by the introduction of the vine and of irrigation. Marseilles was ruined, but Narbonne, Nîmes, Arles, Lyons, Bordeaux, Toulouse, Rouen, and even Paris, owed their beginnings as cities to the stimulus of Roman governmental concentrations, to Roman trade and to the Roman peace. Treves, Cologne, and Mainz served as bases of supply for the great permanent camps of "the two Germanies" and somewhat as bases for the trade with the barbarians across the Rhine.

The most recent authority on the Roman provinces (Chapot, *The Roman World,* Eng. trans., 1928), tells us that, "as regards the economic life of Roman Britain, our sources are remarkably reticent." It appears that Britain, only partly Romanized, remained even more purely colonial than Gaul. Although the network of Roman roads was very dense, they were military rather than primarily commercial. Life remained essentially agricultural without any considerable urban centers. Many rich country houses have been found with artificial heating and several other adaptations to the climate. These were presumably paid for out of the profits of successful business of some sort. Agriculture seems to have been improved by the introduction of the superior Italian techniques. Quantities of cattle were exported. The tin mines were converted into a governmental monopoly, and their productivity and their outlet much improved. Much pottery was also produced.

Gaul and Britain, however, seem not to have been very firmly integrated with the economic life of the empire and were the first to feel the disintegration of the third and fourth centuries. Between cause and effect it is impossible to distinguish, but economic decline and political weakness appear together. By the fourth century, the Franks were able to advance without opposition into wide areas of Belgica that apparently had been abandoned. Britain was only very loosely held from the end of the second century, and when the troops were withdrawn in 407, even less Roman organization was left behind for the Celtic natives and the Germanic invaders to imitate and adopt than in Gaul.

Rome has always remained a regretted loss in the minds of the intensely historical barbarians, our ancestors, who came into its western areas determined to seize its values, to become a part of it, and in the minds of us, who have been puzzled and distressed ever since to see that it vanished as we grasped it. No one ever tries to explain the disappearance of the Persian Empire or of the Egyptian culture, but people are always trying to explain the decline of the Roman Empire. All sorts of "reasons" have been offered, the alleged immorality of the Romans, the decline of fertility, the development of large farms (*latifundia*), operated by slave or unfree labor, etc. From all this plethora of explanations one is driven back to the simple truism that all cultures that have endured a very long time have in the end passed away. Like life and death in biology, the fact remains essentially inexplicable, mysterious. All that is possible is to describe in summary fashion the process of decline.

We have already seen that the decline was a matter of the West. In the East, the Oriental culture remained strong and vital enough to produce great manifestations, the greatest synthesis of law, the code of Justinian, one of the greatest architectural achievements, the church of Sancta Sophia, a new religion of high order, Mohammedanism, and, not least, sheer capacity to survive for another thousand years. What disappeared then, was the culture of the West and the Oriental culture as it was manifested in the West. From the economic point of view, what happened was: (1) a decline in population—towns and countryside alike were deserted; (2) a decline of technique—the art of building, for example, was almost wholly reduced to the very simplest forms; (3) commerce died down to such a point that the arrival of a peddler was the subject of special legislation, as for example, in the early Anglo-Saxon laws; (4) important resources, like the Spanish silver mines, were left unused.

Some of the economic decline is reflected in the attempts to arrest it, such as the famous price edict of Diocletian in 302, the gradual attempt to fix people in their status, to compel shoemakers (and their sons) to remain shoemakers, and the upper middle class (*curiales*) to retain the burdens of tax collection and other governmental duties in the municipalities. It seems fairly obvious that whatever the cause or causes, the burden of Roman government, which had developed as the government of prosperous society, proved to be too heavy for the Western communities when they were no longer prosperous. The functions of government were allowed to fall into the hands of local magnates, senatorials, and churchmen, who had got great land areas under their control. The correspondence of Gregory the Great, as bishop of Rome from 590 to 604, shows how completely that change had taken place in his time. Roman writers from the end of the fourth century tell how men escaped to the barbarians and found life better and easier with them. When the barbarians came in as conquerors, the kind of government they provided—simple government—was adequate for several centuries.

In the history of the economic institutions of modern Europe which is the proper subject of this book, the disappearance of the imperial economic life in the West is perhaps important for its theoretical or philosophical implication rather than for its specific historical connection with those institutions. Valued economic and political institutions, even techniques, can perish although men are seeking to protect and maintain them.

European economic life, as we shall see, "inherited" some important legacies from Rome, notably the Roman law. It was, however, typically by way of rediscovery rather than by way of direct succession that such legacies were realized. By the end of the ninth century, the whole of the great Roman complex of economic forms and ways had disappeared from the European West. In one sense, Western European economic life was far from primitive even then. Techniques such as weaving, cooking, the use of money, the use of iron, continued as a part of the heritage of the human race. In another sense, for us by far the more important sense, the social organization of economic life, which under the Roman Empire attained such high levels, almost completely vanished. In that sense, the economic life of the historic Europe began *de novo* with practically no traditions from the past to determine its forms, its processes, and its evolution. In one word, it was integral with the Western culture.

PART I

PRECAPITALISTIC ECONOMY

CHAPTER I

THE SUSTENANCE ECONOMY

The Character of Economic Life in Western Europe in the Early Middle Ages

In the centuries in which the organization which we know as European civilization was beginning to take form, economic life, like other forms of social life, was very simple. After centuries of decline, the Roman economic system, like the Roman law, Roman learning, Roman art and architecture, had become merely a memory—a glorious memory, which men for centuries tried in vain to recapture. Whatever may have been the reasons for its disappearance, the great system of production and distribution which the Roman roads from England to the Euphrates and the Roman sea routes along and across the Mediterranean had served was gone from the West.

In the eastern part of the empire, the old economic organization had shown itself much stronger and not only maintained itself at a high level for centuries (say, roughly, down to the Crusades), but even evolved in new and significant directions. The great cities, Constantinople, Antioch, Smyrna, were active commercial and industrial centers, while under the Arabs, Bagdad, Damascus, and Alexandria even surpassed the Greek centers. The story of the Byzantine-Arab economy, fascinating as it is, lies outside of the field of this book. It is mentioned here merely to remind the student that while the Europe that now dominates the world was reduced to a condition of primitive simplicity, the eastern Mediterranean lands were relatively and absolutely prosperous and strong. How strange the advanced civilization of the East seemed to

Westerners is illustrated by the stories which Liutprand, the envoy of a tenth-century king of Italy, brought back of the wonders of Constantinople. Of his reception by the emperor, he writes:

> In front of the emperor's throne stood a tree of gilded iron, whose branches were filled with birds of various kinds, made of iron and gilded, which gave forth the different sorts of birds' notes. The throne . . . was guarded on either side by huge lions, I know not whether of metal or wood, but covered with gold, which lashed their tails on the floor and, with open mouth and moving tongue, roared aloud. . . .
>
> At my entrance the lions roared and the birds sang, each after his kind; but I was neither frightened nor even astonished, since I had taken pains to learn beforehand about these things from those who knew about them.[1]

The frightened astonishment, which Liutprand naïvely thinks would have been natural, may safely be regarded as typical of all the society of Western Europe.

Byzantine-Arab industry, strongly organized in gilds or corporations, was technically very advanced and during six centuries possessed an unchallenged ascendancy over the rest of the world. The Eastern Empire kept the monopoly of the international commerce of which the Mediterranean and the Black Sea were the centers. With a great system of land and sea transportation, a vigorous and productive population, its trade reached such heights that during the eleventh century, the imperial treasury had an annual revenue of nearly $500,000,000 in our money. The ports presented a picture of extraordinary activity. The means of exchange were well organized. The bezant was for centuries the only dependable gold coin of Western Europe. Letters of credit were extensively used. Roads and bridges were maintained at a high standard of efficiency.

When the time was ripe, the Westerners were to learn much of the ways of industry and trade from the great Byzantine and Arab centers. For centuries, however, the West was only a rather

[1] Robinson, Readings in European History, I, 341.

poor source of raw materials. Its surplus production was so slight that it offered only very minor attraction to Eastern merchants as a market. It is an error, however, to attribute to the influence of the East that revival of economic energy which becomes apparent in the tenth and eleventh centuries. The "influence" was available in even greater degree while economic life in the West was declining and disintegrating. It was only when new life and productive vigor developed in the West, when it had begun to discover new ideas and invent new institutions for itself, that it began to appropriate the ideas and institutions of the East.

During these centuries, life in the West had become almost purely agricultural. As early as the fourth century, the flourishing cities of the Roman Empire along the Rhine in Gaul, in Britain, and even in Italy, had begun to lose their prosperity. In the succeeding centuries, nearly all of them had become the homes of a purely agricultural population. Mainz, for example, was thus described by Arab travelers about the year 1000. Others had become mere mysterious ruins, strange monuments of a departed glory, as Bath seemed to the wistful Anglo-Saxon poet:

> Windowless is this wall of stone; weirds have shattered it.
> Broken are the burgh-steads, crumbled down the giants' work;
> Fallen down are the roof beams, ruined are the towers.

In 845, Strassburg was described as largely uninhabited. When the empire disappeared from the West, the Italian cities, which had already lost their metropolitan character as industrial and market centers, lost also their functions as centers of government and taxation. The Lombard kings destroyed them when they could. Fredegarius tells us that King Rotharius "commanded that they be called villages"—what they had already become in the economic sense, residences of an agricultural population. The countryside itself was sparsely settled, with wide stretches of waste between scattered villages, hamlets, and manors, where wolves in huge packs preyed on human life. The drainage and irrigation systems of Italy had fallen into decay. "Now the fertile lands, deserted by men and deprived of all cultivation, lie empty in solitude," complained Paul the Deacon, the eighth-century historian of the Lombards. Great forests supplanted human culture over the greater part of Western Europe. Although we have no way of determining, even approximately, the population density of that time, all signs point to a very low figure indeed.

The Village Economy

Under these circumstances, the forms of economic life were, of course, comparatively simple and primitive. Agricultural production was organized in what we have come to call "village economy." The forms of settlement on the land varied considerably among the different peoples who formed the settlements. Slavs had round villages and consolidated holdings. Celts and Normans had homesteads on the undivided holdings. The Germans had irregular villages and scattered holdings in common fields. Roman colonies still existed with stone houses built wall to wall and rectangular fields. Among these diverse external forms, however, we find a common economic idea: production in common for sustenance rather than for profit. The European peoples showed many characteristics of a transition from (or back to) nomadism and pastoral institutions. Their agricultural technique was very low, their groups were still bound together by the idea of blood relationship, and the land was distributed roughly in proportion to the need and the power of each family. The sustenance idea seems to be a mark of this same transition. Just as the pastoral tribe depends upon its flocks and herds for food, clothes, and shelter, so the medieval villager depended upon his primitive agriculture for all his needs. Even the preparation of his raw products for use—industrial production, building, the production of clothes, of tools, of food was an affair of his own household. If a large establishment were needed, his community provided it, as in the case of water mills and smithies. In Domesday Book, Maitland points out, "sometimes the ownership of a mill is so divided that we are tempted to think that this mill has been erected at the cost of the vill." In Bavaria, the mills and the smithies, like the churches and the palaces of the dukes, were protected against disorder and violence by specially severe penalties provided in the law. These public workshops were community property and could be used by each inhabitant in turn as need arose. Very early the smith and the wheelwright appeared in the villages as specialized workers, not, however, as independent craftsmen, but rather as functionaries of the community who performed the necessary smithing and wheelwrighting for their share of the community's agricultural production.

Somewhat more is known of the working of one of these types of village economy than of the others; namely, of the Germanic open-field system, common in western Germany, northern France, and eastern England. It is therefore possible and profitable to examine it somewhat more particularly, but we should keep in mind that this system is not by any means general or even predominant in Europe. What a summary examination of its external features can offer is a notion of the practical working of the sustenance idea, how people in a medieval village were bound together in such a way as was possible only for people who had strong community feeling and a strong sense of mutual interdependence.

The open-field village began to be called by that name very late in its history in order to contrast it with the fenced fields which in the eighteenth and nineteenth centuries at last displaced it. The typical open-field village was a little group of houses, homes of the tillers of the soil, in the midst of, say, fifteen hundred acres of land of various sorts, meadow, marsh, woodland, and, of course, in every case, arable or plowland. Such a village might have thirty families. Each of these thirty families (not each individual) had a set of rights in these fifteen hundred acres, not defined by boundaries as in the case of an American farm, but by dozens, not to say hundreds, of arbitrary prescriptions arising out of the experience of the group of which the family was a part. Only in one part of the fifteen hundred acres could the head of a family stand and say, this is our land up to that line; beyond, it is some other family's land. That was in the arable. This part of the tract was divided into three great fields (in some places, two) cultivated in a set rotation, each field lying fallow once in three years. In each of these three fields, our peasant family would have perhaps ten oblong strips, called acres in England, typically four rods wide and a furlong (furrow-long) in length. Actually it varied greatly in size and shape. The acres of our peasant family were not next to one another but scattered over the whole of the three fields; but it has been noticed that the same families were likely to be neighbors in each part of their holdings. These strips, or acres, were separated from each other only by balks, little ridges of earth. If you fly over England you can still see in some parts the gridiron pattern they make on the countryside. Naturally, such a system was practicable only if every one in the village plowed, sowed, and reaped at the same times and planted the same crop. No one had to puzzle over agricultural college bulletins to decide what crop to plant the next year. It was decided for him by the authority of tradition and custom. The rotation of wheat, oats, and fallow was as fixed as the laws of the Medes and the Persians.

In the other parts of the fifteen hundred acres, our peasant family's rights were even more involved with those of others. In the meadow, after the grass was cut and divided for winter storage, it might pasture so many cows, so many pigs, as it had done for generations. In the woodland, it might cut a certain amount of wood for fuel or for timber for a new hut. All these various rights are different from individual property. They are rights of participating in a common life. If in the other village forms, the external aspect of the organization does not so clearly manifest it, nevertheless the same community feeling existed.

The low technique of agricultural production meant, of course, that the whole community had to devote itself to the raising of food and fibers. For a number of centuries our barbarous ancestors were quite unable to produce a surplus of goods that would have enabled them by way of exchange to participate in the brilliant civilization of Byzantium to the east or of Arab Spain to the south.

It was natural that such a community should be a close and controlled community. Not until comparatively late did the stranger, the "immigrant," have a place in it. This system continued in full vigor for many centuries and only gradually changed as affinity in blood was displaced by propinquity and as inequality in holdings developed an agricultural class that might almost be called an agricultural proletariat, the cotters (crofters, cotsetle) of the English sources. Even after such changes, the mode of agriculture and its spirit persisted over wide areas down to the nineteenth century—a full thousand years from the time of Charlemagne.

The Feudal Economy

The surprising uniformity in this widespread agricultural economic system was also reflected in another set of relations, partly political, partly economic, that we call feudalism. We are not here concerned with the political and constitutional aspects of feudalism, but only with its economic aspect as a form of landlordship. We shall disregard questions like the social status of the agricultural producers—which varied through all possible shades from Roman slavery to the full personal freedom of the English sokeman and the French alodiary—and the forms of tenure, which were even more confused. The economic features of feudalism are separate from these considerations. Whatever his personal status, the agricultural producer had to give a certain part of his product to his lord, he had to serve a certain number of days in the year on the land of his lord; he remained attached to the soil, and his children after him because there was no other place to go. These features of feudalism do not differ substantially from one end of our limited Europe of that day to the other. The common Roman origins of feudal practices, the common racial traditions of the Germanic invaders, the pervasive influence of the church, especially of the monasteries, with their interchange of persons and practices, combined to give the landlord economy throughout the Western European lands an essentially uniform character.

The feudal landlord economy in all lands was a system by which a class of powerful people attained the end of having their need for goods satisfied by the labor of other people in their own establishments. These powerful people were of various sorts: monks, church dignitaries, kings, princes, warriors, and their officers. Their common economic characteristic was leisure. Not even the poorest of them—and some were very poor—would do other than "honorable service," fighting or praying. Indeed, it may be said that his leisure was the economic objective of the feudal landlord. The acquisition of wealth in the modern sense was not the primary objective, certainly not the acknowledged one. The greater lords, whose supply of goods from a county or a duchy far exceeded the needs of a single family, the great abbots and bishops, whose incomes far exceeded the needs of their monks and clergy, used their surpluses to build up courts, to increase their following of knights, to ornament their churches to the greater glory of God, to enrich their own lives with material and spiritual enjoyments, rather than to build an estate as modern men do. Something of the feudal attitude toward wealth remains in modern feeling. A "gentleman" (which is itself a feudal concept) must be rather indifferent to wealth, especially in the form of money. A "debt of honor" is not money owed to the grocer for the necessities of life, but a debt incurred in noneconomic ways. A gentleman, a lord, "lived of his own" and did not have accounts with outside providers. Even in the landlord economy, the need-satisfying principle of the sustenance economy was basic.

Certain external characteristics also gave a distinctive aspect to this economic life. The courts, the monasteries, the cathedral clergy constituted large, unified consumption groups. For these groups there was no correspondingly large organization of production. Apparently technique of management was lacking even in connection with agricultural production. The rich landlord (as for example, the king of England) had to move from manor to manor to enjoy his income of goods. There was no considerable number of professional and independent craftsmen, nor any market system of distribution for satisfying wants. On the whole, the needs of the landlord consumption group were typically satisfied through the products of its own possessions by means of labor which was a part of those possessions, and therefore the landlord economy, like the tenant economy, may be regarded as an individual economy.

The landlord's exploitation of the labor at his command was in general thoroughly involved with the village organization. In part, he took a share of the producing farmer's own product, which was collected for him by the bailiff (*meier, villicus*), who was often one of the farmers, or by subordinate landlords, or, in the case of some great lords, officials who had large subdivisions of his lands in charge. The landlord had also his demesne (inland, *salland, terra dominica*), which he exploited by means of labor due him from his service-bound tenants in amounts roughly corresponding to the peasant's degree of unfreedom. This land in general was not a separate holding, but was just as thoroughly involved in the village economy as the land of the peasant. In the three-field system the lord's demesne, like the peasant's holding, was scattered in strips over the common fields.

Industrial production on the manor was carried on essentially in the same spirit: the landlord's needs were met by the labor supplied by his tenants or by servants in his household. In England, even bread was commonly delivered by peasants, but on the Continent the landlord commonly had his own bakery and brewery, and from a very early date his own mill, or, in some cases, the right of having a certain amount of grain ground or rolled in the village mill as an owed service. Clothes were sometimes delivered "ready to wear," especially in the manors of which monasteries were the landlords (e.g., Prüm, Fulda). More frequently, however, the peasant delivered the cloth, and the sewing was done by the women and maidservants of the households. Occasionally the whole process was carried out in the landlord's household. Fulling and dyeing were generally performed by his own servants. Leather tanning and shoemaking seem also to have been done usually in the household of the landlord. Building involved a whole complex of materials and services. Raw materials came from the lord's own woods, quarries, and fields. Unskilled labor was furnished by the lord's domestics, of whom some were also trained masons or carpenters. The rest of the labor and raw materials was furnished as services owed by the tenants. Naturally such a system was adequate only for the very primitive building of the early Middle Ages. As standards developed, skilled labor had to be secured on special terms. Thus, in the ninth century, the bishop of Salzburg collected master masons, smiths, and carpenters, to build churches. Other skilled labor services were secured as dues for holdings. The wheelwright of South Brent in England had to make a plow and harrow, and to help the peasants keep their wagons in order. The smith of Wermouth in Domesday Book "holds twelve acres for making plowshares." Sometimes the smith and the wheelwright were members of the lord's household.

This simple and personal system of production lasted, with only unessential changes, down to the twelfth or thirteenth century and, in a sense, even down to our own day. Alongside it there developed in the villages the seeds of an independent industrial life, which will be further discussed in connection with the revival of town life. In some places, especially in some of the monasteries, a highly artistic technique manifested itself in beautiful enamels, vestments, tapestries, and "illuminated" manuscripts. The boast of many a lord's daughter was "that in the making of lovely garments she surpassed all the ladies of the region." The Bayeux "tapestry" immortalizes the skill of the duchess of Normandy.

Transport in the early Middle Ages was an affair only of short distances but was organized in the landlord economy, like agricultural and industrial activity, upon the basis of owed services. The scattered holdings of some great lords led them to impose upon certain peasants the obligation of making themselves into professional boatmen and carters, whom we shall encounter as an important branch of the new exchange economy.

This economic organization, so widespread over the Europe of the Germanic peoples, so different in all its external aspects from the organization with which we are familiar, was the external expression of a widely different set of economic notions from those that dominate the mind of modern man. None of us could view a medieval village without wishing at once to reorganize it upon a more profitable basis—redistribute the land in the interest of efficiency, lessen the burdensomeness of the system for the working farmer on the one hand (although we would propose that the number of farmers on a given area should be reduced), and increase the revenue in goods and especially in money for the lord on the other. Such proposals would have been met with a complete lack of understanding on both sides: clever and intelligent men like Sir Thomas More, the great sixteenth century author of the *Utopia,* and even Oliver Goldsmith in the eighteenth century did not understand, or at any rate did not value, the results when such changes were taking place under their own observation.

The reason was the same in both actual cases and in our imaginary offer to some lord of the manor. The object of medieval economic life and the object which concerned More and Goldsmith was not profits but men. In the Middle Ages, this purpose was expressed in an economy the object of which was the nourishment and sustenance of all the individuals in the group. Nourishment and sustenance, it is true, varied from person to person, according to his station in life. If he were a lord, he must have a castle, horses, and above all leisure. If he were a peasant, he toiled as a part of his community and counted upon the community to insure him shelter of a rude kind and food still ruder. After the customary semireligious routine of the crude village agriculture was finished, he never thought of utilizing his wide margin of leisure to improve his economic income. He had worked sufficiently to live according to his station in life. It is not necessary to believe that every peasant or every lord thought or felt in this fashion: the exceptions provided the materials for the fables about the extraordinarily rich and the misers, that so frequently recur in European tales. Even more familiar are the men who deliberately sought to make themselves rich by finding treasure or making gold by alchemic processes: it is hardly necessary to point out that they sought wealth outside the economic nexus.

The standards at which the economic man, that is to say, the generality of men, aimed and the means by which he tried to attain them were empirical, traditional, not rational. "According to his station in life" was the familiar, the customary, the traditional standard. The processes were the familiar, the customary, the traditional village system of agriculture, exploited in equally customary fashion by the lord of the land.

REFERENCES FOR FURTHER READING

General

Sombart, W. Der moderne Kapitalismus (3 vols. in 6 parts; 1916–1927). I, 29–90.

Most of the available literature concerns itself with the physical form of the village and the legal relationships in the manor, rather than with the economic question properly speaking. A convenient and excellent description of an open three-field village is to be found in—

Knight, M. M. Economic History of Europe to the End of the Middle Ages (1926), chap. v.

Interesting general approaches to the problem of the village, distinctly sociological in character, are to be found in—

Weber, Max. General Economic History (tr. F. H. Knight; 1927), Part I, Household, Clan, Village, and Manor.

Cunningham, W. Western Civilization in Its Economic Aspects (2 vols.; 1908).

Thompson, J. W. Economic and Social History of the Middle Ages (1928).

Other Works Containing Useful Material on the Village Economy

Boissonnade, P. Life and Work in Medieval Europe (tr. E. Power; 1927).

Ashley, W. J. English Economic History and Theory (1913).

Cheyney, E. P. Industrial and Social History of England (rev. ed., 1923), chaps. ii, v, vi.

Coulton, G. G. The Medieval Village (1926).

Dopsch, A. Die Wirtschaftsentwicklung der Karolingerzeit. 2 vols. (1921–1922).

Fustel de Coulanges, N. Histoire des institutions politiques de l'ancienne France, tomes III–IV (1887–90).

Gras, N. S. B. An Introduction to Economic History (1922).

Gray, H. F. English Field Systems (1915).

Janssen, J. History of the German People at the Close of the Middle Ages, 16 vols. (English tr., 1896).

Jessopp, A. The Coming of the Friars (1903), chapter on "Village Life in Norfolk Six Hundred Years Ago."

Lipson, E. Introduction to the Economic History of England: The Middle Ages (1915), chaps. i–iii.

Luchaire, A. Social France at the Time of Philip Augustus (Eng. tr., 1912).

Maitland, F. W. Domesday Book and Beyond (2nd ed., 1907).

Meitzen, A. Siedlung und Agrarwesen der West- und Ost-germanen (1895).

Sée, Henri. Les Classes rurales et le régime domanial en France (1901).

Seebohm, F. The English Village Community (1883).

Seignobos, Charles. The Feudal Régime (tr. E. Dow, 1904).

Traill, H. D. Social England (6 vols., 1894–1898).

Usher, A. P. Industrial History of England (1920).

Vinogradoff, P. English Society in the Eleventh Century (1908); Growth of the Manor (1911); Villeinage in England (1892); article, "Village Communities," in Encyclopædia Britannica (11th ed.).

Sources

Bland, Brown, and Tawney, eds. English Economic History: Select Documents (1914).

Translations and Reprints from the Original Sources of European History, vol. III, no. 5.

More, Thomas. The Utopia (Introduction).

Goldsmith, Oliver. The Deserted Village.

CHAPTER II

THE TRANSITION TO EXCHANGE ECONOMY

Definitions and Background

An exchange economy is one in which needs are satisfied by the exchange of products between several economic units. Such exchange may be by barter or by money. Exchange is so universal in the modern world that it is very easy to think of it as a fundamental characteristic of the genus *homo sapiens*. It actually seems that humanity developed the exchange habit very late, and that the distrust with which the trader is regarded by primitive peoples is a reflection of a condition in which peaceful exchange is at best an exceptional practice. Even the Carthaginians, according to Herodotus, still found peoples in the Mediterranean area with whom they could deal only by depositing goods on the shore and withdrawing.

In medieval Europe, of course, the self-contained economy was a reversion to an earlier stage of development under force of circumstances rather than the reflection of a retarded culture. Even the primitive Slavs, Celts, and Germans had known exchange and had learned the use of money from the Romans. The highly developed, centuries-old Roman system of exchange economy did not entirely disappear, but simply declined to a minimal factor in the economic life of the eighth, ninth, and tenth centuries. Thus it is not a question of the establishment or reestablishment, but rather of a redevelopment of exchange.

Three forces seem to have contributed to that redevelopment. (1) The professional traders from the East (Byzantium and Bagdad) exercised then much the same kind of influence upon

Europe as Europe now exercises upon those areas. They were Greeks (more exactly Syrians) and Arabs, who combed especially northern and eastern Europe for high-grade raw materials, such as furs and amber, and exchanged for them the products of Eastern industry, e.g., jewelry and cloth. (2) The surplus production of communities, the occasional surplus production of individuals who benefited by the growing differentiation of holdings, and the surplus production of specialties like fish, honey, wine, poultry, plus an apparent increase in population made exchange a natural and convenient addition to the sustenance economy. (3) Much of the early medieval exchange economy, however, is connected with the landlord system. Landlords early appear as sellers. "So much wine and salt came to our monastery from its estates," says Caesar of Heisterbach, "that it was simply necessary to sell the surplus." The remark illustrates the "sustenance economy." Caesar thought of the function of the monastery's estates as being primarily to supply the monastery, not to furnish an income with which to supply the monastery. Only a surplus created the "necessity" of selling some of the product. The English manors, especially those of the monasteries, from a very early date produced a surplus of wool; the cathedral chapter of Trent collected 14,000 cheeses in the course of a year! It is not surprising then to find frequent regulations for the sale of surplus. The statutes of the monastery of Corby provide that of the garden tithes "what reasonably can be sold, shall be sold for money or for provisions"; the sustenance idea, however, constantly recurs—first supply the need, then sell the surplus.

Even more frequently we find the landlords as buyers, since they alone had money incomes, not only from the sale of their own commodities, but also from their peasants, in the form of money rent, as early as the eighth and ninth centuries. Bobbio, a great monastery in northern Italy, had a money income of about $2,500 (present-day values); Prüm, in Germany, about $1,500; Saint-Germain, near Paris, about $2,500. Another indication that it was the rich (the landlords) who bought, is the character of goods usually listed as merchant's goods: gold, silver, gems, slaves, ivory, and dyes.

The landlords, however, not only turned to the exchange economy themselves. Their desires also constituted a force which ended the individual economy of the peasant. The demand for a money rent itself compelled the peasant to sell his products. He found himself increasingly obliged to use the lord's mill, bakery, and wine press, and thus he was forced into an exchange nexus. The demands of the landlords for special products, agricultural and particularly industrial, forced the peasants to look elsewhere for their supply of the other necessities. From the eleventh century onward the landlord system as such developed tendencies that were destructive to the old individual economy. Money rents were increasingly substituted for rent in kind; the system of management by bailiffs was displaced by a system of leasing, and servile systems of tenure were displaced by free forms. These processes, which were going on all over Western Europe in the twelfth and thirteenth centuries in very much the same way, seem to have been brought about by the conscious desire of the landlords to increase productivity and to be able to apply their increased share as they chose to the purchase of higher-cost goods. They were a phase of the considerable increase in the standard of comfort and luxury noticeable in the Europe of the eleventh and twelfth centuries.

Other aspects of European life in these centuries manifest a decided transformation in the economic effectiveness of the Western peoples: (1) the increase of wealth, especially the increased agricultural and industrial productivity; (2) the increasingly close relations with the Orient, pilgrimages, crusades, commerce; (3) the breaking down of the communal life, especially noticeable in religious institutions, cathedral chapters, monasteries, and abbeys, the offices of which began to be treated as perquisites of noble families; (4) the revival of production of the precious metals, particularly silver, of which the most important mines of the next three or four centuries were brought into operation during the tenth century. The increased supply of silver, by facilitating exchange, facilitated the departure from the simpler individual economy and made possible money rents, money wages, money taxes, money lending, mercenary armies, all of great significance, as we shall see, in the evolution of European economic institutions. Finally, (5) the establishment of towns, which, as presently will be shown, are rather causes than consequences of the development of the exchange economy, provided the entities which were to embody most of these beginnings of exchange economy.

The Rise of the Towns

The exchanges of this developing exchange economy were largely performed by the producers themselves. It was only gradually that commerce was differentiated into a separate occupation. As in all primitive societies, piracy and occasional trading went hand in hand as a rough means of exchange, but in general, in Merovingian and Carlovingian times, the merchant seems to have been a rare person, usually foreign. In the early Middle Ages he was usually a Syrian. Later came the Jews, regarded as foreigners after they had ceased to be regarded as Roman citizens. Besides the Jews, Arabs and Greeks were known as merchants in Italy, as also the North Africans in Spain. London and Paris were known even in the eighth century as "the emporia of many peoples." We hear also of northern merchants, Slavs from Bohemia at Danube markets in the ninth century, Russians in the tenth at Constantinople trading slaves, wax, and furs for precious silks, spices, and jewelry. At a very early date, a certain number of traders who were not producers were to be found. They are mentioned in the laws of the eighth century Lombard King Liutprand. These "merchants by profession," however, were only small fry, indistinguishable from peddlers, with their pack ani-

A Medieval Town: Bauthen
about 1500

mals, barrows, or little boats. They were not very numerous even in such a relatively great commercial center as Constantinople. At one time, only fifty Russian merchants were allowed to be in the city, and each of them was limited in his purchases of silk to the amount of fifty gold pieces (bezants).

In the field of industry, the transition which we have to study is the rise of free and independent craftsmen. The dearth of materials does not permit us to say positively whether there were or were not such workmen before the beginning of town life. It is fairly clear that there were craftsmen who were freemen, but that does not dispose of the question whether or not they owed service to landlords. It is also fairly clear that the industrial worker on a manorial estate gradually acquired some independence in disposing of his products. First he could sell to the public only what his lord permitted; later the lord's claim was limited to a specified amount of his product, and the craftsman's principal occupation was dealing with the public; still later, all obligations to the lord were forgotten or commuted. The existence of such free workers throughout the Middle Ages is suggested by (1) the fact that industrial workers existed before the establishment of manorial arrangements and that not all villagers were brought into the manorial nexus, and (2) the fact of the existence of a certain number of wandering craftsmen. When Charlemagne wished to build churches, he ordered certain of his "primores" to send workmen and to see to their sustenance, but other workmen "who came from afar" were to be cared for by his own officials. Hyde Abbey was finished in 902 after two years of work because a number of craftsmen were "added"—presumably hired. Certainly it can hardly be doubted that there were at least wandering free workers in the ninth century. Probably they were few, but we shall see that they had a great importance in the later history of industrial organization.

The climax of this transition period was the emergence of the town. In the evolution of a society from the purely agricultural conditions of the early Middle Ages to the highly urbanized conditions of the present, it is obvious that the town as such is a factor or a symptom of the highest importance. But what is a town? The definition of this familiar word has taken many different forms; a town must have walls, it must have a market, it must have a university, it must have a population of 2,000 and so on. These variations arise from variations in the point of view and have their utility for the points of view to which they correspond. Our point of view is determined by our problem, the evolution of economic institutions, and our definition of the town is consequently one which emphasizes its economic aspect. A town is a considerable settlement of human beings on a limited area without a general kinship bond, who for their sustenance look to the production of other economic units. "It is the surplus produce of the country only . . . that constitutes the subsistence of the town, which can therefore increase only with the increase of this surplus produce," says Adam Smith. It is obvious then, if our definition is to be at all serviceable, that the principal, constituent elements of the towns are those who are able by power or wealth to command the means of subsistence from elsewhere, a king who can tax, a landlord to whom dues are paid, a merchant who makes profits outside the town, a student who is supported by his parents. These are the "town-builders." After them come what we may call the "town-fillers," those who serve the needs of the town-builders: the shoemaker who makes the king's shoes, the jeweler who depends on the purchases of the merchant's wife, the landlady from whom the student rents his room.

Jean de Long, the fourteenth century author of the Chronicles of St. Bertin, tells a story of the beginnings of Bruges, in his day the greatest urban center of Northern Europe, that portrays in concrete terms the typical development which has been described. After narrating the building of the castle of Bruges by Baldwin, the count of Flanders, sometime in the latter part of the ninth century, he proceeds to explain the origins of the town as a consequence:

> Thereafter, to supply the materials for the castle or the needs of its occupants, merchants, that is, dealers in the dearer sorts of goods, began to congregate before the gate of the castle by the bridge. Then came tavern keepers and innkeepers, who began building houses and inns where those who carried on business in the presence of the count on the occasions when he was present at the castle, and who could not be given hospitality within the castle, could be entertained. Such people soon began to say, "We are going to the bridge" instead of "to the castle." The number of dwellings increased so much that presently a great town had come into being, which consequently had the name of bridge in the language of the country, since *Brugghe* signifies bridge in that tongue.

Jean de Long was not above criticism even when he was not writing about matters that had occurred five centuries before his own time, and the story which we have quoted bears some of the marks of an eponymic myth, a story based merely on the apparent meaning of some place name. Nevertheless, the story may be true and even as a myth deserves some credence as evidence of how fourteenth century people thought of the origins of towns.

When with these concepts in mind we examine the development of the medieval towns, we note at once that they were still largely villages in the economic sense, that is, centers of residence of agricultural producers. Freytag gives a living picture of the agricultural activities in a German town in his *Bilder aus der deutschen Vergangenheit.* Even in London, pigs and oxen were raised as late as the thirteenth century. The so-called towns founded by colonizing lords in France and in eastern Germany were actually agricultural villages, usually with an especially large endowment of agricultural land. Of three hundred such towns in eastern Germany, only thirty ever rose above the level of small farming communities.

In some of these semi-agricultural towns, however, developed groups of town-builders. They were mainly consumers of subsistence which they derived from outside agricultural areas. There were first of all the secular and ecclesiastical princes, bishops, abbots, counts, dukes, and kings. A king was inevitably a town-builder; the king of England alone in the year 1100 supported with his revenue ten to thirty times as many people as the commerce of the very important commercial town of Lübeck. Most of the churches and monasteries which became centers about which towns were developed also were centers to which great incomes were drawn. University students were an important element in the development of many a medieval town; their influence in town development can easily be observed in dozens of small economic communities in the United States today. The attraction to the towns of the essentially agricultural feudal lords was similarly an abstraction of consumption groups from the agricultural organization and their diversion to urban development. In the town they too were consumers of produce from outside. The medieval town grew also as a fortified center; but from the economic point of view it was rather the garrison than the walls that contributed to its evolution.

The important fact is that the consumer comes first in the evolution of the town. The merchant and the craftsman do not settle in the town until it affords them a better market than the countryside.

If the consumer comes first in the evolution of the town, it is nevertheless hard to conceive of a town in which part of the population does not support itself by industrial and commercial activity. Such classes did exist in all the medieval towns, but at first their significance and their size were alike small. The town produced some industrial articles for the peasants, but this was limited by the very small product that the peasant had to offer in exchange. Of somewhat greater significance, for some medieval towns, was international, or more correctly, interlocal commerce. How small it was is illustrated again by the case of Lübeck; if we assume an average income of only twenty-five dollars, and an average profit of twenty per cent, its commerce in the fourteenth century could support only about 6,000 persons. Export industry developed in a few towns—weapons in Milan, linen in Constance, cloth in Florence—but only late in the Middle Ages, so that it has little to do with the first development. Special products, like herring, salt, wine, silver, sometimes contributed to the development of towns, but even Freiburg, the great silver-mining town of the thirteenth century, the largest town of Saxony at the time, had only 379 house properties and at most a population of 4,500 to 5,600.

Only one factor besides the concentration of agricultural income seems to have played a considerable part in the medieval town development, namely, the bankers and usurers. Writes the bishop of Speyer in 1084, "When I decided to make a city out of Speyer, I felt that it would multiply a thousand times the distinction of the place if I would collect Jews there." The money business, however, could have had an essential influence on the growth of population only in the greater centers.

The town-fillers, the part of the population that came because of the presence of the great consumers, consisted of (1) the subordinate clergy, which in an English cathedral town in the fourteenth century numbered as high as 849; (2) the soldiers and officials of the bishops and princes; (3) the craftsmen, who later were a very important part of the population, but who in the eleventh century were only a minor fraction, supplemented frequently when a great church or palace was being built by imported craftsmen; (4) the beggars, who were apparently a more numerous class than in modern times; and (5) the merchants. It is apparent from the frequent granting of market privileges in the eighth and ninth centuries, that at this time peddling was developing into market-trading. A market was a place where periodically (once a week, once a month, once or twice a year) people assembled to buy and sell for a day or a few days. We are here concerned only with its significance for town development, especially because some theories of town development are practically based upon the thesis that a market makes a town. It would perhaps be more correct to say that a town exists only where a market has ceased to be held. It is when (and where) the merchant finds that it is more profitable to settle down in a shop than it is to spend weeks going from fair to fair, that really urban conditions exist. The decisive step from the standpoint of town development was taken when the merchant decided not to move on but to continue to offer his wares for sale at the little booth which he had taken at the fair, to have his wife and children join him and to build a bit of a house behind his booth. To this day, the houses which stand along the market in Münster show by their architecture that they originated as extensions of market booths. Certain it is that the merchant did not settle thus until the town population furnished an adequate and profitable outlet for his goods.

The town in the Middle Ages, like the town of the twentieth century, exercised a powerful attraction upon the country population. The insecurity of the countryside especially during the Norse and other invasions of the tenth century, the increasing burden of manorial service, the widespread tendency to depress the free landholding peasant to dependency, the apparent increase of population from the ninth to the twelfth century, all combined to create that persisting feature of European social life, cityward drift of population. The town offered security and freedom: *Stadtluft macht frei.*

In the town evolved a new economic life, destined to displace the dominance of the agricultural organization which we know as feudalism. Two forces formed this new system—the interest of the petty craftsmen, whom we have seen clustering about the palaces of the princes and bishops in their little market booths, and the interest of the town as a whole. How this interest of the town as a whole expressed itself is our next concern.

The Handicraft Economy

The medieval town was characterized by a strong feeling of unity, shared by all classes, lords, aristocracy, and democracy. The town was home, all the rest of the world foreign. The political organs of the town, as a natural consequence of that sense of unity, were at the same time the organs of control of its economic life. The idea of individual independence in economic affairs was as completely absent as in the agricultural society. It was the community and its representatives that prescribed to the individual his relationships, that cared for the welfare of the individual. From this leading idea of community derived that powerful system of regulation and control to which, as we shall see, all economic processes in the medieval towns were subjected. The idea of community was also the source of the fundamental economic principle upon which the medieval town acted. This principle, which had controlled the economic activity of tribe, village, and manor, was the satisfaction of need. The working of this principle in the town was, of course, determined by different conditions, above all by detachment from the soil. As we have seen, the essential character of the town involved importation of goods rather than production. This import was so regulated as to assure to the community as a whole the necessary supply of goods. All supplies, especially food supplies, must be exposed for sale in the town itself before they might be taken elsewhere for sale. They must be exposed for sale in the public market so that no speculator (forestaller, regrater) could buy them up. By the right of cavil (*droit de part, Ernstandsrecht*) any consumer had the right to buy any part of the wares of the seller, regardless of his desire to sell it entire or in larger portions. Thus a whole system of regulations aimed to protect the consumer as a member of the community against monopolization, high prices, false weights and measures.

The concern of the town government about the supply of industrial products seems to have been much less anxious. Nevertheless, it took care that foreign craftsmen and merchants were attracted to the annual market, that the crafts were kept well supplied, and that industrial production in the town was honestly and skillfully carried on. Especially careful inspection was made of wares for export, so that the community's markets abroad might not be alienated. The same end, the assurance of an outlet, was sought by compelling a countryside as extensive as possible to supply itself with industrial products in the town, even by prohibiting industrial production in the country.

The town, moreover, concerned itself deeply with the organization and maintenance of a specific system of industrial production, the craft gild system. By the end of the Middle Ages it became practically equivalent to the town itself. The craft gild system (*Handwerk, jurandes,* gilds) from the economic point of view, is that form of exchange economy in which the economically active persons are technical workers, legally and economically independent, controlled by the subsistence idea, trafficking under traditional limitations, and standing in a functional relation to a united organization.[1]

The craftsman, unlike the modern industrial wage worker, combines the technical qualifications with the control of the materials of production. He is technician, artist, organizer, and salesman, as well as owner of the necessary tools, raw materials, and shop. As the French gild statutes say in stereotyped form, "Whoever wishes to be of this trade, may do so, provided that he knows the trade and has the wherewithal (*ait de coi*)."

The general organization of the handicraft system was simply a transfer to industrial and commercial relations of the organization of agricultural life. Both the village community and the gild

[1] This and other long definitions scattered through this book are intended simply as useful abstractions to guide the student in laying hold upon the economic essentials of the data which are presented in the succeeding paragraphs and chapters. It might possibly be useful to memorize them, but probably would be more useful to criticize them or to reconstruct them after the data have been examined.

organized the economic activity of individual members in associational forms. Both started from the idea of a given amount of work to be done and a given need to be satisfied. Both combined individual returns with common property. The essential idea of the handicraft, like that of the village, was that the industry should sustain its man. Just as the village community assured to its members a sufficient area for their sustenance, so the gild undertook to assure its members a sufficient outlet for the goods they produced through a monopolistic control of the markets of its own town, and, where possible, of other towns. By corresponding monopolistic methods it undertook to assure them of an adequate supply of raw materials; hence the constant attempt to hinder the export of raw and half-fabricated materials. It undertook also the erection of establishments too expensive for the individual craftsmen, such as dyehouses, sawmills, oil mills, just as the village had its commons. In summary, wherever a common direction of work or common regulation of the means of production was requisite, the gild functioned as a society.

The craftsman's activity was extremely personal. His point of view was essentially that of the artist. His work was his whole life. He functioned as a unit in a productive system, without the degree of specialization that would reduce him to stupid mechanical toil, and on the other hand he had a proverbial contempt for "the jack of all trades, master of none." His craft was supposed to keep him fully occupied and to give him adequate means of livelihood.

In order to assure to its members a fair share of work, to prevent the increase and enrichment of some at the expense of others, the gilds laid down (1) prescriptions governing the purchases of raw materials (no master might buy except on market days at the market; the price of the raw materials was officially set; none might buy more than a specified quantity; any fellow craftsman short of material might share in the purchase of another); (2) limitations upon the individual craftsman's activities and the amount of his production (he might have only so many journeymen and apprentices; he might produce only so many pieces of cloth); (3) regulations intended to equalize and stabilize supply and to avoid competition (goods must be sold at such a time and place, in such a way; the fellow gildman's customer must not be alienated; a task begun must not be finished by another).

The craft consists of the masters, those who understand the craft (just as the village community is constituted by those who possess the land). The master takes apprentices in order to provide for successors to carry on the craft. If he prospers, he needs the help of other persons trained in his craft. He finds them among the journeymen, men who have finished their apprenticeship but have not yet been admitted masters. The handicraft shop, then, is commonly a shop in which several persons work with the master, but in relationships that are peculiar to the craft system. The master, his apprentices and journeymen constitute an organic group much like the family, a production group and at the same time a household group.

The handicraft system was possible only under certain conditions of population and technical development. The craft was a "mystery," a body of technique acquired only by organic and empirical methods. The apprentice grew up in this industrial family, learning from his master as a child acquires family characteristics. His future standing as a journeyman, as master craftsman, depended upon his conformity to established processes, imposed by a vigorous opinion strongly organized in the gild. This conservatively organized system of production could meet the needs of a relatively sparse population increasing very slowly, such as we have in the later Middle Ages, but it could neither transmit its technique nor adjust its methods of production rapidly enough to meet rapidly increasing demand.

The conventional, stiffly regulated processes of production also made the existence of the craft system dependent upon very favorable market conditions. The absence of acute consideration of production costs (such as is necessitated by competitive conditions) made necessary a supply of raw materials at a low and stable price, free from speculative influences. Similarly the rigidity of the craft technique made necessary a very definite equality between demand and supply, a demand that did not vary greatly in quantity or at all in the character of the goods demanded; a supply that above all was not determined by competition, which was prohibited alike by the prescriptions of the gilds and by the fact that the empirical transmission of technique made differentiation in quality a slow and accidental process. Finally, the undeveloped character of transportation served to protect the local crafts from the complexities of outside competition.

A more specific examination of the data will show how these conditions existed during the later Middle Ages. In the first place, let us examine the aspect of the demand for industrial goods. The consumers fall naturally into three classes, the residents of the towns themselves, the surrounding agricultural population which came to the weekly market, and the foreigners who came to the annual market. The first class was small. The largest city in Western Europe was Paris, with a population probably nearer 100,000 than 200,000. London in 1377 had 35,000 inhabitants. The "great" cities of Flanders and Italy had about 50,000. Many important commercial centers, such as Frankfurt-am-Main and Bristol, had less than 10,000. Furthermore the average purchasing power was very low. The figures are only occasionally to be found, but in 1292, ninety per cent of the population of Paris had less than $240 annual income (present-day values). In the Rhenish Palatinate, about the same time, ninety-three per cent had less than $500. The surrounding population also offered only a very small market, since it was absolutely small, while the towns were numerous. The sellers at the "year markets" seem to have been about as numerous as the buyers. It is apparent that the craftsmen, outside of the food industries, worked only for a very small minority of well-to-do people, that is to say, the nobility and clergy, plus a few money merchants in centers like Paris and London. It was the rich, not the generality, who determined the character of the demand for goods. They bought an extraordinarily wide variety of products, scarcely less wide than the range of consumption goods today. Their demand, however, was for lovely, splendid things, but above all for durable, solid things, as many a fourteenth century chest or chair or fabric still testifies. They seem not to have had the modern passion for up-to-dateness, for new fashions. A rapid change of "the mode," for example, is not noticeable in Germany before the middle of the fourteenth century, and then it affected rather the cut of the clothes than the materials. When Joinville was chaffed because he wore finer clothes than his sovereign, St. Louis, he replied that they were the kind of clothes that his ancestors had worn before him, and such as were produced on his estates. All in all the demand for industrial products in the Middle Ages was of a character for which the handicraft system of production was perfectly adapted.

But how was the demand of the population, especially of the town population, for industrial goods, satisfied in this craft economy? In the first place, in large part, by production in the form of individual economy. As late as 1400, the cathedral chapter of Notre Dame in Paris consumed grain grown on its own estates, ground in its own mills, baked in its own ovens. Every household baked, brewed, butchered its own meat, smoked and pickled it, spun its own yarn, sometimes wove it, tailored its own clothes, and cobbled its own shoes. For some of these processes a skilled craftsman was attached temporarily or permanently to the household, but in the later centuries this was frequently forbidden; e.g., by the shoemakers in Frankfurt in 1355. The remaining part of industrial production was handicraft. Part of it was wage work; that is, the customer delivered the raw material for production to the craftsman and paid him for his labor. The miller and the baker were generally paid with a "toll" of the flour or bread they prepared. Most building seems to have been carried on by the wage system. Some building was done by contract, but in 1356, contracting was still so unusual in London that the mason's gild required four or six masters to be associated as guarantors of every contract. Even in the building trade, the craftsman was frequently housed, fed, and supplied with clothes by his employer.

In the textile industry, very frequently the customer took yarn spun in his own household to the weaver, woven cloth to the fuller, the dyer, and the finisher, and the finished cloth to the tailor. Otherwise he bought ready-made cloth of the clothier with the advice of the tailor who was to make the clothes. This tradition of the handicraft economy is reflected by the appellations "tailor to His Majesty," "furnishers to the Queen," and other similar titles which appear in some very modern advertisements. These courtly tailors in England were forbidden by gild ordinance to wear the livery of their lords, but in France wore, as marks of honor, badges of the families that used their services.

Similar arrangements were customary in other industries. The customer brought gold and silver to the goldsmith to be made into jewelry, iron to the shield maker for armor and to the horseshoer for horseshoes, all of whom performed their work for a wage. In other industries, such as baking, butchering, wheelwrighting, the craftsman procured the raw material and delivered the ready-made article for a price.

Then, too, there was a certain amount of production which was not ordered by customers but made in anticipation of demand and disposed of in the shops or at the market. A set of sixteenth century wood carvings in the Germanisches Nationalmuseum at Nuremberg shows very concretely what the craftsman's establishment was. The master's wife "tended shop" in a front room while the master with his apprentices and journeymen worked in another room at the back. In the salesroom lay, hung, or stood a small collection of ready-made wares. The girdle maker has eighteen purses on his counter, the shoemaker about a dozen pairs of boots and shoes, the furrier half a dozen pelts. These wood carvings date from the sixteenth century, and it may be that they represent an advance upon an earlier time when workshop and salesroom were all one and still fewer ready-made products were to be seen. Certainly, however, as early as the thirteenth century, the Parisian bakers displayed their wares in show windows, and the goldsmiths in Stettin put out their wares on their lowered shutters. In Paris, the craftsmen were permitted to display their wares in their shops from Monday to Thursday but were required to take them to the "halles," or markets, on Friday and Saturday. In Oxford in 1319, the University required the craftsman to sell his wares in the market held every Wednesday and Saturday. These wares must have been "ready-made." In the German towns, specialized market houses were established in the fourteenth and fifteenth centuries, especially "cloth halls" (of which the cloth hall at Ypres was perhaps the supreme example). Shoe halls, salt halls, fur halls, linen halls, were also common.

In the towns and fairs, the merchant, the man whose whole profession was buying and selling goods, also played a considerable part in satisfying the demand. In the larger towns, professional, permanent retailers appeared as early as the thirteenth century. They were quite unspecialized, dealing in all sorts of goods in the one shop; but foreign goods, such as silk and drugs, constituted a much larger proportion of their stocks than did local products.

Of more importance were the "year markets," or fairs, which were regularly held in almost every large town. In many places they became great concentrations of merchants devoted largely to wholesale business, where, however, goods were also disposed of to the final consumer. Certainly a very large proportion of the demand for industrial products on the part of the towns, especially the demand for goods not produced locally, was satisfied at these fairs, to which goods came in large quantities and variety and often from very great distances.

The fair was a concentration of an already existing widespread and diversified interlocal trade. Throughout the Middle Ages, craftsmen wandered over the country with their packs and barrows containing a few articles which they themselves had produced. The craftsman was seeking out his customer because he could not find enough consumers grouped about him in a town. As early as the twelfth century, woolen cloth seems to have been widely distributed in this manner from the producing centers. Linens were even more widely distributed and were sold in made-up form. Minerals were carried long distances. The trade in tin from Britain dates back to the Phoenicians. Iron ore was brought into northern Italy as early as the tenth century and exported to Egypt as early as the twelfth. Silver from German mines appeared in Champagne and in England in the thirteenth century. Copper and lead from Germany were articles of trade with England in the eleventh century and with Italy in the tenth. Weapons and armor were distributed all over Europe from Milan, Venice, and Cologne. Other products which are found as material of interlocal trade are woodenware, hides and leather, leather goods, hose, shoes, girdles, felt hats, ivory combs. An interesting index of interlocal trade in ivory is found in A. M. Cust, *Ivory Workers of the Middle Ages,* and in the *Guide to the Medieval Antiquities of the British Museum.*

How all this was drawn together into a nexus in which the producer and consumer sought out each other may be shown by a description of Winchester Fair. William II authorized the bishop of Winchester to hold a fair on the hill outside the city for three days, which by Henry II's time lengthened to sixteen. On the morning of each August 31, the bishop's justiciar, standing on the summit of the hill, declared the fair open. Then he rode through the town, closed the shops and the market, and rode back to the hill. There he named a special mayor and bailiff, and constituted the court of piepowder, (*pied poudré,* dusty-foot) to control weights and measures, to witness contracts, and to settle disputes between merchants. The hill was soon covered with rows of wooden huts, each row devoted to merchants from a given locality or to craftsmen of a given trade. All commerce in Winchester and within seven miles was suspended during the fair. In Southampton, only food could be bought; and in Winchester, all the tradesmen had to move to the hill. The bishop collected duties on all merchandise that was brought into the fair.

The producer obtained his raw material in much the same way as the consumer. When it was not furnished by his customer, he usually was required to buy locally in public halls, markets, and fairs. In almost all towns direct sales outside the public markets were forbidden, and the prohibition was drastically enforced. Buying from samples and buying for future delivery, so important in modern commerce, were almost entirely absent.

The geographical organization of industry was characterized by a very great degree of local specialization, apparently greater than that of today. Lincoln was famous for its scarlet, Doncaster for saddle girths, Bristol for leather, Toledo for its blades, Milan for coats of mail. The basis of this specialization was partly then as now natural resources, nearness to market, accident, but also and especially the empirical basis of technique: only through the migration of masters could technique be transferred. Nevertheless, the quantitative proportion of goods produced for local markets seems to have been larger than at present. Many industries which today are confined to a few localities, were then to be found in every town, notably weaving.

Very little is known of the number of industrial workers; estimates indicate that they constituted a larger proportion of the urban population than now, but a very small proportion of the population as a whole. Certainly their numbers fell far below the demand. Whole towns were sometimes stirred up over the need for a few dyers. Princes and towns offered special privileges to craftsmen settling in their territory. The training of craftsmen was very slow, but no considerable increase in population pressed in upon the industrial trades. When the population was not at a standstill or decreasing because of the lack of hygiene, plagues or famine, the surplus agricultural population at any given point was limited by the colonizing enterprises so frequent in France, Germany, and England in the twelfth, thirteenth, and fourteenth centuries.

The productivity of the craftsmen was very low. This is indicated by the high prices of industrial products; a ton of iron cost 180 shillings in England in the fourteenth century, as compared with $22.75 in the United States in 1928 ($13.60 in 1932), when the purchasing power of money was many times lower. In Wesel in 1428, 342 master weavers (with journeymen and apprentices) produced only 5,140 pieces of cloth. In 1399, the 400 weavers of Beauvais boasted that they produced about 700 pieces of cloth a week. It took fourteen days to finish a good lock. In artistic production, time was ignored. Centuries were taken for the completion of a cathedral, generation after generation labored on choir stalls. Ghiberti worked forty years on the doors of the Baptistery of St. John in Florence.

The question remains, Was industrial life in the medieval town completely organized in gild fashion? Certainly, as we have seen, a significant part of industrial activity, the industries that were carried on in the home, remained outside the officially organized and recognized gilds. The gilds themselves were showing signs of disintegration from the latter part of the thirteenth century. Wide differences in income operated to weaken the fellowship bond among the masters. In 1292, seven craftsmen of Paris had incomes of more than 5,000 livres, and 821 had less than 250 livres. Even production limits were differentiated as between individuals of the same craft. At Frankfurt-am-Main, eleven of the woolen weavers had the right to produce thirty-six pieces each for the fair, while forty-nine others had the right to produce only four each. As the masters grew more plutocratic, the journeymen began to have a less certain hope of being admitted as masters and organized journeymen's gilds, unions based on their interests as wage earners. These journeymen's gilds have a fairly close analogy to modern labor unions of skilled workers.

On the other hand, as industry developed, the craft gilds grew more numerous. The number in a given city was a fair measure of its industrial importance. Another indication that the gilds continued to predominate is the fact that industrial units continued for a long time to be the small personal units of the gild type. Such statistics as have come down always show a smaller number of journeymen in a trade than of masters. In the sixteenth century, in Heidelberg, for example, over half of the masters worked alone and only one had as many as five journeymen. The wood carvings in the Nuremberg museum, mentioned above, never show more than two or three journeymen and frequently only a single apprentice working with the master. When in 1443 Master Tonnies Evers of Lübeck was discovered to have twelve journeymen and seven apprentices in his service, his gild required him to reduce the number.

In general we may conclude that, while a considerable part of production was not organized in gilds, and while, from a very early date, the gild was ceasing to be an entirely equalitarian organization even among the masters, yet the gild continued to be important in the industries that produced articles of commerce down to the sixteenth century. The mutuality and the restrictions of the gild statutes retained less importance than the handicraft ideal of small units and the personal devotion of the master to his craft. The theoretically favoring conditions for the handicraft ideal were still present: an empirical technique, a slowly growing population, a steady demand for industrial goods made to last a long time, and competition in the modern sense almost entirely excluded. Conversely, the conditions necessary for the evolution of a new form of economic life which should dispossess the handicraft system, that is, capitalism, were absent. We shall next see how even in the economic activities where we most expect the capitalistic form, export industry and commerce, the handicraft ideal prevailed.

The Organization of Export Industry and Commerce in the Handicraft System

Production for export and the sale of goods as an occupation seem at first sight to be removed by their very character from the handicraft economy (self-sufficiency, associational form, empirical, traditionally controlled technique). So perhaps they are, in their essential logic. We shall see that it is in these fields that the first phenomena of capitalism appear. A closer examination, however, will show that even in these fields the characteristic customs, relationships, and limitations of the handicraft system prevailed until late in the Middle Ages.

In the fourteenth century, the cloth industry of Flanders had grown into a (relatively) large exporting industry, and new elements entered its organization, *poorters, coomanen, gewandschneider,* who were essentially merchants, great and small, attempting to control the weavers. The attempt was bitterly and successfully resisted by the clothmakers' gild. Their resistance, their persistent effort to secure for themselves and for the other gilds a part in government, and the purely gild spirit of their ordinances even in the fifteenth century, justify the impression that the textile industry of Flanders still had an essentially handicraft organization. The textile industry of Florence, as will be seen, began to have a clearly capitalistic organization somewhat earlier. On the other hand, the silk industry in Venice, Lucca, and Geneva, also largely an export industry, was handicraft in character. The mining industry in the medieval period was generally carried on by associations of craftsmen, and even the small hardware manufacture in Nuremberg, Solingen, Schmalkald, and other hardware exporting centers was carried on in handicraft fashion. That is to say, we always find the group of masters with their journeymen and apprentices, who controlled the industry in their common interest.

It is more surprising to find commerce itself organized in handicraft fashion. The merchant seems to be, by definition, so exclusively concerned with the production of profits, that it is difficult at first to think of him as limited in his efforts by the sustenance idea or by a traditional technique. Yet a direct examination of medieval commerce will easily show us just that. In the first place, commerce was on a small scale even in the greatest centers. Lübeck, for example, in 1384 one of the greatest, exported only 293,760 marks' worth of goods, about $500,000 in present-day values of money. The English export of wool, another major interest, in 1277–1278 amounted to about 3,000 tons. These small figures are the more striking when the number of merchants among whom the trade was divided is taken into consideration. The English wool export was handled by 252 merchants, giving an average business of $4,000 a year in present-day values. The average sum in fifty Genoese *commenda* contracts—of which more subsequently—dating from 1156 and later, was between $250 and $275. In 1429 in the rich commercial city of Basel only five merchants were worth more than $10,000.

Another index of the smallness of export trade in the pre-capitalistic period is the low tonnage of ships, which nevertheless were generally owned and operated in common by several merchants. In the year 1470, seven Spanish ships were seized by English pirates, taken into English ports and reclaimed by the Spanish owners, who under oath catalogued the tonnage and value of their ships. They ranged in tonnage from 40 tons to 120 (three of 100 and 120 tons) and in value from £70 to £180. Land trade was on a still smaller scale. The value of a caravan of Basel merchants pillaged in 1391 on its way to Frankfurt fair, was 9,544 florins, an average of less than $400 for each of the 61 merchants in the caravan. The maximum value of a German merchant's stock at the great fair of Novgorod in Russia in the fourteenth century was estimated to be $2,500.

The merchant appears to have been in thinking and feeling, in social position, in the character of his activity, much like the smaller craftsmen. Nothing lay further from his mind than profit winning in the unrestricted style of modern enterprise. He was dominated by the sustenance idea. As the reactionary Luther put it, in his essay on "Commerce and Usury," "You must be careful to seek nothing but your proper nourishment in such commerce." The merchant was also a technical worker, at least in his own eyes. His technique was a matter of calculation, travel (Andreas Ryff visited thirty and more markets every year), and to a certain extent writing. We have the diary of Lucas Rem, a German who went to Venice shortly after 1500 to learn "reckoning": "da lernte ich rechnen in 5½ monat gar aus." The merchant used the characteristic master-apprentice relationship for the transmission of his technique, which, it must be remembered, was of a very low order. The first chapter of the French Ordinance of Commerce of 1673 related to merchants and their *apprentices.*

The laws and customs of merchants also illustrate this handicraft character. The early combinations of persons, most of them family combinations, had only a common chest from which each took according to his need for support. All the merchant's relations were personal. He faced his customer with his goods and was paid for them in coin or other goods which he likewise saw, rather than by exchange instruments, checks or drafts. If he borrowed money, it was without thought of profit to the lender, frequently his gild: "If any man or woman of the said fraternity without fault on his own part fall into poverty, the said fraternity will lend him a sum of money for trading for a year or two at his convenience without taking anything for gain," ran the statutes of the Gilda Mercatoria of Coventry. The cloth merchants of Florence at first excluded usurers and when money lending and borrowing had become a more usual practice, charged them double fees for admission to the gild. Throughout the statutes of the merchant gilds runs the fundamental handicraft notion that the trade in or from the city was a source of support—sustenance to which all members had an equal right. Perhaps no simple, single character so clearly brings out the handicraft character of commerce in the handicraft period and its differentiation from modern commerce, as the fact that competition, whether by irregular dealings, advertising, solicitation of customers, or departure from standard prices, was everywhere forbidden.

We have now surveyed in very summary fashion the economic character of the two systems which were the antecedents of capitalism in European society. Our problem now is to mark the earliest phenomena of capitalism.

REFERENCES FOR FURTHER READING

General

Sombart, W. Der moderne Kapitalismus, vol. I, pp. 91–309.

Ashley, W. J. English Economic History and Theory (1892), vol. I, chaps. II, III.

Boissonnade, P. Life and Work in Medieval Europe (1927), book II, chaps. IV–VII.

Cheyney, E. P. European Background of American History (1904).

Cunningham, W. Growth of English Industry and Commerce During the Early and Middle Ages (2 vols., 1896).

Day, Clive. A History of Commerce (1904).

Knight, M. M. Economic History of Europe to the End of the Middle Ages (1926), pp. 153–158, chap. VI.

Levasseur, E. Histoire du commerce de la France (2 vols., 1911–12).

Ogg, F. A., and Sharp, W. R. Economic Development of Modern Europe (1926), chap. III.

Risson, P. Histoire sommaire du commerce (1902).

Weber, M. General Economic History, chaps. XIV–XVI, XVIII.

The Rise of the Towns

This is a subject which has given rise to many diverse theories, the principal of which are embodied in the first four books named.

Bucher, K. Industrial Evolution (tr. S. M. Wickett; 1912).
Gras, N. B. S. Introduction to Economic History (1922), chap. IV.
Pirenne, H. Medieval Cities (1924).
Schmoller, G. The Mercantile System and Its Historical Significance (1910).

See also

Schevill, F. Siena (1909).
Cunningham, W. Essay on Western Civilization (1898–1900), vol. II.
Below, G. von. Probleme der Wirtschaftsgeschichte (1907).

The Gilds

Cheyney, E. P. Industrial and Social History of England (1923), chaps. III, IV.
Evans, A. "The Problem of Control in Medieval Industry," *Political Science Quarterly,* vol. XXXVI (1921), pp. 603–616.
Green, Anna S. Town Life in the Fifteenth Century (2 vols., 1894).
Gross, C. The Gild Merchant (2 vols., 1890).
Renard, G. Guilds in the Middle Ages (1919).
Saint-Léon, M. Histoire des corporations des métiers (1923).
Salzmann, L. F. English Industries of the Middle Ages (1913).
Thompson, J. W. An Economic and Social History of the Middle Ages (1928).
Unwin, G. The Gilds and Companies of London (1908).
  Industrial Organization in the Sixteenth and Seventeenth Centuries (1904).

Illustrative Source Material

Bland, Brown, and Tawney. English Economic History, Select Documents, part I, secs, 5 and 6.
University of Pennsylvania. Translations and Reprints, vol. II, no. 1.

PART II

THE FOUNDATIONS OF MODERN CAPITALISM

CHAPTER I

THE STATE AS ECONOMIC ORGANIZATION

The Indirect Promotion of Capitalism

The political organization which we know as the state was of supreme importance for the development of the modern economic system which we know as capitalism.[1] The state is purely a mod-

[1] The word "capitalism," which is used so much in this book as the equivalent of "the economic institutions of modern Europe," means different things to different men. Karl Marx, the great originator of scientific socialism, used it as a sort of epithet for the whole of nineteenth-century European society. A prominent English economist and historian uses the word as meaning an economic system in which capital in large units plays a major part. An American economic historian says, "One of the outstanding facts about the capitalistic régime of today, from the angle of organization, is the presence of capital in the form of negotiable stock, viewed as an investment to yield interest." Both these definitions or characterizations have their utility from certain points of view, the first, from that of a student of the rôle of capital as such, and the second, from that of a student of "the capitalistic régime of today." From the standpoint of this work, the purpose of which is to portray the economic aspects of European society as an evolving entity in world history, it is necessary to go back of today, not merely for differences but rather for evolutionary beginnings; and it is necessary to go beyond negotiable stocks and even beyond capital: these are merely two instrumentalities among many others used in the economic activity of Europeans. On the other hand, a concept more narrowly restricted to the ways of getting and spending than that of Marx is required. The need here is for a definition in terms of society rather than in terms of economic abstractions or devices.

In this work, then, capitalism is a system of exchange economy marked by certain distinctive characteristics. Two groups of the population, the owners of the instruments of production and the propertyless workers, are clearly differentiated, but cooperate in impersonal relations established through the market. The orienting principle of economic activity in capitalism is unrestricted profit, secured or sought in competition with other economic agents by means of instrumentalities fully rationalized with reference to that end.

Several of these characteristics capitalism has in common with the handicraft system. Both are systems of exchange economy, marked by strong occupational specialization. Both operate through the market nexus. Capitalism differs from handicraft (1) in the social differentiation between the directing persons, owners of the means of production, on the one hand, and the technical workers on the other; (2) in its dominating principle, the pursuit of profit, as against the sustenance principle, the satisfaction of the needs of the individual man; and (3) in its rationalism, its elaborate planning and

ern development, quite different from the city-state of the ancients, from the empire of the Romans, and from the quasi-anarchic system that we know as feudalism. It began to appear in the twelfth and thirteenth centuries with men like Henry II of England, Philip Augustus of France, Frederick II of Sicily. In the period with which we are now concerned, it developed toward concentration of authority in one single person, a process which which culminated in the age of Louis XIV of France, with whom is associated the aphorism "L'Etat, c'est moi." It is easy to emphasize too much this concentration in the hands of one person. Whether the state be a single person, an oligarchy (Venice, England in the eighteenth century), or a democracy (France, the United States), the common phenomenon appears of an authority gradually approaching absolutism, as in the democracies of today which, like the United States, certainly at least in principle, undertake to extend their authority over an unrestricted range of subjects. Blackstone declared, "I know of no power on earth that can withstand an Act of King, Lords and Commons in parliament assembled."

In its development the state directly favored the evolution of capitalistic forms, but besides the self-conscious promotion of capitalistic activity, the state furthered capitalism in indirect ways. The state itself was an organization which carried into society a notion which was fundamental to capitalism, the idea of two distinct classes, directors and performers, rulers and subjects, analogous

adaptation of means to specific ends, its thoroughgoing accounting, as against the traditionalism of the handicraft system.

The visible form of the capitalistic economy is the capitalistic enterprise, the business, the concern, which may be a factory or a trading house, an employment agency or a bank, which may be a one-man concern or a combination of the wealth of several persons as capital, which may use slaves or free labor, which may be fully independent or fully bound up with the government, which may, in short, be of any one of twenty different sorts.

The capitalistic entrepreneur functions as the organizer of production: he brings laborers and material together; as a merchant: he finds a market for goods that have been produced in anticipation of demand; and as accountant: since his aim is not directly the customary sustenance of an individual but a sum of money, he watches his activities to see that they result in a balance of money.

to entrepreneurs and workmen. This type of organization was especially exemplified in the army. Medieval fighting forces were made up of feudal elements gathered together for the occasion, who, in general, supported themselves and directed themselves. The army of the monarchical state was a paid army, constantly on foot, and directed by functionaries of the state. An excellent example of a feudal array confronted by an army in which the modern idea was beginning to manifest itself can be obtained from Froissart's story of the battle of Crécy. It was, however, the famous *Ordonnance sur la gendarmerie* (1439) of Charles VII of France which first created an army in the modern sense, a step which meant much for the specially rapid development of the monarchical state in that country. What happened in France in the middle of the fifteenth century, took place in all the European states within the next two centuries. A similar growth took place in naval force. The standard of size for both land and sea forces grew steadily higher. The Normans won the battle of Hastings with not more than 7,000 men. The largest number of crusaders in a single battle in Palestine was 10,200. The greatest army which the Middle Ages saw was that of Edward III at Calais in 1347: 32,000 men. In contrast, the armies of the European states by the eighteenth century ran to the hundreds of thousands.

Austria (peace standing)	297,000
Russia	224,500
Prussia	190,000
France	182,000

In the thirteenth century Genoa dominated the Mediterranean with 65 galleys carrying about 12,000 men, mostly rowers. In 1588, the Felicísima Armada ranked as the greatest of sea armaments the world had seen, with 130 sail and 65 galleys, carrying about 30,000 men. In 1786, the English fleet consisted of 292 warships.

These increasingly large bodies of men and material required a new system of production and delivery. The warrior of the Middle Ages as a rule brought his own weapons and armor with him. This had to change with the introduction of powder and cannon. Arsenals begin to appear in the fifteenth century (Paris, Mons, Bruges). Smaller weapons continued to be bought by the individual soldier, who suited his own taste in muskets. The long pikes of the Spanish infantry in the sixteenth century furnish the first example of uniform weapons in a large force. Similarly, the Spanish government first developed a system of providing food and shelter for troops through government functionaries (quartermaster, *servis*) instead of leaving it to the individual soldier. It was only in the eighteenth century that the clothing of the soldier became the affair of the state.

All of these changes had a direct if unintended repercussion upon economic life: they offered a function to and created a need for the entrepreneur who could bring about the production of the needed goods in adequate quantities and deliver them where and when they were needed.

Mercantilist Policy

The state self-consciously promoted the development of capitalism. The theories and policies used in this promotion we call mercantilism. Unfortunately for purposes of definition, mercantilism never received a systematic exposition to which we can refer with definiteness nor, as a matter of fact, has any adequate history of mercantilism been written. Definition therefore has to be picked out from scattered characteristics. The central idea is embodied in Colbert's expression: "I believe that agreement is fixed upon the principle that it is only the abundance of money in a state that determines its greatness and power." It is first of all to be observed that in one very important respect mercantilism simply extended to the wider area of the state the economic feeling of the town. The aim was the good of the whole rather than the good of the individual. Just as the town had pursued the policy of assuring to its inhabitants the necessary means of life, so the state gradually took over the same function. In England, in Spain, in France from the thirteenth century onward, the kings prohibited intermittently and in various forms the export of food materials, especially grain and meat.[2]

In mercantilist policy, all economic activity was "privileged." Just as in the town the craftsman and the merchant derived their right to produce or to trade from the community, so in the state the prince granted such "rights" and imposed such duties as he, as head of the state, thought proper for its interest. Then, too, the prince had his own special interest as ruler. Since his power was based upon a mercenary army and a salaried bureaucracy, he needed money above all else to pay them. To be able to raise money by taxes or by loans, the country must be supplied with an adequate provision of the precious metals. The supply of precious metals—bullion, the English mercantilists usually termed it—was the good which the mercantilist state took special care to provide for the community, as the town took special care to assure the supply of meat and grain. The state promoted the direct acquisition of silver (and later, of gold). The same purpose underlay the early colonialism. The state naturally associated itself with the early capitalism because both were in opposition to the medieval localism of feudal elements and towns. Both depended upon an adequate supply of the precious metals. Another characteristic of mercantilist feeling is illustrated by the preamble of the French King Henry IV's edict of 1603: the arts and manufactures are to be encouraged as "the sole means of avoiding the transportation out of the kingdom of the precious metals and the consequent enrichment of our neighbors." Since the object of policy was power, and power was relative, the gain in precious metals which made power for a neighbor was a loss to the state.

[2] For a more systematic discussion of mercantilist thought, see Part III, chapter v below.

The mercantilist policy in regard to industry and commerce expressed itself in (1) the granting of privileges, (2) regulation, and (3) unification. Privilege sometimes took the form of monopolies. The practice appears in the "first modern state," Sicily under Frederick II, who claimed for himself the monopoly of all commerce in grain, salt, iron, and raw silk. In the fifteenth century, the absolutist states of Italy claimed a monopoly of all trade. A number of coal merchants, organized into a gild, were given the sole right to sell coal to the ships which came to Newcastle. The Merchants Adventurers alone had the right to sell English cloth in the Netherlands and Germany. All silk trade in France was concentrated in Lyons. The most significant development of this geographical type of monopoly took place in the oversea trade, where it was the basis of the great trading companies, such as the East India companies of England, France, and Holland. Monopoly of production was equally common. Old industries became, by authority of the state, the monopolies of existing gilds. New industries became national monopolies in the hands of the inventors or the men who introduced them, as, for example, the glass industry in England (patent monopoly of 1567) and in France (1551).

Another form of privilege for industry was the widespread control of commerce in such a way as to prevent the export of raw materials and the import of manufactured materials. Philip III of France forbade the export of native wool in 1278, and in the succeeding centuries the prohibition was repeated and extended to other materials (1305, 1320, 1567, 1572, 1577). The Oxford parliament of 1258 also forbade the export of English wool; but England became a great wool-exporting country, and it was not until the time of the Tudors that the series of prohibitions began again, not to cease until 1825. Distinctively "protective" tariffs began to appear in the sixteenth century (England, 1534; France, 1564, 1577, 1581) and became a fully developed system under Colbert. "Colbertism" continued to dominate commercial policy until the commercial treaty of 1786 between England and France. The removal of internal tariff boundaries was another measure that meant much for capitalistic development on a nation-wide scale. Colbert secured the abolition of the Five Great Farms which at least united the northern part of France into a single economic area, and the French Revolution completed his work. In Germany, the barriers between the various states were not broken down until the Zollverein was formed (1834).

Bounties and premiums were freely used to promote and encourage capitalistic enterprise. Colbert expended 5,500,000 francs in this way in addition to considerable sums furnished by provinces and cities. In England, bounties on exported wares became the preferred method. In Austria, from 50,000 to 80,000 florins a year was applied to bounties. Savary in his *Dictionnaire du Commerce* (1726) lists about twenty forms of favors, from ennobling for important entrepreneurs to admission to the mastership for workers, which were used in France.

Regulation was the other aspect of privilege: since industry was a privilege granted by the state, it must be controlled by the state. In England, where the system of control was least extended, the government concerned itself with all these matters in the year 1630:

(1) Only Spanish black shall be used to dye silk.
(2) Bread shall not be eaten on Friday and other fast days.
(3) A commission is to investigate why the fishing industry does not flourish.
(4) Commissions for several shires shall see that cloths for export are made of a certain length, breadth, and weight.
(5) Cloth shall be made only out of native wool.
(6) No logwood or blackwood shall be used for dye.
(7) No foreign thread shall be imported.
(8) No new houses shall be built in London.
(9) No tobacco shall be planted in England.

In France, the government even regulated the size of the leaf and the quill, tools used in weaving. Between 1683 and 1739, 230 different measures were passed regulating industry. It is obvious that the state simply continued the spirit of the old gilds in its minute regulations. Indeed, the gilds themselves continued a vigorous life down to the end of the eighteenth century, more exclusive than ever, more drastic in their ordinances, and, in virtue of the wide power of the state, nationalized in their authority where hitherto they had been local. So in France, in England, and in the German States. The numbers of gilds also increased steadily. Politically, the gilds were being undermined by the general substitution of the state's authority for their own, but the economic ideal which they embodied remained. The flood of regulation in the seventeenth and eighteenth centuries was called forth by and directed at capitalistic industry, but generally it meant a modification of the gild restrictions. Thus the Elizabethan Statute of Artificers continued and generalized the master-journeyman-apprentice relationship, but contained no restriction upon the number of apprentices.

The exercise of the authority of the state involved the nationalization of the industrial system, a process that was completed in England and France about the same time (Elizabeth, Henry III, Henry IV) but did not go as far in German lands. In England, the gilds were made national in extent, but continued under supervision of the central government. In both France and England gilds were formed for the control of the growing domestic industry. In France, the old gilds were nationalized except that a non-Parisian master could not exercise his craft in Paris.

The mercantilist state also promoted the evolution of the capitalistic economy by its intercourse policy—by measures promoting the interest of private entrepreneurs, such as the English navigation act of 1651, by bounties for shipbuilding, and by the establishment of uniform commercial law, weights and measures, and coinage. It also facilitated intercourse by road building and canal building and by the organization of posts. Under Sully, the great minister of Henry IV, canal building was begun in France. Colbert carried out and extended his policies. In the years 1737 to 1769 the French government spent from two to four million livres a year on roads and canals. We shall consider the development of means of communication more fully later.

Money

Another function of the state that had much to do with the development of capitalistic forms was the establishment of money systems. What money is, every one knows by experience, yet the definition of money is something upon which there is no general agreement. It is easily agreed that money (1) is the expression of all exchange values, (2) is a general means of exchange and circulation, (3) is a general means of accounting, and (4) is a means of storing exchange values. The disagreement begins in the attempt to get a single definition for money. If, however, we approach the question from another standpoint, we find two categories under the same name. That standpoint is the question, What makes a thing money? In the one case it is the general consensus of social groups trading together, in the other it is the arbitrary act of a lawmaking power (the state). A simple exchange money can be based upon the value of something as a ware. Money as means of account depends upon an act of the state which authoritatively defines it. The state may take (usually has taken) the ordinary money of commerce and may give it the character of money of account. On the other hand, the state is not all-powerful. If it attempts to establish one kind of money at too high a valuation, the undervalued other kinds will disappear (Gresham's law).

The early history of exchange money (from the thirteenth to the eighteenth century) was characterized by a great simplicity, both on the side of technique and on that of economic control.

Coins were made on a purely handicraft basis and cost from 6 to 25 per cent to manufacture. The English coinage at the end of the seventeenth century varied as much as ten per cent in weight. The understanding of economic forces was equally deficient: the French ordinances repeatedly complain of the stupidity and stubbornness of a people who refuse to accept a depreciated coinage. The state did not conceive its business to be to provide a sound currency, but regarded the control of coinage from a purely fiscal point of view as a source of profit. The English recoinage under Elizabeth was the first designed purely as an economic measure. It was not until well into the seventeenth century that similar measures were taken in France and Germany. The international traders and especially the international money traders developed an organized market for money as a protection against the vagaries of the princes in order to provide a sure goods-equivalent in money. Florence was the market at which rates of exchange for almost all Europe were fixed from the thirteenth to the fifteenth century; Antwerp, from the fifteenth to the end of the eighteenth century; then London.

The circulation of coins was much more international than now. When the Emperor Ferdinand I in 1559 undertook by edict to exclude foreign coinages from Germany, he excepted from the operation of his edict seven different kinds of double ducats, twenty-three different kinds of ducats, ten different kinds of crowns, from Spanish, Portuguese, French, and Italian mints. In 1606, the Netherlands "placards," an early form of business newspaper, contained quotations on almost one thousand foreign coins. England in the eighteenth century used a large number of Portuguese coins.

The relative value of gold and silver was determined partly by law, partly by exchange, and was also affected by the fact that it cost proportionately more to coin silver. This resulted sometimes in the total disappearance of one metal or the other because of a mistake in the legal valuation: so silver disappeared (as money) in Florence in 1345. Furthermore, throughout this period, there was a general, continuing debasement of coins through changes of fineness or of weight. Almost all the coinages of Western Europe derive their form from the pound, solidus, denarius system of Charlemagne, but varying processes of depreciation resulted in widespread differences in value. In Hamburg and Lübeck, the number of coins made from a pound of fine silver rose from 2 marks, 2 schillings in 1226 to 12 marks, 8 schillings in 1506. The English silver penny in 1300 weighed about 22 troy grains; in 1464, 12 troy grains. In 1309, 2 livres 19 sous were made from 234 grains of fine silver; in 1720, 98 livres. The Florentine gulden, the "florin," was the only coin that had an unchanging content through these centuries. This persistent debasement of the coinage was due largely to the need of the state for revenue (in the form here of profits) but also in part to the (at times) increasing value of silver, as in the fourteenth and fifteenth centuries.

As a result of the technical inefficiency of minters, the problem of circulating medium was further complicated by a practice best described in the preamble of an ordinance of Charles I of England (1627): "Some of the goldsmiths have grown to that licentiousness that they have for divers years presumed for their private gain to sort and weigh all sorts of money current within our realm to the end to cull out the old and the new monies, which, either by not wearing or by any other accidents are weightier than the rest; which weightiest monies have not only been molten down for the making of plate, etc., but even traded in and sold to merchant strangers who have exported them."

A new epoch in the history of money as an economic factor opened when the English government removed the minting charge, thus removing the coinage from the field of fiscal enterprise and treating it instead purely as a function to be performed in the interest of an easy commerce. The increase in the supply of gold through the opening of the Brazilian and African gold fields (as we shall see) led to the adoption of the gold standard. The principal steps were:

(1) Declaration of free coinage of silver and gold (1666).

(2) Accumulation of gold by the public treasury.

(3) Gold declared legal tender (1717).

(4) Disappearance of silver in consequence of the overvaluation of gold.

(5) Silver restricted to small money.

(6) End of free coinage of silver (1798).

The vagaries of exchange in the sixteenth and seventeenth centuries led to another device which, like the florin and the gold pound, was intended to assure an unvarying money of account. That was "bank-money." The banks of that day had as their primary function to simplify the matter of accounting by furnishing a uniform and stable money. They were what are still called in Europe "giro-banks" rather than money-lending institutions. The best known of them were the Banco di Rialto in Venice (1587), the Wisselbank (Exchange Bank) of Amsterdam (1690), the Girobank of Hamburg (1629) and the Banco publico of Nuremberg (1621). A contemporary wrote of the Wisselbank of Amsterdam: "It is of so great a convenience for the commercial world, that one would not believe it possible, if he had not lived and transacted business in the city for some time, since accounts of millions can now be settled as a matter of everyday routine by means of simple orders which are called bank billets [i.e., checks]." Bank statements and statistics are wanting from this early period, but Adam Smith estimated the deposits of the Amsterdam Bank at £3,000,000.

Paper money is another manifestation of the interest of the state in the creation of adequate means of exchange. The history of paper money through the eighteenth century is characterized by the incapacity of state organs to handle so delicate a matter and by a deep distrust of paper money by the community, a distrust which was justified by the extraordinary mistakes that were at first committed in connection with this new device. The outstanding examples are the Law System in France and the "South Sea Bubble" in England. The Law Bank, in the short period before it collapsed in 1720, issued two billion livres of notes: it was a half-century before an issue bank was thought of in France again. Similar unjustified issues of notes with similar results took place in Denmark and Norway, in Sweden, in Russia, and in the American colonies. The one exception was the Bank of England, whose right of issue was limited to the amount of its capital. This prevented the misuse of the printing press so general in other paper money schemes, but it also meant that the note issue was only a limited part of the English money supply. Even at the end of the eighteenth century the note issue amounted to less than £10,000,000. Through most of the century, the proportion of paper money to hard money was about 1:50, at the end about 1:10, whereas in the United States in 1921, the proportion was about 3½:1.

Colonialism

Colonial policy was another field in which the state served capitalism. The significance of colonial economy has already been discussed: here we are concerned with the direct action of the state in regard to colonies, their seizure, organization, and control. The word "colony" applies properly to the settlements of the Greeks, to the military settlements of the Romans on the frontiers, and to the settlements promoted by medieval French and German lords to recapture waste lands. In connection with the modern state, however, it has a somewhat different meaning: an outlying possession exploited by the owning power for its own benefit, rather than an integral extension of the original whole. Colonies in the mercantilist policy were to the state as the surrounding country was to the medieval town. The colonies must deliver their products to the mother country, just as the surrounding country must market its products only in the town. The colonies must buy products, especially industrial products, from the mother country; the colonies must not produce what the mother country had to sell; the motherland retained the monopoly of transport. A sharp distinction, however, exists: the medieval town was dominated by the idea of sustenance, the mercantilist state aimed at profits. No limit of natural needs hindered the state in its acquisition and exploitation of colonies. It aimed at unlimited expansion because its objective was not sustenance, but gold.

Colonization in this sense began for modern Europe with the acquisitions of the Italian city-states during the Crusades and the break-up of the Eastern Empire. Genoa, Pisa, and Venice received fractions of the cities conquered by the Crusaders along with corresponding areas of the surrounding country. The colonial empire of Venice underwent a sudden expansion when at the capture of Constantinople in 1204 it received three-eighths of the whole Eastern Empire, including the Ionian Islands, the control of the Dardanelles and the Sea of Marmora, Crete, Cyprus, and, later, acquisitions on the Black Sea and in Armenia. Genoa developed rapidly as a dangerous rival, with a large group of colonies on the Black Sea, Chios, Samos, part of Cyprus, Corsica, Sardinia, possessions in Spain, Greece, on the Armenian coast, in Syria and Palestine. Pisa and Florence also had possessions in Syria and Palestine, in Africa and Greece, but were never serious rivals for supremacy. The discoveries of the Portuguese and the Spanish, opening the new seaways to India and the western continents, made the Atlantic powers the great colonizing states. Spain won all of South America (except Brazil), Central America, and the southern part of North America, as well as most of the islands of the Caribbean and the Philippines. Portugal's empire equaled the Spanish; the east and west coasts of Africa, Brazil, the coasts of the Arabian Sea, and the Moluccas—most of which later became booty for other states. France from the time of Richelieu (1627–1642) built up her immense empire of New France (Canada and Louisiana) with Martinique, Guadeloupe, and Haiti in the Antilles. The Dutch made a great empire out of rich fragments won largely from the Spanish and the Portuguese, plus the Cape of Good Hope, Sunda Isles, New Amsterdam. The English settled on the eastern coast of North America and preyed upon the other colonial empires, to remain as the last and most immovable of holders.

The history of the colonial empires is largely a history of wars: they were conquered. If sometimes a treaty granted admission to traders, the colony soon became the occasion of war with the native peoples, between rival colonizing companies or between rival colonizing states, wars which received their final arbitrament on the battle fields of Europe. It is hardly necessary to name examples: the long struggles between Genoa and Venice, the wars of the Dutch for independence and Spanish-Portuguese colonies, the wars between England and Spain in the time of Elizabeth, between England and Holland in the seventeenth century, between England and France in the eighteenth.

The exploitation of colonies followed several different patterns. Settlement was confined practically to the English and French colonies in North America. All the rest were commercial or plantation colonies, small groups to exploit trading privileges or labor rights over a foreign population. Sometimes this was accomplished by direct state action as in the case of the Venetian and Spanish colonies. More often, colonization companies received privileges and political rights from the state, including the right to carry on war. The earliest form of colonization company was the Genoese Maona. The most famous Maona was that of Chios, which received the control of that island and Phocaea from the government in payment of a debt incurred in the conquest. From the sixteenth century onward the great trading companies fill the pages of colonial history, the English Muscovy, Levant, East India, Royal Africa companies, the French Compagnie des Indes, the Dutch East India Company.

In spite of variations of form, from the time of the Italian colonies in the Levant to the decline of the great trading companies and the abolition of slavery, the colonial system was essentially the same, because it developed on the same bases:

(1) Privilege: feudal grants in the Levant colonies, encomiendas in the Spanish, exclusive trading rights in the English, French, and Dutch.

(2) Proportionately strong military apparatus: "The Dutch factory in Bengal looks more like a castle"; the Dutch East India Company maintained a standing army of 12,000 Europeans; the English East India Company spent over £9,000,000 for forts in India in the years 1765–1771; Jamaica in 1734 had a white population of 7,644, a garrison of 3,000.

(3) Slavery or some other form of forced labor, recognized and supported by the laws.

Religion

Finally, the state became the organ through which religious considerations first became a barrier to economic development, then gradually were eliminated. The development of state churches, accentuated by the Reformation, at first intensified the severity with which variations of belief were repressed, both in Protestant and in Catholic countries. The principles of tolerance began to emerge in the sixteenth and seventeenth centuries as a result of religious indifference (Montaigne), of religious principles (Penn), of logical reasoning (Bayle), or of political considerations (the Politiques in France). In the seventeenth century, however, economic considerations began to operate to the same end. Thus Cromwell admitted the Jews to England after four centuries of exclusion. Thus James II argued in his Declaration of Indulgence that "persecution is unfavorable to population and trade." Holland under William of Orange became the first state to exercise a policy of complete tolerance. Thence the policy of toleration was extended to the Dutch colonies. Maryland, Rhode Island, Pennsylvania, and Carolina were founded with toleration as a part of their fundamental laws. England suspended persecution of dissenters by the Toleration Act of 1689. It was not, however, until the end of the eighteenth century that toleration became a general policy. The Jews were tolerated in Holland from the declaration of independence (1580), in England from 1654, in some American colonies and a few German cities from the seventeenth century onward. Legal distinctions based on religion did not wholly disappear from any of the states of Western Europe until late in the nineteenth century.

The period of active intolerance had produced a cleavage in the populations of most European States: orthodox and heterodox. The heretics frequently found it advantageous or were forced to emigrate (Pilgrims and Puritans in Holland and America, Huguenots in Holland, England, and America) carrying with them technical knowledge and a spirit of enterprise. The "religious" wars themselves were an economic fact of no mean order, in fact obviously destructive, but also, as we shall see, opening the way to new forms of economic life.

REFERENCES FOR FURTHER READING

General

Sombart, W. Der moderne Kapitalismus, vol. I, pp. 334–360.

Boissonnade, P. Life and Work in Medieval Europe (1927), book III, chaps. I, II.

Burckhardt, J. The Civilization of the Period of the Renaissance in Italy (tr. S. G. C. Middlemore; 1898).

Levasseur, E. Histoire des classes ouvrières et de l'industrie en France avant 1789 (2 vols.; rev. ed., 1903–1904).

Ogg, F. A., and Sharp, W. Economic Development of Modern Europe (1926).

Risson, P. Histoire sommaire du commerce (1902).

Sombart, W. Krieg und Kapitalismus (1912).

Weber, Max. General Economic History (1927), chaps XXVIII, XXIX.

Mercantilism

Schmoller, G. The Mercantile System and Its Historical Significance (1910).
Haney, Lewis H. History of Economic Thought (1911), chap. VII.
Clement, P. Histoire de Colbert et de son administration (2 vols., 3rd ed., 1892).
Cunningham, W. Growth of English Industry and Commerce During the Early and Middle Ages (2 vols.; 4th ed., 1904), Appendix.
Day, Clive. History of Commerce (1904).
Mims, S. Colbert's West India Policy (1912).
Sargent, A. J. The Economic Policy of Colbert (1899).
Unwin, George. Industrial Organization in the Sixteenth and Seventeenth Centuries (1904).
Usher, A. P. History of the Grain Trade in France (1913).
Lipson, E. Economic History of England, vols. II, III: The Age of Mercantilism (1931).

Colonization

Morris, H. C. A History of Colonization (2 vols., 1908).
Keller, A. G. Colonization: A Study of the Founding of New Societies (1908).
Leroy-Beaulieu, P. La Colonisation chez les peuples modernes (4 vols., 1891).
Biggar, H. P. Early Trading Companies of New France (1901).
Cawston, G., and Keane, A. H. The Early English Chartered Companies (1896).
Day, Clive. The Dutch in Java (1904).

The Control of Currency

Shaw, W. A. The History of Currency, 1252 to 1894 (2nd ed., 1896).
Ehrenberg, R. Capital and Finance in the Age of the Renaissance (1928). (A bad translation of a good book.)
Sombart, W. Der Bourgeois (1912).

Religious Policy

Lecky, W. E. H. History of the Rise and Influence of the Spirit of Rationalism in Europe (2 vols., 1868).

Campbell, D. The Puritan in England, Holland and America (2 vols., 1892).
Sombart, W. The Jews and Modern Capitalism (1913).
Tawney, R. H. Religion and the Rise of Capitalism (1926).

CHAPTER II

THE TECHNICAL EQUIPMENT OF CAPITALISM

The Tools of Industry

The Faust-spirit of the Western culture manifested itself more definitely in the field of invention than elsewhere. In no field is there a more distinct cleavage between the periods that we call medieval and modern. Medieval technique was empirical, organic, as we have seen. To the persisting medieval mind, the invention of new devices was "black art," the fruit of a too close intimacy with the Devil. The legendary Faust was himself a man of new devices, and participant in such a bargain. The legend expresses the medieval, reactionary aspect of Protestantism. Pascal says of his contemporaries: "Those who invent are rare, those who do not are the more numerous and therefore the stronger. They commonly refuse to grant the inventors the glory which they deserve and which they seek by their inventions. . . . All the inventors gain is ridicule and the name of visionaries."

The sixteenth and seventeenth centuries nevertheless were marked by a new and striking interest in new processes. Leonardo da Vinci would be the supreme example with his profound and thoroughly modern scientific sense and his clever mechanical imagination, but he stands alone. The greatness of Leonardo as an artist, the timelessness of his great paintings makes it difficult to realize him as a great mechanical genius and a great civil engineer. Aside from his achievements as a constructor of fortifications and of canals, about sixty inventions, some of them fundamentally important, are to be accredited to him. He invented several sorts of gears, bevel and spiral, screw-cutting machinery for square-threaded and conical screws; he worked along correct lines toward the turbine waterwheel; he developed anti-friction roller-bearing, band-brakes, a dredge and a pile driver, a rope-making apparatus, and even a power loom. "There is certainly no ground for the view that his scientific and mechanical capacities were in any sense inferior to the artistic powers which afforded naturally a simpler and more direct claim to recognition" (Usher).

Leonardo was not less remarkable for the number of his inventions than for the scientific method that he used. He was a profound student of dynamics and especially of hydraulics, and influenced the scientific method of men of the very first order in science, such as Galileo and Kepler, as well as many men of secondary order. Although he did not publish any treatises, his notebooks had a small but distinguished circulation both in Italy and in the other countries to which they were taken by collectors, especially Spain and England.

A century after Leonardo's time, Sir Francis Bacon attempted to formulate the principles of invention in *The Dignity and Advancement of Learning*. His formulae, like so much of his boasted contributions to scientific method, remain abstract and unreal, in spite of the undoubtedly stimulating character of some of his criticism. His criticism, however, serves to illustrate the degree to which the world of inventors was slow to adopt a scientific approach to problems arising out of experience, the degree to which, in short, Leonardo stood alone.

How devoid the inventors were of the scientific spirit is illustrated by the great Agricola, author of *De Re Metallica* (1556), who believed that demons were important factors in mining, although he displays a surprisingly wide acquaintance with mechanical devices; Johann Joachim Becher, the author of *Närrische Weisheit und Weise Narrheit* (1686), who believed that "common flowing sand, as a mother-source of minerals, has a great affection for metals, in such wise that they, when treated with it, always emerge improved"; the Marquis of Worcester, author of *A Cen-*

tury of Names and Scantlings of such inventions as at present I can call to mind to have tried and perfected (1663). On the other hand the scientific men, such as Galileo, Copernicus, and Newton, were devoid of interest in mechanical applications.

All sorts and conditions of people seem to have been affected by the inventing impulse: princes like Ruprecht, nephew of the English Charles I, the inventor of Prince Ruprecht's metal; nobles like the Comte de Milly who introduced improvements in the manufacture of porcelain; great functionaries like M. Bon, a president of the French *Chambre des Comptes* and inventor of improvements in silk weaving, and Benjamin Franklin, inventor of the lightning rod and the Franklin stove; priests and monks like the inventors of the magic lantern and champagne; craftsmen and laborers, like Humphrey Potter, inventor of the steam governor, and Arkwright, inventor of the spinning jenny.

Inventing was almost a profession or avocation by itself, with an art that could be applied in many fields. The marquis of Worcester (1601–1670) "invented" a stenographic system, a sort of telegraphy with cannons, an unsinkable ship, a boat that could be propelled without oars against wind and current, a floating fort, a water clock, a hoisting machine, a tide machine, a repeating pistol, a flying machine, a calculating machine. Réaumur, Papin, and Becher similarly dabbled in many fields. What they wanted to do brings out the contrast of their methods with that of the modern technician. "Eight things there are," wrote Becher, "after which the learned and curious strive: the stone of the philosophers, the licquor Alcobest, flexible glass, a perpetual light, the hyperbola in mirrors, the length of the degree, the squaring of the circle, perpetual motion." Even Papin, who in 1698 produced a working steam engine, knew nothing of stresses. They were modern in their desire for technical advance, medieval in their mode of thought. Technique remained empirical. "Coal for iron making must be not too heavy, not too light" (Bergius, 1776). Paul Hoche, the Jesuit teacher of mathematics, wrote in his *Theory of Ship Construction* (1680), "It cannot be denied that often the most unscientifically built ships are the best." What had changed was the partial substitution of a rationalist spirit for the traditionalism of the handicraft system.

The actual advances in technique were considerable, even before the eighteenth century. In general, the materials of production remained as before, animal and vegetable products, with some changes as newly discovered parts of the earth offered new materials. It was distinctly still the age of wood: even the first steam engines were made of wood. The forces used also remained the same, men, animals, wind, and water. The most important technical improvements which we have to note during this period lie in the field of improved applications. It was the age of "mills," wind, water or tread-mills. The Dutch windmills for grain date back to the middle of the fifteenth century although cruder forms are still older. Sawmills with one saw also date back to the Middle Ages but were much improved in the end of the sixteenth century. In 1633, a Dutchman erected a wind-driven sawmill on the Thames in which one man and a boy could cut as many boards as hitherto twenty men, but this enterprise was closed down "lest our laboring people want employment." Water-driven wire mills are first heard of in Nuremberg in 1532. Water-driven hammers for metal working appeared in the fifteenth century, and water-driven blasts for furnaces appeared about the same time. A hammer was lifted by cams on the shaft turned by water power. As the cam passed the head of the hammer, the hammer was released and delivered its blow. The same principle was used in a number of devices, such as fulling, stamping, and crushing mills. Power transmission was also much improved. Cogwheel transmission had long been known but was much improved in the sixteenth century. Leonardo da Vinci and Agricola knew the flywheel as a recent invention. The belt is first mentioned by Leonardo da Vinci on January 1, 1496. The first transmission systems in which several machines were driven by one power machine, appeared about 1500 and are described by Agricola and Biringuccio (*Pirotecnica,* 1540). The improvement of chemical processes belongs, with some exceptions, to the period of fully developed capitalism.

In agriculture, some very notable advances were made. The essentially urban prosperity of the northern Netherlands throughout the sixteenth century stimulated the market for agricultural goods. By means of dikes and windmill pumps, great areas were reclaimed from the sea. These "polders," as they were called, lent themselves to a very intensive agriculture. Everything favored the adoption of technical improvements, such as careful manuring and moisture control. Breeding of cattle also reached a high development. Many a village owned four thousand cows; bullocks weighing two thousand pounds were not exceptional. In France, numerous treatises on agriculture were published in the sixteenth century. The most important were *The True Recipe for everybody in France to get rich* of Bernard Palissy (1563) which, in spite of its silly title, contained the excellent advice to use manures to maintain fertility rather than to attempt to restore it by the wasteful and ineffective practice of leaving each field fallow every two or three years. Even more popular was the treatise of Olivier de Serres, *Le Théâtre de l'agriculture et ménage des champs* (1600), which went through nineteen editions before 1675. He advocated artificial meadows instead of the native grasses, artificial drainage, and fruit raising. Probably both these Frenchmen just wrote down what they had seen or heard of in Holland. Certainly it was a Dutchman, Gabriel Plattes, who wrote the first theoretical work on agriculture in England (1638). These works, however, in spite of their popularity, could have little effect, because the medieval system of communal operation and communal rights persisted as a solid obstacle to any departure from traditional methods. Perhaps it would be more correct to say that it was individual rights in communal things which prevented the application of better methods. A single individual could prevent,

A—Shaft. B—Bottom pump. C—First tank. D—Second pump. E—Second tank. F—Third pump. G—Trough. H—The iron set in the axle. I—First pump rod. K—Second pump rod. L—Third pump rod. M—First piston rod. N—Second piston rod. O—Third piston rod. P—Little axles. Q—"Claws."

The Early Development of Mechanical Technique: Sixteenth Century Mine Drainage Practice

for example, the planting of the fallow, even if every one else in his village was in favor of doing as M. Palissy advised. Nevertheless, in the sixteenth century, many individuals in France tried and many in England succeeded in "enclosing" the open fields by moving off the peasants regardless of their rights and raising sheep with five men where perhaps fifty had farmed. All the preachers and public moralists protested: sheep are eating men, they said. The great Sir Thomas More protested against it in his most famous work, the *Utopia.* Laws were passed against it. Actually it did not amount to much. Before it had gone very far, the profits in wool raising declined and regular farming became more profitable. More than nine-tenths of the land remained to be enclosed in a later movement. It was not until the eighteenth century that the passion for improvement in farming grew strong enough to give some general effect to the teachings of such men as Serres, Palissy, and Plattes.

Although the common pasturage and the lack of artificial fodders made any improvement in breeds of domestic animals difficult, the interest of the rich, the nobles, and the kings did lead to some specialized efforts to improve the breed of horses. Marx Fugger in 1578 and Lohneisen in 1609 laid the foundations of horse breeding in Germany.

In industry, the greatest technical change came in mining and metal refining. Horizontal shafts appeared in Bohemia in the fourteenth century. Before 1560, hoist pumps made it possible to work at the great depths necessary in silver mining. Boring machines were mentioned by Bernard Palissy in 1550. Powder blasting was first tried in 1613. Railways and ventilating machines were known to Agricola (1566). Until about 1519, ores were very crudely worked by hand; then the stamping mill at the same time reduced the labor required and made possible the utilization of lower-grade ore. Most important of all was the invention in the fifteenth century of iron casting and the development of blast furnaces, which made possible large-scale production. Scarcely less significant, in a very different way, was the discovery (1567) of the amalgam process for the reduction of silver, which made the American mines fully available. Iron working also underwent important changes: tinning (first half of sixteenth century), rolling (1615), hammers of six to ten hundred pounds for making anchors and cannon, cannon-rifling machines, appeared in the sixteenth and seventeenth centuries. Even more important for economic life at the time were the improvements in the working of the precious metals, beginning with the rolling machine of the Frenchman Brulier in 1552 and culminating in the milling machine, first used in England under Cromwell and in France in 1685, which made possible accurate coinage. Sombart says, "Without it [accurate coinage] the full development of capitalism is not conceivable."

In the textile industries a similar series of improvements is to be noted. Foot-driven spinning wheels were introduced about 1530. Mechanical weaving appeared in ribbon making in Holland at the end of the sixteenth century. Becher claimed to have invented a weaving instrument with which two persons could make a hundred ells of cloth a day. The flying shuttle of John Kay (1733) was more practically significant. Cloth (cotton) printing was first introduced into Europe by Jakob ter Gower in Amsterdam (1678). A knitting machine was invented by an English theological student named Lee and was gradually brought into use in the course of the seventeenth century. New products, of course, were more susceptible to the application of rational technique than old ones and also, as we shall see, to the application of new principles of industrial organization. Chocolate making, tapestry weaving, lace making, coach making, clavichord making, wall paper are only a few examples of the many.

Military technique, especially weapon making, was of wide significance. The interest of the state assured protection and reward to the inventors of improvements in weapons. Such improvements contributed enormously to the development of the state. With the increase in the size of armies, uniform weapons, and increase in size of cannons, these new processes required large capitalistically organized factories. The quantity production of powder apparently began at Spandau in 1578. Some of the important changes in weapons may be listed:

Iron cannon balls (instead of stone)	1471
The German wheel lock	1515
Drawn barrels	About 1550
Exploding bombs	1588
Breech-loading cannon	16th century
The musket	Before 1600
Cylindrical shells	1627
The flintlock	1630–1640
Cannon casting and boring	1740

The technique of measurement also underwent an evolution of essential importance for the development of economic life. We are concerned here only with measurements of time and space, because in this period the measurement of weight remained unchanged from primitive forms. Wheel clocks and water clocks existed in some of the medieval monasteries, but the modern timepiece is the work of the fifteenth, sixteenth, and seventeenth centuries. In 1500 Peter Hele invented the first "pocket clock," the essential principle of which was the elasticity of a given element, the spring. At the beginning of the seventeenth century the balance wheel was introduced; in 1674, the spiral spring; at the beginning of the eighteenth century, the second hand. The pendulum clock was invented by Huygens in 1656.

Space measurement, especially in the form of orientation, underwent even more radical change. The compass came to Europe at the end of the twelfth century, although its use became general only after 1500. Polydore Vergil did not know it when he wrote his book on inventions (1499); Cardano in 1560 calls it the crown of all inventions. Columbus first noted the declination of the needle, and successive observers in the following century worked out a fairly complete set of observations. The astrolabe was worked out from Zacuto's *Almanach perpetuum* (1473) by Joseph Vecinho and the mathematician Moses working with two Christian colleagues. More than two hundred years later (1714), a device for the measurement of longitude finally took a prize offered by the English Parliament. An effective telescope was invented in 1608. Maps steadily improved from the crude sea maps of Mario Sanuto and Pedro Vesconte. Mercator (1560) introduced the form which still bears his name; at the end of the sixteenth century Halley published a map of air currents, and in 1665 the Jesuit Kircher published one showing the ocean currents.

In the field of transportation, technique developed very slowly, except on the inland waterways. Seagoing vessels were improved in detail and in size, and the deepening and narrowing of keels increased their stability and manageability. Thus Elizabeth's navy was able to outmaneuver the Spanish Armada of 1588. Later development in this same direction permitted the American clipper ships to carry larger power plants, that is, to increase their sail area. On land, roads were much improved in certain areas, especially near Paris. The invention, late in the sixteenth or early in the seventeenth century, of the "fifth wheel," the element which makes it possible for the front axle of a four-wheeled vehicle to be turned independently of the body, led to the production of various elaborate forms of carriages. The sail-wagons of Holland in the seventeenth century received a great deal of attention but were of only local significance. The railway, known in the sixteenth century, was long confined to the mines of Germany and of England. Inland waterways, which had been preferred lines of travel from time immemorial, have a very different record. Locks, first in the form of sluices and then in the form of chambers, became common in Italy in the fifteenth century, "long in use" in Leonardo's time. Dredging machines were mentioned as early as 1545. A patent was issued in 1618 to one John Gilbert in England for an improved dredge, and eighteen other improvements were patented during the seventeenth century. The Chinese invention of printing was appropriated, but progress in it was very slight, except in regard to the casting of type. Even the ingenious Franklin printed very much as Gutenberg did. Qualitatively the work of some of the sixteenth century printers has never been surpassed.

The Instrumentalities of Exchange: Gold and Silver

Modern economic life is not more dependent on the tools of industrial production than upon the instrumentalities of exchange, gold and silver. The ambition of the inventors of new devices was paralleled and more than equaled by the zeal of the searchers for gold and silver. From the tenth century up to a very recent date successive increases in the supply of precious metals kept pace with the expanding economic life. The names Kuttenberg and Goslar, Schwaz and Joachimsthal, Potosí and Guanajuato, Brazil and Guinea, California and Australia, Klondike and Witwatersrand, characterize so many stages in the evolution of the European economic system. We have in this connection to study not only the record of the production and geographical distribution of the precious metals but also the effects of that distribution upon the whole of economic Europe and upon its parts. That impact, of course, was primarily in the field of prices. This necessitates some definition of our answer to the perennial question of economic theory, What is the relationship between the quantity of money, materials, and prices?

Although in this section on the "foundations of modern capitalism" we are concerned generally with the beginnings of its institutions, it seems appropriate to continue the story of the supply of the precious metals down to the nineteenth century. To labor the figure of speech, the superstructure of the European economic system grew so rapidly that this particular element of the foundation had to be continuously reinforced in order to bear it. It was the good fortune of Europe that it could be reinforced with the same materials. How good that fortune was, is illustrated by the multitude of remedies and the paucity of agreement now that the supply of gold has fallen short of the needs of the economic world and silver has ceased to be a precious metal.

The history of the supply of precious metals during the six hundred years may be summarized very briefly.

(1) From the break-up of the Roman Empire to the eighth century. The Roman Empire had been fairly rich in the precious metals: its supply at the beginning of the Christian era is estimated at about 2.5 billion dollars, or about half the supply in the United States in 1924. Most of this was lost by the western part of the empire in the succeeding centuries. The low point seems to have been reached in the eighth century.

(2) From the eighth to the end of the thirteenth century. During this period, there was at first a slow increase, then a relatively rapid one. The Arabs brought back many of the abandoned Spanish mines, and in 938 Abderrahman III was able to send to the caliph 400 pounds of pure gold and a large amount of bar silver. New silver mines were discovered in Alsace (ninth century), in the Black Forest (tenth century), and in the Harz Mountains (970). Still richer in new discoveries were the twelfth and thirteenth centuries: the Mansfeld, Saxon (Freiburg), Bohemian (Kuttenberg), and Tirol silver mines, the gold mines of Goldberg, Löwenburg, Buntzlau, and Hungary were discovered in these centuries and became the Mexico and Peru of the earth before the discovery of America. Gold and silver, however, continued to flow eastward until the crusaders and the Italian colonizers corrected this tendency by their plundering and exploitation of the Eastern populations.

(3) From the end of the thirteenth to the middle of the fifteenth century. During this period most of the European silver production ceased on account of technical difficulties. King Wenzel of Bohemia in the year 1300 thanked God for Kuttenberg's continued productivity "while in almost all the kingdoms of earth, the sources of His grace to men are dried up." It was the time when nearly all the cities and lands of Europe began to prohibit the export of gold and silver. The coinage of gold and especially of silver by the English mint (the only statistics we have) shows a decided decline until the end of the fifteenth century:

Average Coinage per Year

Period	*Silver*	*Gold*
1272–1377	8,906 lbs.	2,538 *
1377–1461	1,157	1,845
1461–1509	3,184	4,338

* Average for period 1345–1377 only.

The effect of this cessation in the silver supply was intensified by the increased (net) flow of precious metals toward the East resulting from the decline of the crusading movement, the advance of the Turks, and the increase in the Levant trade.

(4) From the middle of the fifteenth century to 1545. In this period new and richer mines of gold and silver were opened in Germany. The Portuguese established themselves in the gold lands of Africa and Asia, and the Spanish plundered Mexico and Peru. The gold mines of Salzburg flourished from 1460 to 1560. Some very great silver mines were opened. Schwaz in the Tirol began to produce about the middle of the fifteenth century, reached its maximum in 1523 with more than 53,000 marks of fine silver, and by 1570 had declined to 2,000. Schneeberg (1471) and Annaberg (1496) developed a very great production. Joachimsthal in Bohemia was opened in 1516, rose to a production of 254,259 "thaler" in 1532, and as rapidly declined.

In the fifteenth century the Portuguese smashed the Arab control of commerce between Europe and the East and established themselves in control of the sea routes. In 1415 they took Ceuta, in 1511 they had reached (and conquered) Malacca, with effective control of the intervening routes. The first consequence of this direct connection with the East was to accentuate the drain of precious metals from Europe. The Westerners had nothing to sell. At first every carrack took 40,000 to 50,000 Spanish dollars to pay for the pepper that was bought. Colonial establishments, however, soon made possible tribute and extortion in various forms. In Africa, Senegal and Sofala produced large quantities of gold which the Portuguese conquerors brought back at the rate of $2,000,000 a year between 1493 and 1520, and $1,750,000 from 1521 to 1544. The plundering of the Aztecs and Incas gave the Spanish great sums of which we have no accurate index except in the case of some individuals.

(5) From 1545 to about 1620. The opening of the great American mines, Potosí, Zacatecas, Guanajuato, and their exploitation by means of the amalgam process (see page 86) was in effect a great revolution in itself. Silver became the predominant money metal and remained so until the discovery of the Brazilian gold fields. While the gold production of the world remained substantially the same, its silver production rose from a yearly average of about 200,000 pounds in 1521 to about 925,000 pounds in 1621. Most of the increase was due to Mexican and Peruvian production. Potosí alone produced over 150,000 pounds a year in the last two decades of the seventeenth century. While the German sources were diminishing, the Spanish were increasing. Production in Spanish lands, however, did not mean distribution in Spain. Colonial administration costs, capture, consumption (plate, jewelry, etc.), foreign trade, diverted the silver stream to the fructifying of the economic soil of Holland, England, and France. As an example, Philip II's fleet in 1577 carried 800,000 ducats to Antwerp for the Fuggers. A century after the discovery of Amer-

ica, the other countries mentioned probably had more gold and silver money than Spain.

(6) Seventeenth century. The seventeenth century saw a decline in silver production with the almost total disappearance of European mines, and a slight increase in gold production. The total production by periods (gold and silver combined) was as follows:

1621–1640	$470,000,000
1641–1660	452,000,000
1661–1680	432,500,000
1681–1700	457,600,000

(7) Eighteenth century. The eighteenth century was a period of rapid increase in the world supply of precious metals. The Brazilian gold fields, which began to produce just before the turn of the century, raised their annual production from 150 million marks a year in the first two decades to 816 million a year from 1740 to 1760, reaching their maximum in 1764 and then declining to almost nothing by 1800. Silver production, however, was correspondingly increased by the discovery of Valenciana (1760) and Bonanza (1764), so that the total production rose to the year 1800.

1701–1720	$ 499,000,000
1721–1740	654,200,000
1741–1760	823,100,000
1761–1780	876,300,000
1780–1800	1,039,400,000
1800–1820	526,500,000

In other words, a steady and substantial increase through the century, and in the first decade of the nineteenth century.

(8) From 1810 to 1848. In this period, political disturbances cut Mexican silver production to about one-half the 1810 standard,

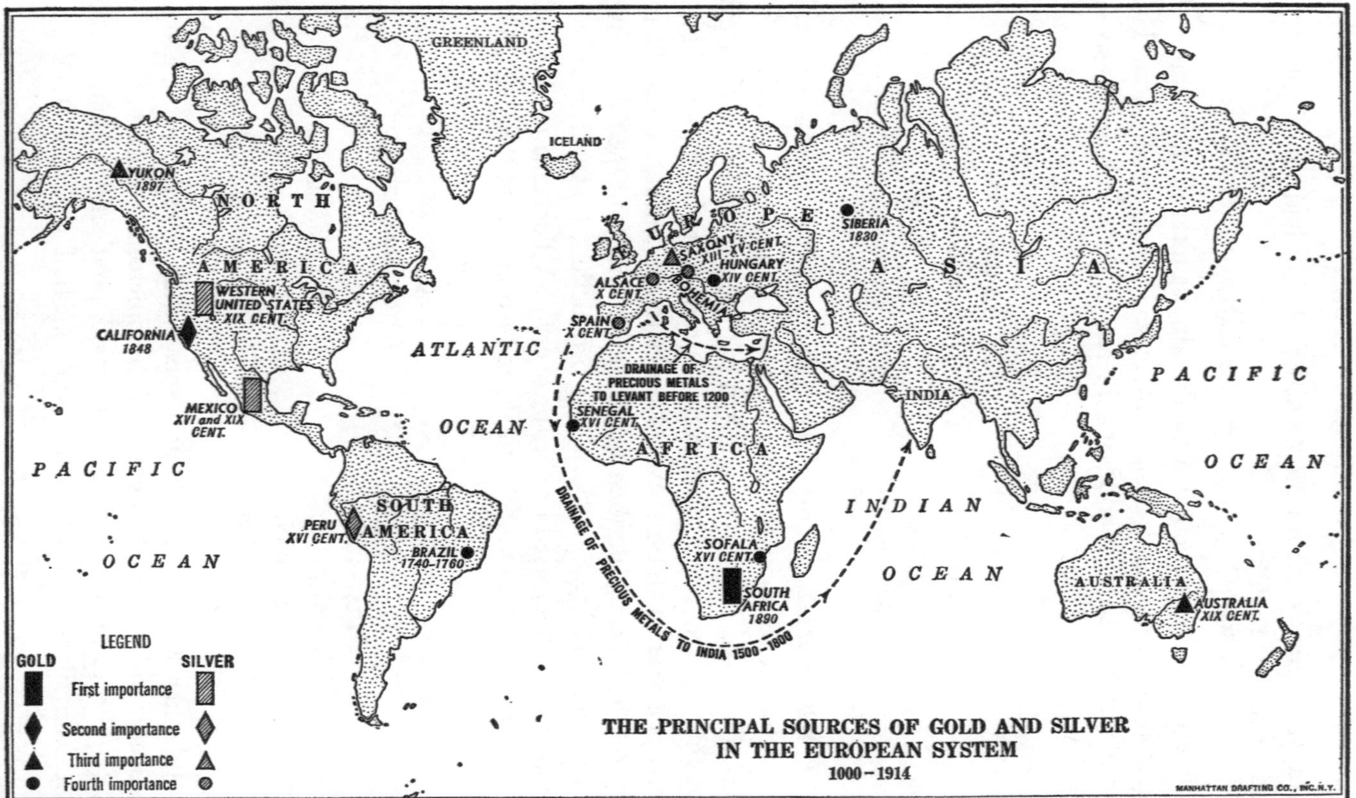

THE PRINCIPAL SOURCES OF GOLD AND SILVER IN THE EUROPEAN SYSTEM
1000–1914

and even the new Russian gold fields did not bring the total production up to the mark of the first decade. In the year 1848, however, the discovery of the previously unequaled California field introduced the "golden age of capitalism."

So much, or so little, for the data. What is the significance of silver and gold, in particular of this increasing supply, for economic life and civilization in general? It seems, in fact, chimerical, as though men had agreed upon these metals as a symbol for which they should strive and labor, fight and die. The myths, the Golden Fleece, Midas, the Rheingold, show us the desire for gold acting as a powerful impulse among quite simple societies. It entered into the ambitions of Darius and of Alexander, into the conflicts of Rome and Carthage. It was in the mines of the new world that modern slavery received its first development. The desire for gold led to the invention of powder and the whole development of modern chemistry. It spurred the explorers of the unknown Atlantic, the conquistadores of Mexico and Peru, the founders of modern states. The whole question has psychological and metaphysical implications which we may forgo to turn to the purely historical question, the influence which the use of the precious metals in these varying quantities has had upon social organization and social relationships.

That is itself a question of wide importance. It is possible only to suggest here some of the many complications. The effect of precious metals used as jewelry and plate is quite different from their effect when used as money. Gold or silver won by piracy, tribute, or direct production from the mine is one thing; that won by commerce is another. Its influence varies according to the social relations of the persons who acquire it and according to the kinds of things for which it is expended. (For example, consider the very special consequences of high wages in the United States.) Naturally, its influence varies also according to the circumstances among which a given amount of the precious metals is introduced (again, for example, the United States has developed a capacity of resistance to the effects of the introduction of amounts of gold absolutely and proportionately so high that they would have produced very radical changes even fifty years ago).

The necessities which limit our consideration to the general form of economic life, dictate also the character of our discussion of the significance of the precious metals. What is the connection between the constantly increasing supply of precious metals which accumulated in Europe after the Middle Ages and the general form of economic life which developed during that same time, and which as a whole we call capitalism?

We have already had occasion to note the importance of money supply in the development of the modern state, that Siamese twin of capitalism (in Chapter I above). Money for salaried officials and for mercenary armies was a *sine qua non* of state development. Psychologically, the increasing quantity of money contributed to development of that unlimited striving for gain, culminating in phenomena like the Law affair in Paris and the South Sea Bubble in London. On the other hand, the increasing definiteness of money made possible exact accounting, likewise essential to capitalism as we know it, the development of which we shall discuss elsewhere. The increasing fluidity of wealth which increasing money supply brought about made possible accumulations on a larger scale and at a more rapid rate. Finally, the increasing supply of precious metals appears as a factor in that elaborate evolution of the market system as a result of which the most ordinary demands are satisfied by supplies from the end of the earth. Money supply made possible production for the market, as we shall see (page 126). It made possible a more than local demand. As more wealth became available in fluid form, demand on the part of individuals for consumption goods increased. With the extension of markets, came more radical changes in prices and the development of systematic extension of price changes. Most of these connections are obvious, and in any case will be discussed in another place.

The problem of money and prices, however, requires somewhat more attention. Real "laws" of price we shall not discover, because price is the product of so many incommensurable forces. Traditionalism, ignorance, legal, social, and natural barriers, and similar forces have as much to do with price as economic factors. Still through the chaos of price run certain large tendencies connected more or less with the supply of money values. This notion, elaborated in many different forms, is the basis of the "quantity" theory. In its most naïve form as elaborated by Locke, Hume, Montesquieu and others of their time, price was simply the proportion between the amount of money in a country and the amount of the goods-sales. Among the classical economists and their successors, this was restated in their psychological formula: "The law of supply and demand governs the value of these metals as of other things" (Horace White). Certain logical and historical difficulties, however, have led to a reaction from this extreme position. In the first place, money is not an ordinary commodity, for it is obvious that not only the static quantity, but the dynamic velocity of money enters into the determination of its value. The course of this special commodity in society is also different from all others: it *circulates,* while all the others proceed in more or less rectilinear fashion from producer to consumer. Then, too, although in a simple exchange it functions just as any other commodity might, in other respects it is unlike all others, for its value depends not on its use as a consumption good, but almost wholly upon the possibilities of exchanging it for other goods. In judging the value of gold or silver, "We have to deal only with relative purchasing power. We do not reckon a utility in the metal itself, but in the commodities it will buy. . . . We must first inquire the relative circulating value of gold and silver before we can know at what ratio we ourselves prize them." (Irving Fisher, *The Purchasing Power of Money,* p. 377.)

In the economic society that we are studying, money has been the formula into which has been translated the demand for other goods implicit in all production beyond sustenance production. "Out of the depths of the gold and silver mines, came, in the material sense, so much metal, came in the economic sense, so much demand for goods." Finally, it is apparent—and was apparent to the mercantilists—that, in contrast to the course of other commodities, increase in the supply of money increases the demand, or, in other words, stimulates business and creates new need for circulating medium.

This is one of the most serious objections to the defenders of the classical theory, who insist that their principle must be read "all other things being equal"—as if one were to say, "All other things being equal, the addition of yeast to warm dough does not increase its volume."

It is obvious, then, that in the money metals we have a commodity that is wholly special in character, and that creates logical difficulties when it is caged within the ordinary formula of supply and demand. We are reduced to a more skeptical formula: the quantity of money metal (either in coin or in bullion) is one of the elements that enter into the determination of price.

Certainly this more cautious formula is borne out by the history of prices, which have risen rather steadily along with the increase in the supply of gold and silver. After a period of rising prices from some time in the twelfth century, the period 1350 to 1500 saw a rapid decline. The sixteenth century, which saw the first really great addition to Europe's stock of the precious metals (through the conquests and exploitation of the overseas lands), saw also a rapid rise in prices. Grain prices, for example, rose about 155 per cent in England, about 300 per cent in Saxony, and about 500 per cent in Spain. From the end of the sixteenth century, the problem of prices is more complicated, and the data are not much more complete than before. It seems that a part of the seventeenth century was a period of stable prices, but that from the end of the century to about 1815 prices rose quite steadily and generally.

If we take the price level of 1800 as 100, we have a course of prices somewhat like this:

1500	35
1600	75
1700	90
1800	100

It is safe enough, then to adopt as a basic principle that changes in the quantities of precious metals produced tend to affect the purchasing power of money.

The careful observation of the gold and silver supply has been carried out only in the economic society of Western Europe, that is to say, in a society which has not only been expanding internally and externally, but to which a large expansiveness has been dictated not only by external circumstances but by its own social psychology, its *Geist.* It would be a great advantage in defining this obviously important character in our own history, where it is still a sort of "mysterious stranger," to have adequate statistical indications of the functioning of the money metals in one or more societies that were economically at a standstill or declining. In European society, it seems fairly clear that the increase in the supply of gold and silver has been both cause and effect. On the one hand, it seems to have contributed to that characteristic and persistent expansionism of economic Europe. On the other hand, that expansionism has itself constituted a steady and insistent social demand for a larger equipment of exchange instrumentalities, that is to say, over most of our period, a simple demand for more gold and silver.

Thus, a change in the price level can be effected only through a change in the conditions of production of the precious metals, particularly in the cost of production. Thus, in a period of rising prices (declining exchange value of the precious metals), a mine owner will continue producing until the costs of operation (wages, cost of transportation, etc.) become greater than his returns. He then shuts down the mine; that much demand is removed from the markets, and prices decline (i.e., the exchange value of his product goes up). When they have declined sufficiently to reduce the costs of operation below the amount of silver or gold he can get out, he reopens his mine and the cycle begins again.

Of course, the generalization of the price changes through changes in the amount of precious metals produced, depends upon the general proportion between the amount of precious metal production and the range and intensity of the economic activity into which it comes, particularly, the amount of wares being produced, the rapidity of exchanges, and, finally, the previously existing supply of money.

Any systematic presentation of the operation of gold and silver in society must be recognized as purely abstract and idealized. The historical actuality is characterized by radical irregularities. For example, the world's supply of gold and silver has probably been produced at a net loss to the producers and would-be producers. Every one knows the characteristic fate of gold-mining stocks. We happen to have some statistics from the exceptionally rich Joachimsthal area which indicate that from 1525 to 1575 the expenditure in getting and trying to get silver was between three and four times the yield. On the other hand, much was produced for Europe without production costs that can be reckoned in any system of accounting, as when it was obtained as loot and plunder (the Italians and the Crusaders in the Levant, the conquistadores in Mexico and Peru). At times, the money metals ceased to be increasable goods (fourteenth century, early nineteenth century) and the question of cost of production disappears from the determination of their value. Even when the supply is being increased, the exchange value of the precious metals is determined by the cost of production in the highest-cost mine, sometimes by that in the lowest-cost mine, depending upon the course of prices, whether rising or declining.

With this brief theoretical definition (which does not in the least pretend to be complete) of the characters of the precious metals as an element in economic theory, it is possible to turn to an examination of their record in the course of economic history.

The realization of a money income by the miner of precious metals was not always a simple process, nor has it been a uniform process throughout European history. While gold panned from the sands could nearly always be taken directly to the mint, ore, the only form in which silver is found, had to be smelted. Apparently in America, a smelter was normally a part of the equipment of each mine. In medieval Europe this was not the case. The mining was done by individuals, sometimes organized in gilds, but often working quite separately. The typical arrangement for disposal of the ores was sale to a smelter owner, or more commonly to a middleman, an ore buyer. The legislation (1300) for the Kuttenberg workings shows a sort of weekly market. The ore buyers were apparently in a position to dictate prices. Much is heard of their exploitation of the miners; the Kuttenberg legislation refers to their practices as a "detestabilis conspiratio." In the fifteenth century, *Fürkauf,* buying for others, was forbidden at Gossensass and Schwaz.

At a very early time, this exploitation led to the development of what we would call public smelters. One was erected for the Silesian mines as early as 1203. About the same time the landlords of the mines in the Tirol erected one at Innsbruck. In the second half of the fifteenth century, the duke of Bavaria erected one at Brixlegg which not only smelted the product of the ducal mines near by, but also attracted ore from the Tirol and even from more distant sources.

Although it is apparent that there was a social justification for political monopoly, the objective of these establishments was, like that of the mints of the time, fiscal, revenue for the sovereign or lord who had the power to concentrate the right of coinage in his own hands. Generally speaking, the sovereign rights thus concentrated were "farmed out," entrusted for a longer or shorter time to favorites, associations, or individual business men. The concern of such minters was naturally to mint as many coins as possible and to buy the raw material, gold and silver, as cheaply as possible. Free coinage, in the sense of unrestricted coinage, was assumed rather than prescribed. Many ordinances in all of the countries of Western Europe provide that any one bringing so much metal to the mint shall receive so many coins.

The freedom, however, was only with reference to the amount coined. It was generally provided that the precious metals produced should be coined within the kingdom, duchy, or other sovereignty in which they were mined. Prohibitions of export are found in the great producing areas, such as Silesia, Saxony, and Bohemia. In 1534, Ferdinand I as king of Bohemia prohibited export except when the royal mint was unable to take the metal offered, and, in any case, the royalty, something over seven gulden for each mark of fine silver, was to be paid. The example is important because it shows how the prohibitory attitude persisted even in case of surplus production. The same requirement of coinage on the spot explains at least in part why Mexican silver was exported in the form of Mexican dollars, which were dispersed all over the Americas and the Far East.

This general prohibition of export would have meant that the countries which had no mines would have no raw metal to coin. In fact, there were markets for bar gold and silver, and therefore they were exported. The much used Viennese pennies were made of silver brought from sources quite distant from Vienna. Foreigners carried metal to and from Strassburg without interference. The prohibitions were gotten around by smuggling and by contracts. The dispersion of American silver (see Chapter I) was accomplished in the main by smuggling and the same practice appears in medieval Europe. Contracts permitting exportation were numerous in the fifteenth and sixteenth centuries.

Antony von Ross in 1486 paid 4,000 florins to the duke of the Tirol for one year's permission to export as much as he chose. Similar arrangements were made by the Augsburg financiers with the king of Bohemia and by the great Fugger house with the kings of Spain.

It is obvious from all this that there was trade in gold and silver; even gold was bought with gold coins and silver with silver coins. The transportation costs, the royalties, the mint charges, the changing precious metal content of coins, all combined to create a wider margin of difference between the metals and the coins than we are accustomed to, and to make it possible to speak of the price of the money metals themselves. The lack of any permanent relation between the coins of any given coinage area and a given weight of metal made the exchange of metal for coin something else than a mere change of form, a real market exchange. The number of coins given for a unit of gold or silver varied widely but still within effective limits. The upper limit was the number of coins that could be made from the given unit minus the costs of manufacture and the royalties and other dues collected by the political powers. The lower limit was determined by the ability of the minters to raise their share by lowering prices of the metals. The varying prices were, of course, in part determined by contracts and bargaining, but mostly by the legislation of the mint lords or even of the minters.

In contrast with present practice, the variations were frequent and considerable. In Florence, where monetary practice generally was of a higher standard than in the generality of coinage centers, 132, 140, and 111⅗ grossi were paid at different times between 1345 and 1347 for one pound of silver. In Breslau from 6 florins 3 grosse groschen to 7 florins 7 grosse groschen were paid for one mark of pure silver. Even prices determined by contract varied widely. In 1449, Duke Sigmund of the Tirol contracted with the smelters of Gossensass and Schwaz to give them 6½ florins for each mark of silver minus 2½ florins for exchange; in

1488, by a similar contract, the Fuggers were to receive 8 florins, 3 for themselves and 5 for the smelters. These prices obviously were determined by a combination of political and economic forces. When silver was scarce in the fourteenth century, the French ordinances directed the mints to return the whole number of coins to the metal owner minus only the actual cost of minting. Sometimes, as in the case of the Fuggers' contracts in Spain, it was the economic situation of the mint lord that occasioned specially favorable terms.

Free coinage meant something quite different from what it means at present. The owner of gold or silver could be sure of getting his metal coined, but the market to which he brought it was very uncertain. Every variation in the exchange value of the precious metals must have been reflected much more rapidly in their "price" than in a time of mechanized free coinage like our own. The fixed and automatic exchangeability of money metals into an identical amount of coin must necessarily attenuate the effect of changes in the purchasing power of money in determining the price of money metals. Conversely, the changes in purchasing power in this earlier time must have exercised a direct and immediate influence on the production of the precious metals.

Certainly what little we know of the connection between cost of production and the variations in the price in the centuries before the eighteenth bears out this idea. In the twelfth and thirteenth centuries new and more productive mines were opened, gold-bearing sands were exploited and gold and silver were brought back from the East as booty. In other words, the cost of production was low, the exchange value of gold and silver declined, and prices rose. In the fifteenth century, when the precious metals grew scarce again, the minters generally complained that "silver was dear" and remedied the situation by debasing the coinage. From the end of the fifteenth century, cost of production declined again, when precious metals were looted from the Aztecs and Incas and Joachimsthal and Schwaz surpassed the mines hitherto known in Europe. The well known rise in prices in the sixteenth century was the inevitable consequence.

Alexander von Humboldt, the great scientist and traveler of the early nineteenth century, has a table comparing the cost of production of the richest mine in America with the richest mine in Saxony in his time. In the Mexican mine, the cost was 14 livres tournois; in the Saxon mine, 24 livres tournois a pound.

When the amalgam process of refining silver had been developed, the price of quicksilver became a large element in the cost of production. When the price of quicksilver was cut in half by the large importations from India in the latter half of the eighteenth century, and by the improvements in the Spanish mines, the American use of quicksilver rose from 37,750 hundredweight in 1762 to 59,000 in 1782.

The low cost of production promptly found expression in the immediate lowering of the subjective valuation of the precious metals in the hands of the producers. Every one is familiar with the fantastic tales of extravagance and high prices in such areas as the Klondike and California in the days of easy production. A fifteenth century chronicler tells us in pinched phrases of a gold strike in his time when money was hardly valued any higher than goods that the miners could buy of the peddlers. The Spanish grandees who got the cheap money from America acted the same way, spent their easily won silver as rapidly as they could. The result was that prices in Spain rose even more rapidly than elsewhere. The Brazilian gold discoveries led to such outrageous prices (at the gold washings) as one pound of gold for a pair of cats. Toward the end of the century, the price level had been adjusted to the changed conditions of silver production. The Mexican revolution and the general stabilization of the price level after the Napoleonic wars correspond closely enough. In general, from 1250 to 1850, the price movement followed substantially the variations in the production costs of gold and especially of silver.

REFERENCES FOR FURTHER READING

General

Sombart, W. Der moderne Kapitalismus, vol. I, pp. 463–571.

Industrial Technique

Usher, A. P. A History of Invention (1929).

Taylor, R. A. Leonardo the Florentine (1927).

Dircks, H. The Life, etc., of the Second Marquis of Worcester (1865).

Georgius Agricola. De re metallica (trans. by Herbert Clark Hoover and Lou Henry Hoover; 1912).

Haskins, C. H. Studies in the History of Medieval Science (2nd ed., 1927).

Thurston, R. H. History of the Growth of the Steam Engine (1902).

Smiles, S. Lives of the Engineers (1861–1862); Men of Invention (1884).

Weber, Max. General Economic History (1927), pp. 302–314.

Feldhaus, F. M. Die Technik der Vorzeit, der geschichtlichen Völker und der Naturvölker (1914).

Fournier, E. Le Vieux-Neuf: Histoire ancienne des inventions et de découvertes modernes (2nd ed., 3 vols., 1877).

Knight, M. M. Economic History of Europe to the End of the Middle Ages (1927), pp. 246–253.

Gold and Silver

Del Mar, A. History of the Precious Metals (2nd. ed., 1902); Money and Civilization (1886).

Humboldt, A. von. Essai politique sur le royaume de la Nouvelle Espagne (1811).

Soetbeer, A. Edelmetall Produktion und Wertverhältnis zwischen Gold und Silber seit der Entdeckung Americas bis zur Gegenwart (1879).

Lexis, W. "Beiträge zur Statistik der Edelmetall nebst einigen Bemerkungen über die Wertrelation," in *Jahrbuch für National Okonomie,* 34:361–417.

Ehrenberg, R. Capital and Finance in the Age of the Renaissance (English trans., 1928).

Lamprecht, K. Deutsche Wirtschaftsleben im Mittelalter (3 vols., 1879–1899).

Rogers, T. A History of Agriculture and Prices in England, 1259–1793 (7 vols., 1866–1892).

Steinbeck. Geschichte des schlesischen Bergbaus (2 vols., 1857).

Adams, Brooks. The Law of Civilization and Decay (1895); The New Empire (1902).

Fisher, Irving. The Purchasing Power of Money (1913).

Taussig, F. W. Principles of Economics (2 vols., 2nd ed., 1917); "The Quantity Theory of Money in Modern Form" (book III, especially chaps. XVII–XIX).

Hobson, J. A. Gold, Prices and Wages (1913).

Foster, W. T. "The Circuit Flow of Money," *American Economic Review* 11:460–473 (1921).

CHAPTER III

THE ADAPTATION OF POPULATION GROUPS TO CAPITALISM

The Organization of Labor

The development of a wage-working class is one of the essential prerequisites of the capitalistic economy. The problem is twofold: first, how the propertyless class, the potential wage-workers, came to be, and second, how they were organized into a suitable and responsive labor force.

We are confronted in the centuries from the sixteenth to the nineteenth with two apparently contradictory phenomena: a large mass of unemployed persons and a great dearth of labor supply. The numbers of beggars which investigators such as Levasseur, Rogers, and Perthes have established for France, England, and Germany are appalling even to modern ears, accustomed to postbellum unemployment crises. In the fifteenth century, a contemporary estimated the number of beggars in Paris at 80,000; in 1634, another set their number at one-fourth of the city's population. Voltaire and Mercier regarded the number of beggars as an incident of wealth. In the provinces, conditions were equally bad. In 1482, Troyes numbered 3,000 beggars in a population of 15,000. In 1678, Amiens had from 5,000 to 6,000 laborers who depended on alms. The bishop of Montauban wrote in 1694, "We find six or seven dead at the gate of the town almost every day, and in my diocese of 750 parishes about 450 persons die every day from lack of food." Gregory King (1696) estimated the number of persons in England dependent on alms at one-fourth of the poulation. The money collected for poor rates equaled a quarter of the whole export trade. In Holland, "the whole country swarmed with beggars." In the German ecclesiastical states in the eighteenth century, it was estimated that in each thousand of population there were fifty clergy and 260 beggars. Cologne had 20,000 beggars in a population of 50,000.

The factors to which this vast number of paupers have been attributed are many. Sixteenth century Englishmen thought it was due to enclosures, the concentration of the open fields into single holdings. The classic expression of this feeling is More's introduction to the *Utopia*. Only about three per cent, however, of the area of England was affected by the enclosures of the sixteenth century. The suppression of the monasteries turned out about 88,000 paupers to the mercies of lay charity. Overpopulation was much blamed, when the population of England amounted to from five to eight million. The gradual impoverishment of independent agricultural and industrial producers was certainly a factor—one which needs to be taken into account. We shall see that many of them went directly into a dependent relation as producers in their own homes for "putters out." The decline of villeinage from the fourteenth century onward detached many from the soil and drove them to the freedom of the roads. In France and Germany, the long succession of wars (especially the Thirty Years' War and the devastations of Louis XIV) seems to have been even more disastrous than the last war in Western Europe. In France, taxation, although not as high on the whole as modern taxation, fell unequally and disastrously upon the classes least able to bear it. An interesting list of alms takers at Neuenkirchen an dem Stor (Schleswig-Holstein) classifies them: war cripples and wounded, mutilated men, dismissed officers, worn-out chaplains, people who had been "burnt out," shipwrecked or impoverished by drought, unfrocked preachers, schoolmasters, organists, preachers' widows, wandering students, blind people, lame people, insane and other ill persons, apostate Jews and Catholics.

On the other hand, through the memoirs of entrepreneurs,

the reports of officials, the comments of industrialists, runs the one complaint: lack of workers. At the States-General of 1614 the Parisians complain in their cahier of a lack of workers for the woolen industry. Colbert and his corps of intendants used every method from cajolery to fines to compel people to work in the new industries. Defoe declared, "There is in England more labor than hands to perform it and consequently, a want of people, not of employment." Even in 1784, Dale found it "no light task" to collect a population for New Lanark. In Germany, the iron industry in Baden was handicapped by lack of labor. "Often must the industrious farmer divide his hard-won patrimony with these loafers, since he is not in a position to get laborers for his fields even with money," wrote Johann Wilhelm Klein in 1792.

The reasons for this apparent contradiction of lack of employment and lack of workers is not far to seek. In the first place, the lack of connection between communities made possible directly opposite conditions in localities quite near to each other. Then, too, the problem of training workers was a difficult one on account of the purely personal character of skill and the methods of acquiring it. For instance, the hats of the cardinals of the Catholic Church were made only in Caudebec by hatmakers who became Protestant in the sixteenth century. When the Edict of Nantes was revoked in 1685, the hatmakers migrated to England; and thenceforth cardinals' hats had to be bought in Protestant England until, in the middle of the eighteenth century, one of the descendants of the original hatmakers returned to Paris and set up an establishment there. Throughout the early capitalistic period, the transmission of technique remained personal, organic, empirical, as it had been in the handicraft system. Still more obvious was the widespread disinclination to work—to work at all, or to work in the manner or at the tasks which the arriving capitalistic entrepreneurs demanded. The old sustenance idea, as distinguished from the idea of gain, led the workman to abstain from labor when he had enough to eat and drink. In France, Colbert and his intendants constantly complained of the "do-lessness" of the people of this town or that. In England, nearly all contemporary observers speak of the idleness of the poor. "We have thousands of people miserably poor, yet will not work." The Manchester manufacturers, according to Arthur Young, wished to have prices, especially of food, remain high enough to keep their employees at work six days a week. In Holland, "the whole summer through, the weavers did nothing but wander from village kirmess to kirmess, getting drunk at each and recovering in the intervals." In the Catholic countries, at least, this inclination to idleness was organized somewhat in the form of religious celebrations. In the seventeenth century, the Carinthian iron industry operated with only 100 eight-hour shifts in a year. In Paris 103 holidays were celebrated in 1660. The propertyless groups obviously worked to live; they did not live to work. The problem of Mussolini, to teach Italy to work, was in effect the problem of those individuals whom the feeling for gain, the rationalistic attitude toward economic activity, the passion for enterprise, which we call the capitalistic spirit, had made "friends of industrial progress."

This was partly accomplished by the labor legislation of the rising absolutisms. The motive that impelled the first Renaissance monarchies in this legislation was neither the desire for class advantage nor humanitarian concern but "the good of the state"—which, of course, was easily and often confused with the good of the monarch, or with the good of the well-to-do. Some of the legislation was humanitarian in effect, as for example the prohibitions upon "truck," or payment in provisions, in England and elsewhere. In general, however, the avowed and conscious aim, registered in thousands of preambles and pamphlets, was the power and welfare of the state—the monarch.

The state undertook to regulate and control the relation of the worker to the economic cosmos, just as it undertook to regulate all other economic relations, in its own real or supposed interest. That the relations between employer and employee were a purely private affair that concerned only them would have seemed to every one at that time a monstrous notion. On the contrary they had to be regulated and the regulation had to come from those in power.

Forced labor was supplied to the early capitalistic industries under the authority of the state. The old agricultural serfdom, which disappeared in England very early, lasted in the rest of Europe until the end of the early capitalistic period and in the eastern part of Europe well down into the nineteenth century; and it was widely used by early capitalists. The Fuggers of Augsburg in the sixteenth century held wide territories in lordship whose inhabitants were obliged to weave for them. As late as 1788 mining in Silesia was carried on largely by peasants bound to labor, as were also the cloth factories in Austria and in Poland and the new manufacturing enterprises of the nineteenth century in Russia. There the lord usually "hired out" his serfs to other persons, owners of factories or mines.

A sort of state serfdom also was established in most European countries. In Spain as early as the sixteenth century, the beggars and vagabonds were rounded up and put to work in the workshops of Valladolid, Zamora, and Salamanca. In France, in addition to the corvée, a kind of road labor tax, compulsory labor was enforced upon the *paveurs* and quarry workers. On account of lack of labor for cloth factories in Silesia, the government ordered all persons, especially soldiers' wives and children, to devote themselves to spinning. In Bohemia, the Regency decided on August 5, 1717, that, in order to introduce fine cloth making, it would be desirable to establish a "poor, orphan, and work house." In England, under the statute of apprentices (1563), "in order to banish idleness," any unmarried person under thirty years of age, trained in a trade or fit for agricultural labor, could be forced to take employment at a wage established by the justices of the peace; and any untrained person of that age could be forced to enter apprenticeship.

The handling of poverty by the state offered special opportunity to solve the labor problem by compulsion. From the fourteenth century a long series of often repeated laws in each country of Western Europe declared that the beggar and the vagabond must be put to work. In the sixteenth century, workhouses began to appear, where the pauper could be put to work. In 1539, the Albergo dei poveri in Genoa already had 500 men and 1,300 women employed in spinning. In France a workshop for beggars and vagabonds was opened in 1576, but the system was first effectively developed under Colbert. The Elizabethan Poor Laws provided authority for the establishment of workhouses by the justices of the peace in each county, but it was not until the end of the next century that the first was actually built at Bristol (1697). An advocate of the system declared, "This would prevent poverty and in a little tract of time bring up hundreds to be able to gain their livelihoods." The occupants of the Paris workhouses were exploited in various ways, ranging from direct production for the market by the institution itself to hiring out to independent manufacturers. Hiring out in various forms became very common in England and ultimately a gigantic abuse. Basel in Switzerland turned the occupants of its orphan asylum over to the manufacturer who promised to support them best.

An interesting phase of the organization of the labor supply is the earnest competition of the several countries for one another's trained workers. Foreigners were important in all countries both as entrepreneurs and as laborers, because they brought new ideas and processes. Of that aspect, the last section of this chapter will treat in more detail. At this point, we are concerned with the measures taken to attract and hold trained workers. Venice confiscated the goods of glassworkers who migrated. A French ordinance of 1682 imposed a penalty of death (!) upon workers who left the kingdom. English statutes penalized enticing or contracting with laborers to go out of the kingdom. The prohibitions of export of tools and machines from 1666 onward are of the same general significance.

Attraction of foreign workers was the counterpart of the prohibition of emigration. Almost all English industry was built upon the influence of alien immigrants. Edward III brought over Flemish weavers (fourteenth century). Henry VI (1452) admitted Saxon, Bohemian, and Austrian miners. Henry VIII introduced weapon manufacture almost solely with the aid of German workers. England, like Prussia, fell heir to numberless French craftsmen after the revocation of the edict of Nantes. In France, the silk industry was established by the importation of Italian workers; tapestry weaving, by Flemish and Italian workers. Prussia under Frederick II sent agents all over Europe to capture workers and methods in silk making, damask weaving, leather working, and other industries.

The various states took over also the regulation of industrial relations from the craft gilds and nationalized it, specifying the duration of the ordinary contract, prohibiting change except under certain conditions, regulating wages, regulating the conduct of workers away from their work, and heavily penalizing combinations of workmen.

The Development of Bourgeois Wealth

Between the Middle Ages and modern times there exists a curious distinction in regard to the concept of personal wealth, obvious enough at first glance but somewhat difficult to put into words. An aphorism of Sombart's puts the problem neatly. If, in the Middle Ages, you had power, the inference was that you were rich. If, now, you have wealth, the inference is that you are powerful. Then, power brought wealth; now, wealth brings power. But what does the word "wealth" mean? Obviously, in this connection, something different from what it signifies in the expression "the wealth of nations," a shading that is perhaps best expressed in the English word "means" (German, *Vermögen*). But "means" to what end? Essentially, means to command the services of others. These means may be individual in character, a pair of strong hands, a capacity for domination, or they may depend on social sanction—relations with family, right to the labor of slaves, or (to come to the connotation that is most frequent in modern speech) the right to dispose of material goods. This social wealth derives its primary meaning from the fact that through it the owner can command the services of other men.

Historically, of course, individual wealth appears first, then social wealth. The men endowed with special powers and capacities, the medicine man, the military leader, are endowed by society with larger shares of land or of booty. The powerful become the rich. Such was the wealth of the feudal lord—whether it was land or movable property or money. But money, as it came into Europe in increasing quantities from the ninth century onward, effected a gradual transformation in the essential character of wealth. The possession of money gave power to every one who had it. This new power first developed alongside the feudal power and then displaced it with a power system—the state—adjusted to its own characteristics and forms. The agents of this new power are the *nouveaux riches,* the *gente nuova,* the *homines novi, quos fortuna faece tulit.* They stand from the first outside the feudal nexus; their wealth is bourgeois wealth.

The evolution of bourgeois wealth is a historical problem. The sources, the means, and the tempo of fortune building are all determined by historical circumstances, and in turn determine in varying ways the course of events, especially the forms of economic life. We shall consider first the distribution of wealth (in the modern sense) among feudal persons, then turn to the evolution of bourgeois fortunes in restricted (legal) forms and finally to the free (unlegal) forms of fortune building. We are not here concerned with the development of fortunes in capitalistic activity, but rather with fortune building as a part of the historical background, a precedent condition of modern capitalism.

Feudal wealth consisted to such a large extent of power relations that it is difficult to evaluate in terms of modern wealth. Lamprecht and D'Avenel have given estimates of land values which show a radical advance from the ninth to the sixteenth century; but the complete revolution in landed property since that time makes the figures more than doubtful both in fact and in significance. Income figures seem more comparable, but are not available before the fifteenth century. In the reign of Edward IV (1461–1483), the nominal income of an English duke was estimated at £4,000; that of a marquis, £3,000; that of a baron, £500; that of a simple squire, £50. Gregory King in 1696 estimated the average income of the peers to be £3,200; that of the squires, £450; that of a great merchant, £400; that of a retailer, £45; that of a craftsman, £38. The Italian nobles were more wealthy. The Orsini and Colonna families of Rome had incomes of about 25,000 florins a year in the fifteenth century. Milan counted five families with incomes of from 10,000 to 30,000 ducats. In the fourteenth century, six Spanish dukes had incomes of over 100,000 ducats.

Among public establishments, still larger aggregations of wealth were common. The papacy at the end of the Middle Ages was regarded as the most wealthy—the *mater pecuniarum,* it was called. Of peculiar significance for economic history, as we shall see, was its development as an international financial system and its strong tendency to "monetization." The Templars at their suppression early in the fourteenth century were said to have 10,500 manors; the Hospitallers, 19,000. Philip Augustus, king of France, left an estate of $10,000,000. In 1574 the annual royal income was about $5,700,000; by 1715 it had grown to about $60,000,000. The English crown was by far the most effective financially of the secular governments of the Middle Ages. William the Conqueror had about $2,000,000 a year at his death; a century later Richard

From J. Savary, *Le Parfait Négociant* (1675).

A French Consular Court in the Seventeenth Century

Cœur de Lion had nearly as much. Some of the city states were almost as rich as kings and popes. These figures are all open to a great deal of criticism, but together they illustrate the fact that the scale of wealth was much lower than today and that the relatively great incomes were to be found among the politically powerful rather than among merchants, manufacturers, and bankers.

A priori, it would seem that the traditional and legal and technical limitations of the handicraft economy would have made any considerable accumulation by "trade" impossible. The fact remains that some merchants and craftsmen did become rich. The German folk tales tell us of peddlers who "became so wealthy that they had great sums of money standing out with almost every one." Andrew Bate, the butcher of Lynd, one of the leading wealthy men of the place, famous for his great herds, his land purchases and sales, and his ruthless extraction of tribute from the "western men"; Hans Waldmann, the tanner and iron dealer of Zurich, who carried on also an extensive money-lending business; Hagnel, the butcher of Orléans, who "was so enriched by money-lending that a great part of the houses of the town were pledged to him and he bought ovens, mills, and châteaux from the nobles"—all these like the Fuggers and the Welsers of the sixteenth century are examples of hundreds of craftsmen who became rich. It seems, however, almost as if not quite universally true that their fortunes were made not so much in the exercise of their crafts as by incidental speculation, above all by money-lending, so that the rich craftsmen are not exactly examples of the wealth-building possibilities of the crafts.

In commerce, profits seem to have been comparatively small: Vickos von Gelderson between 1370 and 1376 averaged 19 per cent on his cloth sales. Tin was bought in London at 8 florins and sold in Florence at 13½ florins a hundred pounds. In industry there was a wide "spread" between raw material costs and the selling price of finished products; but, as we have seen, the producing shops were characteristically very small and their product even more limited. Occasional monopolies, especially natural monopolies like salt beds, were the source of fortunes, sometimes for nobles, but also sometimes for lesser folk. Great fortunes were made by transport operators especially in the Italian ports. Oriental goods commanded a peculiar market among the especially rich and therefore were the source of many a merchant's fortune.

As we have seen, money-lending played an important part in the building of great fortunes in the later Middle Ages. In spite of the hostility of church and custom and economic structure to gainful money-lending, it appears to have been continuously practiced. Even in the ninth century, when money economy was at its lowest point, it was the subject of some legislation on the part of the later Carolingians. The market for loans was among the nobility, secular and ecclesiastical, whose consumption demands exceeded their natural income from their estates—a lord who wished a fine coat of mail, an abbot who wished to indulge his taste for building a fine church. All over Europe, proverbs, poems, and the reflections of moralists from the tenth to the thirteenth century tell us of the fatal inroads of the usurer upon the feudal economy. If the money of a usurer were put into the same coffer with that of an abbot, ran the monastic legend, it would devour the whole, so that in a little while nothing could be found in the coffer. A repentant Parisian usurer on his death bed remitted all his outstanding loans: the list consisted almost exclusively of loans to spiritual and secular lords. The Crusades gave an enormous stimulus to the needs of the nobility for money and to this way of satisfying them. Between 1295 and 1304, bishops had borrowed over 4,000,000 florins from five Florentine houses. By the middle of the fourteenth century, the Bardi and Peruzzi had lent the king of England $3,000,000. These sums, comparatively insignificant to modern eyes, were enormous in contrast with the annual value of the export trade of a great seaport like Lübeck (less than $650,000) and that of the whole export of wool from England to Italy (only about $500,000). In short, money-lending was the "big business" of the merchants and Jews all through the early capitalistic period.

The profits were enormous. Interest was ordinarily 20 to 25 per cent, rarely as low as ten. The count of Provence in 1243 forbade interest in excess of 300 per cent. Frederick II in 1244 paid 173 per cent. Even the papacy, with its great financial system, paid from 8 to 35 per cent. Louis XIV paid 15 per cent. In form the loans were usually conditional transfers of property, generally a prince's revenue, a lord's banality (right to the patronage of his peasants at his mill, wine press, etc.). The result was the development in the rising state of a widespread publican economy, the collection of revenues by money-lenders who regarded them simply as property. France was the classical land of the tax farmer. From the thirteenth through the eighteenth century, the system developed until the farmers-general became a terrible incubus. In the seventeenth century, it was estimated that only one-fifth of the taxation reached the king's coffers. In the sixteenth, the Fuggers made profits of from 175,000 to 525,000 ducats a year by advancing money to the kings of Spain and collecting their revenues. The great family syndicates which made Augsburg the successor of Florence as the financial capital of Europe, and of which the Fuggers are only the best known example, were all money-lenders. The French farmers-general all built up enormous fortunes. La Bazinière, the son of an Angevin peasant, came to Paris, became the lackey of a "financier," rose to be treasurer of the king, and died a rich man. Camus, who began with nothing, left $400,000 to each of nine children. Of the 726 *gens d'affaires* penalized in 1716 for unsavory financial operations, 105 had from 50,000 to 100,000 livres, 13 from 1,000,000 to 2,000,000 livres, and 6 more than 2,000,000 livres.

The forms of fortune building with which we have been concerned above obviously rested upon the transfer of wealth from certain individuals and classes to others, rather than upon the creation or accumulation of new wealth. Of this latter category, the important sorts were the accumulation of city real estate and mining profits. The differentiation of city tenures from agricultural tenures is in itself an interesting study, but here it must suffice to say that there was in the towns a general tendency to substitute for the tenures on condition of actual services, tenures on condition of money payments. Burgage in the English towns is an example of this development. Sometimes, as in Flanders, Italy, France, bitter struggles were necessary, but substantially the same end was attained everywhere in Western Europe. Down to the fourteenth century, city land was still held of the lord for this money service, as indeed it still continues in many cities to be in the form of leases. The general reduction of services to money then brought about something practically identical with modern sales. Meanwhile increase of population within city walls led to very stiff prices. In Florence, for example, at the end of the thirteenth century, building sites commanded from $2.50 to $5.00 a square meter (present-day values).

Although in general more has been spent in the search for precious metals than has been won, yet in many individual cases great fortunes have thus been won, not only by poor miners who became millionaires overnight, but also by the owners of royalties, kings and landlords, by the refiners, and by the mint lords, the mint superintendents, and the minters. The more valuable of the German mines of the thirteenth and fourteenth centuries were very productive, and the American mines of later centuries even more so. Alexander von Humboldt tells of single Spanish-American mines that produced over $1,000,000 a year in the eighteenth century. Royalties (i.e., shares due to the crown) were especially high. In the Brazil gold fields they ranged from one-fifth to two-thirds. They were often diverted into other hands because they were particularly suitable for pledging to money-lenders. The Fuggers thus took over the mines of the archduke of Tirol in 1487 and later extended their activities to Hungary and Silesia.

The miners themselves were originally organized in gild

fashion and considerable fortunes were acquired in this way; but the gild organization was soon supplanted by the individual adventurer. "In fact," says the Kuttenberg mine ordinance of 1300, "frequently two miners, who don't have enough to say where they will lay their heads the next night or where they will find tomorrow's food, get into conflict over a lease that may produce several thousand marks of silver." The wealth of the Weitmoser family was founded by Erasmus Weitmoser (died 1526), the son of a poor wood-hewer, who, with the help of a hundred thalers lent him, opened a rich vein of gold on the Radhausberg. Finally we meet also, especially in the mines of the Tirol and of Hungary, rich burghers acting practically in a capitalistic function. Between 1495 and 1504 the Fuggers took from their Hungarian mines a dividend of 119,500 Rhenish florins; between 1504 and 1507, 238,474 florins. From the pledged quicksilver mines of Almadén, they took 600,000 ducats between 1595 and 1604. The wealth of the great German houses came out of mining in so far as it did not come from money-lending. The American mines were much richer: the count of Valencia sometimes got $1,500,000 a year from his Mexican mines.

The refiners and the minters also got rich from the increased flow of the precious metals through their hands. The refiners usually were accused of a "detestable conspiracy to beat down the price of ore." Minting rights were commonly farmed or pawned and treated, of course, as a purely profit-making enterprise. Reminting was a much favored source of profit. In Görlitz, for example, seven recoinages were effected in the year 1308.

Still more indirect fortune-building consequences of the increased gold supply were the increased number and amount of public loans, the high profits, notably at the American mines, where Seville merchants made profits of from 100 to 500 per cent on a single expedition lasting from nine to twelve months, and the opportunities offered in the exchange business by the variations in the prices of gold and silver. "There are so great abuses of late yeres growne by corrupt dealing of sundry Merchants and Brokers as well strangers as English upon bargaines of exchanges and rechanges of Moneyes to be payed both out and within the Realm," reads the preamble of Elizabeth's proclamation of September 20, 1576.

Money-lending, real estate, mining ventures seem to us conventional enough ways of acquiring wealth; but even methods which seem lawless to us were also of importance. Cheating, larceny, and embezzlement produced some of the greatest fortunes. The old tradition that power brought wealth continued to be exemplified in the dishonest officials who were the rule rather than the exception. Pierre Remy, French superintendent of finances, left a fortune of $14,000,000 at his death in 1328. Æneas Sylvius describes the chancery of the Emperor Frederick III as "a hungry crowd, who turn every opportunity to the greatest possible advantage." In Spanish Naples, officials with salaries of 600 ducats a year presently retired with great wealth. The trial of Sir Francis Bacon brought out the fact that the English judges expected bribes from both parties in cases before them. The semipublic trading companies were honeycombed with corruption, as is illustrated by the fortunes which Clive and Hastings brought home from their service with the East India Company. Robbery, especially in the form of piracy and plundering, became significant in the economic sense when Western Europeans came in contact with increased supplies of gold and silver. Genoa and Pisa owed their wealth to the piratical exploitation of their control of the Mediterranean. Venice plundered the cities of the East, especially Constantinople. Albuquerque brought back a million ducats of booty from Malacca in 1511, one-fifth of which went to the Portuguese king. Elizabeth was proud to share with Drake and Hawkins the results of their freebooting upon the Spanish galleons bringing home the booty wrung from Peru and Mexico. In 1717, there were 1,500 pirates on the coasts of the Carolinas.

Forced trade was equally common and only another form of

robbery. The Arabs for a time enjoyed a forced trade in Oriental goods at the expense of Western Europe but the Portuguese discoveries turned the flank of their position. The Western Europeans after the discoveries turned upon the natives of the Americas, Africa, and India, and by virtue of their military dominance bought the native goods with European goods at fantastic valuations. While the apparently excessive spread between cost and selling price was considerably reduced by operation costs, the large dividends of the East India companies over long periods indicate plainly that they converted their power into profits. The Hudson's Bay Company bought beaver pelts for goods costing seven to eight shillings. In the Altai, the Russians sold iron pots to the natives for as many beaver skins as would fill them. The Dutch East India Company paid the native producers of pepper about one-tenth the price it received in Holland. The French East India Company in 1691 bought Eastern goods for 487,000 livres which sold in France for 1,700,000 livres. The profits of the East India companies were enormous: the Dutch company paid an average of 18 per cent over a period of 198 years in addition to its payments to the government, the stealings of its officials, and a considerable multiplication of its capital.

Slavery in the colonies was another source of great fortunes. We are not here concerned with the fine legal distinctions of status connected with servitude, but include all forms of forced labor.

The Crusaders in Syria and Palestine and the Venetians in the Byzantine territories maintained a system of slavery as brutal as American slavery at its worst. In the transoceanic colonies, the Dutch and the English imposed forced labor upon the native populations in the East. The Spanish attempted to utilize the American Indians in their mines, but humanitarian considerations led the Spanish government to interpose a protective policy. The labor supply problem was solved with wonderful rapidity by the introduction of Negroes. Through the Middle Ages the Moors had carried on the Negro slave trade across the Sahara, and from 1445 onward the Portuguese began to displace the Moors. In 1501 the first Negroes were introduced into the Spanish colonies; in 1510 the Portuguese began to supply Negroes for the mines; in 1619 the first Negroes were brought by a Dutch ship to Virginia. From the beginning Negro slavery was supported by the State; and the Church also supported the system in spite of a long tradition of hostility to white slavery, because it gave an opportunity to convert the Negroes. In 1517, Charles V granted the first privilege to introduce Negro slaves into the Spanish colonies at the rate of 4,000 a year; in 1715, by the terms of the Asiento Treaty, the English South Sea Company undertook to furnish 144,000 in the course of the next thirty years.

White servitude was also common in the English colonies. Persons guilty of common law or political crimes or of the crime of poverty were sent to the colonies as bound servants, or indentured servants. In 1620, Sir Edwin Sandys sent to Virginia 100 children "appointed for transportation" by the City of London. After the battle of Worcester (1745), 610 Scotch prisoners were sent to Virginia. By far the greater number of these "indentured servants" accepted the status voluntarily as a way of securing passage across the Atlantic. With the growth of the plantation system the use of forced labor increased rapidly and steadily. Sugar, tobacco, and cotton culture rested upon Negro slavery. By 1830 the number of Negro slaves in the Americas was estimated to be about 5,739,000, plus about 1,082,000 freedmen. The number in the United States grew rapidly until 1860, when it reached 4,400,000. The increase was furnished by an active slave trade, itself a source of great fortunes. In 1769, British ships carried 53,100 slaves; French, 25,000; Dutch, 11,000; British-American, 6,500.

The fortune-building significance of slavery was of course very great. The slave trade was enormously profitable, as slaves were cheap in Africa, and usually fairly dear in the plantation colonies. In the seventeenth and the eighteenth centuries, French slavers made about 1,000 per cent. In 1786, Liverpool ships handled 31,690 Negroes with a profit of £298,462. Slave labor was profitable under certain conditions:

(1) In the plantation system, i.e., with the concentration of considerable groups under single management.

(2) Noncompetitive prices assured by some monopolistic position, such as climate: it was especially true that slave labor could not compete with white labor.

(3) Exhaustion of the slaves: the slave was not only used, but used up; it is a well known fact that the slave population never reproduced itself but had to be kept up, after the slave trade became illegal, by smuggling and by purchases from specialized breeding areas.

(4) Exhaustion of the soil: slave labor could not be used in such a way as to keep up the fertility of the soil.

Under these conditions, slave plantations showed profits of from 15 to 25 per cent.

In the Dutch East Indies, the natives were forced to produce a "contingent" for which they received a low fixed price. In 1762, the contingent of Java was purchased for 82,223.6 rix-dollars and sold for 215,874.8 rix-dollars. The system of the English East India Company was more complicated. By getting the diwani, or financial administration, of Bengal into its hands, the company had the collection of £20,000,000, of which £7,000,000 went to the rajah and £9,000,000 to expenses, leaving a net of £4,000,000 for "investment" in native goods. As a contemporary pointed out, all these goods were drawn to England "without sending an ounce of silver from hence."

White servitude in the English colonies across the Atlantic was profitable because of the extraordinarily high cost of labor. In tobacco culture indentured servants came into competition with Negro slaves, and the servant was expected to produce several times as much as the slave.

On the whole, the pictures of plantation life that have come down to us show a great wealth-building force in slavery. Manoel de Salvador tells us, of the Brazilian planters about 1600, that "one who doesn't eat off of silver, passes for a poor man." Defoe wrote in the beginning of the eighteenth century: "We see now the ordinary planters of Jamaica and Barbados rise to immense estates, riding in their coaches and six, especially in Jamaica, with twenty or thirty Negroes on foot running before them whenever they please to appear in public."

The Development of Bourgeois Demand

In the course of European history, the demand for goods underwent a complete transformation. From one point of view the new aspects of demand are a significant manifestation of bourgeois forms of wealth and bourgeois attitudes toward it. From another point of view, they were so many new opportunities for the accumulation of bourgeois wealth.

We have already had occasion to note the development of wealth among new classes of society, who demanded new and more numerous forms of enjoyment; the rise of the great armies, whose support and equipment demanded large quantities of uniform goods; the increasing number of ships in navies and in merchant fleets, whose building requirements far transcended local sources of provision; the development of great towns, whose dense and extensive concentrations made dependence upon foreign sources of supply a major fact in their own lives and the lives of the communities from which they drew; the colonists, whose wealth and whose longing for the things of home made them eager customers of the merchants who followed them across the world.

These new demands, potently expressing themselves in terms of money, easily accumulated in the hands of kings and burghers and easily disbursed, required for their satisfaction a non-local, broadly based and intensely active organization of production and exchange. In what respects did the character of demand change? How much did it amount to? How did it affect the rest of the economic process? In the terms of the classical economy, this discussion is concerned with the margin between socio-psychological demand (desire) and economic demand in the strict sense of that word.

The increase in luxury demand is well illustrated by the social history of the courts of kings and princes. The papal court at Avignon was perhaps the first modern court with a nobility whose whole life was devoted to its activities and with beautiful women, "often distinguished in manner and wit," who gave the tone to the court life. The papal court carried its new manners back to Rome, and the great Renaissance popes from Paul II to Leo X maintained courts that were not surpassed in their time. The other Italian princes followed their example, and Charles VIII, Francis II, and Catherine de' Medici carried the new standard to the wider terrain of the court of France. The château of Blois shows how the Italian influence operated to produce new standards of luxuriousness in building. The peace that returned to France with Henry IV made possible new advances, and under Louis XIV, luxury expenditures reached their peak. The Sun King spent altogether about $60,000,000 for his palaces. Clothes were correspondingly magnificent. Louis himself wore one outfit which was decorated with $2,800,000 worth of jewels. The royal mistresses of the eighteenth century depended upon their capacity for brilliant expenditure for the security of their positions. Louis XVI's queen, Marie Antoinette, spent from $30,000 to $40,000 a year on her clothes.

Through the short period from the opening of the mines of Potosí and Guanajuato to the reign of Philip IV, the Spanish royal court even surpassed that of France in luxury, and the Spanish style manifested its influence everywhere. The English court, even when the Stuarts attempted to copy French standards, never reached the height of extravagance there maintained. The German courts even more sedulously imitated the Grand Monarch but were less wealthy and had a predisposition to emphasize quantity rather than quality in luxury.

The demand for luxury spread from the courts to general society. "It is a plague," Saint-Simon tells us, "which, once introduced, has become a cancer growing at the vitals of every individual, because from the court it is promptly carried to Paris, to the provinces and the armies, where men of position are appraised only by their tables and their general scale of magnificence." Luxury in eating, especially appreciation of quality, seems first to have become widespread in Italy, then to have been carried into France, where on the whole the highest standards have been maintained ever since. The new tropical products, coffee, cocoa, tea, tobacco, grew in popular demand until they became psychologically indistinguishable from necessities. In 1668, 100 pounds of tea were brought into England; in 1786, 14,000,000 pounds. The individual consumption of coffee in Europe in 1800 was at the rate of about one pound per year (now it is about six pounds). Three to four pounds of sugar per person were imported into Europe, but France used only about one pound per person. The English used 10,000 tons in 1700, and 81,000 tons in 1790. Clothes and dwellings show a similar rising curve of costliness and luxuriousness.

The towns were more marked by this tendency to luxury than the villages. The characteristic city amusements, the theaters and music halls, began to flourish in the seventeenth century. The Opera at Paris dates from 1673; the Comédie Française, from 1689; the first playhouse in London, from 1576. Fine restaurants and hotels appeared first in London. Beaumarchais said that more money was spent in a single winter evening in the public houses and restaurants of London than the population of the seven United Provinces spent in six months. The shops, especially the luxury shops, shocked Defoe with the growing extravagance of their settings and furnishings.

Luxury had become domestic, an affair of the residence rather than of the cathedral or of the market place; things had taken the place of people; servants had taken the place of retainers; the wood carver and the embroiderer had supplanted the architect and the sculptor. The tempo of luxury had changed: instead of the periodic feast day with its concentrated splendors, any day was appropriate for a great banquet, a masquerade, or a ball. The deliberate production of the Middle Ages had given way to a demand for the immediate personal satisfaction of the consumer. The Milanese family of Sacci had worked for eight generations, over two hundred years, on the altar silver of the cathedral: for Louis XIV, workmen were busy day and night against time to finish his château of Versailles. Demand had learned to change from year to year, almost from month to month. The "mode," the "fashion," introduced variation as a persisting element in demand. In the thirteenth century, Joinville might justify the cut of his clothes by the retort that his ancestors had worn them that way. In the sixteenth, Jovius Pontanus wrote, "Clothes we admired four months ago, we now despise and refuse to wear." Montaigne noted that the changes in fashion were too rapid for invention and the tailors had to return to old fashions. The English Parliament attempted to resist the demand for change with sumptuary acts, six of which were passed between 1511 and 1570. It was with the luxury-loving court and society of Louis XIV's time, however, that the "age of the mode" effectively began: in 1672 appeared the first fashion magazine.

An important incident of the luxury demand was the interest in foreign things. The French valued things brought from Italy, the Italians, those brought from France. The English "millinery" shops were full of French, Milanese, Spanish, Flemish, Venetian goods. Ben Jonson wrote, in his comedy *The New Inn,*

> I would put on
> The Savoy chain about my neck,
> The cuffs of Flanders, then the Naples hat,

With the Rome hat band and the Florentine agate,
The Milan sword, the cloak of Geneva set
With Brabant buttons; all my given pieces,
My gloves the natives of Madrid . . .

The development of the great cities involved a great concentration of demand. In the sixteenth century there were probably fourteen cities in Europe with populations of more than 100,000. While a few, like Lisbon and Antwerp, declined thereafter, most of them steadily grew. English kings tried to stop the growth of London; French kings, that of Paris. In spite of royal edicts, both cities continued to grow; and in 1801 London had nearly 1,000,000 inhabitants, and Paris nearly 700,000. Substantially all these people, as well as those of lesser cities, depended on outside economic (producing) groups for their sustenance. Londoners bought about 650,000 muttons annually between 1736 and 1770; they paid £330,364 in taxes on the distilled liquors they drank in 1784, and used about 1,000,000 tons of coal a year. The supply of Paris was carefully studied by committees of the Constituent Assembly at the beginning of the Revolution: they reported that 90,000,000 pounds of meat were consumed each year, and a total of 260,000,000 livres a year was spent for all provisions brought into the city.

In the minds of their European rulers, a colony existed partly to give a new and larger form to demand. The colonies exercised a powerful influence on shipbuilding and the shipping industry. In 1769, England employed 1,078 ships and 29,000 seamen in the trade with the North American colonies alone. All the colonies were rich and bought even beyond their direct purchasing power by the industrious use of credit. Each European country restricted the trade of its colonies as far as possible to the mother country, and often the trade was concentrated in single ports of entry, notably in the Spanish colonies at Porto Bello and Vera Cruz. The Asiatic culture lands, such as India and Malacca, had already a fully elaborated system with which the European merchant had to compete. It was not until the nineteenth century that Indian industry was destroyed by the English. The American culture lands, on the other hand, were devoid of all industrial equipment, and their new colonial populations demanded the goods to which they had been accustomed at home. The Negro population required clothes and food, which in the sugar colonies, where the population was densest, had to be brought from the mother country. Where the interest of the colonists dictated the seeking of cheaper sources of supply, as the French colonists in Haiti sought flour and salt fish in the United States, or manufacturing for themselves, as the New England colonists attempted to manufacture beaver hats and iron, repressive laws were made to hold them to the market of the mother country. Smuggling counteracted most of the restrictions on trade. On the other hand, manufacturing developed only very slowly even in the United States. When the restrictive laws were nullified by the American Revolution, the scarcity of labor and the higher rewards of capital and labor in agriculture and the extractive industries caused the Americans to continue to depend on England and other European countries for manufactured goods.

The needs of the fighting forces increased, of course, roughly with the increase in the forces. Large weapons (cannon) were used in steadily increasing numbers. English naval vessels carried 2,087 cannon in 1548 and 8,396 in 1700. Under Colbert the guns of the French navy increased sevenfold, from 1,045 in 1661 to 7,625 in 1683. The need for food supplies grew with the extension of military action beyond the local limits of feudal warfare. Philip Augustus, for example, bought eight months' supplies in Genoa for the force which he sent to Palestine. The function which the capitalistic organization was destined to perform is plain when we see the agents of the French king going from bailliage to bailliage in 1304, requiring each to deliver a specified amount of grain and wine at Calais. Supplies for the war vessels were handled in the old local fashion until the opening of the

Atlantic made long cruising the rule, instead of simple ventures out from port. The Armada again serves as an example. For the voyage to Flanders, 110,000 hundredweight of biscuits had to be collected. The increase in military and naval budgets expresses for us the revolutionary increase in demand. In the beginning of the seventeenth century, the French king spent an average of $2,000,000 a year on his armies and fleets; in 1680, $40,000,000; in 1784, $160,000,000.

The development of shipping bears significantly upon the new forms of the demand for goods in two different ways. Its increase reflects the greatly increased territorial range of demand, and the building of ships in itself required many different kinds of goods in new forms. The number of ships built per year increased steadily from the sixteenth century to the eighteenth. They also increased in size, necessitating new technique and organization. Down to the nineteenth century the typical vessel used in European waters weighed only about 100 tons. The oceanic cruises, however, required larger vessels. The typical East Indiaman ranged from 300 to 500 tons. War vessels also grew larger: by the end of the seventeenth century, the English fleet contained forty-one vessels of over 1,000 tons, the largest having 1,739 tons. This meant larger shipyards, larger groups of workmen, larger concentrations of material. The "tempo" of shipbuilding also rose rapidly: Cromwell and Colbert both built up their navies with extraordinary rapidity. The assembled character of ships extended the economic influence of shipbuilding over a wide range of products: wood, tackle (flax and linen), sails, iron (anchors, chains, sails, wire), tar and pitch, brass, copper, and tin. The costs give a summary index of the quantitative alteration in shipbuilding as a source of demand: in the sixteenth century, a medium-sized English war vessel cost £3,000 to £4,000; under James I, £7,000 to £8,000; under Charles I, £10,000 to £20,000; in the beginning of the eighteenth century, £15,000 to £20,000.

The demand for goods had been vastly transformed:

(1) Greater quantities of goods were demanded with increasing wealth.

(2) The demand for goods had transcended the purely local character of demand in the Middle Ages: the city drew on the country; foreign goods were demanded along with native goods; colonial goods were demanded in Europe, European goods in the colonies.

(3) The demand for goods was concentrated in increasingly great cities, the great entrepôts of the colonies, the great shipyards.

The Emergence of the Entrepreneur

Capitalism was the work of dominating individuals. While, like other economic forms, it grew out of the needs and circumstances of the times, its development was marked by the activities of revolutionary individuals and groups overthrowing the old systems or distorting them for their own purposes. These were the *entrepreneurs*—a class for whom we have no favored English word, since "enterpriser" is not liked, and "undertaker" has come to be associated with a quite different concept. Feudal enterprise, the achievement of lordship, had much in common with capitalistic enterprise, in that in both the entrepreneur bent other men's wills to the problem of supplying him with income. They differed fundamentally, however, in that the activity and influence of the feudal entrepreneur, the strong-willed man who made himself lord of a community, was local and personal, whereas the activity and influence of the capitalistic entrepreneur extended itself over thousands and millions of men whom he would never see. The type was the same in both groups; the vigorous, the clever, the strong-willed. It existed among all the people who have made European history, in France and England, in Germany and Italy, in Spain and Holland as well as among the Jews. It appeared in all classes of society—princes, lords, merchants, craftsmen, and beggars—and in all religions.

The capitalistic entrepreneurs, however, fall naturally into two distinct groups, according to the means they used to carry through their plans: those who used political power—the princes, the nobles, and officials—and those who, without political power, depended upon their own powers of persuasion and organization. The two groups shade into each other, as we shall find, for the latter group, with increasing frequency, depended upon the state for direct support, and generally molded the law of the state to favor their activities. Among the second group certain elements appear with special significance—elements which have the common characteristic of strangeness to the general society in which they lived: the heretic, the immigrant, and the Jew.

Circumstances, ambition, and even a conception of duty led many monarchs of the Old Régime into capitalistic activities. Gustavas Vasa of Sweden not only encouraged mining, but operated a great sea-trading organization. Edward IV of England carried on an extensive wool trade. Elizabeth and James I shared in the freebooting ventures of Drake and Raleigh. Charles I sent agents all over England to make profit-sharing bargains with various industrialists. Colbert, the great minister of Louis XIV, gave strong support to all sorts of capitalistic ventures—enabling his sovereign to share in the profits of many of them.

The nobility—the landlords—although their feudal origin involved a negative attitude toward gain-seeking, drifted very naturally into capitalistic enterprise. Sometimes they were actuated, like the abbot of Ossegg, by a humanitarian desire to have their dependents kept busy and correspondingly comfortable. In general, however, the landlord turned to capitalistic enterprise just as other enterpreneurs did, in response to the attractions of unlimited gain and the increasingly favorable conditions which were facilitating the evolution of capitalism. The abbots of Closterrode, for example, developed what was not only in all probability the first coal mine on the Continent, but the largest, with eight hundred men underground and about as many occupied above the ground.

The nobles in all European countries were becoming urbanized. Old families were dying out, and the new nobility were coming from the wealthy families of the bourgeoisie. The decline of feudalism was bringing the nobility to the courts. In England, the restrictions of primogeniture were effecting a coalescence between the younger branches of noble families and the upper middle class. James I sold baronetcies. In France, this practice was even more widely developed in the reign of Louis XIV, when 800 titles were sold; in the eighteenth century, the mere purchase of a "noble" estate carried nobility with it. In other words, the successful capitalist was displacing the military man in the nobility. There remained, however, a tradition that barred even the descendant of a drug clerk or an old-clothes seller from "trade" after he became noble. It was proper for him only to organize his control of the soil in capitalistic fashion. It was proper, of course, to raise agricultural products or stock through the tenant system or even by wage labor, to exploit mineral and timber wealth, to use his power over labor. He might also properly invest in the stock of the great trading companies.

In England the mining and smelting industries were almost wholly the enterprises of nobles. The great sheep growers were often cloth makers as well, and converted into cloth the wool they had grown. In France, nobles founded mining enterprises, foundries, spinning and weaving establishments. The thirteen owners of smelters in the generality of Tours in the eighteenth century were all noble. Nineteen nobles, of all ranks from the princes of Croy down, had and exercised the right of mining coal. In Silesia in 1785, of 243 mines, 20 "belonged" to the king of Prussia, 14 to a duke and two princes, 191 to "other counts, barons, and noble estate owners," and only two to the Breslau merchants. Porcelain and glass making were introduced into

Germany by small princes. So in Austria we find nobles busy as organizers and exploiters of the quicksilver mines and the iron industry. In Bohemia, the first paper mill was established by Count Nostiz (1644). In Russia the various industries introduced under the auspices of Peter the Great were not shared in by the nobles, but in the second half of the eighteenth century they became a considerable factor in industrial production because they could utilize the labor of their serfs. In 1809, of 98 cloth factories, 12 belonged to merchants, 19 to the high nobility, 55 to simple nobles, 12 to foreigners. Nobles were usually the leading adventurers and beneficiaries of colonial establishments. The Spanish colonies were granted out in *encomiendas*. Lord Delaware, the earl of Clarendon, the duke of Albemarle, the earl of Shaftesbury, and many other nobles for reasons of philanthropy and profit participated in the founding of English colonies.

The bourgeoisie as a whole contributed to the entrepreneur class not only directly but indirectly through the recruiting of the nobility from the more wealthy, the more successful, and, it may be presumed, the more enterprising of their class. The bourgeoisie steadily became a larger and more important element in enterprise until in the end it attained political and economic dominance. It had the advantage of the bourgeois virtues, industry and frugality, and the steady development of bourgeois wealth opened opportunities for the enterprising type to use his own and others' wealth in capitalistic fashion. The bourgeois entrepreneur did not, like the noble, depend upon power and privilege to bring him wealth, but depended upon money to bring him power and privilege. He was properly the first capitalistic entrepreneur, because for him capital, especially money capital, was the essential prerequisite of all enterprise. Through him, the "bourgeois wealth," the development of which we have studied, became significant for the building up of the capitalistic system.

The bourgeois entrepreneur evolved along two distinct lines: first, through the gradual expansion of some handicraft business directed by him, which might be farming, industry, commerce, or transport. The original entrepreneur in a family appears as a small capitalist; his son or grandson begins to emerge as an important merchant or manufacturer. A great part of the handicraft *negotiatores*—Florentine wool merchants, English tradesmen, French *marchands,* Jewish piece-goods merchants—became capitalistic entrepreneurs. Similarly, rising industrial merchants became what the English called manufacturers, the French, *fabricants.* The other principal line of development was through "putting out" (German *Verlag*). Appearing at first as a sort of obligation of the rich masters to furnish materials for their less fortunate brethren, putting out became a system by which the rich masters or, more frequently, merchants, organized the labor of the less enterprising and prosperous workers. It was especially common in the cloth industry and spinning, but also existed in mining and smelting, in the manufacture of notions, especially of paternosters, and tailoring.

It was the bourgeois class that furnished another distinct type of entrepreneur who found his opportunity in the opening of distant vistas by the development of overseas commerce. This was the founder of new enterprises, the projector or promoter. "About the year 1680," writes Defoe in his *Essay on Projects,* "the art or mystery of projecting began to creep visibly on the world." We have already noticed the type, however, at least a century earlier in men like Johann Joachim Becher (see Chapter II). A certain Benevento appeared at the court of the Emperor Ferdinand, and then at that of Philip II of Spain, offering to increase the revenues of these monarchs without any new taxes and without any innovation of significance. Defoe's time was nevertheless the *Blütezeit* of the promoter. The supreme examples, perhaps, were William Paterson, who successfully solved the financial problem of the expanding monarchy of England by founding the Bank of England, and John Law, who less fortunately tried to solve that of the expanding monarchy of France, not to speak of the wag who, at the height of the South Sea Bubble, invited subscriptions to a project, the objects of which were to be disclosed later.

Finally, the strangers—the heretics, the immigrants, and the Jews—in all countries played an important part as entrepreneurs. The development of state churches, Catholic or Protestant, after the Protestant Revolution, brought a cleavage in the citizenry, the orthodox and the heterodox, the full citizens and the half-citizens. The heretics were excluded from all official life and existed only upon sufferance. Their position was essentially a defensive one. They were forced to turn for their livelihood to business and to cultivate a special standard of honesty and sobriety. The Spanish proverb declared, "Heresy promotes business spirit." William Petty, an English observer of the seventeenth century, cannily noted that "trade is not fixed to any species of religion as such; but rather to the heterodox part of the whole." In Mohammedan India, the Hindus; in Turkey, the Jews and the Christians; in Italy and Spain, the Jews and the Protestants; in France, the Huguenots; in England, the Dissenters—all played a part in business wholly out of proportion to their numbers. In France this unequal distribution was forcefully brought out at the revocation of the Edict of Nantes (1685), when nearly every branch of capitalistic industry was seriously injured by the emigration of Huguenots.

Some observers, notably Max Weber and R. H. Tawney, find a special connection between Protestantism, especially its Puritan aspects, and capitalism. Certainly it seems obvious that the religious notion that all human activity was a "calling" lent a powerful psychological sanction to the enterprising Protestant business man. In another sense, Protestantism and capitalism were akin to each other because they were both heresies, both "nonconformities," both products of the innovating spirit.

At any rate, whatever the reasons, it is apparent, both from statistical evidence and from the judgment of contemporaries, that the European "heretic," especially the Protestant, was disproportionately important in the new forms of business. Closely associated with religious heresy is another social fact of the sixteenth and seventeenth centuries, namely, migration. At that time, migration was most general among nonconformists, French Huguenots and English Separatists, who fled from their homelands to England, to Prussia, to Holland, and to America. The vigorous minority with the courage to make new homes in the old world or in the new found themselves not only in a state of half-citizenship that put a premium upon economic enterprise, but also detached from the customary and traditional limitations that governed the natives of the countries to which they went. The one measure of their success in life, the one future that lay before them, was the accumulation of significant wealth.

It is not surprising then to find the foreigner a prominent participant in the development of new enterprises. The "Lombards"—Italians from Genoa, Florence, Pisa, and Venice—were the foremost financiers of England, France, and the Netherlands from the thirteenth century to the sixteenth. The silk industry was organized in something like the modern factory system in Genoa, Bologna, and Lyons by immigrants from other cities, especially Lucca.

Migrations *en masse,* such as those of the Jews from Spain, of the colonizers of North America, and of the persecuted Christians, provide even more obvious manifestations of this characteristic function of the foreigners. The migration of persecuted Christians in the sixteenth and seventeenth centuries involved some hundreds of thousands of individuals, the largest group of whom were the 300,000 Huguenots who left France after the revocation of the Edict of Nantes. Scotch refugees, Catholic and Protestant, were the big business men of Cracow, Bromberg, and Posen in Poland at the end of the sixteenth century. Fugitives from the devastated Palatinate and from Holland founded the silk business of Krefeld upon a capitalistic basis. French Huguenots founded factories in Saxony, in Hamburg, in Hesse-Cassel, in Prussia. Holland, perhaps, offers the classic example of the influence of foreigners. The tolerant policy of that country made it the refuge and haven of Jews, Flemings, Walloons, English, French Huguenots, all the persecuted of Catholic countries, without, on the other hand, excluding Catholics themselves. The foreigners became characteristically the founders of factories—cloth factories, pot factories, paper mills, printeries. In England, Italians, Portuguese, French Huguenots, Flemings, Walloons, and Dutch immigrants participated in the founding of such important industries as cotton spinning, cotton printing, and cutlery manufacture. A conspicuous example of this same phenomenon nearer our own time is the large part played by foreigners in the economic development of Russia in the nineteenth century.

The Jews, of course, during most of the early capitalistic period, combined the characters of stranger, heretic, and half-citizen, and we find them playing a remarkably large part in just those phases of economic life in which capitalistic forms were most rapidly developing. One-twelfth of the English foreign trade passed through their hands during the first half of the seventeenth century, when they were still legally excluded. At the Leipzig fair, they were always prominent, and during the last days of its greatness one-third of the merchants were Jews. They controlled the Levant trade of Spain, and when they were expelled, carried the control with them to the Netherlands and to the Levant. Luxury trades, such as diamond cutting and silk, bulk trades, such as cotton goods, alike seemed to fall into their hands. They played a significant part in the colonization of new lands. Hardly had Columbus discovered America, before a colony of Portuguese Jews settled in St. Thomas and began exploiting slave labor. They poured into Brazil in spite of prohibitions and were strongly reenforced during the Dutch occupation. Jewish refugees from Brazil made the greatness of the sugar industry in Martinique and Haiti.

Similarly we find the Jews disproportionately prominent in that most capitalistic of economic enterprises, the supplying of armies. "The great Jew," Antonio Carvajal, was one of the principal contractors who supplied Cromwell's armies. Similarly, "the great contractor" of William III's time was "the jew Medina," who was knighted. In France, Jacob Worms was known as the principal war contractor of Louis XIV. Marshal Saxe declared that his army was never better supplied than when he depended on the Jews. Cerf Beer was naturalized as a French subject for his services in connection with famines in Alsace. In German lands, the same story. In 1537, Isaac Meger was permitted to live in Halberstadt on condition that he supply the Cardinal Albrecht's army with "good weapons, harness and armor." "From thenceforth all commissaries are Jews, all Jews, commissaries," wrote a German biographer in 1677. Jews were the principal commissaries of the American troops in the Revolution as well as in the Civil War.

These examples illustrate the prominence of Jews as entrepreneurs without touching upon their activity as financiers and bankers, which was an equally important factor in the evolution of capitalism, but which hardly belongs here.

REFERENCES FOR FURTHER READING

I. Labor

General

Sombart, W. Der moderne Kapitalismus, vol. I, pp. 785–919.

England

Cunningham, W. Growth of English Industry and Commerce During the Early and Middle Ages (2 vols.; 4th ed., 1904).

Ballagh, J. C. White Servitude in Virginia (1905).

Bowden, Witt. Industrial Society in England Towards the End of the Eighteenth Century (1925).

Cheyney, E. P. History of England from the Defeat of the Armada to the Death of Elizabeth (2 vols., 1924–1926); Industrial and Social History of England (rev. ed., 1923).

Cunningham, W. Alien Immigrants to England (1897).

George, D. London Life in the Eighteenth Century (1926).

McCormac, E. I. White Servitude in Maryland (1904).

Prothero, R. E. English Farming, Past and Present (1912).

Unwin, George. Industrial Organization in the Sixteenth and Seventeenth Centuries (1904).

Webb, S. and B. English Poor Law History, part I, The Old Poor Law (1927–1929).

France

Levasseur, E. Histoire des classes ouvrières et de l'industrie en France avant 1789 (2 vols.; 2nd ed., 1900–1901).

Clément, P. Histoire de Colbert et de son administration (2 vols., 1892).

Martin, G. La Grande Industrie sous la règne de Louis XV (1899).

Renard, G., and Weulersse, G. Life and Work in Modern Europe (1926).

Rambaud, A. Histoire de la civilisation française (2 vols.; 9th ed., 1921).

Sargent, A. J. The Economic Policy of Colbert (1899).

Sée, Henri. Economic and Social Conditions in France During the Eighteenth Century (1927).

Germany

Marriott,, J. A. R., and Robertson, C. G. The Evolution of Prussia (1915).

Schevill, F. The Making of Modern Germany (1916).

Sources

Defoe, Daniel. Giving Alms No Charity (1704).

Mandeville, Bernard. Fable of the Bees (1714); Essay on Charity and Charity Schools (1723).

Statutes of the Realm, 5 Elizabeth c. 4.

Young, Arthur. Six Months Tour through the North of England (4 vols., 1770).

II. The Emergence of the Bourgeois

General

Sombart, W. Der Bourgeois (1912). Tr. by M. Epstein as The Quintessence of Capitalism.

D'Avenel, G. La Fortune privee à travers sept siècles (1897).

Rogers, Thorold. A History of Agriculture and Prices in England (7 vols., 1866–1892).

Law, Alice. "The English *Nouveaux Riches* in the Fourteenth Century," Transactions Royal Historical Society, vol. IX (n.s.), p. 49.

Hall, Hubert. Society in the Elizabethan Age (4th ed., 1901).

Perkins, J. B. France Under the Regency (1892).

Robbery as a Source of Wealth

Prescott, W. H. History of the Conquest of Mexico (2 vols.); History of the Conquest of Peru (2 vols.).

Exquemelin, A. O. The Buccaneers and Marooners of America (1891).

Gasquet, F. A. Henry VIII and the English Monasteries (2 vols., 1889).

Slavery as a Source of Wealth

Wilson, H. History of the Rise and Fall of the Slave Power in America (3 vols.; 4th ed., 1875).

Cairnes, J. E. The Slave Power (2nd ed., 1863).

Bassett, J. S. Slavery and Servitude in the Colony of North Carolina (1896).

Day, Clive. The Dutch in Java (1904).

Heyd, W. Geschichte des Levantehandels (2 vols., 1879).

Helps, A. A. The Spanish Conquest in America (4 vols., 1900–1904).

The Bourgeois as Consumers

Defoe, Daniel. The Compleat English Tradesman (2 vols., 1725–1727); The Compleat English Gentleman (1890).

Sombart, W. Luxus und Kapitalismus.

Neuberger, Otto. Die Mode: Wesen, Entstehen und Wirken (1913).

Tilley, A. Modern France (1922).

Weeden, W. B. Economic and Social History of New England (2 vols., 1890).

III. The Entrepreneur

Clément, P. Histoire de Colbert et de son administration (2 vols., 1892).

Sargent, A. J. The Economic Policy of Colbert (1899).

Clark, H. W. History of English Nonconformity (2 vols., 1911–1913).

Cunningham, W. Alien Immigrants to England (1897).

Baird, C. W. History of the Huguenot Emigration to America (2 vols., 1885).

Berg, W. E. J. De Refugies en de Nederlanden (2 vols., 1845).

Elgas, B. A. The Jews of South Carolina (1903).

Hyamson, A. A History of the Jews in England (1908)

Sombart, W. The Jews and Modern Capitalism (1912).

PART III

EARLY CAPITALISM

CHAPTER I

THE TRANSFORMATION OF ECONOMIC MOTIVE AND OF ECONOMIC FORMS

The Epoch of Early Capitalism

The definition of epochs in history is a difficult problem. As a matter of fact, they are fictions—necessary fictions, evolved out of the minds of the historians as a means of expressing the past—rather than consciously felt experiences on the part of the people who were contemporary with their beginnings. On the other hand, it is quite inevitable for persons with any intelligence, reading about, say, William the Conqueror or Periclean Athens, to realize that there is a distinct individuality in the conditions of that time, in other words, that it is a distinct epoch. It is when the attempt is made to mark the beginning or the end of an epoch that this inevitability disappears and disagreement and uncertainty enter. Any given date on the rather wide margin belongs to the earlier or later epoch according to the principle or principles in the mind of the person looking at it.

It is then necessary to have in mind the principle being used in this reconstruction of the past, embodied in summary fashion in our definition of capitalism. This gives us two conditions which have to be met before it can be said that capitalism exists. The first condition is that the wills of strangers, through the compulsion of money, shall have made economically active persons serviceable to a profit purpose; the second condition is that there shall be a disposition to reorganize economic activity, rationalizing it with a view to the highest possible profits. From this point of view, the beginning of the capitalistic period cannot be set very far back. We should guard against the notion that the coming of occasional individuals who act capitalistically, or of certain conditions that might fit into a capitalistic society, marks its arrival.

Capitalistic practices of this exceptional character are not difficult to discover in the thirteenth and fourteenth centuries. The Sienese bankers whom the papacy was using in the thirteenth century to handle the revenue which it derived from widely scattered sources had a system which extended all over Western Europe, and which *could* have been serviceable to a highly developed international commerce, just as modern banks are. It was not thus serviceable because international commerce had not then developed to the point of needing such a system. In the fifteenth century Leon Battista Alberti taught bourgeois economics in his *Libro della Famiglia.* The same century saw at least the beginnings of rationalistic accounting, that is, double entry bookkeeping. Professor Byrne in his excellent study of *Genoese Shipping in the Twelfth and Thirteenth Centuries* (1930) states that in the thirteenth century Genoese shipping ventures were often financed by the distribution of *loca,* or shares, which were treated much as negotiable shares are today—divided, sold, and used as security for loans; and he shows that the Genoese collected capital in much the same way as do modern entrepreneurs. If modern capitalism were merely that, merely the use of a certain device, there could be no answer to his charge that Sombart is in error in putting the beginning of capitalism so late as the end of the fifteenth century. But he proceeds to show that, as accumulations of wealth in single hands grew sufficiently large to finance voyages without such associations, the use of loca declined and disappeared. Nothing could demonstrate more clearly the uncapitalistic *spirit* of these Genoese. Here obviously is no "disposition to reorganize economic activity, rationalizing it with a view to the highest possible profits."

At the end of the fifteenth century, however, the manifestations of capitalistic enterprise become numerous and consistent.

The obvious phases of a new spirit and a new organization of economic life—in a word, of capitalism—become so numerous that even a bare catalogue is too long. A large number of gold and silver mines were opened in Germany and Austria in the late fifteenth century. This aspect was intensified by the discovery of America and the exploitation of the large stocks of gold and silver in Mexico and Peru. America also offered the opportunity for unlimited exploitation of labor in these areas, where European custom had never reached. The discovery of sea routes to India increased capitalistic opportunity in that great trade. The religious persecutions of the Jews in Spain and of the Protestants in France and parts of Germany was accompanied by the displacement of large numbers of economically active individuals. It is worthy of note that Antwerp, destined to be for a time the great capitalistic center of Europe, then began its growth. The establishment of great modern states under monarchs like Louis XI of France, Henry VII of England, and Ferdinand the Catholic of Spain brought various kinds of material and financial needs which could be satisfied only by capitalistic arrangements. Other phases of the change were the distinct advance of technique in engineering and industry (of which Leonardo da Vinci and Agricola are the great examples) and in accounting, notably, double entry bookkeeping. The concept of the "firm" began to spread; great central markets and wholesale houses appeared, and also the solicitation of business, and the operation of collective services like the postal service. Entrepreneur types appear, Puritanism furnished a philosophy for capitalism, and luxury increased at a great rate. The modern stock company began to develop, especially in the oversea trade, business publications began to appear, purchase began to be made by sample, discount and deposit banks began to function.

The end of our epoch of early capitalism, of course, comes with the beginning of what we shall call "full capitalism." It is marked by fully developed rationalization, by purely objective business practices, by the ideal of combination, by "liberty," by centralized markets and long-distance buying, by speculative practices and crises, and in short, by the application of capitalism to all forms of economic life. Applying these tests to the chronological sequence of events, we may regard the period of early capitalism, then, in its largest extent, as the period from the middle of the fifteenth century to the middle of the nineteenth, or, more narrowly, from the sixteenth to the eighteenth.

It will be noted that in defining our period, we have ignored such important political milestones as the French Revolution, although a very great economic history of France, that of Levasseur, divides its four substantial volumes at that point. As a matter of fact, the French Revolution marked no general change in the economic life of France, that is, in its modes of production, distribution, and consumption. Capitalism won some very important political victories in the French Revolution, but its own development had been greater and more crucial in the seventeenth and early eighteenth centuries and was destined to be greater in the middle years of the nineteenth century.

Economic Motive

"Style" is a useful concept in thinking about economic history as well as in thinking about art or clothes or manner of writing. In its present use, a style consists of the psychological attitudes and the intentions manifested in putting together the parts of a whole, whether it be a life or a picture, a poem or a contract. Style is a social fact. Sometimes rather asocial persons have somewhat individual styles. In general there is in any given society a community of attitudes and intentions that pervades and determines the form of its activities.

The style of economic life during the epoch of early capitalism is best characterized by the word "bourgeois." The word, however, has today a connotation of sobriety, dullness, and conservatism, which certainly were not characteristics of the leading agents in the transformations of economic life that are the subject of this section. They were "adventurers," as easily pirates and freebooters as merchants. In Elizabethan England, we meet John Hawkins as discoverer, queen's official, pirate, ship captain, and merchant. Carrying on business meant battle, imprisonment, diplomatic negotiations, as well as trading. Like their medieval forbears, these adventurers won their conquests at the expense of the foreigner or of the lesser breeds, with the idea of sharing them with their own community and people. Comparatively small elements of the population went on these freebooting-trading expeditions, but the fundamental idea, to get rich quickly, led many of the stay-at-homes into "adventures" as bold and disturbing in the economic sense, the "projects" of which we hear so much in the seventeenth and early eighteenth century. Hence the financing of so many of these piratical voyages; hence the strong preference for mining ventures; hence the numerous associations for raising sunken ships; hence the rapid development of marine insurance (bottomry). The primary capitalistic impulse was there, to get rich quickly; what was lacking was the rational and deliberate calculation of the fully developed capitalistic spirit.

More sober, less fantastic characteristics of the bourgeois were also developing. Along with the medieval community notion and the feudal power notion, was developing a system based upon the idea of individual responsibility and the contractual connection of individuals. The exercise of power by and through political agencies was still destined to make important contributions to the upbuilding of the capitalist organization, but this was to be in increasing degree the service of the state to the business interests, to that contract-bound society that ultimately was to ask anarchical exemption (*laissez faire*) from the action of the government. Independently of it, the contract organized the powers of whole sections of society outside of government, on the one hand, and outside of the community organization of village and gild, on the other. The "country merchants" who came from the towns into the villages and, as strangers to its communal life, made arrangements with the village weavers or file makers for a portion of their product had different principles of action, different purposes, different ethics from either the communally minded craftsman or the communally minded villager. Their distinctive virtues were faithfulness to contract and thriftiness.

Leon Battista Alberti in his *Libro della Famiglia* (*Book of the Family*) in 1450 gave the first distinct literary expression to that pride in solidity, dependability, which is for the capitalistic bourgeois the highest of virtues, a pride that curiously parallels the noble's pride of birth. "Never," he declared, "has there been any one in our family who has broken his word given in a contract." Alberti's "never" was probably an exaggeration, but the spirit of this and similar utterances illustrates how virtues get domiciled in this world. The increasing literature of mercantile virtue through the succeeding century all puts faithfulness to contract first. Not all business groups had the virtues in the same degree: it is interesting to note that the English business moralists of the seventeenth century constantly held up the Dutch as models for their countrymen, whose lack of honesty they deplored. Even Defoe, who was not troubled by the moral scruple, gives a very poor impression of the state of business honesty in England (*Compleat English Tradesman*).

In general, we may assume that this virtue of "solidity" grew with capitalism. The more business relations developed on the basis of contract and credit, the more essential the virtue came to be. To us, it seems like a universal virtue, unconnected with the economic system. To a German poet of the latter seventeenth century, the connection was obvious:

> When Truth and Honor else no more is known,
> Still in the honest merchant's breast can it be found
> Whose joy and health on strangers' trust is built.

Bourgeois Virtue: Hogarth's "The Industrious Apprentice out of his time and married to his Master's daughter." Plate VI of his series, "Industry and Idleness."

"Poor Richard" summed up in a word the bourgeois ethical principle: "Honesty is the best policy." In this concept of solidity we have the basis of a professional business ethics, purely utilitarian in origin and registered in our notion of commercial honor and the customs of the exchanges.

Honesty and those other prime bourgeois virtues, industry and frugality, were urged upon the world in countless books of what in modern days is called the inspirational type. A classical example is to be found in the advice of Robinson Crusoe's father to his son.

Another ethical notion of great importance for the development of capitalistic society was that of the honorableness of gain. The pious merchants, like the pious kings, began their contracts with an invocation of the Trinity and regarded their profits as "the blessing of God." This religio-ethical approval of profit seeking was limited to honestly won gain, and the historical question is, What did this idea include?

First of all, the fundamental idea remained the same as in the subsistence economy and the handicraft system. Gain must not be unlimited, but determined by an ideal objective; namely, the sustenance appropriate to one's station: "To every class and every individual God has assigned his sustenance." Another mercantile moralist wrote, "We must rigorously abstain from seeking more than is necessary and sufficient for us and ours." "Enough" is "enough for his station in life." Defoe illustrates this limited standard by the ideal which he presents as the natural objective of a successful business man. "If he has gained twenty thousand pounds, he can buy a pleasant estate and become gentry, spending one half his thousand-pound income and using the rest to increase his landed estate." Franklin thought that "a wise man will desire no more than what he may get justly, use sparingly, distribute cheerfully, and live upon contentedly." The time that he devotes to business will be limited: Franklin held that six hours was the proper limit.

The notion of a just price held over from the canon law until about the middle of the seventeenth century, at any rate in England. Petty recognized a distinction between utility and exchange value. Savary, the great French mercantile writer, still held in 1724 that price should be determined by what it was *just* that the merchant should gain. The German *General Treasure House of the Business Man* (1742) held that it was permissible to make a profit out of scarcity, provided that it was a "Christian" profit and the merchant "in his soul felt no shame."

Competition remained under a certain disparagement. A Paris ordinance of 1761 ran as follows: "Some merchants of this town have assumed to scatter among the public letters in their names to announce the sale of their goods at prices which they allege to be lower than that at which the same goods are customarily sold by other merchants. Such contraventions, which are almost always the last resort of a faithless merchant, cannot be too severely repressed." Gerard Malynes (1686) condemned as "dangerous and prejudicial" all "striving to undersell." The *Compleat English Tradesman* (1745) complained that "this underselling practice is grown to such a shameful height that particular persons publickly advertise that they undersell the rest of the trade." Advertising, of course, was "mean and shameful."

A combination of this moral prejudice against competition and the mercantilist insistence that the population be employed led to considerable action against the introduction of technical improvements in industry. In 1561, the Cloth Makers' Gild of London rejected a finishing device invented by an Italian, because it would throw numerous workers out of employment. Until 1685, knitting machines were forbidden in France, lest they destroy the knitting industry from which many poor people made their living. Colbert regarded the inventors of labor-saving machinery as the "enemies of labor."

In short, the business style of these centuries that we call early capitalistic was only partly free from the older idea of need-satisfying, of subsistence, as the proper aim of economic activity. The pursuit of profit and the economic rationalism which are characteristic of fully developed capitalism were alike in an undeveloped state. Many of the men who furnished the enterprise and leadership were themselves from the quasi-feudal nobility and ran their enterprises as private rather than as market affairs. An observer wrote of the Silesian mines in the beginning of the nineteenth century, "The lord is here owner of the iron ore and annually smelts only so much as can be smelted with that part of his wood supply which he has no other use for." Most of the noble founders of enterprise lacked any inner urge to bring them to great success. Among the non-noble, bourgeois entrepreneurs, economic life was still an ordered regular conventional thing, and novelty, new devices or arrangements were repugnant and unpopular. Marperger (1717) declared that "without doubt, at the present day, it must be recognized that all modernization, even when it is advantageous, is distasteful to most people."

"Retirement" at as early an age as possible was preached by Defoe and was certainly practiced to a large extent. The number of seats in Parliament bought by retired business men like Brice Fisher and Nicholas Linwood or by the heirs of such men, like Sir Samuel Romilly, is a fair statistical index of this tendency in England. An intelligent observer of Hamburg life in the late eighteenth century noted that while business absorbed the whole population from birth, there was a large number of individuals who, having won their fortunes, were "content to sit within their walls and enjoy two and one-half per cent interest." Even in their active careers, the business men did not work all day or all week or all year: the English week end and the French midsummer holiday are vestiges of the early capitalistic "style." An Italian mercantile writer of the sixteenth century even advocated a sabbatical year for business men.

The modern notion of large sales and small profits was foreign to early capitalistic motivation. "Strive not to undersell others," is the constant refrain of the commercial moralists. A strong prejudice existed also against the expansion of business by the free use of credit. The handicraft tradition of "solid goods" still governed extensively, although Josiah Child protested against it as a handicap of English trade in competition with the Dutch. (The most capitalistic country was furthest advanced in the art [?] of providing cheap goods. Compare the complaints of English and American merchants against the German and Japanese "shoddy" production, especially before 1914.)

Finally, early capitalistic business was extremely secretive, a mystery. With the development of the trade journals and new publications in the eighteenth century, came also a whole series of complaints and protests, the general purport of which may be summed up in the complaint of the Hamburg merchants that publication of such news "made the outsider too wise."

Business Forms

It is inherent in the division of any historical process into periods that many of the characteristics of the older period should persist in the new. So it is with the development of economic life. In order to understand exactly what was distinctive in the epoch of Early Capitalism it is desirable to examine briefly the persistence of medieval forms. The individual industry of the separate craftsman as a distinct form persisted in important respects throughout the epoch, and in a less important way down to our own day. The more distinctive forms of medieval economic life, however, were the various types of association which had been worked out, the union under the lords, the craftsmen's association, the family associations, and the occasional combinations of merchants for this or that particular venture. What remained of these in unchanged or in modified form? Economic union under the lord, of course, received its greatest manifestations in the manorial system, which has already been discussed. With certain modifications, it remained the important form of agricultural life down to 1800, although it had almost disappeared in England. In many cases the manorial organization was the center of long-distance commerce. Thus, the Bohemian Glass Association in the beginning of the eighteenth century was not carried on by free and established merchants, but by unfree residents of the glass-producing districts. This feudal medieval idea was carried out also in the colonies. The Genoese and Venetians carried themselves as lords of the manor in their colonies in the eastern Mediterranean. The so-called *encomiendas* and *repartimientos* in the South American colonies of Spain were based upon this idea, as also the captaincies in Portuguese Brazil. A curious example of the persistence of the feudal idea is the organization of the postal system in the Holy Roman Empire as a feudal tenure of a noble family, Thurn und Taxis. On July 27, 1615, Lamoral von Taxis represented his function to the emperor as an imperial regality and fief. The associative character of labor persisted also, to a very late date. The village community of farmers persisted well toward the end of the early capitalistic epoch, although heavy inroads had been made upon it in England. Similarly, in the field of industrial production, the gilds had retained many of their old characteristics, although many of them had been modified by the competition of capitalistic forms of production, and by their own adoption of capitalistic methods. Thus, the London Hosiers' Gild in 1657 became essentially a capitalistic producing society. The Company of Hoastmen at Newcastle had become a coal monopoly. In the field of transport the boatmen's associations on the rivers persisted, generally almost unchanged until the end of the epoch.

The merchant associations gradually lost the personal character which was so prominent a feature of the early organization. They developed into "regulated companies," membership in which was based upon purely formal conditions. The family association underwent a substantially similar change. In the early centuries of our epoch this family association was very prominent. The

Bardi, the Peruzzi, and the Medici in Florence, the Soranzos in Venice, the Fuggers and the Welsers in Augsburg, the Imhofs in Nuremberg, the Rulands in Ulm, are only a few examples of this interesting form of economic organization. They were not exactly firms or corporations, nor did they have the idea of separate individual property in the different members of the family. Gradually they came to take in outsiders, but the personal character of the association was marked by the common provision that members of the family should have larger shares of the profits.

The occasional association for a specific venture remained fairly common down to the eighteenth century. Savary in his *Dictionnaire du Commerce* gives some typical examples: (1) A merchant may desire to join with another in the purchase of a cargo; or (2) three or four merchants at a fair may join to purchase on a common account, and at the close of the fair, divide the purchases in proportion to the purchase money each has put in; or (3) several merchants may unite, for example, in the case of rising prices in France, to buy large quantities of corn in Poland and bring it to France. This occasional combination was important for the development of capitalistic forms of combination, because of its purely contractual and impersonal character, although it plays a very small part in modern capitalistic life.

On the other hand, in the fifteenth century, and at an increasing rate during the next three centuries, new forms of business were established which we may call capitalistic. The establishment of capitalistic forms was marked especially (1) by the development of the notion of business as a legal entity, the Firm; (2) by the notion of the business as an accounting entity, and (3) by the notion of business as a credit entity, the *ditta*.

The notion of the Firm, that is, of a business enterprise as a legal entity, gradually developed during the sixteenth century. The word itself is derived from the Late Latin *firmare,* to sign, and came to imply, by the sixteenth century, the group or combination with a common legally binding signature. As early as the sixteenth century we find merchants in France each of whom was a member of several firms. The French Ordinance of 1673 first settled this relationship by systematic legislation, but even in the eighteenth century its form was not sharply defined by law.

The development of the concept of the business enterprise as an accounting entity is marked by the development and spread of double entry bookkeeping and the introduction of the idea of the balance sheet. Regular bookkeeping seems to have orginated in the government of the Italian cities, rather than in the business circles, as such. As early as the thirteenth century, Florence, Milan, Venice, and the papal government seem to have had something that might have been called a system of bookkeeping; and from these governmental institutions the practice seems to have extended to the bankers, who were closely bound up with the governments. The second step in the development was the introduction of double entry. Although some beginning of double entry can be seen in the bookeeping of Genoa and of the Venetian house of Soranzo as early as the fourteenth century, the first systematic exposition of double entry bookkeeping was that published in 1494 by Fra Luca Pacioli. Fra Luca himself, however, did not include a complete system of double entry bookkeeping and balance sheet. The idea that a balance should be struck yearly, or more frequently than at the death of the merchant or the dissolution of the business, was first introduced by one Simon Stevin, a Hollander, in 1608. It was only at the end of the seventeenth century, apparently, that the system of business accounting was completed by the introduction of the inventory, probably by Savary, the author of *Le Parfait Négociant,* in the Ordinance of 1673.

The significance of systematic bookkeeping for the development of capitalism, that is, for the rationalistic pursuit of unlimited profits, can hardly be exaggerated. One Wilhelm Meister (not Goethe's) declared, "It is one of the most beautiful inventions of the human spirit and one which every good business man should introduce into his business." Sombart declares, "Double entry bookkeeping is born from the same spirit as the systems of Galileo and Newton, as the teaching of modern physics and chemistry." It reduced the gain idea to an abstraction by putting the profit in a specific form, a definite sum of money in contrast to the natural aim of subsistence which was in the forefront of the medieval business man's mental attitude. It was this abstraction of profit that first made the concept of capital possible.

From this abstract formulation of the results of business activity, it was only a step to rationalization. Systematic accounting made it possible for the capitalistic entrepreneur to formulate his aim, to recognize the degree to which he was attaining it, to determine the plans for his future activity. Notions like fixed capital and cost of production were practically impossible without accounting.

Another aspect of capitalism which depends upon complete accounting is the mechanization and depersonalization of business. The entrepreneur and enterprise were separated from each other. As a modern authority on accounting puts it: "It is not necessary to confuse the enterprise with the capitalist, its proprietor. The two are separated by accounting, which conceives the proprietor of the enterprise as the third person, as the creditor of the enterprise for the capital which he has put into it."

Systematic bookkeeping spread over Europe from Italy as a center. Its expansion was conditioned in part by the development of elementary instruction. In Florence, a fourteenth century writer tells us that from 1,000 to 1,200 boys were learning to reckon in six schools. In Paris, there were several thousand pupils in elementary schools in the fifteenth century. For arithmetic they studied the *Liber Abbaci* of Leonard Pisano, principally the "rule of three." In the next century, Italian boys were taught to compute interest and discounts. It would be easy to exaggerate the education of the Italian merchant in bookkeeping; the few examples of bookkeeping that have come down to this day are

Distinctio nona. Tractatus. xi°. De scripturis

Casi che acade mettere ale recordançe del mercante.

Tutte le masseritie di casa o di bottega che tu ti truoui. Ma vogliono essere per ordine. cioe tutte le cose di ferro da perse con spatio da potere agiongnere se bisognasse. E cosi da segnare in margine quelle che fussino perdutte o vendute o donate o guaste. Ma non si intende masseritie minute di poco valore. E fare ricordo di tutte le cose dottone da perse comme e detto. E simile tutte le cose distagno. E si mile tutte le cose dilengno. E cosi tutte le cose dirame. E cosi tutte le cose dariento e doro &c. Sempre con spatio di qualche carta da potere arrogere se bisognasse. e cosi dadare notitia di quello che mancasse. Tutte le malleuerie o obbrighi o promesse che promettessi per qualche amico. e chiarire bene che e comme. Tutte le mercantie o altre cose che ti fosseno lassate i guardia o a serbo o i prestança da qualche amico. e cosi tutte le cose che tu prestassi a altri tuoi amici. Tutti li mercati condittionati cioe cõpre o vẽdite comme per exẽplo vno cõtrato cioe che tu mi mandi con le prossime galee che torneranno dinghilterra tanti cantara di lane di lim[illegible]stri a caso che le sieno buone e recipienti. Jo ti daro tanto del cantaro o del cento o veramente ti mandaro alincontro tanti cantara di cottoni. Tutte le case o possessioni o bottegbe o gioie che tu affitassi a tanti duc. o a tante lire lanno. E quando tu riscoterai il fitto alora quelli dinari sanno a mettere al libro comme di sopra ti dissi. Prestando qualche gioia o vasellamenti dariento o doro a qualche tuo amico per otto o quidici giorni di queste tale cose nõ si mettono al libro. ma sene fa ricordo ale ricordançe. perche fra pochi giorni lai bariauere. E cosi per contra se a te fossi prestato simili cose non li debbi mettere al libro. Ma farne memoria ale ricordançe perche presto lai a rendere.

Comme si scriuono lire e soldi e danari e picioli e altre abreuiature.

Lire	soldi	danari	picioli	libbre	once	danarpesi	grani	carati	ducati	fiorin larghi.
₰	ß	ð	p̃	libbre	ő	ðp	g°.	₭	duc.	fio.laf

Cõme si debbe dettare le ptite de debitori.

M cccc° Lxxxxiii°.

Lodouico di piero forestãi de dare a di xiiii. nouembre. 1493. ₰. 44. ß. 1. ð. 8. porto contãti in prestãça. posto cassa auere. a car. 2 ₰ 44 ß 1 ð 8.

E a di 18. detto ₰. 18. ß. 11. ð. 6. promettemo p lui a martino di piero foraboschi a suo piacer posto hẽre i qsto. a c. 2. ₰ 18 ß 11 ð 6.

Cassa i mano di simone da lesso bõbeni de dar a di. 14. nouẽbre 1493. ₰. 62. ß. 13. ð. 2. da francesco dantonio caualcanti in qsto a c. 2 ₰ 62 ß 13 ð 6.

Martino di piero fora boschi de dare a di. 20. nouembre. 1493. ₰. 18. ß. 11. ð. 6. porto lui medesimo contãti posto cassa a car. 2. ₰ 18 ß 11 ð 6.

Francesco dantonio caualcãti de dare a di. 12. di nouẽbre. 1493. ₰. 20. ß. 4. ð. 2. ci pmisse a nostro piacer p lodouico di piero forestãi a c. 2. ₰ 20 ß 4 ð 2.

Cõme si debbe dittare le ptite di creditori.

M cccc° Lxxxxiii.

Lodouico di piero forestãi de hauere a di. 22. nouẽbre 1493. ₰. 20. ß. 4. ð. 2. sõno p parte di pagamento. E per lui celia promissi a nostro piacere frãcescho dãtonio. caualcãti posto dare a c. 2. ₰ 20 ß 4 ð 2.

Cassa in mano di simone dalesso bõbeni de hauere a di. 14. nouẽbre. 1493. ₰. 44. ß. 1. ð. 8. alodouico di piero forestani in qsto. a car. 2. ₰ 44 ß 1 ð 8.

E a di. 22. nouembre. 1493 ₰. 18. ß. 11. ð. 6. a martino di piero foraboschi. a ca. 2. ₰ 18 ß 11 ð 6.

Martino di piero fora boschi di hauere a di. 18. nouẽbre. 1493. ₰. 18. ß. 11. ð. 6. gli pmettemo a suo piacere p lodouico di piero forestani posto dbbi hẽre i qsto a c. 2. ₰ 18 ß 11 ð 6.

Francescho dãtonio caualcanti de hauere a di. 14. nouẽbre. 1493. ₰. 62. ß. 13. ð. 6. reco lui medesimo cõtãti posto cassa dare a. car. 2. ₰ 62 ß 13 ð 6.

THE BEGINNINGS OF DOUBLE ENTRY BOOKKEEPING: A PAGE OF LUCA PACIOLI'S TREATISE OF 1494

The first debit entry (left) reads: "1793. Lodovico, son of Piero Forestani, shall give on the 14th day of November, 1493, L 44, S 1 D 8 for cash loaned, posted cash shall have at page 2, L 44 S 1 D 8." The first credit entry reads: "1793. Lodovico, son of Piero Forestani, shall have on November 22, 1493, for L 20, S 4 D 2 for part payment. And for him Francesco, son of Antonio Cavalcanti, promised to pay it to us at our pleasure. Posted shall give at page 2, L 20 S 4 D 2." Kindness of Mr. J. B. Geijsbeek Molenaar, Denver, Colorado.

very incomplete and unclear. An anecdote of the Albertis shows that the merchant who kept books was exceptional, and that the function was not at all specialized: the head of an establishment did it for himself if it was done. The introduction of Arabic figures, which was a long process, not complete in the sixteenth century, facilitated bookkeeping as well as general arithmetical education.

It was quite customary for German merchants to go to Italy to learn bookkeeping. The first works on bookkeeping which appeared in Germany (1518–1531) were still behind Pacioli: it was only later in the century that double entry established itself widely in Germany. The first English manual of double entry appeared in 1543, but the practice was still regarded as a novelty in 1569. About the same time, Pacioli was translated into French and Flemish. In Holland, Nicholas Petri Van De Venter broke new paths with his *Manual of Reckoning, Ciphering and Bookkeeping* (1588). In the seventeenth century more than 400 works on bookkeeping appeared in the Dutch language. Holland thenceforward remained the leading country in accounting standards. Benjamin Franklin tells how he learned bookkeeping from the Dutch widow of one of his friends (1730). In France, the advance of accounting went far: in 1673, bookkeeping was prescribed by the great ordinance of that year for all merchants, wholesale and retail. Even before the ordinance, Savary assures us, it was customary among the greater merchants.

The notion of the association as a credit unity was marked by the development of a word which has hardly gone into English practice, *ditta*. This Italian word was widely used on the Continent, as in the phrase, "When one begins a new business or changes the ditta." It appears in this sense first in the sixteenth century and was used especially to express the relations of commercial firms to money-lending institutions. The expression "ditta of the Bourse" was used to characterize a firm in good standing, that is, one whose obligations could be sold easily.

In these centuries we see developing also forms of associations thoroughly impersonal in character and capable of persisting as entities independently of the persons participating in them or ceasing to participate in them. These characteristics identify them as capitalistic associations. The earliest form was the partnership, which in French law was called the public business association. Systematic bookkeeping was substantially essential to make this possible as a substitute for the very personal combinations of the medieval period. It first appeared as a legal institution in the sixteenth century and at that time it was necessarily based upon specific contract. At the end of the seventeenth century it seems to have become the principal capitalistic form of association, and in the Italian, French, and Dutch business writings of the time the public business association is spoken of as the customary and natural form of association. The great French Ordinance of 1673 provided for the distribution of responsibility among all the members of the association. Article seven provided that all the associates would be obligated as a whole for the debts of the association; and this provision applied even if only one had signed, in all cases in which he had signed for the association.

The stock company is the fullest development of the capitalistic association. It is not surprising, however, to find that stock companies were comparatively rare until the end of the eighteenth century. From the end of the sixteenth century to 1720, considerable development of stock companies took place in England. They appeared in France under Henry IV (1589–1610), but they seem to have had no success. Savary des Bruslons, the compiler of the *Dictionnaire du Commerce* (1732), does not notice them. In Germany very little was seen of the stock company until the nineteenth century. In England the financial disaster resulting from the mad outburst of speculation in company shares in 1719 and 1720 led to a law forbidding this form of organization, which remained unrepealed until 1825, although for many years it had not been enforced. These stock companies were generally small.

Of the forty-nine in England before 1680, only four had more than one hundred stockholders. Two of the great colonizing companies, on the other hand, the African Company and the East India Company, had from nine hundred to a thousand members each. The relationship of the stockholders was on the whole very personal in spite of the fundamentally impersonal character of the association. The stock was issued to persons and transfer was strictly limited. Even the dividends were unequally distributed, commonly in the order in which the shares were bought. The shareholders were called "brothers." Corporation accounting, even in Holland, was remarkably primitive down to the end of the seventeenth century, and it was only in the middle of the eighteenth century that the capitalistic characteristics reached full development.

The securing of capital for these companies also shows this personal character. It was localized, and at first the subscribers were primarily great persons. For instance, the capital of the French East India Company was furnished in the first place by the king, who subscribed six million livres, while the financiers subscribed two million, and the Merchants' Gild subscribed six hundred and fifty thousand. Similarly, a smelting establishment in Silesia in 1609 was financed by the margrave, who took forty shares, several towns which took a total of thirty shares, nine residents of Beuthen who together took ten shares, and so on.

The state also participated directly and indirectly in the development of capitalistic forms of business. Some of them were entirely under State management, profit enterprises pure and simple, like the imperial mirror factory at Neuhaus after 1720 and the Prussian arms factory at Potsdam founded in 1722. Some of them were combinations of the state and private capitalists. In some, the capital was provided in part by the government as in the case of the Prussian Bank of 1765. In other cases the authority was furnished by the government and the capital was furnished by private persons, for instance the Bank of England and the bank organized by John Law in France. The privileged companies are somewhat similar to this last group, such as the Royal Manufacturers in France, the Gobelins tapestry makers and the monopolistic companies which usually purchased the monopolies from the king. Other examples are the publisher of the *Encyclopedia,* and the publisher of the final edition of Voltaire.

REFERENCES FOR FURTHER READING

General

Sombart, W. Der moderne Kapitalismus, vol. II, pp. 23–173.
Fagniez, G. L'Economie sociale de la France sous Henri IV (1897).
Weber, Max. General Economic History (1927), chap. XVII.

"Firm," "Ditta," Bookkeeping

Anderson, Adam. An Historical and Chronological Deduction of the Origin of Commerce (6 vols., 1790).
Child, Josiah. A Discourse of Trade (1668 and many later editions).
Ehrenberg, R. Capital and Finance in the Age of the Renaissance (1928). See index, s.v. *ditta di Borsa.*
Jager, E. L. Luca Pacioli und Simon Stevin (1876).
Postlethwayt, M. The Universal Dictionary of Trade and Commerce (2 vols., 1754).
Geijsbeek, John B. Ancient Double-Entry Bookkeeping. Lucas Pacioli's treatise . . . reproduced and translated, etc. (1914).
Savary des Bruslons, J. Dictionnaire universel de commerce (1732).
Scott, W. R. The Joint-Stock Companies (3 vols., 1912).
Weber, Max. Die Handelsgesellschaften des Mittelalters (1889).
Woolf, A. H. A Short History of Accountants and Accountancy (1912).

Business Style

Defoe, Daniel. The Compleat English Tradesman; Robinson Crusoe.
Franklin, Benjamin. Autobiography.
Namier, L. B. "Brice Fisher, M.P., a Mid-Eighteenth Century Merchant and His Connections," English Historical Review, 42:514–532.
Savary, J. Le Parfait Négociant (1675).
Tawney, R. H. Religion and the Rise of Capitalism (1926).

CHAPTER II

THE TRANSFORMATION OF THE MARKET: (I) ITS EXTERNAL ASPECT

The Change in the Form of the Market

The epoch of early capitalism was marked by a very radical change in the form and character of markets, especially in the geographical range and the intensity of the process of buying and selling. More goods came into the market as a natural consequence of the increasing demand, which in its turn seems to have been partly due to the increase in the supply of gold and silver, averaging about six million dollars a year, and also to the increase in population, so marked throughout the entire period. Furthermore, new consumer groups were beginning to appear in such forms as to affect the demand for goods. The prosperity of the bourgeois and of the nobles was beginning to manifest itself in expenditures for objects of comfort and luxury. The charming and expensive domestic architecture of Elizabeth's time in England is a case in point. As the kings on the Continent succeeded in centralizing power and developed great armies, they required huge supplies such as only elaborate organization could provide. The cities were growing into great aggregations of population which drew upon wide areas for their food and raw materials. The oversea colonies, both as buyers and as sellers, necessitated new organizations to handle their business relations. At the same time, they introduced a whole new series of materials into ordinary commerce. The predominance of Florence in the cloth industry led to the growth of great wool and dye markets there. Shipbuilding necessitated the concentration of considerable materials for building the ships and for the support of workers at the shipbuilding centers. We shall see also that in this period the growing definition of national restrictions and of national encouragement of business increased the range of markets as compared with the old town markets. It also set limits to the old interregional trade, as is exemplified by the decline of the Hansa and of the other interregional organizations.

Price determination also changed from the rather irrational and erratic methods of the precapitalistic period, when custom and the notion of the just price predominated, to the more rational basis exemplified by organizations like the exchanges, where prices were determined by means that seem almost mechanical. It changed also from the rather personal character, illustrated by the haggling so common in the medieval market, to the practice of fixed price. In 1786, the Six Corporations of Paris condemned the Petit Dunkerque, the first modern shop in that city, for selling its goods at an established price: "The public, seduced by the fixed price which it does not dare to dispute and which is presented as the real value of the object on sale, is attracted without any justification to the shop in which it thinks its incapacity is protected from all deception, and by means of this notion defective merchandise is sold."

Price determination, however, did not become fully rationalized. The "just price" notion did not die out; and even where the will existed to rationalize prices, the habit of secrecy and the consequent lack of information, and technical deficiencies such as the lack of uniformity and exactness in weights and measures, prevented the attainment of anything approaching the standards of the present. The remnants of monopoly, some of which persisted until the end of the early capitalistic period, also interfered with rational price determination.

Cycles and Crises

The early capitalistic markets did not experience the rather short cycles of expansion, crisis, and depression with which the modern capitalistic market is so familiar. Market connections were not yet so close that the economic world moved as one. Even more important, technique and information service were not developed to such a point that the rapid expansion that now occurs after a period of depression was possible. Consequently, the crisis that now occurs at the climax of a period of rapid expansion was then out of the question.

Nevertheless, partial manifestations of this ebb and flow are to be noticed. A steady and widespread expansion marked the general economic life. The general absence of industrial statistics leaves us short of evidence to be summarized conveniently, but one very important sign of an expansion phase is constant through the centuries from the fifteenth to the end of the eighteenth, that is, steadily rising prices. The great speculative outbursts of the early eighteenth century, the tulip craze in Holland, the South Sea Bubble in England, the Law schemes in France, show only a superficial similarity to the later expansion-crisis-depression cycle, on the one hand because they are purely local in character, and on the other because they are purely financial affairs, indeed, hardly more than new and attractive forms of gambling, as a contemporary characterized them. Their importance for our present purpose is principally this, that the market had at least reached such a point of organization that large groups of people could be brought together as buyers and sellers through the impersonal nexus.

In a very real sense, however, it may be said that the nature of demand, which, as we have seen, still expressed itself in the form of orders for goods still unmade, and the character of production technique, which was still almost wholly dependent upon organic materials, limited expansion to a very slow rate. No aspect of economic life, no industry and no trade during these early modern centuries, shows such increases as are familiar to the modern statistician, amounting often to one hundred per cent in five or ten years.

On the other hand, early capitalistic industries often experienced crises that were peculiar to that epoch. Such development of the market as had taken place made them susceptible to many accidents of fortune. Sumptuary laws, changes of fashion, periods of mourning for royal persons, lack of raw materials, poverty throughout the country, scarcity of bullion, were various causes which produced crises in the Lyons silk industry at various times in the course of the seventeenth and eighteenth centuries. These crises were really not at all the crises of modern economic life but merely conditions in which markets with a narrow range among "regular customers" turned sluggish from local and temporary causes.

From another point of view, it is possible to see a broad cyclic movement among the several nations of Europe (as economic communities) during these centuries. At the end of the Middle Ages, the leading regions of capitalistic development were southern Germany, Italy, Spain, and France. Germany, Italy, and Spain after the middle of the sixteenth century fell back, while France and Holland rose to an ascendency, and reached their highest relative point in the end of the seventeenth century. Then they began to give way to England, whose supremacy was complete by the middle of the eighteenth century and continued until it was challenged by Germany at the end of the nineteenth century and, perhaps, ruinously crippled by the Great War.

The Means of Intercourse and Trade

The early capitalistic centuries were characterized by a steady advance in the means of communication, in the improvement of roads, rivers, and canals, in technical devices of land and water transportation, in the organization of transport services. Naturally, the sea as a means of intercourse can be changed only through the development of man's technique in using it and through the development of its approaches. The progress which navigation in the widest sense made during the early capitalistic epoch has already been discussed in Part II, Chapter II. Beyond subordinate improvements in map-making and the incidental increase in knowledge of the sea, technical development of this character was very slight indeed. The development of the vessels themselves had to wait until the nineteenth century. Although buoys and lighthouses were known as early as the Middle Ages in Western Europe, their establishment was comparatively slow until the nineteenth century. In the sixteenth century there were some eighteen lighthouses. Thirty-five new ones were established in the seventeenth century, 29 between 1700 and 1750, 39 between 1750 and 1775, and 64 between 1776 and 1800. It was only in 1792 that the Argand light replaced tallow lanterns. The development of ports was also comparatively late. Henry IV of France began the safeguarding of various French ports by dredging and building moles, and the French monarchy had a real predominance in this field of economic promotion down to 1789. Liverpool had the first artificial harbor, the Old Dock which was begun in 1710. London up to the end of the eighteenth century had only four hundred sixty meters of "legal wharves" between the Tower and London Bridge. The West India docks, the first great modern artificial harbor, were begun in 1799. In Amsterdam, Hamburg, and Bremen down to the end of the eighteenth century and even later, ships anchored in the river to load and unload. This limitation of harbors served, of course, to limit ship development very sharply.

France led also in road development until the nineteenth century. In the sixteenth century, there were a few stretches of built road; in the generality of Paris, about forty kilometers per thousand square kilometers of area. The built roads were most numerous near the capital, but were generally in bad condition, as inadequate provision had been made for their upkeep. The eighteenth century saw a very considerable improvement, and Arthur Young liberally testifies to the superiority of France in that respect. In England, road building hardly began until the middle of the eighteenth century, when the turnpike, that is to say, the toll road built as a private concession, became the popular object of investment. In the first fourteen years of the reign of George III, four hundred fifty-two laws authorizing road construction were passed by Parliament, and by 1821 England had a hundred miles of built road for every hundred square miles of area.

If France was first in road building, England easily was the first in the development of interior waterways, especially in the development of her rivers. As early as the sixteenth century, nine concessions had been granted for improvement of stretches of river; in the seventeenth century, twenty-four were granted, and in the eighteenth century, thirty-six. Although as early as 1563 a small canal was constructed between Topsham and Exeter, it was not until 1759 that the era of canal building really began. In that year the Bridgewater Canal from Worsley to Manchester was built by Brindley; and before the end of the century not fewer than one hundred fifty permits for canal building had been granted, and the canal system furnished convenient transportation of goods between all parts of the country. In France, canal building had begun as early as the reign of Henry IV, whose great minister, Sully, was so much interested in internal transportation. Colbert built several canals, notably, the great canal of the South which connected the Mediterranean and the Atlantic. In 1770, eight canals were finished, and by the end of the eighteenth century, the network of usable canals had attained 1,000 kilometers. In 1688, Germany had 185 kilometers of canals and 330 kilometers of canalized rivers; by 1836, it had 649 kilometers of canals and 1,225 kilometers of canalized rivers.

These channels of transportation were used in ways that were very much less systematized than is modern transportation. Except for rather narrowly controlled packet lines between Holland and England and the transportation of pilgrims and crusaders across the Mediterranean, regular passenger service on the sea seems to have been unknown until late in our period. In 1525, an official prescription at Trieste forbade the carrying of passengers by vessels carrying freight. The rivers seem to furnish the earliest examples of regular passenger service. In England, passenger boats were available on the Thames above and below London as early as the beginning of the sixteenth century. By the end of the seventeenth, an established tariff was in existence. By the end of the eighteenth, the traffic was so dense that it was often days before a boat could work itself through. In France, "market ships" appear as early as the end of the sixteenth century on the Seine between Melun and Paris, between Corbeil and Paris, and between Sens and Paris. Other rivers had similar services. It took four hours to go from Saint Ésprit to Avignon on the Rhone. By the eighteenth century some service was found on the Loire, the Canal de Briare, and the Garonne. These river lines remained throughout the period private enterprises, while, as we shall see, the land transport became a state enterprise. In Holland, the *Treckschyten* which were drawn by horses on the canals maintained hourly service and were regarded as especially luxurious. On the German streams, especially on the Rhine, passenger service was known in the Middle Ages. Regular service began as early as the seventeenth century. In the eighteenth century, the journey from Mainz to Cologne lasted two and one-half days and cost three thalers. Between Frankfurt and Mainz the market ships ran twice a day. Similar service was available on parts of the Danube.

Travel by river, of course, was limited by the fact that the rivers would not carry everywhere and, as a rule, one traveled on horseback well down into the eighteenth century. Until the sixteenth century, it was necessary for the traveler to use his own horse or horses. Then, however, a very great advance in organization of horse-travel took place through the establishment of posts which made possible travel by hired horses over wide stretches of Europe. This word, "post," of course, has only accidentally come to be applied to the transmission of mail. The original meaning of "post" was simply a place where horses could be hired. In the sixteenth century, the post system was spread over the most important commercial routes of the whole of Western and Southern Europe. Rome was the center of some sixty-nine post-routes. Between Rome and Madrid there were one hundred seventeen posts, between the Netherlands and Madrid, one hundred seven. "In England towards the southern and western parts and from London to Barwick on the confines of Scotland, post houses are established at every ten miles or thereabouts," we are told in a guidebook of the beginning of the seventeenth century. The cost in the English system amounted to about threepence a mile. Between 1637 and 1779 the English post was a state monopoly.

Carriage travel first became general in the sixteenth century, but by the end of the seventeenth century it was as customary in Western Europe as travel by horseback. A very considerable organization developed. At first private concerns simply rented coaches for entire journeys, but the postmen began to compete first by furnishing horses and carriages and later by establishing the "ordinary post," that is, carriages in which single seats could be taken. The great period of the post system was between 1820 and 1840. The annual capacity then seems to have reached about one billion passenger kilometers (for all Western Europe), which may be compared to the corresponding figure for the German railroads in 1913: 41.2 billions. Carriage transportation within the cities developed correspondingly. London in the middle of the eighteenth century had nine hundred hackney coaches. Paris in 1781 had eighteen hundred fiacres.

The care of the traveler developed in somewhat the same way. In the Middle Ages, the ordinary traveler took care of himself. This was one of the reasons for the living quarters that were connected with the foreign trading establishments all over Western Europe, such as the Steelyard in London and the Fondaco de' Tedeschi in Venice. Piety provided hostels for pilgrims, and soon other travelers were provided for in the same way. Erasmus described establishments which he had seen in Germany, accommodating eighty to ninety guests of all classes and functions of society, eating and sleeping in one common room. The monasteries also functioned as agencies of hospitality. During the seventeenth century the inns were much improved: the eating and sleeping rooms were divided according to classes, and individual bedrooms were introduced. The posthouses became natural places of hospitality for travelers. Hotels as such were developed in the great cities as early as the fifteenth century, but at first were confined to people of rank. Lyons, with its great fair, had ten as early as the first half of the fifteenth century. In the second half of the sixteenth century it had thirty-one. It was not until the end of the eighteenth century that continental hotels introduced what Goethe called "the greatest invention of the century," namely, *à la carte* service.

The transportation of goods was similarly systematized. Ocean transportation was carried on by small vessels which averaged less than one hundred fifty tons. As we have already noticed, their size was limited by the lack of harbor development. Such small vessels were very numerous in Great Britain, where nearly eighteen hundred ships of commerce were found. The Dutch fleet, about the year 1700, totaled nine hundred thousand tons. While the Dutch fleet was about nine times as great as the French, and almost double the size of the English fleet, the other fleets were still farther behind these three greater sea powers. The crews were relatively numerous. Holland used one man to about twenty tons, England, one to seventeen, while the typical modern proportion is one to fifty. Because the ships were small, the crews were small, and they preserved the handicraft tradition the more easily on that account.

During the whole early capitalistic epoch, it remained customary for the merchant to own his ships and even to build them. In the seventeenth century, eighty per cent of the Baltic trade from Emden was carried on in vessels owned by the merchants engaged in the trade. In the eighteenth century, the typical French oversea trader not only fitted out his own ships but had his own group of captains. In Hamburg, in 1830, it was a sign of a merchant's prosperity to own his ships. The chartering of ships, however, reaches far back into the Middle Ages; it is reflected in the Tables of Amalfi. In the sixteenth century, the Hamburg merchants complained that the English Merchant Adventurers rented all the ships available over the heads of the Hamburg traders. It was in Holland that ship chartering reached its highest development in the early capitalistic epoch. By the seventeenth century, the industry had become sufficiently organized to support a whole profession of ship broking. These brokers made it their business to find cargoes for ships sailing to particular points. There were also commissioners who similarly made it their business to find ships to charter for any part of the world.

While in a sense regular ship lines reach back to the Middle Ages, they were rather slow in development. Amsterdam began in the seventeenth century to develop as a center of regular lines with periodic sailings to various parts of Europe. The packet boats of England began to run regularly in Queen Anne's time. Local lines developed very early in the northern Adriatic. By the beginning of the eighteenth century, England had several lines to various parts of the Continent. The beginning of the eighteenth century also saw the establishment of regular transoceanic lines from England. The last Thursday of every month a ship left the Thames for Barbados, Montserrat, Nevis, St. Christopher, Antigua, and Jamaica. The Asiento ship, which after the treaty of Utrecht took its annual cargo to Porto Bello, may also be regarded as a liner. The French government attempted without success to establish a packet line across the Atlantic just before the Revolution. The cargo capacity of the fleets was, of course, very small by modern standards, although it grew rapidly during our period. At the end of the sixteenth century, the total capacity of the British merchant fleet was about 50,000 tons; at the end of the seventeenth, about 300,000 tons; at the end of the eighteenth, 1,725,000 tons; at the end of the nineteenth, over nine million tons.

The speed of transport did not show much advance. While the vessels improved in the eighteenth century, the organization of the ports and trading relations made the "turn around" very slow. The Spanish galleons took twelve months to cross the Atlantic and return. In the seventeenth century the trip between Portugal and the East Indies took eighteen months. The Dutch ships in the seventeenth and eighteenth centuries took from seven months to a year. For their trips to India and China, the English East India ships took from eighteen to twenty months.

The dangers of ship travel were very great. Illness was common. It exceeded 100 per cent [1] in the Austrian commercial fleet in 1760 and in the English West India war fleet in 1780 and 1781, as compared with 11 per cent in the French navy during the years 1890–1896. Shipwreck was common, and capture by pirates or privateers was a real danger down to the end of the eighteenth century. The Amsterdam Insurance Company maintained sixty ships of war in order to protect the vessels it had insured. Marine insurance to cover shipwreck and capture began to appear as a requirement toward the end of the fourteenth century in Portugal. The same century saw the beginnings of the insurance business in Italy. At first it was rather a form of occasional investment for persons with surplus cash. The insurance firms appeared about the end of the seventeenth century: Savary notes them as new phenomena. Marine insurance is, in fact, one of the first occasions for capitalistic organization in large form, and from the end of the seventeenth century in various lands we see the found-

[1] That is to say, the number of cases of illness during the year exceeded the number of persons in the crews.

ing of these insurance companies. In France, the Chambre des Assurances, founded in 1668, was transformed in 1686 into a stock company. The "Bubble" period in England at the beginning of the eighteenth century brought a whole series of projects for the founding of marine insurance companies, two of which were successfully developed. It is evident, from the full development of insurance law and from the slight statistical indications, that by the end of the eighteenth century, insurance had become a regular part of the shipping business.

The cost of ocean transport declined very substantially (about one-half between the fifteenth and eighteenth centuries), although it remained fifteen to twenty times as high as at the present time. Insurance premiums remained higher than freight charges even toward the nineteenth century, especially on the more costly goods. A considerable cost, avoided under modern conditions, was due to the deterioration of perishable goods, such as tobacco and flour.

Land transport of goods continued to be very simple down to the end of the eighteenth century. Peddlers carried a large amount of goods throughout the country on their own backs. Hand barrows and pack animals remained usual for the transport of bulk materials like coal and wood down to the nineteenth century. Carts and wagons were not generally utilized until the road improvements of the latter part of the eighteenth century. The organization went through a development somewhat like that of passenger transport. Originally, the merchant who was prosperous enough to use a pack animal owned his own. As early as the thirteenth century, however, we find independent organizations of carriers, especially in the cities of Italy. Free or unorganized interlocal freight carrying appears, however, to have reached its highest development in the eighteenth century, although it probably had developed before that time. The farmers seem to have carried it on as a side line in England and in Germany. In France, at the end of the seventeenth century, Savary tells us of the "powerful figures who have several horses and carts and send their carters to conduct them." In the year 1705, we hear of three commissioners who bought for a hundred thousand livres the monopoly of freight carrying in France. Long-distance freight services appear in England, France, and Germany from the seventeenth century.

The business of freight dispatching developed rapidly in connection with other businesses. The freighters seem to have been dispatchers from a rather early date, and stage houses became freight dispatching stations. Savary speaks of commissioners at the stage houses as common phenomena. Bankers early developed a function in connection with the transfer of goods, which is naturally collateral with the transfer of money. It was in Amsterdam, however, that freight transporting became a separate and distinct business by the eighteenth century. A contemporary observer tells us that when a merchant of Amsterdam wanted "to send merchandise into one of these countries, he has only to send his *expéditeur* a signed order, showing to whom and where it is to go." The capacity of the ordinary lines seems to have been very considerable. In the eighteenth century, a thousand pack horses were alleged to have passed through Hettersheim in a single day; through Nuremberg, 72,000 passed in a year. On the other hand, when, in 1769, a coal shortage occurred in Cleves and a contractor undertook to bring in twenty-seven million pounds in a year, he found himself able to bring in only three million. Theoretically, the capacity was about one one-hundred-thirtieth of the railway and waterway transport of Germany in 1913.

The use of the inland waterways, of course, dates far back to the most primitive times. The shipping industry on the rivers was thoroughly organized in the Middle Ages, and the merchants complained a great deal of the dearness of the charges of the boatmen. Regular periodic service had obtained full development on most navigable streams by the seventeenth century. The cost was about three or four times the present charges. It was greatly reduced where canals were built; for instance, Colbert's Canal of the South and the Bridgewater Canal in England. Although the rivers and canals were very heavily used where they were available, the land transport, of course, far exceeded the inland water transport in the larger continental countries.

News and Information Service

The individual communication of news is as old as the race, and, as a simple human habit, is, from our point of view, practically without a history. Ancient Babylonian letters on clay tablets, dug up by the spades of the archaeologists, are not particularly different from modern letters. It is with the development of two social aspects of news-commerce that we are here concerned; namely, the means of transmission, especially the postal systems, and the public agencies of information, especially the newspapers.

In Europe the development of the postal system as a collective messenger service for the community dates back to the private postal systems of merchants which began to appear in the end of the sixteenth century. In southern Germany, the business of carrying letters became associated with the peddling butchers and remained so down to the end of the seventeenth century. In England, the common carriers and peddlers were used for the purpose. Private messenger service for the public became available in Paris in 1653, and in London in 1685. Some of the cities developed postal systems of their own, Venice as early as 1300. Nuremberg, in 1570, had lines to Breslau, Frankfort, Leipzig, and Lyons. Leipzig, in 1608, had thirty sworn messengers with ten substitutes. Two interlocking systems connected Barnstaple through Exeter with London. Postal treaties were made between towns, and in some cases towns maintained postal agents at the various terminals of the postal routes. The state postal systems appeared in Spain, France, and England at the end of the fifteenth century. Their function was especially to carry official letters. In some cases they were forbidden to take private letters.

The imperial system carried on by the family of Thurn und Taxis gradually evolved into an international system. In 1633, the English postmaster-general and the postmaster of Ghent made a treaty for an express mail service between Antwerp and London. At Rhinhausen between March 28 and December 25, 1597, the passage of thirty-six postal couriers from the Netherlands and thirty-nine from Italy was recorded. By the beginning of the seventeenth century, the principal places of Europe were connected, although not always directly. For example, Prague was connected with Warsaw only through Vienna. The ordinary schedule was a weekly one, but even so, the postal system seems to have been ahead of the demand except on the routes northward through Italy. Rhinhausen, in September, 1598, reported the transmission of two hundred sixty-six letters. The English postmaster-general in 1633 estimated that each of the five hundred twelve market towns would send fifty letters a week to London, that is to say, about a million letters a year, equivalent to the correspondence of a modern town of about four thousand. In the eighteenth century, the English network was developed to such a point that no substantial market town remained unreached. The frequency of service was increased until by 1800 there were daily departures. The increase in revenue reflects a very rapid development in the use of the postal system.

The speed of the service depended, of course, upon the development of transport. In the fifteenth century, a letter took eighteen to twenty-two days from Genoa to Paris. In the sixteenth century, one from Antwerp to Amsterdam took from three to nine days. In England, in 1666, the estimated speed was three to four miles per hour. The cost was very high and hardly declined until the nineteenth century. It increased rapidly with the distance. In England, by the tariff of 1657, letters were carried within a radius of eighty miles from London for eightpence per ounce, to Scotland for one shilling, sixpence per ounce, to Constantinople for three shillings, ninepence, to Stockholm and Copenhagen for four shillings per ounce.

The publication of news was conditioned upon many changes that were taking place in the sixteenth and seventeenth centuries, such as the extension of printing and the development of postal service. It is not surprising to find the earliest appearance of newspapers in the beginning of the seventeenth century. The Strassburg *Zeitung* appeared in 1609. In 1702, the first daily journal, the London *Daily Courant,* appeared. By the end of the eighteenth century, the newspaper had had a great development, especially in England. It is estimated that in 1753 the total sale of newspapers from the various European countries had reached about 7,400,000, and in 1792, slightly over 15,000,000 copies. Even the English colonies in America had thirty-seven newspapers in 1775. The significance of the newspaper for the evolution of economic institutions lies in the fact that it is a medium of advertising and a medium for the transmission of commercial news.

The older forms of advertising by street criers and shop signs lie, of course, outside our immediate concern. Printed bills of advertisement appear in the seventeenth century in London. A London merchant offered a "bill of advertising" free to every customer who bought a guinea's worth of goods. In France, the word *affiche* does not appear in the first edition of Savary's *Dictionnaire de Commerce* but does appear in the supplement published in 1732. The definition of the word is, "a placard put up in a public place to make something known to everybody." Newspaper advertising appeared first in Holland in the beginning of the seventeenth century. In the course of the seventeenth century, advertising news sheets had a considerable development in all countries. The *Publick Advertiser* of London began to appear in 1657.

Advertising on the whole, however, attained only a very limited development in the early capitalistic epoch. The range of the newspaper was extremely limited as measured by the present standards, perhaps one four-thousandth to one six-thousandth the present range. The subjects of advertising were also limited, principally to such occasional matters as are likely to be handled in the "want ads" of the present-day newspaper. New books, quack remedies, new products, and occasional bargains were the principal subjects. The idea of competition and, therefore, the idea of competitive advertising, claiming superior service, superior quality, lower prices, were still not respectable in the world of business, and belong rather to the beginning of the period of full capitalism. In the first number of the London *Times* on January 1, 1788, three such advertisements appear, like a monument dividing the old age from the new.

Commercial and industrial information in the Middle Ages was confined to the gild and shared within it. This idea persisted to a considerable extent in the early capitalistic period. For example, a new post came to Emden from Lisbon sometime in the sixteenth century. The burghers came together in the borough house and the letters were read aloud without any concern as to the persons to whom they were addressed. In one case a caution had to be observed: "It was not possible to communicate the whole because many burghers were present." As the gild idea weakened, however, groups of merchants associated themselves together with the idea of supplying one another with important information. Then each merchant tried to provide himself with "correspondents" in other centers who would inform him as to the market affairs in those places. "There is the secret of the merchants and brokers, that every post day they learn promptly not only the prices of wares but also the rates of exchange" (Ludewig, 1743). These merchant letters were often duplicated and transmitted to a circle of business associates. They included principally the price lists and especially the price of exchange. In 1634, John Day, citizen and sworn broker of London, was granted a patent for the sole right to sell a weekly market list of wares at the principal places of Christendom. The grant of the patent stated that the "publication of market lists had never yet been brought here to that perfection answerable to the other parts beyond sea by which neglect within our city of London, our said city is much disgraced and all our merchants hindered in their commerce and correspondence." This practice had developed especially in Amsterdam by 1700. Savary tells us that some of the "price currents" published thirty different lists of prices. It had become a substantial, paid service. Toward the beginning of the nineteenth century, we find it rendered as a favor to desired customers.

It was still a service rather than a publication of news in the general sense of that word. With the collective transmission of commercial news begins the third period. The newspaper in its beginnings was anything but a medium of commercial news. Even in the middle of the eighteenth century, when a journal at Frankfurt-am-Main published a list of exchange prices, the brokers promptly protested that it was the business of the publisher "to publish affairs of state, of war and of peace and not to concern himself with commerce and exchange." The Frankfurt brokers were somewhat behind the times, as the regular publication of commercial news had begun in Holland in the first half of the eighteenth century. In London and Paris it began somewhat later. The first number of the London *Times* devoted about one-sixteenth of its four pages to commercial news, including the movement of ships and the market prices for some thirteen stocks. A few so-called commercial journals began to appear in the latter half of the eighteenth century. One in Hamburg, besides commercial and shipping news, had the cost of exchange, the prices of stocks in Amsterdam, and the prices of agricultural products, but filled in most of its space with articles on the history of the opera in England, public notices, and mixed news. The early capitalistic period ended before either the newspaper became fully involved with mercantile life, or mercantile life with the newspaper.

REFERENCES FOR FURTHER READING

General

Sombart, W. Der moderne Kapitalismus, vol. II, pp. 185–418.

Cunningham, W. Growth of English Industry and Commerce, Modern Times (2 vols.); Western Civilization (2 vols.).

Day, Clive. A History of Commerce (1904).

Geistbeck, M. Der Weltverkehr (1895).

Gras, N. S. B. Introduction to Economic History (1922), sec. 41.

Hewins, W. A. S. English Trade and Finance.

Knight, Barnes, and Flügel. Economic History of Europe in Modern Times (1928), chap. II. See also pp. 363–368.

Levasseur, E. Histoire des classes ouvrières et de l'industrie en France avant 1789 (2 vols., 1901).

Renard and Weulersse. Life and Work in Modern Europe (1926). See index, s.v. Monopolies, Trade, Canals, Roads, River Transport, Postal Systems.

Ricard, J. P. Le Négoce d'Amsterdam (1710).

Weber, Max. General Economic History (1927).

Westerfield, R. B. Middlemen in English Business (1915).

Cycles and Crises

Aftalion, A. Les Crises périodiques de surproduction (1913).

Ashley, W. J. The Economic Organization of England (1914).

Juglar, C. Des crises commerciales et de leur retour périodique en France, en Angleterre et aux Etats Unis (2nd ed., 1889).

George, M. Dorothy. London Life in the Eighteenth Century (1926).

Mitchell, W. C. Business Cycles (1913); Business Cycles: The Problem and Its Setting (1927).

Transport Ways

Forbes and Ashford. Our Waterways (1906).

Foville, A. de. La Transformation des moyens de transport et ses conséquences économiques et sociales (1880).

Jackmann, W. T. The Development of Transportation in Modern England (2 vols., 1916).

Letaconnoux, J. "Les Transports en France au XVIIIe siècle," Revue de l'histoire moderne, 11:97, 269.

Porter, G. R. Progress of the Nation (new ed., 1912).

Pratt, E. A. A History of Inland Transportation and Communication in England (1912).

Sax, Emil. Die Verkehrsmittel in Volks- und Staatswirtschaft (2 vols., 1878–79).

Smiles, S. Lives of the Engineers (3 vols., 1861–1862).

Postal Systems

Rothschild, A. de. Histoire de la poste aux lettres (1873).

Hemmeon, J. C. The History of the British Post Office (1912).

Joyce, Herbert. The History of the Post Office (1893).

Newspapers and Advertising

Datz, P. Histoire de la publicité (1894).

Sampson, H. A History of Advertising from the Earliest Time (1875).

Williams, J. B. Early History of London Advertisement in the Nineteenth Century (1907).

Besant, W. London in the Eighteenth Century (1902).

Karwill, V., ed. Fugger News-Letters, being a selection of unpublished letters from the correspondents of the house of Fugger during the years 1568–1605 (2 series, 1924, 1926; trans. by P. de Chary from Fugger-Zeitungen, Vienna, 1923).

CHAPTER III

THE TRANSFORMATION OF THE MARKET: (II) BUYING AND SELLING

THE selling of goods in the Middle Ages had three distinctive features: (1) periodicity; (2) extensive peddling and other migrant forms of merchandising—the merchant wandering in search of the buyer; (3) a highly personal exchange, which was always performed by direct contact between buyer and seller. In this chapter we have to inquire where and to what extent these characteristics of distribution persisted in the period of early capitalism and what changes they underwent during these centuries. We shall see the transition from the periodical exchanges of the markets and fairs to permanent selling establishments open all the year round; and the transition from the personal contact of the buyer and seller to what we shall call long-distance buying. In summary, we shall see depersonalization, materialization, mechanization. This development was favored by the increasing luxury demand, which affected powerfully the forms of retail trade, by the increasing bulk demand of the armies and the cities, and by the increasing importance of oversea commerce, which contributed greatly to the development of warehouse commerce. Without the development of the means of communication which we have just surveyed, it would have been impossible.

THE DEVELOPMENT OF SETTLED RETAILING AND WHOLESALING

Peddling remained important throughout the early capitalistic period. Tobacco, tea, coffee, sugar, and spices, during the seventeenth and especially the eighteenth century, were distributed throughout the countryside by peddlers. On the Continent they bought their wares in Amsterdam or other importing centers and sold them to the village shopkeepers or directly to the consumers. In England in the first decades of the nineteenth century hundreds of young Scotchmen carried on this "tea trade," especially in the industrial communities of Lancashire. Small hardware was similarly distributed by the "Sheffield men," who "would travel from one market town to another, and there at some inn they would proffer their wares to sell to the shopkeepers of the place." Similar methods were used in the small hardware business of the Rhineland. Watches were a favorite stock for the peddlers. Textile goods were peddled in all countries. The Bohemian glass industry had perhaps the most highly developed peddling system, extending through the whole of Europe.

Peddling was especially significant in two ways. It developed a demand for new kinds of goods among remote elements of the population. Justus Möser calls the peddlers "the milliners of the farmers' wives." Peddling was also a form in which the free mercantilist spirit of modern times developed most easily. The peddlers were characteristically foreigners, Scotchmen in England, Frenchmen in Germany, and, above all, the Jews in all countries. In Hamburg about 1800, it was estimated that one-fourth of the Jewish population were peddlers. A German observer estimated that in 1885 "of the wandering merchants in the whole of America hardly one-twentieth are Christian." The general conditions of peddling detached the peddlers from the limiting traditions of the gilds.

On the other hand, settled retailing seems to have extended to almost every country town and indeed to most villages in the countries of Western and Central Europe by 1700. Justus Möser again tells us that "thousands of people have given up farming and have taken up shopkeeping without having learned the business." It was, of course, in the great cities that the development was most rapid and most extensive. In 1528 an Italian observer declared that in Paris "there are many beautiful streets that are full of marvelously beautiful shops, and there are an infinite number of rich merchants." In Paris, however, and in London as well, the great development came in the seventeenth century. In 1633, the number of mercers in London was not more than fifty or sixty. In Defoe's time, about 1700, there were three to four hundred. Similarly, the number of linen drapers had "monstrously" increased. On the whole it is obvious that the number of retail businesses increased in the seventeenth and eighteenth centuries much more rapidly than the population. At the end of the eighteenth century a very competent German observer noted that the shopkeepers had increased at the expense of the craftsmen.

Specialization of shops came rather slowly, in the great cities earlier than in the smaller towns, and in London earlier than in Paris. Specialized shops appeared in London as early as the reign of Henry VI (fifteenth century); in Paris, toward the end of the seventeenth century, and in other continental cities, only in the nineteenth century. Specialization seemed to develop according to methods of measurement (pound goods, yard goods, piece goods), somewhat according to the origin of the goods, and to a lesser degree according to their use. A directory of Paris at the end of the seventeenth century gives a list of about twenty-five different kinds of shops: bookshops, curiosity shops, jewelry shops, gun shops, furniture shops, various sorts of food shops, etc. Specialization according to the character of the demand seems to have come first in the eighteenth century. An English observer tells us that the mercers in 1745 were offering for sale "an innumerable train of expensive trifles for the ornament of the fair sex." The trade in luxury goods, such as jewelry, was also organized in this way. House furnishings were similarly combined in Paris and in London. This specialization, however, remained essentially exceptional until the end of our period.

The character of dealing in these specialized shops was very personal. As Defoe put it in his *Compleat English Tradesman,*

"Customers love to see the master face to face in the shop." In Paris, the finer shops in the Palais Royal became a place of resort for the fashionable world. In the eighteenth century the furnishing and decoration of shops became a subject of much remark. Voltaire remarked of the Petit Dunkerque, an early department store, on his last visit to Paris, that nothing could be more brilliant to the eye. The improvement in the shops was accompanied by a disposition to locate them in the more elegant parts of town (Bond Street, London) or in luxury centers like Wiesbaden.

Markets and fairs persisted, in the early capitalistic period, only in declining and changing forms. The middlemen, the professional merchants, as they developed, displaced the original producers in the retail markets. Mass articles like grain tended to disappear. In Central and Eastern Europe the original character of fairs where the agricultural population supplied materials which the industrial producers needed for the ensuing year persisted much longer than in the West. Memel, Tilsit, Danzig, Berlin each gathered together more than one thousand merchants and as many as fifty thousand buyers as late as 1820. Wholesale business, as it developed, utilized the market system through the eighteenth century even in the West. The fairs at Stourbridge and Bristol in England, Beaucaire and Lyons in France, Leipzig in Germany, Bozen in the Tirol all retained importance as annual wholesale markets well into the nineteenth century, Lyons and Leipzig even to our own day. Porto Bello, Vera Cruz, and Havana similarly persisted as wholesale fairs until the decline of Spanish control. Some of the fairs were specialized, like the wine fair at Bordeaux and the fish fair at Yarmouth. Cloth fairs in the various manufacturing centers of England came to be held weekly rather than annually, and in permanent "halls" rather than in temporary structures. Savary tells us that these halls were also an ordinary feature of French towns. At the general fairs, not only manufactured goods but also raw materials were to be found and were dealt in, in considerable quantities. The agricultural dealings at the fair of Frankfurt-am-Oder in the years from 1781 to 1789 amounted to about two million dollars. Business at these fairs retained the old personal character. The buyers and the sellers met face to face with the goods between them.

As commerce grew in volume, wholesale trade, like retail trade, began to be continuous rather than occasional. It also retained for a long time the essentially personal character, remained "hand trade." Savary insists that "the presence of the wholesaler is necessary both at the purchase and at the sale of his wares." Even in Amsterdam, where mercantile technique was most highly developed, as late as the eighteenth century, actual coins were exchanged in almost every transaction "to bind the bargain"—so personal was the conception of buying and selling.

Auction sales, which were widely used by the great colonial companies to market their goods as they arrived, constitute a transitional form between the intermittent fairs and markets on the one hand and settled wholesaling. They differ from the fairs in that their dates were determined by the arrival of goods from abroad rather than by custom or charter. The English East India Company sold its imports "by the candle," [1] after it had been announced on the exchange that at such a time and place, such and such goods would be sold. By the eighteenth century, it was an established practice in the sale of all sorts of goods, especially in the great importing centers, such as London, Amsterdam, Copenhagen, and Hamburg, and also in interior centers, such as Leipzig. In Hamburg by 1760, the auctions were held as frequently as once a week, and in 1790 no fewer than 196 were held.

The "halls," originally built to house occasional markets, by the eighteenth century were also becoming permanent places of wholesale business. The best known of these institutions is Blackwell Hall, in London, opened in 1397 as a place to which the "country clothier" resorted and offered his goods for sale on the appointed

[1] That is, at auction. Nominally, bids were received only until a candle had burned down to a certain point.

market day. About 1660, the Blackwell Hall factors, agents who undertook selling commissions for clothiers unable or unwilling to come in person, began to function and soon developed as the controlling jobbers.

"Country buying," or purchase of materials from the producer by purchasers who went directly to him instead of waiting for his products to appear at the market in a neighboring town, appeared in the grain trade in France and in England during the seventeenth century, and in Germany somewhat later. Similarly, wool was bought in England by "broggers" who made a farm-to-farm canvass. The preamble of a decree of the margrave of Brandenburg of 1581 complains that foreigners buy all the good wool and take it out of the country, wherefore it is ordered that no wool be contracted for or sold outside of the yearly fair.

Industrial products were similarly bought up. Lombard wholesalers in the latter part of the seventeenth century went from village to village in Swabia buying linens. English merchants periodically went into the weaving districts to buy cloth. In France, a sort of broker's business developed in this connection: a wholesaler from one of the towns would get into touch with some man who knew his community and could give information as to the materials available in the community. Small hardware was bought up by the same method in Germany and in England.

Continuous, all-the-year-round wholesaling from the constantly collected stores of goods was just a step beyond the country-buying which outflanked the customary markets and fairs. It was still apparently an extremely new thing in the sixteenth century. Guicciardini described Antwerp, which at the time was far in advance of other centers in almost every form of commercial institution, as a "perpetual fair." This wholesaling from stores, to which the retailer or the industrial producer came, developed first of all in the import and export businesses, and then in internal commerce along with the markets and fairs; and by the end of the early capitalistic epoch, it had attained a significant position in every branch of business. Thus, cotton (a new product and therefore susceptible to new methods) was sold from warehouses from the start of its importation. The Dutch weavers bought their supplies of wool from warehouses in Holland, where the Spanish wool had been sent by Spanish growers or brought by Dutch importers. Other colonial wares followed a similar course: purchase at auction in Amsterdam, London, or elsewhere, warehousing at the port where they were imported, transfer to some interior warehouse, whence they were sold to the shopkeepers for retailing.

In the export business, a similar change took place about the same time. The English Merchant Adventurers originally sold their exports to the Continent at markets and fairs. In the sixteenth century they still appeared at four markets a year in Antwerp. In 1601, however, they were notifying their foreign customers of the arrival of new shipments, from which purchases could be made at any time. Thus, too, the Bohemian glass merchant traveled with his goods to some distant country like Portugal, "rented a cellar as a store for a few months, unpacked his goods, and sold them as quickly as possible." In London and in Amsterdam, by the eighteenth century, exporting and importing business in this form had commonly been combined in one firm. The same development in internal trade is illustrated by Defoe's statement that the industrial products of the country were sent to London, and sold by the warehouse keepers to the retailers.

By this gradual expansion of settled retailing and wholesaling, the occasional trading of the Middle Ages, institutionalized in markets and fairs, was displaced and reduced to a very minor form.

The Development of Contract Buying

The personal character of exchange, the barterlike face-to-face meeting of buyer and seller and hand-to-hand exchange of goods and money, which characterized medieval trading, was radically altered in the course of the early capitalistic epoch by the development of "future" buying, that is, buying upon contract for delivery at some future date, which permeated ordinary commercial buying and gave the necessary basis for systematized speculation in commodities and stocks. Frequent prohibitions of purchase before production in the Middle Ages show that while it was not literally unknown, at the same time it was not a part of the ordinary business practice. A whole series of comments from the end of the seventeenth century, however, shows us the practice rather suddenly becoming common, at least in England, France, and Germany. A French memorial of the year 1699 tells how the grain market of Paris was outflanked by the farmers, who brought samples in their pouches and met would-be buyers outside the market in hotels or cafés, negotiated with them as to price, then went to the market and, over a few bags, pretended to perform the transaction in public. This done, the grain the farmer had on the market was taken away by the dealer, but he later went about to the farms and collected the much larger quantities which he had actually bought in the same transaction. Similarly, Defoe tells of the "utterly unlawful" new method of selling and buying grain and malt "by samples only as 'tis called."

Apparently, the pressure of the increasing demand for grain was responsible for a desire of both the buyer and the seller to avoid the burdensome restrictions and physical inconveniences of the customary markets. London and Paris and other cities had grown to unprecedented size, with correspondingly increasing demand for foodstuffs. The wars of Louis XIV, especially the War of the Spanish Succession (1702–1714), were accompanied by a very sharp rise in the demand upon the grain supply. In France, the consequence was a practical disruption of the closely restrictive Colbertian system. In England, the export figures rose from an average of about 18,000 quarters for the years 1697–1700 to an average of 112,000 for the years 1710–1720.

The cloth trade also saw a beginning of this trading by sample and contracting for future delivery. The new organization of Blackwell Hall, to which reference has been made, favored the practice, as did also the improvement in the carrying trade, "the carriers and waggoners" who traveled "constantly from their countries to London and so back."

It is obvious that long-distance selling had begun. It was only a beginning. Savary in his *Parfait Négociant* does not mention selling by sample, but *echantillon* (sample) is the subject of a lengthy article in his son's *Dictionnaire universel de commerce.* Even in Amsterdam, the sample was used in the corn exchange as a preliminary to an actual, personal exchange in the warehouse. The commercial traveler, the great carrier of samples, did not appear until the end of the eighteenth century, and belongs really to the epoch of full capitalism.

The great force, however, which lifted the commercial world out of its old customs and traditional practices and made contract buying "big business," was the demand of the growing states, especially their demand for supplies for their growing armies.[2] Even before 1500, delivery of subsistence and outfitting materials had played a considerable rôle in Italy, where the great banking houses usually participated. In France up to Henry III's time (1574–1589), the *manutentionnaire,* an officer of the court, had charge of the collection of materials requisitioned directly from the villages. In 1575, the first contract for provisioning the army was made with a rich bourgeois of Niort. Gradually through the seventeenth and eighteenth centuries, all the military nations went over to the contract system. By the end of the eighteenth century, army contracting had become the principal form of contract selling.

Instruments of Payment

The forms and conditions of payment also underwent a con-

[2] See pages 63–64.

siderable modification in this period. Sales on credit (on trust, on time) seem to have been more usual in England and France than in Holland or Germany. Defoe declared that two-thirds to four-fifths of all business in England was transacted on credit. Where fairs and markets persisted, as in Germany, buying for cash was more common, and continued to prevail as late as the nineteenth century.

The forms of payment also show considerable development. Barter, which has practically disappeared from Europe, remained fairly common throughout our period. The German fairs that attracted Poles and Russians, such as Breslau, saw a great deal of direct exchange. Hard money was also used to a greater extent than now. An economist in 1725 estimated that the total amount of transactions in England was £126,199,328, for which about £15,000,000 of coin was available. Certainly, the withdrawal of coins for reminting in England at the end of the seventeenth century caused much more disturbance than we should expect from a similar operation today. A general distrust of paper money and preference for "ringing coin" was widespread among most classes of people. Purchases among farmers and craftsmen had to be made with hard money. The whole transoceanic commerce which went through the auction rooms of the great trading companies was handled with coin.

Nevertheless, various substitutes for money came into use. Where circulation banks developed, bank notes became the rule with the wholesale trade. At the fairs, a system of clearances was created by which purchases were offset against each other in such a way that considerable transactions were effected without any cash or currency passing from one hand to another. "Bills of Debt or Bills Obligatory, which one merchant giveth to another for commodities bought or sold," mentioned by Gerard Malynes (1622), were common in most Northern European centers, but not in England.

The use of drafts grew extraordinarily toward the end of the period. The form of draft which became most important was what might be called a "merchant draft" rather than a bank draft. Originally, exchange was money exchange, that is, a sort of arbitrage between the different kinds of coins that circulated in Europe. From the fifteenth century down to the end of the seventeenth century, Italian and especially Genoese bankers bought and sold credits at a high rate of interest: that is, an individual desiring to transmit a payment, might buy of the banker a draft on some other place where it would be paid to his creditor in coin of that place. For this service he paid a high price, as much as 20 per cent. This business developed into "exchange fairs," at Lyons (the principal example in the sixteenth century), Antwerp, Besançon, Piacenza, and finally in the eighteenth century Santa Margarita, near Genoa. This form of exchange was of purely financial significance and only indirectly affected the general course of commerce—for instance, by serving as the channel through which the flood of gold and silver from America was made available for Europe as a whole.

The merchant draft was a different thing, more like the clearance system practiced at some of the fairs, and on the other hand, like the bills obligatory described by Malynes. In its earliest form, during the thirteenth, fourteenth, and fifteenth centuries, the draft was essentially an instrument stating that the signer had received at one place a specified sum of money and would pay such and such a sum at some other place. From the fifteenth century, it began to be a means of clearing debts. One merchant in payment of a debt gave to a second a draft on a third, who owed the first merchant an equivalent or larger sum. The utility of this draft in this stage was limited by the fact that it was not indorsable and therefore had only a limited circulation. When Behaim was a student in Bologna and received a draft on Venice, he could get it cashed only by going there. When the merchant Lion in Honfleur received a draft on a merchant in Dieppe he sent it back, "not having any need of money in Dieppe at present" (seventeenth century). At the end of the sixteenth century, the use of such drafts had become general. By the beginning of the nineteenth century it had received such extension that in Manchester, for example, it was estimated that nine-tenths of all settlements were effected by means of drafts (1820). Drafts of £10 came back with as many as 120 indorsements.

The "turnover" of such drafts was extremely slow as a result of the undeveloped state of transportation and the awkward forms of distribution and payment. In the oversea trade Bremen merchants counted on one turnover in three years. Devices intended to shorten this period were the "loan banks," several of which were founded in the eighteenth century. The customary time between the draft and the actual return of cash even in Europe was from two to three months. Discounting of drafts appeared about 1700 in France and in England, about 1750 in the more advanced commercial centers of Germany. Regular discount banks existed only in England and Vienna, until in 1783 a discount company was organized in Sweden. The charges were inordinately high, 10, 15, and 20 per cent—and they were naturally little used. "They are a pest for commerce" which the private merchants would do well to avoid, wrote a German in 1796.

The Differentiation of Merchants and of Business Services

The number of professional merchants increased steadily through this epoch, and with that increase came a progressively increasing differentiation. The craftsman who sold his own wares was becoming more and more rare, although he did not disappear until well into the nineteenth century. The occasional trader, so common in the Middle Ages, disappeared first.

The first great differentiation was that between the wholesaler and the retailer. In England, where this development first is manifest, the distinction appears in the Mercers' Company of London, the members of which are classified as (1) merchants, (oversea traders), (2) tradesmen (inland wholesalers), and (3) shopkeepers (retailers). The distinction was well established in France by the time of the elder Savary, who in his *Parfait Négociant* advises wholesalers not to sell to any but dealers because the cost would become known among the public.

Wholesaling itself became specialized. It was shown in the preceding chapter how transportation, communication, and lodging had early become separated from the function of trading as such. By the end of the early capitalist period, personal differentiation according to function had also progressed considerably in forms that correspond to the impersonal organization there described. In the import trade there were (1) the buyers and (2) the exporting houses in the foreign country, (3) the importing houses and (4) the sellers in the country to which the goods were imported, (5) the inland wholesaler, the "second hand," who sold to the manufacturer or to the retailer. In export commerce, there were (1) the wholesaler (the engrosser), like the Breslau merchants who bought up the Silesian linen, (2) the exporter in the seaport, (3) the importer, commonly native to the exporting country like the Merchant Adventurers in Antwerp and Hamburg, later natives of the importing country. In the *commerce d'économie,* that is, trade between two countries carried on by natives of a third, which Hollanders developed so extensively, another element appears. In interior commerce, the wholesaler intervenes regularly between the retailer and the producer. As Defoe (1727) put it, the retailers in the provinces no longer buy their goods of the producer, but "they correspond with the wholesale dealers in London, where there are particular shops or warehouses for all these."

Differentiation according to materials handled also developed. Among the "merchants," the oversea traders, we hear of Hamburg merchants, Turkey merchants, Eastland merchants, East India merchants, who imported all products of the regions with which they dealt. Internal commerce differentiated more specifically: coal merchants, wool men, silk men, Birmingham hardware men, yarn men, drapers, mercers, grocers.

The banking of the early capitalistic epoch also was a specialization from general business of the large sort. Aside from the Bank of England and the Vienna *Banco dei depositi,* which were the only banks resembling modern banks in function, there were many private "bankers," who were essentially dealers in exchange, but who ordinarily combined with this the commission and forwarding business. In the year 1823, there were in Frankfurt-am-Main 275 merchants who thus occupied themselves with "exchange, commission and forwarding." The firm of Shickler Brothers in Berlin is an example of this combination somewhat more than ordinarily extended, as they carried on the following branches: (1) forwarding goods, (2) buying and selling on commission, (3) "putting out"[3] in the iron and weapon industries, (4) exchange, (5) management of the estates of the Prussian kings, (6) financial underwriting, (7) shipping. In the larger towns like Paris, dealers in exchange were specialized still further according to the regions with which they dealt.

Retailing also underwent a thoroughgoing differentiation which has already been described and to which it is not necessary to make further reference here.[4]

One of the most distinctive symptoms of the development of impersonal business relations is the development of agency business in various forms. During the sixteenth century, even in such an important commercial center as Venice, it was the regular thing for a merchant to accompany his goods to such distant ports as Antwerp. In 1517, provision was made that any merchant who sent as much as 15 ducats of cargo (as one might say, $35.00 worth) on the Flanders fleet, was to be carried with it. As the contacts of individual business men widened, it became necessary for them to multiply themselves and to be effectively present at

[3] See Chapter IV, below.

[4] See above, pages 186–188.

several places at the same time. This was accomplished by the development of agency.

In a sense, the members of the old merchant gilds, of family associations, and even of commercial firms acted as agents of the associations of which they were members; but this relationship was purely organic and personal. A second stage toward agency business properly speaking was the use of factors, which appears in Italy and in France (Jacques Cœur, the great merchant prince of Bourges, in the fifteenth century, had one hundred thirty-five factors), and developed especially in Germany during the sixteenth century. All the great south German commercial houses, such as the Fuggers and the Welsers, were really great factor systems. The great colonial companies were built up in much the same way. The final stage was specialization of agency business as a separate service which was bought and sold, just like that of the exchange bankers and of the transportation services. Brokers, that is, men who made it their business to arrange contracts between buyers and sellers, appear in Italy and in the Netherlands during the Middle Ages, although with somewhat different functions from that of the modern broker. They were sometimes intermediaries between foreigners who were not permitted to deal with each other, more usually insurance brokers or exchange brokers. Around 1600, however, a very important expansion took place. The French King Henry IV established a sort of brokers' gild, limiting the number in each city, for example to eight in Paris. By 1634, this number had grown to twenty; by 1638, to thirty. A similar development took place in the German cities. In Frankfurt-am-Main, there were twelve brokers in 1582, forty-eight in 1589, forty-two in 1610, although the business had begun less than a century before. Brokerage seems to have reached its height in the two great commercial centers of the Netherlands. In Antwerp, even in the middle of the seventeenth century, one hundred twenty-four brokers were officially recorded. Amsterdam, a little later, was said to have about twelve hundred, specialized into many different groups: two hundred fifty exchange brokers, one hundred stock brokers, eighty wine and brandy brokers, and so on. In England the development was slower; the proverb ran, "A crafty merchant needs no broker." Purchasing brokers were comparatively rare in this period, and generally were limited to the purchase of raw materials or of half-finished goods, for example, Silesian raw linens. Selling brokers, sellers on consignment, on the other hand, developed very considerably and constitute the distinctive characteristic of internal trade and importing trade especially in the eighteenth century. The Blackwell Hall factors who began to perform this function for the cloth trade have already been discussed. Defoe, in *The Compleat Tradesman* (1727), wrote of the clothiers, "as soon as they can finish their goods, they hurry them up to London to their Factors and immediately follow them with their bills of the money." Similarly there were in London factors (consignees) for all sorts of products, "who deal by commission and sell the goods of other people consigned to them for a customary premium." In Paris, according to the elder Savary, there were "almost no merchants of importance who do not sell on commission for foreigners and merchants of the realm." Foreign trade, of course, was the peculiar field of the consignment trade. It was especially favored in the trade with the Spanish colonies through Cadiz, where it made it possible to circumvent the laws excluding foreigners from the colonies. The products of the Slavic and Magyar hinterland of eastern Germany "were entrusted to trustworthy houses, who either sent back goods as ordered or settled with the sender in hard money." The commission trade was limited to areas in which exchange systems and means of intercourse were fairly well established.

The Development of the Bourse

The general organization of the mercantile population reveals a similar transition from the personal organic union of the medieval gild to the impersonal bourse or chamber of commerce. Some of the gilds remained down to the end of the early capitalistic period, for example, the "Six Corps de Marchands" of Paris, some (in form) down to the present, for example, the livery companies of London. Besides the gilds, there were the "nations," found in the various foreign ports during the Middle Ages, which persisted to some extent during this period. These gradually lost force as unions and began to be displaced by commercial companies.

Around 1600, exchanges or bourses began to appear in all the principal commercial centers of Western Europe. As yet they lacked the close organization and discipline which the name connotes in later times. They were simply places where buyers and sellers of goods and, in a minor way of stocks, forgathered. In the exchanges, the old local and personal idea of "an honorable merchant" had been displaced by the idea expressed in the inscription on the Exchange Building at Antwerp: "For the use of merchants of whatever nation or tongue" (*in usum negotiatorum cuiusque nationis ac linguae*). The exchanges had not yet developed very complex methods. The merchants who met on Change still negotiated personally, still went to the warehouse and completed their deals with the goods in view. "After the bargain is struck, the merchants or the brokers go to the warehouse with their samples in order to show the buyers that the goods conform to the samples, whereupon delivery is completed." The international character of the exchanges moved many would-be literary lights to eulogy, some in the form of poetry. Even Addison wrote on the subject: "It gives me a secret satisfaction to see so rich an assembly of my countrymen and foreigners consulting together upon the private business of mankind."

The new organization developed an official aspect through the establishment of chambers of commerce, either under the auspices of the government, as in France, or independently, as in Great Britain.

The management of commercial business took several new

forms. To a great extent, perhaps in the greater part of business, the old handicraft idea persisted. At the end of the seventeenth century, the Six Corps of Paris were composed of 2,752 "masters" who had some 5,000 assistants. Similar proportions existed in Breslau and Berlin well into the nineteenth century. This was especially true among the small retail businesses. Wholesale business was commonly organized in some associational form, either partnerships or some more distinctly capitalistic form of organization. In the foreign and oversea commerce, because of the heavy investment in "factories," fleets, armies, and political relations, and because of the slow turnover, the great privileged companies were apparently the only type of organization that could operate effectively.

The geographical organization of business was characterized by an increasing specialization among towns. At certain points, such as Exeter, Norwich, Sedan, Rouen, Hirschberg, the "putters-out" (Verleger) concentrated the products of the industrial workers in the surrounding region.[5] "Inland houses," especially in Germany, collected these materials at "second hand," and forwarded them to national centers of metropolitan character. Leipzig and Breslau were great "inland house" towns. Paris, London, Hamburg, Amsterdam were great metropolitan concentration points. Transfer points (entrepôts) were places "in which goods arrived, not to be sold, but only to be transshipped," such as Lyons, Orléans, Smyrna, and Batavia. Banking, that is, money lending, was somewhat localized in cities like Genoa, Augsburg, Amsterdam, and, at the end of the period, London.

REFERENCES FOR FURTHER READING

Sombart, W. Der moderne Kapitalismus, vol. II, pp. 419–585.

Anderson, A. Origins of Commerce (6 vols., 1790).

Cunningham, W. Growth of English Industry and Commerce (2 vols., 1915–1921).

[5] See Chapter IV, below.

George, M. Dorothy. London Life in the Eighteenth Century (1926).

Gras, N. S. B. Introduction to Economic History, sec. 39; The Evolution of the English Corn Market (1915).

Hazlitt, W. C. The Livery Companies of the City of London (1892).

Kerr, A. B. Jacques Cœur (1927).

Levasseur, E. Histoire du commerce de la France (2 vols., 1911–1912).

Postlethwayt, M. Dictionary of Commerce (2 vols., 1754).

Renard and Weulersse. Life and Work in Modern Europe (1926). See index, s.v. Fairs, Amsterdam, and Antwerp.

Ricard, J. P. Le Négoce d'Amsterdam (1710).

Savary (the younger). Dictionnaire universel de commerce (1726); Supplément (1732).

Savary, J. Le Parfait Négociant (1675).

Usher, A. P. The History of the Grain Trade in France (1913).

Vidal, E. The History and Methods of the Paris Bourse (1910).

Weber, Max. General Economic History (1927), chap. xxv.

Westerfield, R. B. Middlemen in English Business (1915).

Wright, Richardson. Hawkers and Walkers in Early America (1927).

CHAPTER IV

THE TRANSFORMATION OF PRODUCTION: FROM THE HANDICRAFT SYSTEM TO THE FACTORY

The Persistence of the Old System

In the development of the system of markets and exchange, we have noted the rapid emergence of new forms of activity—specialization, increase in range, new devices of transportation and organization—along with the persistence to a marked degree of the old personal spirit of the craftsman. In the study of production, we have to note a longer persistence not only of the old spirit, but of the old technique, the old organization, the old forms. It is as though industrial custom, the custom of the man working with his hands, were somehow tougher, less susceptible to change than the custom of the merchant. At the same time, we shall see, alongside the old, radically important new features developing.

One of the most obvious signs of the essentially unchanged character of the production system of Europe, is the fact that, at the end of the early capitalistic period as at the beginning, the population was predominantly agricultural. Even the England of the eighteenth century, by far the most industrialized of European countries at the time, had three times as many inhabitants outside the towns as within them. France in 1818 was estimated to have a rural population of 23,000,000 as against a town population of about 6,000,000. Germany was essentially agricultural territory down to the middle of the nineteenth century. Saxony in 1846, the most industrialized of the German states, had twice as much rural population as urban. This agricultural character would appear even more marked if estimates were possible (1) of the considerable number of town dwellers who managed agricultural establishments, like the residents of Paris who in the seventeenth century got their grain directly from their own properties, had it ground and baked into bread for themselves, in amounts equal to one-third of the grain handled through the markets; and (2) of the persons who conducted agricultural operations in the towns themselves.

Agricultural production continued to be dominated by the sustenance idea. As a whole, more than half of the products of the farms were consumed by the agricultural population. As late as 1862 a competent German authority reckoned that the agricultural consumption of agricultural products throughout Germany amounted to two-thirds of the whole. It is probable that this proportion was general throughout Western Europe a century earlier. The vast preponderance of the agricultural population and the small dimensions of the export trade in grain support this conclusion. Traditionalism substantially controlled all the agricultural processes, as Arthur Young testifies in his various writings on England and France. New agricultural methods were "treason toward God," according to a Bohemian critic of the first decade of the nineteenth century. The open-field system continued to prevail (except in England) and to bar the introduction of new crops and of new methods. In parts of Italy and in Flanders and Brabant, the need of systematic controls of irrigation or of drainage and the cultivation of special crops such as the mulberry and the olive made a certain degree of rationalism inevitable. Some of the foundations of scientific agriculture were laid by Olivier de Serres in France (1600) and Samuel Hartlib in England (1633), but no fundamental revolution in agricultural method took place in either country until well toward the end of early capitalism. The slow advance of new technique in German agriculture is illustrated by the history of the potato: from 1588 to 1648, a curiosity; latter half of the seventeenth century, cultivated as a garden crop in Austria, Saxony, on the Rhine, and in Swabia;

from 1719, grown as a field crop in a few regions; from 1771, generally grown as a field crop. Stock raising shows a similarly low curve of improvement. Sheep raising caused what seemed to contemporaries to be serious inroads upon the traditional agriculture in England, but the methods of the industry remained essentially unchanged from the Middle Ages, indeed from ancient times. Dairying, particularly cheese making, began as handicraft industry in Switzerland and the Netherlands about the fourteenth century and remained the most conservative of industries, especially in Switzerland. Horse breeding was somewhat earlier developed because of the special interest of kings and nobles. Frederick II and Renaissance princes of Italy had famous stables. Louis XIII of France and Charles I of England made the owning of fine horses an obligation of their nobility. It was only in the eighteenth century, however, that stock was generally provided with artificial fodder during the winter. Forest industry remained also comparatively undeveloped because it was bound up on the one hand with the traditional village economy, and on the other with the predominant hunting interests of lords and kings. When the increasing demand due to the expansion of industry fell upon the forests in the late eighteenth century, the numerous forest ordinances and customs were quite inadequate to prevent rapid destruction.

To almost the same degree as agriculture, industrial production retained the old forms. Throughout the period of early capitalism the major part of the demand for industrial goods continued to be met either by household or manorial industry or by handicraft shop production. The ordinary cultivator of the soil still aimed to support himself directly, "care being taken to want as little as possible that is not supplied by the ground." His food, clothes, dwelling, even his tools, were produced by his own labor and that of his family, occasionally with the aid of the village baker, smith, miller, etc., who were members of the community and shared in the subsistence which the farmer produced as a perquisite of their positions rather than as payment in any impersonal sense.

All well organized manors included all the necessary craftsmen. In Germany, even after obligatory services had disappeared, the estate workman was commonly paid in kind out of the products of the estate. The countess of Rochefort (end of the seventeenth and beginning of the eighteenth century) is an excellent example of the noble lady whose life was filled with the superintendence of a wide range of industrial activities in her household. Even the golden wigs of her lackeys were made up out of raw silk in her château. Her diary tells a long story of managing wool-carders, spinning women, sewing women, weavers, masons, and many other sorts of industrial workers.

In the cities, the ordinary household slaughtered its own supply of beef and pork. This was especially true in German towns. In France, the practice was declining. Parmentier noted in 1778 that "in most of the large towns, private persons no longer make their bread themselves."

The handicraft system remained firmly established to the very end of early capitalism and collapsed only with the coming of full capitalism. Although important changes in the legal status of the gilds had been made in the England of Elizabeth (Statute of Apprentices) and in the France of Colbert (state regulation), the gild organization was generally displaced only in two fields; namely, in the nonurban crafts which produced for distant markets and in the gilds of the larger cities. Traces of the older system remained in these fields. Although mining and smelting had to a very great extent been converted to capitalistic forms, examples of the persistence of gild organization are to be found in France, in Germany, and in England. The outstanding example is the Company of Hoastmen at Newcastle-on-Tyne. The small hardware industry in Remscheid and Schmalkalden in Germany, nail making in southern France, and some of the glass industry in Bohemia and France retained the gild character. The textile industry was at one and the same time the industry which offered the best opportunity for capitalistic development and the most considerable refuge for gild forms. In the cities, the gild form often remained long after the spirit of gild relations had departed. Differentiation of rich and poor masters, the development of the gain purpose as distinguished from the notion of mutual helpfulness, the reorganization of personal functions with a view to the highest material results—all this had made the gild something different from the medieval gild. Nevertheless, the proportion of employees (journeymen and apprentices) continued very low, from one to four per master. They were still counted as members of the master's family. In eighteenth-century London, though industries like brewing, distilling, building had become definitely capitalistic, and others like the fur business, saddlery, and upholstery had become partly capitalistic, many crafts such as the smiths, the bakers, and the butchers retained the gild character and the gild forms.

The Putting-Out System

Through the resistant fabric of the traditional handicraft system, the growing institutions of capitalistic industry pushed their way, like trees through rock. Their characteristic form was the association of workers, not only on a larger scale and in more significant ways than had ever been seen before, but, it is even more important to note, in response to the will of a new factor, the capitalistic entrepreneur, armed with a new force, the power of wealth.

The "putting-out," or domestic, system (for which the German language alone has a specific and adequate term, *Verlag*) was the first stage in the transition to industrial capitalism. This was a practice by which an owner of accumulated wealth furnished the materials of production, either in money or in goods, to a craftsman and received in return either a fixed sum or a share (sometimes the whole) of the craftsman's product. This practice was widespread over all of Europe and in all of the more important industries as early as the sixteenth century. Thus the Fuggers in 1527 had such interests in no fewer than 142 small silver mines. The economies of the costly blast furnaces gave the capitalist a favorable opportunity in the iron industry. In the textile industry, the putting-out system took the form of domestic industry, in which the capitalist or putter out, kept the weaver or spinner busy in his own home.[1] In the Florentine cloth industry, for example, contracts by which impoverished weavers gave up their ownership of their machines to creditors but retained them upon payment of a part of their product, were common. Others purchased looms and instead of paying for them, undertook to deliver a certain amount of their product. The silk industry of Venice was characterized by this kind of contract as early as the fourteenth century, and that of Genoa as early as the fifteenth, while it continued in Lyons well into the nineteenth century. An English law of Mary Tudor's time (1553–1558) declared that the "rich clothiers do oppress the weavers . . . by engrossing of looms into their hands and letting them out at such unreasonable rents as the poor artificers are not able to maintain themselves by and much less their wives and families." In Holland, putting-out contracts generally included a provision that the craftsman should not work for any one else. Spinning, which hardly had attained gild organization, was almost completely organized in putting-out fashion in every country of Western Europe by the eighteenth century. Book printing from an early date took on this form, which is reflected in the current German word, *Verlag,* for a publishing house. The establishments of the most famous printers, such as Hans Froben, were hardly larger than the average craftsman's establishment—a reader, a proofreader, five or six typesetters, and a similar number of pressmen. In England of

[1] The name "domestic industry," however, is important rather because of the wide usage it has obtained than because of any real distinction between the practice in the textile industries and that in other industries. The former were more domestic than ironworking, for example, from physical rather than from economic reasons.

Elizabeth's time (1583), we learn, "The provision of letter and many other things belonging to printing was so exceedingly chargeable, that most of the printers were driven through necessity to compound before with the booksellers." The paper industry in France was organized on this principle in a slightly more complicated fashion: the owner leased the paper mill to a wholesaler of paper, who in turn advanced a sum of money to a craftsman, to be used in the production of a given amount of paper. This paper the master craftsman sold to the wholesaler at a fixed price, returning the original capital. The putter out made his profit from the resale of the product. The putting-out system is still used in some great industries, notably in a great locomotive works in Philadelphia.

In a sense, the putting-out system represents a more purely "money-power" relationship than even later factory systems, in which the capitalist-entrepreneur furnishes not only the means of production, but also direction and management of the work. The putter out was concerned with none of this, but only put out a certain sum of money (or materials), and required the return of a certain product. The direction of the industrial process itself remained in the hands of the master craftsman. Putting out was capitalism in abstract form imposed upon the handicraft system. Essentially, however, the putter out was more of a merchant, as, indeed, he was commonly called wherever the putting-out system obtained, than a director of industry. The influence of the putter out was a stimulation to industrial productivity. His interest demanded as many and as productive craftsmen as possible.

Especially in the eighteenth century, however, we see the putter out, the *Verleger,* developing a new character as a center about which craftsmen-producers begin to associate themselves in somewhat higher and more complex forms, and as an influence upon the quantitative and qualitative production of the workman. The Sieur Dartalongue, master and merchant tailor at Paris, for example, announced that he was "able to satisfy the wants of his customers almost without delay, because of the numbers of workers he employed." The putter out was also the source of new standards. Here he had to fight against the custom and statute-sanctioned standards of the old industry, as when the French hatmakers' gild prevented the introduction of hats made of a mixture of beaver and wool. The putter out frequently effected economies in the use of instrumentalities of production, as, for example, when, in the textile industry, he owned a bleachery which handled the product of a whole group of weavers. He contributed to the development of specialization, as in the production of needles, which passed through the hands of seventy-two workers, most of whom were domestic workers, coordinated by the putter out.

This analysis and these examples serve to show how the putter out was a stage in the evolution to the fullest form of cooperation and specialization in industry: the association of workers in large units under a common direction and discipline, or, as we may briefly call it, the factory system.

The Concentration of Production in the Factory

The next problem is to trace the beginnings of these large industrial organizations and to obtain some measure of the degree of factory development and the extension of the factory form over the various branches of industry and in the various countries down to the end of the early capitalistic epoch. It will be readily recognized that in the case of many industries, factory organization had to await the development of power-driven, semi-automatic machines, a process that was hardly begun until the last quarter of the eighteenth century, even in England. Nevertheless, as we shall see, it would be an error to suppose that the essential ideas of the factory system had received no application before that time. The economic institution was present in wide ranges of industry long before the sudden advance of technique gave it its great impulsion.

An example so early as to seem somewhat detached and meaningless as far as the general development is concerned, is the transformation of the silk winding industry of Bologna between 1341 and 1371 by the utilization of a machine driven by water power and winding four thousand threads at once. This mechanical winding seems not to have spread very far until the seventeenth century, when it was carried to Holland or a similar device was invented there by the famous Johann Joachim Becher. He tells us that a building 300 feet long and costing 40,000 florins was put up at Haarlem to house his machines. In 1680, another was built in Utrecht with thirty-seven winding machines. Defoe found such a "silk mill" in Sheffield and refers to another in Stockport, which employed 200 hands. The first silk spinning factory in England was set up in 1719 at Derwent, near Derby, with machines that used with every turn of the mill wheel (water-driven) 73,726 yards of fiber. Piedmont in 1708 had 125 silk winding establishments which employed 6,990 persons; in 1787, it had 272, with 16,143 employees. Although these figures reflect practically no increase in the degree of concentration during the century, they prove the existence of units of production utterly unlike the typical handicraft shop of four or five workmen.

The last part of cloth making—the various processes of "finishing"—was the first to be organized factory-wise. The putter out commonly finished the rough cloths delivered to him by his weavers in a mill which he owned. The English East India Company had the cloths which it bought dyed and finished under its own direction. In Silesia and Saxony, the commercial houses commonly had their own finishing machines. Bleaching of linen and cotton cloths came to be concentrated in factory fashion, especially at Haarlem in Holland, where unbleached cloths were sent from "every place in the world," at least from places as widely separated as England and Silesia.

Stocking weaving became a machine industry without becoming in this period distinctly a factory industry. In 1789, for example, a stocking factory at Orléans employed 800 stocking weavers within the factory, but more than double that number outside. Sawmills in some cases were organized in large units: a Belgian sawmill in 1764 employed 102 workers.

Factories making the basic products of chemistry hardly developed before the nineteenth century, except in the case of sulphuric acid. The first modern sulphuric acid factory was established in 1736 at Richmond near London. Before the end of the century, various improvements had led to a great expansion: the era of chemical "big industry" had begun.

More important for our present purpose are the food and drink industries resting upon chemical processes. The sugar industry from the beginning concentrated large instrumentalities of production, if not large groups of workers. The typical investment was from $5,000 to $25,000, although the typical number of employees was from ten to twelve. Brewing remained essentially a handicraft and home industry well into the nineteenth century, but a few breweries emerged during the eighteenth century, especially in England: Whitbreads, a brewery established during the reign of William III, brewed 3,007 barrels of beer at one brewing. In the middle of the eighteenth century two breweries in London were producing 1,000 barrels each per week. Distilling establishments required "not less than two thousand pounds" of capital and were sources of great wealth. In soap making and candle making also, some concerns grew into large establishments. In Marseilles in 1760, thirty-eight soap factories employed a thousand workers.

The smelting and refining industries in the metal trades, which were at the same time mechanical and chemical, on account of their technical advancement and the expensive character of the establishments, were particularly suited to capitalistic concentration. The transition to the factory system came correspondingly early—in the iron and copper industry during the sixteenth century, and in the other metal industries during the seventeenth. A survey of the iron industry will illustrate the general course of the development in the other industries.

It really consisted of several different branches: (1) the production of raw iron in the blast-furnaces; (2) the production of wrought iron; (3) the refinement into higher-grade forms, such as steel; (4) the conversion into finished forms, such as tools, anchors, and chains; and (5) the production of castings. A part of the iron industry remained small handicraft industry, or else putting-out industry, to the very end of the early capitalistic epoch. The smelting as a whole, nearly all the founding and refining, and a considerable part of the production of finished materials took on the large associational form. Much of this transformation was accomplished by rulers, by cities, or by feudal landlords with the assistance of the rising capitalistic entrepreneurs. The establishment of blast furnaces instead of the small furnaces of the individual craftsmen is a fair index of the transition in the case of the smelting industry. In several of the most important iron-producing regions, including England, Liége, Namur, and Lorraine, the small furnaces were displaced by blast furnaces in the early part of the sixteenth century. Little is known of these early blast furnaces. In the Harz, the first blast furnace was established by the ruling count in 1551; in Saxony by the Elector Augustus I in 1575; in Hesse, by a hospital as a part of its endowment about the same time; in Sweden by Gustavus I (1523–1560); in Nassau by one Wilhelm Wilking under the protection of the prince; in Carinthia, by the city of Veith, which at a later date disposed of its smelter to private capitalists. The smelting process throughout the early capitalistic period remained dependent on wood as fuel, but some technical improvement, especially in size and capacity, came about in the furnaces themselves. Smelting remained distinctly a seasonal occupation: in Sweden and in Carinthia, the season was only twenty to twenty-five weeks. The forges where the iron was wrought also grew steadily larger, but without any great concentration of workers. Among the more important branches of finished production, anchor making developed into the factory form toward the beginning of the eighteenth century; wire mills and file-making establishments, in the course of that century. About the same time, the combined ironworks, carrying on several different processes from smelting to steel making all in one place or, at any rate under one direction, began to appear. The largest ironworks in France during the century was that of La Chaussade at Guérigny, which he purchased in 1781 for 3,075,099 livres, and which included two blast furnaces, four heavy forges, nine smaller forges, five shops for making anchors, two foundries, several forges for small hardware, and a number of nail-making shops. Similar establishments existed in Lorraine, in Norway, and in Sweden.

Manufactures proper—that is, industries in which the application of manual technique rather than the operation of automatic machines and processes was the mode of production—in some cases also showed the tendency to concentration. The Paris book-printing industry reflected it very clearly. In 1600 there were 270 establishments; in 1694, there were only 60, and this in spite of a great increase in business. In London, forty was regarded as the smallest number of workers and £500 to £1,000 as the minimum capital with which a press could be operated. Cotton printing, which was still a hand process, showed an even greater concentration of laborers, if less of capital. An establishment with 44 tables which employed 250 workers required a capital of only 30,500 thalers. A typical establishment included a printing shop with tables at which each printer worked by himself, a block cutting shop, a dyehouse, a bleachery, a drying house, and a mangle, commonly power-driven. Ten cotton-printing establishments in Chemnitz (Saxony) employed 1,437 workers. Tobacco manufacture (especially in the form of snuff) showed rather more concentration in the eighteenth century than did the later cigar making until late in the nineteenth century. A Belgian establishment had 151 workers; a Bavarian, 120; a Saxon factory, 130. Reveillon's tapestry printing establishment in the Faubourg Saint-Antoine, Paris, employed three to four hundred. Lace making was organized factorywise under the patronage of Colbert at Rheims in 1665 and furnished employment to 120 lace makers by the end of the first year. A French ropemaker employed three hundred; in London, a capital of £10,000 was thought necessary to establish a ropewalk.

The combination of various technical processes under single management was earliest developed in the cloth industry. *The Discovered Gold-Mine,* an English publication of 1685, recounts how "manufacturers at great cost build whole great houses, wherein the wool sorters, combers, spinners, weavers, pressers, and even dyers work together." A would-be poet of the sixteenth century tells us,

> Within one room being large and long
> There stood two hundred loomes full strong,
>   Two hundred men, the truth is so
> Wrought in these looms
>   All in a row.

Besides the weavers, the poet tells us, 100 carding women, 200 spinning maidens, 150 sorters, 50 shearers, 80 combers, 40 dyers, and 20 fullers were employed. In Scotland the factory form was apparently even more fully developed and more frequent before the eighteenth century than in England. In 1681, a cloth manufactory was founded at New Mills, Haddingtonshire, with a capital of £5,000, which in one year produced over 55,000 ells of cloth with a net profit of £1,413. A Glasgow woolen mill in the year 1700 employed not fewer than 1,400 persons. Before 1720, several joint-stock companies had been formed for carrying on woolen and linen manufacture. In France the cloth manufacture of Saptes employed about 800 workers during the last years of the seventeenth century. The Van Robais had 1,692 workers in one establishment in which the wool was carried through twenty-two

A GREAT FACTORY IN 1789: The Revillon factory in Paris at the time of the riot of which it was the center

processes. In Austria in 1775, the imperial woolen mills of Linz employed 26,000 persons, of whom 1,000 worked in the factory.

Building as an industry had early manifested the characteristics of the transition to exchange economy [2] and was similarly quick to take on capitalistic forms. Up to about the fifteenth century it was purely handicraft in its organization; then the revival of the professional study of architecture led to the differentiation of the architect, who undertook production of a building from materials furnished by the prince or proprietor who wished it built, a practice somewhat analogous to putting out; then as early as the beginning of the sixteenth century appeared the architect as contractor, producing the building as a whole for a fixed price. By the end of the seventeenth century, at least in the cities, the building industry had taken its present associational form under the direction of the capitalistic entrepreneur. All building, however, was still done at the behest of the prospective owner. Speculative building, except for slight manifestations in Paris and London, was a phenomenon of fully developed capitalism.

In the shipbuilding industry, the large-scale private enterprises did not evolve directly from the small handicraft establishments. In Venice, in England, and in France the industry underwent expansion in the first place, not as capitalistic, but as state enterprise. A travel diary of the fourteenth century describes the Venetian shipyards in great detail: about one thousand workers were employed. In England there is evidence of a royal "arsenal," or navy yard, as early as the thirteenth century, and by the sixteenth there were four. From Elizabeth's time, the contract system was commonly used; that is, the contractor was furnished with the materials and built the vessel at a set price per ton. Richelieu built great "yards," and at Brest, a contemporary tells us, "a whole world" of workmen operated under the direction of the royal shipbuilders, *les constructeurs de la Couronne*. Coach building, which like shipbuilding, utilized the services of a wide range of

[2] See p. 47.

artisans, seems to have rapidly concentrated during the latter half of the eighteenth century. From the time of Colbert and the founding of the Gobelins tapestry works (1667), the making of fine furniture was transformed into a "big industry." Charles Boule in Paris estimated the work in progress in his shops at 80,000 livres. Names like Sheraton and Chippendale, the great furniture artists of eighteenth century England, reflect also the development of comparatively large enterprises under their direction. Furniture production was still "upon command" of the purchaser and therefore still under the influence of the artist. It was only in the latter part of the eighteenth century that production in anticipation of the demand led to his elimination and to the degradation of standards.

In the mining industry a considerable degree of capitalistic concentration was manifested early in the history of capitalism. From the sixteenth century the progress of technique led to deep-shaft mining with water-raising machines that required large concentrations of power and labor force. Agricola describes three machines that required ninety-six horses to operate. Labor force of corresponding size worked in some of the mines—as many as 6,850 in the silver mines of Falkenstein (Tirol) in 1556, from 500 to 1,000 in a Newcastle (England) coal mine in 1649. In that same year, "Master Beaumont . . . adventured into our [Newcastle] mines with his thirty thousand pounds." In other words, the mines, because they were organized in this concentrated form, offered thus early an occasion for purely capitalistic investment.

The weapon industry, however, was the one which reached the highest degree of technical and business organization. The demands of the growing states, with their increasing armies, required the organization, the planned production, the effective delivery, that the capitalistic direction alone could give. From the middle of the fifteenth century, the production of military weapons gradually lost its handicraft character. In 1640 a Swedish factory was making 10,000 muskets a year. In the time of Peter the

Great, one Russian factory employed 683 workers. The Spandau arms factory had 252 workers at the time of its founding in 1722.

This discussion of early instances of concentrated, associational forms of industry has been extended to such a length because nearly all the general histories and economic textbooks give the student the impression that the factory system as such was the product of the so-called "Industrial Revolution" of the late eighteenth and early nineteenth centuries. It is true, of course, that the technical devices (automatic machines, steam power, etc.) combined with a set of economic conditions then existing to give the factory system a very rapid extension in a very short time; but this long discussion will have been in vain if the reader does not understand that the factory form of production had already become a part of the history of Europe when the extension which we call the Industrial Revolution began.

The Geographical Redistribution of Industry

The geographical distribution of industry underwent a transformation that corresponded roughly to the changes in form that we have just been studying. It can readily be understood that the large and costly plants that were characteristic of the factory industry did not lend themselves to the moving about that was habitual in some of the trades of the handicrafts period. At the same time, the range of the individual establishment became wider, and, aided by the increasing favor of the statesmen, the entrepreneurs came to conceive of their market as the nation, rather than the locality or, on the other hand, some foreign market. Practically all of the state-founded and state-subsidized industries were national in their range of outlet. Many forms of industry left the towns, with their gild traditions and restrictions, for the countryside. This is especially true of the cloth industry, in which the putter out played a large part. In England, Holland, France, Spain, and parts of Germany, by the eighteenth century, spinning and weaving had become, in major part, industries of the villages and hamlets. At the same time, the fact that the finishing processes were commonly handled on the factory basis led most notably in the case of the cloth industry, but also in other industries, to a division of the process between country and town. Birmingham and Exeter in England, Rouen and Sedan in France, Hirschberg in Germany, Eupen and Verviers in Belgium, became finishing centers for a large number of surrounding villages. A certain concentration in particular localities also occurred, as for example the English woolen industry in Yorkshire and the German linen industry in Silesia. This development, however, had only begun and can hardly be said to be characteristic of the early capitalistic epoch. Some industries, however, were definitely localized in one or a few of the great cities, as the making of fashions in Paris and the colonial industries in London and Amsterdam.

The Organization of Labor

The transformation of industry involved also the transformation of the relations of labor. Indeed, it is hardly too much to say that from this transformation developed the concept of "labor" in the abstract as a distinct element in the process of production. The whole process may be profitably summed up by way of preliminary:

(1) A capitalistic group devoted wholly to the function of enterprise (the entrepreneurs) comes to stand out in distinction to a group of wage workers who have no ownership in the instruments of production.

(2) Both groups are entirely capitalistic in feeling, the entrepreneur concerned only with the highest attainable profit, the wage earner only with the highest attainable wages.

(3) The relationship between the worker and the entrepreneur comes to rest upon a free contract, easily terminable, in which the

productivity of the worker is measured against a definite standard, money wages.

(4) Within the producing organization (the factory or mine) the labor force is organized in rational fashion for the highest attainable profits, without direct reference to personal need and desires.

Early capitalism saw only a partial approach to this capitalistic standard of labor organization. In the first place, the laborers were only in part, perhaps in small part, both propertyless and free. The unfree, the serfs, whom we encounter in the mines of Sweden, Scotland, and Silesia, and in the factories of Bohemia, Moravia, and Russia through the whole eighteenth century, and the occupants of public institutions, workhouses, orphanages, prisons, were not at all in a position to conclude a free contract, but were, in one form or another, compelled to labor. Among the free, we encounter impoverished craftsmen who owned a part of the tools of production, and who therefore cannot be regarded as wholly propertyless, and (probably the largest class of all) industrial workers who owned land. Statistical information is rare, but a little table analyzing the population of a German circle in 1830 gives an idea of this distribution. There were 9,718 families, whose sources of income were as follows:

Farming alone	3,055 families
Business and handicraft	1,763
Day wages alone	666
Day wages in combination with farming	933
Industrial establishments without farming	346
Industrial establishments with farming	2,167

The table is not very illuminating except on the one point that the combination of some kind of agriculture with labor in industry was predominant among the industrial workers. In 1840, Banfield, an English observer, wrote, "The German is still in that kind of dependence on the soil which apparently secures subsistence and, consequently, independence, even if accompanied by poverty." Banfield considered irrational and primitive a relationship which had disappeared from England two generations before. In France, the paper industry was carried on only in the winter, while the laborers took care of their fields during the summer. An ordinance of 1783 for the arsenal of Saint-Étienne forbade the workers to interrupt their labor "except in case of illness and of urgent need to cultivate their land."

The attitude of the laborer toward his work was undergoing a change but was still far from the attitude of the modern laborer: he still thought and felt in terms of the sustenance idea. When he had food and drink, he did not choose to work, and all that he did earn, he consumed, principally in the form of food and drink. From the standpoint of the entrepreneur, who demanded continuous labor, "the workman who earned too much was seldom a good workman." In general, there was an absence of proletarian class feeling: the workman felt his identity with his craft and with the entrepreneur who directed and furnished his work, but not with "the working classes."

The labor contract, while it became to a very large extent a free contract, was not yet free from old ideas. It was still largely colored by the idea that the workman was the employer's domestic, a part of his family, and should naturally turn to him for his food and shelter and his care in illness or old age. Even in a seasonal occupation like smelting, a Prussian ordinance required one-year contracts. In the accounts which have survived of French factories, especially paper mills, the supplies of food and wine for the workmen are a prominent part of the cost of operation. Many French establishments had large agricultural areas for the direct supply of this food material. In Sweden, it was common to assign each workman a dwelling and a small piece of land.

The *Verlag* (putting-out) relationship was also influential in the form of these early wage contracts, developing into something like the modern piecework contract. This was especially true in the mining and smelting establishments.

The determination of wages was still so irrational and so lacking in uniformity that it is difficult if not impossible to discover any general principles or standards. It has been shown, however, that the changes in industry themselves did not bring disaster upon workers, previously in a condition of prosperity, but rather that the new industry offered attractive opportunities to a class theretofore economically depressed.[8]

With the development of the factory concentrations of the industrial process, came also a change in the organization of labor in the factory. Early capitalism did not see any considerable development along systematic lines of the "division of labor" which Adam Smith described so well from so few examples. It was rather along two other lines that the change came; namely, in the organization of expert direction and in the utilization of untrained workers. These two tendencies together meant the evolution of the "master" into the "foreman."

Women and children were used as workers much more extensively than at present, but it is necessary to understand that this was rather the extension of an old custom than the introduction of a new one. In the thirteenth century, some fifteen industries in Paris were carried on by women alone and eighty by men and women. The utilization of children was assumed to be valuable both to themselves and to society. The spirit of earlier times is illustrated by a patent granted to two gentlemen in 1678 for "a new spinning engine," one of the chief advantages claimed for it being that "by means of it a child of three or four years of age may do as much as a child of seven or eight years old." Nevertheless, the factory system did draw more heavily upon child labor than the gild system. The educational device of the handicraft apprenticeship was transformed into a device for providing cheap labor. One of the earliest examples of this exploitation of

[8] Bowden, *Industrial Society in England,* chap. IV, sec. 3.

child labor comes from the book-printing industry in Paris and Lyons in the sixteenth century. A protest by the journeymen printers complained that the presses upon each of which five workers were employed were being run by one journeyman and four apprentices, sometimes five apprentices, and demanded that the entrepreneurs be allowed to take not more than two or three apprentices for each press. We have seen how in England legislation favored apprenticeship as a means of utilizing child labor. Children were also employed in industries like mining where apprenticeship, properly speaking, never obtained. Boys of ten to twelve years worked in the silver mines and copper mines of Germany and the coal mines of England. (A contemporary picture of the frightful development of the employment of children may be found in Cheyney, *Readings in English History,* pp. 692–695.)

The Social Demands to Which the Transformation of Production Responded

It is well at this point to turn back and review the early development of the factory, the typical capitalistic industrial unit, in order to see if possible just what were the interests and social demands that promoted the replacement of the shop by the factory. In personal terms, it was the interests of the princes (the state) and of the industrialists; in impersonal terms, war and luxury favored—one might almost say, caused—the development of the factory system.

The monarchs themselves often turned to capitalistic industries for the purpose of increasing their revenues, as in the case of the Bohemian gold and silver mines, which the ruler claimed as a part of his right and then simply "put out" for the sake of the revenue. The demands of the princely court for high-grade luxury goods led to another sort of royal enterprise of which the Gobelins tapestry works—"The Manufacture for the Production of the

Furniture of the King," as it was called—is the great example. Sometimes, as in the silk industry in France, enterprises were established as an example and stimulus to private enterprise in order to keep money from being drained out to other lands, and in some cases, in order to assure income "to the poor subjects who had to pay the taxes." Similar motives led to the establishment of war industries: "Peter the Great needed a regular army; it embarrassed him that he should have to depend upon the Hanse cities, Holland and England for a supply of cloth, weapons, powder, ships, and naval stores. He formed the determination to have all the factories established in his own state which were necessary for the army, the artillery, and the fleet." This formula operated in all the greater continental states and led to the establishment of state factories for the production of all sorts of military necessities: the Prussian monarch even had great bakeries for the supply of his armies.

Putting out, which, as we have already noted, constituted an almost pure abstraction of the capitalistic relation in spite of its essentially transitional character, was based in part upon a simple and definite need of the worker for funds to carry himself over the period between production and sale. Two contemporary comments out of many illustrate the point: "Most of the artificers are poor men and unable to provide such store of materials as would serve their turn," states the preamble of an English statute of 1550. A Brandenburg statute of 1687 states that "some of the weavers have not the wherewithal to supply themselves with wool," and those who have, "have not the means to carry their product to the markets and fairs." In France (time of Louis XIV) we hear of four families who possessed the only glass-making outfits in the whole country, but were "not in a position to maintain their industry," and therefore asked three merchants to finance them with a putting-out contract.

We are more concerned here, however, with the development of the concentrated industrial establishment under the direction of the capitalistic enterpreneur. Just one thing led men to attempt to produce goods upon a capitalistic basis: the hope of a profitable disposition of the goods produced. This disposition depended upon the existence of an adequate demand. Two questions emerge: (1) Where did effective demand exist for finished goods that would promise adequate returns to the entrepreneur? (2) Where and when did this primary demand create secondary demands for means of production?

We have already discussed the revolutionary effect of the development of new demands for goods by the rich, the armies, the shipbuilders, the cities, and the colonies. Most of this new demand can be summed up under the two heads, luxury demand and army demand. Practically all the important "finished product" industries of a capitalistic character were either luxury industries or army industries or industries supplying the means of production for such industries.

A simple examination of the list of capitalized industries shows how completely it covers the luxury industries. Sugar (then a luxury), chocolate, silk, lace, embroidery, novelties, tapestries, mirrors, porcelains, jewelry, watches, book printing, are examples of pure luxury industries which were almost wholly capitalistic in form by 1800. Industries which were only partly capitalized provide us with an even more illuminating comment: "handicraft" and "luxury industry" were completely opposed ideas in the consciousness of contemporaries. As Mercier puts it, "One would say that being devoted to occupations more useful than that of the arts of luxury, the craftsmen are recompensed by a calm conscience and by the tranquillity of their lives." This distinction is quite concretely illustrated in many industries. In England, bottled beer was made in the big breweries. The early woolen mills made only fine cloths (John Winchcombe in England, Van Robais in France, Vilets d'Aignan in Montauban). In Scotland, coarse linens for the colonial trade were made in the country, fine linens in the big establishments in Edinburgh. Cotton cloths, which were at first and for a long time luxury goods, as a new product, offered a field for almost exclusively capitalistic organization. "Every man must have a hat," runs an eighteenth century German prospectus; most hatters made "only small and mean hats for the common kind of people," therefore "a fine hat factory" is to be established.

In building, as we have seen, and in the furniture industries, the story is the same. It was the Chippendales, the Sheratons, the Adams who developed the capitalistic organizations, while, on the other hand, the production of ordinary furniture and ordinary houses remained a handicraft industry well into the nineteenth century.

Army industries show about the same development in this period. It has already been sufficiently shown how the purely military demand for missiles, for powder, and for muskets was from an early date met by groups of wage workers under state-capitalistic direction in factories rather than by craftsmen. Other industries were also affected. All large iron foundries up to the eighteenth century were primarily gun foundries. The army demand for cloth and for uniforms was in large measure met by large concentrated industrial units. In Russia, from the time of Peter the Great, weaving mills which produced exclusively for the army were established. In England, in France, and in Prussia, the army demand for cloth affected various branches of the weaving industry. Capitalistic clothing industry, in the form of factory production of ready-made clothes, owes its beginnings almost wholly to the military demand for uniforms. This military demand, in contrast to the luxury demand, was a demand for quantity rather than quality.

The expanded demand for consumption goods and the intensified technique pressed upon the production of production instrumentalities, of tools and machines. For example, the utilization of chemical materials in various processes from gilding and fur-treating to dyeing and bleaching necessitated large quantities of saltpeter, vitriol, alum, potash, borax, and many other chemicals.

Ships were growing in size, and merchant and naval fleets were growing in number: a necessary incident was the increased demand for iron, for sails, for the hundreds of different articles that go to the making of a ship. In terms of our present concern the demand for each article was also a demand for large-scale, concentrated production of the capitalistic kind. The iron industry in Sweden was elevated to the predominance which it enjoyed until the middle of the eighteenth century by the royal promotion of the production of high-grade iron for the cannon foundries. The development of weaving in England seems quite directly to have resulted in a self-conscious demand for better spinning devices. The jenny and the mule, which satisfied that demand, were produced, organized, and operated under purely capitalistic conditions. Arkwright was in many ways the first modern large-scale manufacturer. When the growing demand for iron, as we shall see, pressed hard on the supply of wood and fuel, coal produced by capitalistic mining companies was rapidly brought into use.

Capitalistic production was still for the rich, for the state, for the entrepreneur. Not yet had it come to depend, as it did later, upon widespread demand made possible by cheapened production.

What were the advantages of capitalistic industry that brought it victory in so many fields of industry over the handicraft shop system, which had the sanction of long usage and in many cases a corresponding legal sanction? In part the answer is the obverse of what we have already noted as the necessary conditions of capitalistic development. (1) The necessary men with the spirit of enterprise had developed, and (2) they had got control of the capital necessary to introduce the new modes of industrial organization. (3) The necessary market had developed, especially in the great military organizations and the luxury-demanding town populations. (4) A technique of production had elaborated itself into the complex we call the factory, and (5) an organized labor force had been developed. (6) A supply of the necessary materials and means of production was assured. (7) Supply and outlet to market were assumed by the development of transportation and of commercial organization. (8) The state had granted many industrial capitalists a privileged position, especially in the industries newly introduced by the enterprise of private individuals or by economically minded statesmen.

The handicraft system was unable to compete. It was bound by its very principle of being to the old ways, and could not be adjusted to the new methods. The craft gild with its principle of limited productivity in traditional ways, made and could make no place for the entrepreneur. On the other hand, it could not adjust itself to the demand for new sorts and new qualities of goods: the distinction, handicraft for coarse goods, factory for fine goods, has already been sufficiently mentioned. It could not produce upon the large scale required by the armies, the cities, and the industrial plants themselves. Price differences played only a small rôle in this struggle between the new and the old: capitalistic industry did not so much underbid in price as it overbid in productivity.

In some cases, only capitalistic enterprise could produce the desired goods; this was true of pig iron, which could be produced only by large and costly establishments. In the case of other goods which were produced both by handicraft and by capitalistic enterprise, the latter alone could produce them in sufficiently large quantities and with sufficiently uniform quality to satisfy a single large demand, such as that of a military force. Even the merchant who gathered, as we have seen, the product of a hundred weavers, was not able to supply a product so uniform as the entrepreneur could obtain from his disciplined establishment. The capitalist-producer alone had sufficient flexibility to meet the changing fashions. Large-scale production commanded better raw materials (for example, Holland linens); it made possible elaborate division of processes of production, and it made possible a closer supervision and more adequate training for the worker.

In conclusion, the capitalistic organization of industry had made itself a definite and a large place in economic life before the end of the eighteenth century. That organization was in large measure independent of advances in technique. It was, rather, due to the intervention of a new psychological factor between the demanding consumer and the individual worker—the will of the entrepreneur, which through the market nexus, the power of money, brought the workers to produce in concentrated and disciplined groups for unknown consumers, themselves unaware at the time of production of their demand for the goods. The new organization was destined to evolve into greater and more elaborate forms during the nineteenth century. In particular, its development and application of new technical devices was to make possible an extension of economic activity such as had never been seen. But, independently of the major advances of technique, the essential economic relationships of capitalism had made their place alongside the older handicraft relationships in large areas of industrial activity.

REFERENCES FOR FURTHER READING

General

Sombart, W. Der moderne Kapitalismus, vol. II, pp. 589–908.

Clapham, J. H. The Economic Development of France and Germany, 1815–1914 (1921).

Cooke-Taylor, R. W. The Modern Factory System (1891).

Gibbins, H. de B. Economic and Industrial Progress of the Century (1903).

Hobson, J. A. The Evolution of Modern Capitalism (1926).

Knight, Barnes, and Flugel. Economic History of Modern Europe (1928), chaps. III, IV.

MacGregor, D. H. The Evolution of Industry (1911).

Mantoux, P. La Révolution industrielle au XVIIIe siècle (1906). English translation, 1930.

Ogg and Sharp. The Economic Development of Modern Europe (1926), parts I and II, *passim*.

Renard and Weulersse. Life and Work in Modern Europe (1927). See index, s.v. Domestic Industry, Factories, Industry.

Ure, A. The Philosophy of Manufactures (1835).

Schultze-Gaevernitz, G. von. The Cotton Trade in England and on the Continent (1895).

England

Ashley, W. J. The Economic Organization of England (1914), Lectures VII, VIII.

Bowden, W. Industrial Society in England Towards the End of the Eighteenth Century (1925).

Boyd, R. N. Coal Pits and Pitmen (1892).

Cheyney, E. P. Industrial and Social History of England (rev. ed., 1923).

Clapham, J. H. The Woolen and Worsted Industries (1907).

Cunningham, W. The Growth of English Industry and Commerce (6th ed., 1915–1921).

Curtler, W. H. R. A Short History of English Agriculture (1909).

Gonner, E. C. K. Common Land and Enclosures (1912).

Halevy, E. A History of the English People (2 vols., 1924–1927).

Hammond, J. L., and Barbara. The Town Laborer (1917); The Skilled Laborer (1919); The Rise of Modern Industry (1926).

Prothero, R. E. English Farming, Past and Present (1912).

Slater, G. The English Peasantry and the Enclosure of Common Fields (1907); The Making of Modern England (1913).

Toynbee, A. Lectures on the Industrial Revolution in England (1884).

Unwin, G. Industrial Organization in the Sixteenth and Seventeenth Centuries (1904).

Usher, A. P. The Industrial History of England (1920).

France

Levasseur, E. Histoire des classes ouvrières et de l'industrie en France avant 1789 (2 vols., 1901–1920). Also continued under the same title, 1789–1870 (2 vols., 1903).

Chaptal de Chanteloup, J. A. C. De l'industrie française (2 vols., 1819).

Kovalewsky, M. La France économique et sociale à la vieille de la Revolution (2 vols., 1909).

Laribe, A. L'Evolution de la France agricole (1912).

Lavergne, L. de. Economie rurale de la France depuis 1789 (1921).

Forrester, R. B. The Cotton Industry in France (1921).

Germany

Dawson, W. H. The Evolution of Modern Germany (1914); Industrial Germany (1912).

Deliux, R. M. R. The German Cotton Industry (1913).

Sombart, W. Die deutsche Volkwirtschaft im XIX Jahrhundert (1903).

Wendel, H. C. M. Evolution of Industrial Freedom in Prussia, 1845–1849 (1921).

Sources

Bland, Brown, and Tawney. English Economic History, Select Documents.

Bourgin, G. and H. Le Régime de l'industrie en France de 1814 à 1830 (1912). Texts.

CHAPTER V

EUROPE AS AN ECONOMIC SOCIETY AT THE END OF THE EIGHTEENTH CENTURY

THE purpose of this chapter is to review in summary fashion the operation as a going organization of the economic society which was the outcome of the development portrayed in the earlier chapters. How was European economic society functioning? What were its fundamental ideas? How did these ideas work out in practice? How did the economic transformations of the sixteenth, seventeenth, and eighteenth centuries affect the political and social structures of the European peoples?

MERCANTILISM AS THOUGHT AND FEELING

The basic thought and feeling in regard to economic relations in the eighteenth century is covered by the name "mercantilism." Mercantilism has already been referred to as the basis of the economic policies of the early capitalistic state, of rulers such as Colbert and Cromwell. Here the problem is somewhat different: What was mercantilism as a body of systematic thought? In a way it was the first of the series of European systems of economic thought, the antecedent of physiocracy, classical economics, and socialism. Mercantilism is less a system than the others, partly because it was not the product of a deliberate synthesis by any great thinker, and partly because it received no deliberately conceived exposition such as Adam Smith's *Wealth of Nations,* or Karl Marx's *Capital.* Indeed, it is still rather difficult to refer the college student to a convenient and correct statement of mercantilist thought. Perhaps the greatest of the mercantilist writers was

Charles Davenant; but he was only the most important of a number of English writers on economic subjects in the latter part of the seventeenth century and the first part of the eighteenth. Daniel Defoe, whom we have so frequently quoted, Thomas Mun, whose *England's Treasure by Forraign Trade* (1664) is a very characteristic production of this school, George Chalmers, and Lord Sheffield at the end of the eighteenth century, are all cardinal figures. In France, Montchrétien, Forbonnais, Necker; in Germany, J. J. Becher, Schröder, Justi are the great names of the mercantilist school.

A general misconception of mercantilism is so common that it is proper to begin by denying it. Mercantilism is not the theory that bullion is wealth or the only form of wealth. It is true that the mercantilists were all keenly alive to the importance of a generous supply of circulating medium in active economic life. But to erect this into a cardinal doctrine of the school is to misunderstand the essential concern of the mercantilists.

That primary concern was the strengthening of the state. All their thought was of the common interest as embodied in the state. "One loves his country and serves it," is the starting point of Thomas Mun's well known work. The power of the state was the primary objective of their "political arithmetic," the economic advantage of the individual subject only secondary. "The power of a state consists not in the extent of its territory but in the prosperity and the number of its inhabitants." Economic life was for the mercantilist no "play of free forces," but the direction of the economic activities in organized society to provide power.

The economic method by which the power of the state was to be increased was, in principle, simple: the increase of the productiveness of organized society in the state (rather than of the individual worker—the mercantilists always disapproved of any improvement in technique that seemed to them likely to reduce population). Productivity should be increased by the employment in productive activity of as many individuals as possible as much of the time as possible. Beggars, vagabonds, women, even children must be utilized. The working time must be lengthened, holidays and "blue Mondays" eliminated. The productive powers must be applied to the greatest possible range of lands, materials, and forces. The utilization of the productive powers of the nation must be increased by increasing the productivity of the soil, of the worker, and of exchanges (by improvement of commercial organization and transport). Foreign commerce must be developed to take care of the surplus production: "The exportation of our products is the foundation of all our trade," wrote Davenant. The best trade, of course, is that which returns the most goods, especially bullion, for the least export, that is, the forced trade of dependencies.

Karl Marx discovered capitalism for science in the nineteenth century; to have discovered its character and its significance for economic practice was the achievement of the mercantilists. They recognized the value of the entrepreneur: for Becher, the *Verleger* (the putters out) were the "foundation pillars of the commonwealth." The mercantilists recognized the importance of adequate fluid capital, especially in the form of money, and of labor supply: "We want hands, not manufactures, in England" (Davenant). They had in mind the importance of outlet for goods: a minister of Frederick the Great argued that his twenty thousand soldiers were no burden for Prussia, but a source of well-being, because satisfying their needs gave the employment necessary to increase the population.

To the question, What will give the great economic machine the necessary impulse? their answer also was simple. In their time, when the expansion of business was pressing hard upon the necessary supply of intruments of exchange, when gold and silver were still the principal instruments of ordinary payment, when the devices by which we have learned to increase the efficiency of a given amount of the precious metals were still comparatively undeveloped, their doctrine was essentially correct. For any national economic society in the seventeenth or the eighteenth century, the mercantilist emphasis on the importance of increasing the stock of the precious metals was simple recognition of an obvious fact. It was not the fundamental element of their teaching: it was means to the great end of increased power. Davenant again supplies the classical expression, "Trade brings in the stock [of precious metals]; this stock, well and industriously managed, betters land and brings more product of all kind for exportation; the returns of which growth and product are to make a country gainers in the balance."

The mercantilist economists thought in terms radically different from those of the classical economists. It has already been noted that they had no concern with the "free play of economic forces" which was the whole concern of their successors from Adam Smith onward. Their thought was essentially organic, sociological, as contrasted with the mechanical conceptions of the classicists. The comparison of the state, which for them was the one organized form of society, to the human organism appears in almost all their writings. "There is an important relation, a close similarity between the body of a well organized state and the body of an animal."

The attention of the mercantilists was fixed on the production of goods, while the classicists were equally held by the problem of distribution. None of the mercantilists had a theory of value; on the other hand, by the time of Ricardo, it had become possible for him to write his *Principles* without even a chapter on production. For the classical school, economic principles were static; for the mercantilists, dynamic. For the latter wealth was the capacity for production, not, as for their successors, the total of collected goods. Even money was wealth only as it served "to keep the wheels of the machine in motion." Their aim was the achievement of an ideal, not the mere observation of a condition.

In a sense, the mercantilists were the pioneers of scientific economics, in that they applied thoughtful consideration to economic problems. In a truer sense, however, they performed a different function from the scientific economists and are rather the predecessors of men like List, Dühring, and Henry Carey, who were essentially propagandists, rather than of Adam Smith, Quesnay, and Ricardo, the real founders of scientific economics; that is, economics as a set of static principles.

The great monuments of mercantilist influence are the numerous laws and treaties by which governments attempted to organize the economic process in such a way as to increase the activity and prosperity of their subjects. An index of the growth of that influence may be taken by comparing any fifteenth century government's activity with that of any eighteenth century government. For example, the Intercursus Magnus, the treaty which Henry VII of England made in 1498 with the duke of Burgundy to facilitate the commerce of their respective subjects, invites attention because it is almost unique in its time; in the eighteenth century, it was only the exceptional statute or session of Parliament or treaty that was not devoted wholly or in major part to such subjects.

The navigation acts of England and the restrictive system of France were perhaps the most deliberately mercantilist systems in Europe. Eighteenth century observers, English and non-English, agreed that the ascendancy which England was able to win on the sea over Holland and over France, was facilitated if it was not brought about by the navigation laws. Between 1715 and 1789, France enjoyed a period of steadily rising prosperity and economic expansion which as an advance upon what preceded has hardly been surpassed down to our own day. It cannot be said that mercantilist policy was disastrous. Mercantilism like most bodies of doctrine held by large groups, lasted too long, outlived its usefulness, became false doctrine. By the end of the eighteenth century, the problem of circulating medium had been substantially solved for the countries of Western Europe; the problem of organizing economic power in subordination to and in support of the state had equally been solved; and the increase of production had created a new problem, that of distribution, which it was the function of the classical school to recognize (and for the future to solve). Nations have learned that their best markets are not in colonies but in profitable mutual exchange.

Mercantilism in Practice

Mercantilism in practice was a struggle for foreign markets, especially colonial markets ("export is the life of our trade"), and for the precious metals.

The end of the early capitalistic period saw a very rapid increase in the amount of foreign trade. The average total of exports and imports of England rose between 1700 and 1792 from about $12,-000,000 to about $36,000,000. Between 1716 and 1788, French imports sextupled and French exports quadrupled. The total export and import trade of the three most important countries, England, Holland, and France, rose from about $300,000,000 to about $500,000,000.

These three nations far outranked the others. Portugal had about $25,000,000, Italy, $37,500,000, Spain, $40,000,000, Germany, $60,000,000 of foreign trade at the end of the eighteenth century. Holland stood easily first at the beginning of the century, France, second, and England, third. During the century, however, the relative positions of these three were just reversed, Holland losing its ascendancy about the middle of the century and England pushing far ahead of France in the last decade.

In proportion to population, nevertheless, Holland still remained as it does today, first. The following table shows the per capita export and import trade about 1790 in round figures.

Holland	$75.00	Spain	$5.00
England	17.50	Germany	3.75
France	10.00	Italy	2.50
Portugal	7.50		

It should be understood, of course, that these figures are based on mere estimates both of the trade and of the population, since accurate figures are lacking. It is of some interest to compare them with the 1910–1911 figures, which show Holland first with $425.00 per capita, England fourth with $137.50, France fifth with $87.50, the United States ninth with $37.50. (In 1924, this last figure had risen to about $70.00.)

International trade had also broadened considerably in its territorial extension, partly in consequence of the discoveries of the fifteenth century. The Indies trade, spices in the sixteenth and seventeenth centuries, sugar and tobacco in the eighteenth, had become "the axis about which the overseas trade revolved." Anderson wrote of England: "Our East and West India trade are by far the most eminent, the two great pillars of our stupendous commercial fabric." In Holland, the Indies trade had grown from about one-tenth of the total trade in the beginning of the seventeenth century to about one-fourth at the end of the eighteenth. English trade with the colonial areas rose from 21.9 per cent in the first decade of the eighteenth century to 40 per cent of her total trade in the eighth decade; French trade with similiar areas, from 18 per cent of the total in 1716 to 33 per cent in 1787.

All international commerce aimed at the enrichment of the respective states in the precious metals. The three richest sources of the precious metals during the period were the Spanish colonies (for silver), Portuguese Brazil (from the end of the seventeenth century) and Africa for gold. Humboldt in the latter part of the eighteenth century estimated that about 42,000,000 piasters' worth of goods (inclusive of smuggled goods) was taken by the Spanish colonies, for which about 38,500,000 piasters of precious metals was returned to Europe. Directly or indirectly, substantially all of this went into the channels of European commerce. The Dutch appear to have secured the chief share in the silver of the Spanish colonies, either by sending their goods to Cadiz, using Spanish merchants as nominal agents and trading under their names with the colonies, or by smuggling through their own American possessions, especially Curaçao. In 1688, the French minister Seignelay in a memoir to Louis XIV estimated that the Dutch took home every year 5,000,000 florins as profits from the first sort of trade and a similar sum from the direct trade with Spain, as well as the unknown profits from smuggling. The French at the same time and especially after the ascent of the Bourbon Philip V to the Spanish throne, were permitted by his favor to participate directly in the trade with the colonies. The flow of silver from Spain to France thus begun continued in full strength down to 1789. In that year, the French exported 87,000,000 francs' worth of goods to Spain and imported from Spain only 41,000,000; the balance was paid in coin. England participated, directly and through her North American colonies, in the smuggling trade, and in 1713 secured the assiento by which she was permitted to send one ship a year of 500 tons to Porto Bello. This was less important for the legal trade done in this way than for the basis it offered for further smuggling. The legal and half-legal trade with Spain and with the colonies through Cadiz resulted in a constantly more favorable balance for England, $2,230,000 annual average imports from Spain and $4,500,000 exports to Spain in the years from 1770 to 1780. Lord Sheffield estimated that between 1700 and 1773 England exported $150,000,000 worth of goods to the North American colonies and received from them about $50,000,000. The balance was paid largely with silver and gold won in the complex channels of the smuggling trade with the Spanish colonies.

Trade with Portugal became of great importance for the second time at the beginning of the eighteenth century after the discovery of the rich gold and diamond fields in Brazil. The Methuen Treaty of 1703 bound Portugal to England in such close relations that Portuguese gold almost all went to the London market. "We gain a greater balance from Portugal than from any other country whatever," wrote a contemporary observer. "By the treaty we have increased our exports thither from about £300,000 to near £1,500,000." In the eighty years from 1700 to 1780, this favorable balance of trade together with other means of getting Portuguese gold such as colonial investments by Englishmen in Brazil, brought perhaps £120,000,000 of gold into England.

The trade with Africa was another great source of "a favorable balance" and of a net profit in specie for both England and France. For both countries, it was bound up with the slave trade, and the results were derived not only from the trade with Africa itself, but also from the contact with the Spanish colonial markets which favor assured to the French and the assiento, to the English. The statistics which have come down show that by the end of the century, the balance in favor of each country in the African trade approached $5,000,000 annually.

Germany and Austria were still in a minor way producers of gold and silver. The Hapsburg dominions kept their exports and imports about balanced, but the trade with Germany in the years 1787–1789 netted France a balance of about $10,000,000 in a total trade of $111,000,000, and England a lesser amount in a similar proportion.

The effect of this inflow of gold and silver was somewhat reduced by the steady draining away of precious metals to the East. Humboldt estimated that something over half the annual inflow of gold and silver from America to the Western European countries found its way to India, China, and the Levant. The English imported from India and China about $5,000,000 worth a year in the middle of the century against exports to those areas of only about one-third that amount. In 1787–1789, the French imports were about 34,000,000 livres, the exports about 17,000,000 livres.

The balance of trade among the three leading commercial states was strongly against Holland, in favor of France, and especially in favor of England as against the other two. In France the balance against Holland for the years just before the Revolution amounted to about 15,000,000 livres in a total trade of about 65,-000,000. Between 1700 and 1780, it is estimated that the debit of the Dutch against England rose to £116,000,000.

The discharge of unfavorable balances among these European nations was accomplished, primarily, by the export of capital, which in the eighteenth century was beginning to take on a large aspect. It had already appeared in the sixteenth century as a catastrophic phenomenon in the emigration of religious refugees. In the eighteenth, however, these more highly organized states, especially Holland, began to pay with certain invisible exports. In the case of Holland, the foreign exchange business, which still centered at Amsterdam, amounted to about 200,000,000 florins. Discounting and marine insurance, as we have seen, were also developed on a large scale. The direct exportation of capital (as distinguished from financial services) took the form of (1) mortgage loans, especially in English, French, and Danish colonies; (2) direct capital investments, as in England, where in the middle of the 1700's, one-third of the stock of the Bank of England was owned by Dutchmen; and (3) public loans to sovereigns, a field in which the Dutch and the Swiss had long before displaced the Italians and the south Germans.

England also had become a creditor country in the eighteenth century, although, as we have seen, a good part of the public debt (one-eighth to one-seventh) and much of the stock of English companies were held abroad. The principal financial items in the English creditor position were the foreign loans, profits from ocean transport and marine insurance, in which fields England was displacing Holland, taxes out of India, profits from trade carried on between other countries (e.g., between India and China), profits from investments in the colonies of foreign powers. On the other side of the account stood a very considerable item, the expenditures in foreign lands for war aims, in the form of subsidies, and the hiring of mercenaries. This expenditure, however, had the advantageous result of opening up new markets for English goods. The resulting increase in the cost of exchange put a premium upon the export of goods.

Apparently most of the silver and gold acquired by England was converted to consumption uses. The connection with the rich gold supply of Portugal and Africa led gradually to the elimination of silver from the money supply (under George III down to 1780 only £7,126 in silver was minted) and to the establishment of the gold standard. It was in the eighteenth century that the great plate collections of well-to-do English families were begun.

In France, the supply of specie rose from a low point in 1715 of 730 million livres to about 2,200 million in 1784. This was the result of acquisitions of gold and silver during the century of over 5,490 millions. According to Arnauld, a competent contemporary statistician, the utilization of this five and one-half billion was distributed as follows:

	livres
1. Coinage	1,268,614,000
2. Consumption (plate, jewelry, etc.)	1,752,000,000
3. Sent to Asia	617,481,000
4. Payments of foreign subsidies, pensions, etc.	1,095,000,000
5. Papal court	262,800,000
6. Remelted coins	216,000,000

The distribution of specie among the several countries of Europe is significant.

Country	Date	Amount (in Francs) per Capita
Great Britain	1800	63
France	1791	75
Netherlands	1823	107
Spain	1782	50

Country	Date	Amount (in Francs) per Capita
Portugal	1788	50
Prussia	1805	22
Russia	1815	4

Capitalism and Society

By the end of the eighteenth century the development of capitalism had produced drastic effects in the social and political institutions of Europe. In the first place, it had contributed greatly to the vastly increased power of the state. The new business men were nationalistic in their thought, neither localistic nor international. They furnished the motives, the means, and the methods by which the monarchies destroyed the feudal localism of the nobility and the economic localism of the communes. On the other hand, international economic organization was not yet in question. Even in finance, the decisive steps toward internationalism had not yet been taken. Holland alone, because of the disproportion between her stock of capital and her soil, had begun the systematic practice of international finance.

The states were rendered more nearly self-sufficient by virtue of the specific direction which mercantilistic trade policy took, the development and sale of surpluses produced from the soil.

Population, the great concern of the mercantilist, increased greatly, especially during the eighteenth century. The following table shows the increase in particular countries (in millions):

England	5.5 in 1700	7.9 in 1780
France	19.0 in 1700	23.0 in 1787
Holland	.98 in 1737	1.9 in 1805
Italy	14.0 in 1700	17.0 in 1800
Prussia	3.3 in 1740	5.6 in 1790
Austria	6.1 in 1754	7.9 in 1784

An even greater increase occurred in the revenues of the States. The income of the French kings rose from about 10,000,000 livres at the end of the sixteenth century to about 200,000,000 at the beginning of the eighteenth and to nearly 500,000,000 at the end. The revenues of the English State were about £500,000 in Elizabeth's time, £4,000,000 in 1700, and £34,000,000 in 1801. Furthermore, the various states had greatly increased their use of public credit. The French monarchy owed over 4,000,000,000 livres in 1789. The English public debt in 1793 was over 261,000,000 pounds sterling.

Social relations and social strata were radically affected by the very considerable increase in wealth. Only estimates are available; but, however inaccurate they may be, all agree in representing a very decided increase of wealth. English total wealth seems to have nearly doubled; French wealth seems to have more than doubled, and similar expansion is evidenced by all the signs and contemporary estimates in most of Western Europe.

It is one of the most important and most characteristic features of early capitalism that all the countries of Europe remained throughout "export lands," that is, exported voluntarily the surplus of the productions of their soil in raw or manufactured forms and imported freely chosen goods which for the most part served for the embellishment of existence: export and import were not yet vital to any of them. Holland and Norway may have been exceptions. The grain import into Holland was enormous, but most of the grain imported was again exported. Norway depended to a greater extent than any other country upon foreign food supplies, but even its export was soil-produced surplus of lumber. Even so industrialized a country as Switzerland produced five-sixths of its grain demand in the middle of the nineteenth century. Only in one field, the shipbuilding industry, were the Western European countries forced to turn to other countries for timber and for iron. In the forest industries they had ceased to be soil-lands.

Foreign trade fulfilled the function which the mercantilists assigned to it: (1) it provided the commercial nations with the bullion necessary for capitalistic development; (2) it served to distribute the surplus production of the soil among the several peoples and to stimulate the productive energy necessary to win a share in this surplus; and (3) it flooded the Western European lands with the products of the exploited oversea areas and with those of the Middle and Eastern European countries.

Productive power had been increased by the expansion of enterprise and the increase in the labor supply both through the increase in the population and through the employment of hitherto idle or half-idle parts of the population. People seem to have worked longer and more intensively than in the Middle Ages. More soil was brought into cultivation, new products were introduced, and the forests especially were more intensively exploited. An example of this development of new areas of population is the growth of the fishing industry, which was developed first by Holland and which meant so much also to the economic life of England and France. Power, especially water power, was extensively utilized in the factories as we have seen (see Chapter IV), although the application of steam power remained unimportant before 1815. The improvement of waterways and of roads also meant much in the development of productivity.

Labor was increased in effectiveness, not merely by the development of industrial technique and organization, but also by the development of the technique and organization of commerce and intercourse.

Much of the wealth of Europe came from the unrestricted exploitation of other peoples. The plantation system was largely based on forced labor, especially Negro slavery, and the East India trade upon the forced delivery of goods by native population. Davenant wrote: "Whoever looks strictly and nicely into our affairs, will find that the wealth England once had, did arise chiefly from two articles: 1st, our plantation trade; 2ndly, our East India traffic."

Society was not only growing more wealthy, it was also beginning to take on the characteristics of capitalistic organization. It was becoming mechanical, in the sense that the personal contact in economic relations, the eye-to-eye, hand-to-hand trading, the domestic relations of employer and workman, the family associations (as firms) were being displaced by the impersonal market. The highly organized market was a machine which determined the merchant's price, the laborer's wage, the investor's return, without reference to their needs or their deserts, without prejudice or favor.

Wealth, the control of productive power, was bringing about also a new stratification of society. The middle class was becoming the top class. The old division, *la haute noblesse, le peuple moyen, le peuple menu,* was wholly disrupted in the eighteenth century. The old forms were preserved from dissolution for a while by the modification of the old symbols to include the new powers. The financiers of France, the nabobs of England, took over the titles and the perquisites of the old aristocracy. On the other hand, the ancient nobility itself became largely capitalistic bourgeois, middle-class, in its activities and its relation to economic life. The marquis de La Fayette was a member of one of the proudest of the French noble families: he spent the years after the American Revolution trying to correct the bad organization of Franco-American trade relations.

It was this middle class (become top class) that ruled France in spite of antiquated forms and, when the contradiction of form and fact became too flagrant, made revolution to break the forms. The merchants and manufacturers became the dominant elements in the English Parliament. The Dutch merchants, as the Estates General (and provincial) and as the East India Company, ruled Holland.

As a counterpart of the "middle class" was emerging also a proletariat. The proletariat was far from the class consciousness of the present, but the drifting population that formed the bulk of the enormous increase in population in such centers of the new order as Birmingham and Manchester consisted of essentially propertyless laborers, economic objects at the disposal of the entrepreneur by means of the impersonal wage system.

The Limiting Conditions of Early Capitalism

The evolution of capitalism before the nineteenth century was amazingly slow, as compared with its final stages in the last century. The fields of economic activity which had been won for capitalism were limited and special. Not only agriculture, but the major part of industrial production and of distribution was still in the bonds of the traditional forms and processes of the Middle Ages. Economic productivity in all fields, capitalistic and non-capitalistic, remained petty as compared to later standards. This was not due to the unavailability of modern methods. We have seen wholesale trade in Holland showing almost completely modern characteristics, industrial organizations in all lands with the traits of the modern factory, large-scale iron production on the same ideological basis as the modern smelter. Why then does eighteenth century economic life seem so different, fall so far short of the development which was so gigantic in the nineteenth? Occasion has often been taken in this book to say that cause in historical sequence is unknowable, not to say irrelevant; it is possible in this case only to point out some of the psychological and intellectual conditions which are a part of this comparative retardation.

Let us glance first at the psychological conditions that held individuals back from full capitalistic living. The eighteenth century capitalist still retired as soon as he had gained a certain competence. In England, he bought a country estate and became a gentleman. In France, he purchased nobility for himself, or, more usually, for his son. In Holland, he invested his capital in foreign loans. This potential capital itself was perhaps not less significant for the development of capitalistic activity in the hands of the state than it might have been in the hands of the "proprietors." The diversion of the "proprietors" and potential entrepreneurs from enterprise, on the other hand, was a net loss of some importance when entrepreneurs were still comparatively rare.

The political conditions were, as we have seen, on the whole very favorable to capitalism, and even where handicraft organization retained the support of legislation the enterprising capitalist did not allow himself to be hindered. Nevertheless, the state retained much of its feudal origins and in many ways fell short of that complete service to the capitalistic economy which is normal in our day. It was only at the end of the seventeenth century even in England that money and finance were organized in a helpful and reasonable way. In Spain, in France, in Germany, irrational taxation and equally irrational expenditure operated to handicap business ventures. One needs to think only of the numerous interior tariff barriers which the modern business man of 1789 still had to sweep away in France. The state did not even perform adequately the function of police. Robbery and piracy were considerable parts of the risk of doing business in 1800. In many areas, marine insurance against piracy ran as high as 10 to 20 per cent.

The passion for religious unity led more than one state into measures disastrous to its economic life in general and to the development of a capitalistic economy in particular. The comparatively easy tolerance and hospitality of Holland and England meant a constant reinforcement of the capitalistic class in those countries; the expulsion and exclusion of heretics, infidels, and Jews from Spain meant a great loss of capital and of capitalistically minded men. The revocation of the Edict of Nantes (1685) almost visibly removed a large segment from the new economy which Colbert had labored to build up, and set France back some decades in capitalistic development.

War contributed powerfully to the organization of capitalistic enterprises of some sorts, to the disorganization of other sorts. The devastations of the Thirty Years' War in Germany, and of the wars of Louis XIV and his successors, involved the destruction of many a budding capitalistic enterprise. Worse still, they tended to disturb the capitalistic spirit. "No one works, and the war is the reason," wrote a burgher of Nîmes in 1689. The breaking off of commercial relations paralyzed whole branches of industry and commerce, not infrequently destroyed them. Such was especially the case in the trade between Holland and France. All in all, while war needs and war methods historically contributed to the development of capitalistic enterprise, it is probable that as great or greater and more rapid advances would have been made in peace.

The technical deficiencies of eighteenth century civilization were even greater handicaps for evolving capitalism. The deficiency of hygiene cut sharply across the apparently vigorous reproductive power of the European populations. The plague itself did not disappear from England until after 1666, from the western continental countries until the eighteenth century. Typhus, smallpox, and cholera did not cease as persistent dangers, especially in the large cities, until the latter half of the nineteenth century. Yellow fever has just been brought under control. The economic significance of these facts is most conveniently illustrated by the conditions under which the Panama Canal was built: without the highly organized technique of sanitary control, it would have been impossible. In the eighteenth century, the deficiency of sanitary control meant frequent catastrophes that decimated organized labor forces and a constant wasting of population through the cities, where the death rate was normally well above the birth rate. In London, which may be taken as an extreme example, 16,000 births were registered in 1761, and 21,000 deaths.

The incomplete development of technique in the fields of transport and production also operated in diverse ways to limit capitalistic development. The persistence of the empirical, rule-of-thumb methods has already been discussed (pp. 82–83). The general dependence on organic forces (men, animals, water) and on organic materials (wood, cotton, wool) involved the recognition of a very definite limit fixed by the productivity of the soil. Every man, every beast, required, in effect, so much soil devoted to his sustenance, and in the absence of a highly developed transportation system the amount of soil available was very restricted.

The deficiency of industrial technique furthermore involved a restriction of complex processes to the rate of the slowest element in each process. Before the invention of the spinning machines in the middle of the eighteenth century, weaving was restricted by the comparatively small production of the spinners. It is estimated that in general it took ten spinners to keep one weaver busy. Similarly in the iron industry, the production of the smelters, technically the most highly developed phase of the industry, was limited by the less highly developed ore production and fuel supply (of which more below). This unequal pressure upon the different elements of the production process led characteristically to high costs of production, therefore to a narrowing of the market, hence to still higher costs and in general to a sharp limitation of the development of the capitalistic organization. The cost of producing a ton of iron in the Harz rose from 50.14 marks in the beginning of the eighteenth century to 67.38 marks in 1801. The price of a ton of steel in England rose from £21.11s.8d., in 1566, to £50 in 1753. The whole situation was well put in the *Reminiscences of the Worsted Man, by an Octogenarian,* a manuscript of the early nineteenth century: "The manufacture was necessarily restricted, and an increased demand could not be met by a proportionate increased supply."

The ultimate limit, however, was set by the approaching and visible exhaustion of the forests. European economic life depended upon its supply of wood. Wood was the raw material of dwellings, of tools, of wagons, and of ships; it was the source of important auxiliary materials, pitch, turpentine, potash; it was the ordinary fuel not only of domestic use, but also of industrial establishments, potteries, glassworks, lime and brick kilns, and above all of the mining and smelting industries. The glassworks commonly moved from place to place as the woods were consumed. It required from 350 to 1,400 pounds of charcoal to produce 100 pounds of iron bars. A smelter in Lorraine which employed twenty-one men used up 345 acres of timber a year to supply half of its demand for fuel.

The threat to the supply of wood began to be recognized in nearly all Western European countries as early as the sixteenth century, as numerous ordinances and regulations testify. In Venice, the lime burners had been forbidden to use wood "unless it were from Istria." In 1560, the burghers of Nevers petitioned the king of France to "demolish, suppress, and destroy" all forges within three leagues of the town, in order to insure the domestic supply of wood. Their petition was granted. A whole series of ordinances through the seventeenth and eighteenth centuries forbade the industrial use of timber which could be used for building or heating. In the various German states, smelting was restricted to a limited season of eight to twelve weeks a year. In the seventeenth century numerous ironworks ceased operations because of the lack of fuel. In England, aside from the house-building and house-heating demand, the concern for the shipbuilding industry led to legislation (1559) forbidding ironworks within fourteen miles of the coast. The scarcity of fuel grew so severe that the eighteenth century saw a decline in the English iron industry. In spite of legislative restrictions, however, the forests declined in size all over Europe. Tuscany had 3,474 square miles in 1400 and 2,435 square miles in 1842. France had 7,500 square leagues in 1750 and 2,213 in 1825. England in the Middle

Ages had sixty-nine forests, in the beginning of the nineteenth century only Windsor, Dean, Sherwood, and New Forest.

The growing deficiency was met by the importation of forest products and timber from the forest lands. One of the principal items for which the North American colonies of England were valued was their forest production: timber, turpentine, and pitch. It was the Scandinavian peninsula, however, that offered the most available resources: the trade across the North Sea and the Baltic became of the greatest importance. Attempts were also made to introduce more economical ways of using wood and to replace wood by other materials. These had some results, especially in the substitution of soda and alkaline products for potash. The substitution of coal as fuel was important only for the domestic heating supply. Men had not learned to smelt metals with coal or to build ships of iron and steel. It was in these industries that "the crisis of the woods" made itself most clearly felt. Anderson in his *Origins of Commerce* tells us that about 17,350 tons of iron was produced in England in 1730, "the quantity of which, it was said, we could not increase by reason of our woods being so far exhausted as to have greatly enhanced the price of cord-wood used in the refining of iron-stone." In France, "many furnaces have had to be shut down because the cost of wood absorbed more than half the value of the product" (1836).

In general, European mankind lacked the wood which under the circumstances of the time was necessary to the development of its economic life and institutions. The growing wealth which had made the brilliance of eighteenth century life was derived from the systematic exhaustion of resources the limits of which were already appearing. The woods were going, the colonial areas were closing up as expansion areas because of the increasing cost of ships, in the homelands the soil was fully exploited and productive power restricted by the limited supply of men and the limited supply of materials. "Europe's economic culture had apparently attained the same point of development which all previous cultures had attained and which none of them had surmounted." From this point, all of them had collapsed in catastrophe or had declined into a peaceful, individual economy of small agriculture. How Western European civilization surmounted its crisis and developed what none other of the historic cultures had, even in analogous forms—namely, the institutions of "high capitalism"—is our next subject.

REFERENCES FOR FURTHER READING

General

Sombart, W. Der moderne Kapitalismus, vol. II, pp. 943–1107.

Bourne, H. E. The Revolutionary Period in Europe (1915).

Cunningham, W. Western Civilization in Its Economic Aspects (2 vols., 1898–1900).

Kovalevsky, M. Die ökonomische Entwicklung Europas bis zum Beginn der kapitalistischen Wirtschaftsform (7 vols., 1901–1914).

Ogg and Sharp. The Economic Development of Modern Europe (1926).

Renard and Weulersse. Life and Work in Modern Europe (1927). See index, s.v. Aristocracy, Imports, Monopolies, Population, Trade (foreign), Work-people; and, especially, see the conclusion.

Smith, Preserved. The Age of the Reformation (1920), chap. XI.

Oddy, Jepson. European Commerce (1805).

Mercantilism

Gide, C., and Rist, C. History of Economic Doctrines from the Time of the Physiocrats to Our Own Day (1915).

Schmoller, G. The Mercantile System and Its Historical Significance (1910).

Sheffield, Lord. Observations on the Commerce of the American States (1784).

Smith, Adam. The Wealth of Nations (1776).

Spengler, Oswald. Preussentum und Socialismus (1921).

Thomas, P. J. Mercantilism and the East India Trade.

Social Restratification

Botsford, J. B. English Society in the Eighteenth Century as Influenced from Oversea (1924).

Corti, Egon (Count). The Rise of the House of Rothschild (1928).

Feuchtwanger, L. Power (1926).

Gillespie, J. E. The Influence of Oversea Expansion on England to 1700 (1920).

Gretton, R. H. The English Middle Class (1917).

Kovalesky, M. La France économique et sociale à la vieille de la Révolution (2 vols., 1909–1911).

Namier, L. B. "Brice Fisher, M.P., a Mid-Eighteenth Century Merchant and His Connections," English Historical Review, 42:514–532.

Nussbaum, F. L. Commercial Policy in the French Revolution (1923); "American Tobacco and French Politics, 1783 to 1789," Political Science Quarterly, Dec., 1925; "The French Colonial Arrêt of August 30, 1784," South Atlantic Quarterly, Apr., 1928.

Sée, Henri. Economic and Social Conditions in France During the Eighteenth Century (1927); La Vie économique et les classes sociales en France au XVIIIe siècle.

Young, Arthur. Travels during the years 1787, 1788, and 1789 [in France] (2 vols., 1794).

PART IV

CAPITALISM DOMINANT

CHAPTER I

THE RELEASE OF ECONOMIC ENERGY

WE now approach the period in which the capitalistic forms of economic activity attained their maturity and full development. This was, roughly speaking, the nineteenth century. Certainly we cannot with exactness use the year 1800 as a starting point nor 1900 as a terminus. Indeed, it would be misleading to emphasize any two dates as definition for our period. In different parts of the European world, the characteristic features of "high capitalism" appear at various dates from 1750 to 1850. In general, the student of historical processes will do well to make his concept of the beginning or end of a period very flexible. A garden affords a fair analogy: who can say when the growing period begins? Is it when the first shoot pushes above the ground, or when a majority of the plants have appeared, or when they have all emerged? None of these points is exactly satisfactory, and yet "growing season" is a useful concept to any one who thinks about a garden.

The terminus of this period of high capitalism is more definite, 1914. The catastrophe of war affected the economic fabric of Europe so radically that no observer of the current economic life can feel that it is not something different, a new phase as compared with prewar life. But what? It is still too early to judge the direction which the latest developments are taking. Hence this book contains no attempt to answer that question. Reference is occasionally made to matters later than 1914 to illustrate the institutions of earlier development.

What are the characteristics of fully developed capitalism? It may be useful to attempt a summary answer before the more extended answer to the same question which is implicit in the whole content of this Part. In most summary fashion they may be said to be:

(1) The complete disappearance of all precapitalistic institutions: obviously, communal agriculture, gild industry, town commerce, the whole sustenance economy vanish as well as most of the compromise shifts which characterize transition.

(2) The complete attainment of capitalistic character by all forms of economic activity, rationalization, depersonalization, abstraction of the aims of activity as profit. Where these characteristics are found, there is the territory of fully developed capitalism.

Less abstractly, we shall see a unique development of technique, new mechanical inventions, new devices of money and banking, new systems of transportation, new organization of labor force. We shall see the state become the instrument of economic society, its whole activity conditioned by the purpose of promoting prosperity—in contrast to the mercantilist idea that the purpose of economic activity was to contribute to the strength of the state. We shall see new types of men attain the controls of economic life and, consequently, of the state: democracy!

Quantitatively, the nineteenth century saw a great release of economic energy. More people, more different sorts of people, became leaders of capitalistic enterprise and devoted themselves more thoroughly to the economic life.

In 1872, Walter Bagehot in his book *Lombard Street* complained that the older merchant families "who inherited nice cultivation as well as great wealth—are pushed out so to say, by the dirty crowd of little men . . . These men want business at once and they produce an inferior article to get it." Bagehot's complaint reflects one of the great features of high capitalism: the extension to new strata of society of opportunities for economic leadership.

The economic leader is perhaps as much the creature as the creator of his own conditions. Yet, as Bagehot suggests in the case of the new men of his day, something always results from the character of the men at the centers of power. The driving force of capitalism is the capitalistic entrepreneur.

Certainly the personnel of economic leadership, in the periods of development that we have already examined, shows distinct characters in the several periods. In the Middle Ages, the feudal prince, the ecclesiastical lord, the head of the village, was the natural head of the organically organized agricultural community; the patrician merchants were the foremost gild councilors, the energetic city officials. In early capitalism, enterprising individuals from every grade of society manifested activity in the new economic forms, but it was the princes and their ministers who "dragged the plebs by the nose and the arm to the new sources of profit." In the later day of capitalism, that function was no longer necessary: the market enabled the entrepreneur to control the forces necessary to capitalistic enterprise.

Through the market, he was able to command the capital of other people, instead of or in addition to his own. Through the market, he was able to command the services of high-grade technicians, accountants, salesmen, efficiency engineers, upon whom devolved many of the functions that eighteenth century and earlier entrepreneurs regarded as their own particular concern. Thus the entrepreneur or business man tended to limit his activities to generalized problems of policy and direction, the choice of men and of measures, as against participation in the making or selling routine of his establishment.

Because the margins of the concept "entrepreneur" are rather uncertain, it is necessary to make two rather fine distinctions. A cost accountant, discovering that a certain reorganization of a business will save 10 per cent of the costs of production, may report his discovery to the manager. He has shown the quality of enterprise and indeed has performed one of the functions of enterprise, but he is not the entrepreneur. The man who, at the risk of profits, decides that the change shall be made is the entrepreneur. On the other hand, an entrepreneur who has risen from the ranks is very likely to participate in the operation of some function that was interesting to him, as a general might continue to be a sharpshooter: in so far as he does this he is not pure entrepreneur.

This abstraction of the function of enterprise has made possible a "lateral" integration of the function. A comparatively small number of directors act as leaders for a whole series of enterprises. In 1912, the ten members of J. P. Morgan & Co. held sixty-three directorships in thirty-eight corporations with a total capital of over $10,000,000,000.

Among modern entrepreneurs, three types may be distinguished: the technician-specialist, the seller, the financier. The technician-specialist starts with a product, an invention or a combination; the salesman takes the point of view of the market; the financier provides the necessary capital. Ford, in his first phase, was an example of the first type and later also of the second; Edison was especially an example of the first type in almost pure form; Carnegie, Krupp, Siemens, Sir Alfred Pearson, of the first type; Raskob, Schulte, Penney, Woolworth in America, Selfridge and Lipton in England, Rathenau in Germany, of the second type; Morgan and Vanderbilt in America, Sir Alfred Mond in England, Loucheur in France, Stinnes in Germany, are or were examples of the financial entrepreneur.

To a surprising extent, these groups are "first generation"—that is, made their position as leaders without the aid of social or property inheritance from their families. Chapman and Marquis have shown statistically that about three quarters of the leading figures in the English cotton industry were "first generation." In the United States, Carnegie, H. H. Rogers, J. C. Penney, Harriman, Ford, Firestone, Raskob, are only types, many times repeated, of this same phenomenon. In Germany, the majority of leaders seem to come rather from the moderately poor. Ballin, the great shipping magnate, began life as an emigration agent;

Dernburg and Helfferich, financial magnates, came from professional families; Siemens, one of the great founders of the A.E.G. (Allgemeine Elektrizitätsgesellschaft), was an artillery lieutenant when he started as a builder of telegraph lines with 6,000 thalers which he had to borrow.

On the other hand, active economic leadership continues dynastically in only a few cases: the Rothschilds were exceptional as long as they maintained their active leadership, as are the younger Rockefeller and the younger Morgan in this country.

The leadership in economic enterprise seems to have passed rather definitely to lands at least nominally and traditionally Germanic. England, Germany, and the United States in 1910–1911, produced 75 per cent of the cotton yarn, 78 per cent of the steel, 82 per cent of the coal. Another racial character obvious everywhere is the prominence of Jews: in Germany before the war, 13.3 per cent of the directors of industrial enterprises were Jewish, although the Jews formed only about 1 per cent of the population.

A characteristic of capitalism has been the intensification of activity. "Time is money" might be a very modern proverb. It was only in the nineteenth century that the careful measurement of time in relation to industrial and commercial processes became general: the culminating example, perhaps, is the efficiency engineer studying the movements of the coal heaver with a split-second stop watch. All industry has been permeated with the most accurate methods of adjusting effort to aims. At the same time, capitalistic enterprise has extended itself over all sorts of economic activity, among the laboring and salaried classes, and over the whole face of the earth, to the innermost parts of the most remote areas: the fur trapper of the Siberian wilds is linked to the London market.

This huge release of economic energy, which is perhaps the most characteristic feature of "high capitalism," seems to rest first of all on certain new psychological attitudes. The democratization of enterprise which has been noted, must of itself have brought opportunity to more individuals of the entrepreneur type than was offered by a society in which such opportunity was dependent on the possession of wealth. The Faustian impulse of unlimited attainment "grew by what it fed upon," and especially among Germanic peoples and Jews led to the intense devotion to business with which we are familiar. In the second place, the specialization of function already noticed made possible the "pure" entrepreneur, while the devolution of collateral functions opened a way of approach to the function from below. In the third place, for traditional religion has been substituted a belief in "progress" and a concept of economic activity as in some way a form of duty, even as an object of love, to which the capitalistic man turns as a source of joy, to which he religiously devotes his life.

External influences also favor this release of energy. The "new men," whether from lower ranks of society or from colonial areas, are free from limiting traditions and customs. They are free, under modern conditions, from the timidity of the owner of capital: they characteristically work with the capital of others, who, even when legally in a position to act, like the common stockholders of the American Telephone and Telegraph Company, generally do not even trouble to send proxies. They are free from traditional morality based upon religion. This is not to say that business men have no morality, but that their morality has only a weak connection with the historical morality of, say, the Middle Ages. An example that serves as well as any: on nearly every Gothic cathedral is found a representation of the virtues and vices, and among the latter is nearly always found the vice of —ambition!

Then, too, the increasing technical difficulty and complexity of economic life has called forth great energy. Competition has necessitated more exact control of costs, more rational price-setting, more intense advertising. The increasing cost of labor along with other factors has compelled the transition to higher technical forms—machines, elaborate discipline, "efficiency." The scarcity of labor in the United States, for example, has made the introduction of "labor-saving" machinery almost everywhere profitable. Labor agitation has imposed upon industry the need for more intensive management to increase gross profits and to cover the increased costs. "Fortunate those capitalisms which are confronted by an aggressive proletariat" (La Gardelle). The increase in population has meant an increase in the number of each generation who are compelled to turn to economic activity. Social pressure leads even the already wealthy to an active participation in economic life.

In more positive fashion, modern economic society seeks out its leaders and in a sense creates them. Every expansion necessitates new recruits: they are obtained by systematic efforts. For example, the Westinghouse Electric Company, the Standard Oil Company, and many other corporations and firms formerly sent representatives to the colleges every year to pick men who with training might become the "executives" of the future. Every technical novelty wakens and extends the spirit of enterprise: witness the movies, the radio, the airplane.

The constantly increasing size of economic units increases the productivity of their leaders. The characteristic projection of plans and policies into the future increases the range of the entrepreneur's activity. The necessity of rapid turnover means a demand upon the entrepreneur for more rapid processes of business. The increase of wealth experienced by individuals leads them to seek still greater wealth. The hope for "extra profit," by the improvement of some process, leads to the restless pressure for improvement regardless of personal considerations.

The capitalistic enterprise becomes wholly materialized, depersonalized. The beginnings of the concept of the "business" as a legal, accounting, and credit entity have already been discussed. The economic establishment now transcends the individual economically active man who is a part of it, and lives after his life has ended. The single aim of the capitalistic enterprise is profit.

Ford, who insists that "service for the common good" is his personal aim, says that "my work wouldn't be of consequence if I did not also produce a measurable profit for myself and my associates." The other motives, desire for power, reputation, sense of duty, common good, are subordinate to, conditioned by, the one necessity for profit. Lest this seem to be invective, it is well to recognize the literal truth of Mr. Ford's statement. Granted that his activity is beneficial to society, it is obvious that if it had been unprofitable or were now unprofitable the investment in it would be converted to other uses. The profit that has passed into his and other private hands might conceivably be used as endowment to make up losses due to selling the product below cost: that would not be "business" but charity, and in the rationale of capitalism would have to be justified as charity. This "objectified" system has its own rationale promoted by business magazines, schools of business, mechanical office devices, etc. It has its own virtues: Industry, Frugality,[1] Stability. This purely objective, material character of capitalistic motivation means simplification and therefore intensification. It means the unification of economic life: the common single aim obliterates differences of detail.

In one sense personality has disappeared before the all-enveloping uniformity of the economic machine. Japanese are wearing trousers and straw hats in order to fit into the capitalistic scheme. The whole earth is covered with countless establishments erected after the same pattern, as the best available means to the common end, profit. Variety, individuality, are impossible except as eccentricity.

In another sense, personality is even more important than ever. The huge organizations that modern businesses have become require strong hands to guide them and control them. "The modern system requires for its administration a higher intelli-

[1] Mr. Ford has adopted the new principle that saving is economically disadvantageous. This doctrine is one of the signs that we are passing out of the conditions of "high capitalism" to something else.

gence than the old." When the capitalistic entrepreneurs were driven out of Russia by the Revolution, the whole capitalistic economy stopped until the new government developed functionaries to take their place and do their work.

NOTE: *In this section, the United States and Japan will be referred to, without further explanation, as parts of the modern capitalistic Europe. It is perhaps in the United States that capitalism developed first its most characteristic and its purest forms. From the standpoint of this book, a common economic-historical character is more important than geographical or political separation.*

REFERENCES FOR FURTHER READING

General

Sombart, W. Der moderne Kapitalismus, vol. III, pp. 3–41.

Capitalistic Leadership

Bagehot, Walter. Lombard Street (1872).

Brookings, R. S. Industrial Ownership, Its Economic and Social Significance (1925).

Carlioz, J. Le Gouvernement des enterprises commerciales et industrielles (1921).

Chapman, S. J., and Marquis, F. "The Recruiting of the Employment Classes from the Ranks of Wage-Earners in the Cotton Industry," Journal of Royal Statistical Society, 5:75 (Feb., 1912).

Dobb, Maurice. Capitalistic Enterprise and Social Progress (1925).

Hammersley, S. S. Industrial Leadership (1925).

Hawley, F. B. Enterprise and the Productive Progress (1907).

Kuh, Felix. Arbeiterschaft und Unternehmertum in Wirtschaft und Staat (1923).

Sombart, W. The Quintessence of Capitalism (1913); The Jews and Modern Capitalism (1913).

Tarbell, Ida M. The History of the Standard Oil Company (2 vols., 1904).

Taussig, F. W. Inventors and Moneymakers (1915).

Veblen, Thorstein. The Theory of Business Enterprise (1904); Absentee

Ownership and Business Enterprise in Recent Times (1923); The Instinct of Workmanship (1914).

Biography

Barrett, Walter. The Old Merchants of New York City (2 vols., 1862–1863).

Ford, Henry. My Life and Work (1926).

Hendrick, B. J. The Age of Big Business (1920).

Hughes, John. Liverpool Banks and Bankers (1906).

Myers, Gustavus. History of the Great American Fortunes (3 vols., 1911).

Pinner, Felix. Deutsche Wirtschaftsführer (1924).

Riedler, A. Emil Rathenau (1916).

Smiles, Samuel. Men of Invention and Industry (1884); Life and Industry (1887).

Wiedenfeld, Kurt. Die deutsche Wirtschaft und ihre Führer (announced).

CHAPTER II

THE NEW MERCANTILISM AND THE NEW IMPERIALISM

The state became the servant and instrument of economic society capitalistically organized, rather than its master and director as it had been in the period of early capitalism. Regardless of variations and changes in the political forms, from the democracy of England to the czarism of Russia, in all the countries of Europe, the same general policy was followed, the same laws were established to protect and further the institutions of capitalism.

The nineteenth century state contained in itself two mutually contradictory principles. On the one hand, it pursued a power policy, much after the manner of earlier capitalistic states *à la* Machiavelli, the object of which was "prestige," "a place in the sun," "manifest destiny"—expressions that only modernize Machiavelli's "glory of the Prince." On the other hand, at the same time, in domestic affairs its avowed purpose was the promotion of "progress and prosperity." The contradiction between these two aspects of the state was not, of course, fully visible until the World War, but even in 1914 many people, with perfectly sound logic, declared that the financiers and the industrialists would not permit war. That they were mistaken only illustrates the profundity of the contradiction.

The state had become purely secular, independent of any external sanction, completely sovereign, and therefore indifferent to religious divisions, although state churches survived as relics of an earlier time. It had become thoroughly individualist. Citizenship had become purely citizenship in the state, free of any connection with local or personal bonds. The community solidarity which was characteristic of the Middle Ages was pushed aside and replaced by the principle, "Every man for himself." To the conflict of individual interests, the state remained purely neutral. It was nominalist: that is to say, it rested, so far as internal politics was concerned, upon the philosophic concept that reality existed only in the individual, that the state had no reality, but was only a name for certain relations between individuals. In external policy, however, it rested upon the opposite concept, that the state was a real entity, which had purposes, interests, desires, which transcended the interests, purposes, desires, of any individual citizen or subject or combination of them. This general characteristic becomes more concrete and more obvious as the acts of the state in internal and in external politics are examined.

Economic Legislation

In internal politics, the following general characteristics are observable. (1) The notion that a public office was the private possession of its holder disappeared. With its disappearance, came a sharp distinction between public law and private law: all economic activity became a matter of private law. Specifically, the purchase and inheritance of offices disappeared, and the official became a public servant, in clear contradistinction to the private, economically active person. (See *The Fall of Feudalism in France,* by Sydney Herbert). (2) As corollary, economic life was freed from the restrictions of public law. The legal regulation of economic life was abandoned and replaced by a system of subjective rights, unrelated to any duties. The action of the French Constituent Assembly in 1789 is typical. When it was urged that a declaration of duties should accompany the Declaration of Rights which established the modern right of property in France, the Assembly rejected the proposal by 750 votes to 433. When, in the course of the nineteenth century, many labor laws were passed in various countries of Europe, always over strong opposition, both advocates and opponents used the argument of "liberty." The opponents alleged that the measures proposed interfered with liberty of contract. The advocates of the measures argued that such measures were necessary to give the weaker elements "liberty" in the face of the more powerful. (3) In content, economic legislation was characterized by a thoroughgoing support of the essential capitalistic principles. Freedom of industry, that is, the right to labor as, when, and where the individual chose, freedom of contract, freedom of ownership (the right to use, abuse, or destroy), the right to dispose of property at will, the indestructibility of property right, became the common law of all European countries and expressed their complete acceptance of capitalism as the norm of economic life.

The mere catalogue of the legislation in the several states designed to clear the way for capitalistic construction would in itself run to several large volumes. What can be attempted here is only a summary reflection of the range and general character of that legislation.

Agricultural economy was modernized by the abolition of serfdom, the dissolution of communal agriculture, and the abolition of privilege connected with property. In England, serfdom had become obsolete by the sixteenth century and never was abolished by any specific legislation. In France, the Revolution swept away the vestiges of serfdom, already in large measure obsolete. In Germany, the reforms of Stein and Hardenberg included the destruction of serfdom. Slavery was abolished in the English colonies in 1833 and in the United States in 1865.

Communal agriculture, the old medieval village system, lasted in all European countries until the nineteenth century. In England private enterprise, after an outburst of "enclosing" in the interests of the wool industry in the sixteenth century, which affected about three per cent of the soil, completed the process between 1700 and 1850. The Enclosure Acts, which were private acts of Parliament, obtained by agreement among all concerned, converted the open-field systems of specified villages into "enclosed fields," that is to say, from the economic point of view, into private property to be used as the owner chose. The following table is a fair index of the disappearance from England of that most uncapitalistic institution, communal agriculture:

NUMBER OF ENCLOSURE ACTS BY DECADES

1760–1769	385	1810–1819	853
1770–1779	660	1820–1829	205
1780–1789	246	1830–1839	136
1800–1809	847	1840–1844	66

In France, the Revolutionary confiscations of feudal and church property involved the establishment of the concept of full private property in land. In Prussia, the process was begun by Stein and Hardenberg in 1807, but not completed until the decade 1850–1860.

Commerce and industry were similarly freed of the old restrictions. In England, again, the process began early; as early as 1650, complaints are heard of the "complete freedom" of the country weavers. In 1624, the English Parliament abolished monopolies, but in the same act made provision, in a wholly modern spirit, for the protection of monopolies granted to inventors. Turgot attempted to abolish the gilds during his short ministry (1776); after his fall they were restored, to be abolished again in 1791. Napoleon attempted to reconstitute them in much modified form (1801), and after his fall they gradually disappeared (the Printers' Gild in 1870). Industrial freedom was decreed in Prussia in 1810, but did not become effective and general in Germany until 1869.

In the field of commerce and transportation, the characteristic act was the abolition of interior tariff barriers. This problem had never, properly speaking, existed in England as a hindrance to capitalistic development. In the United States, the Constitution of 1789 put an end to all tariff barriers between the several states. The Constituent Assembly swept away the whole complex system of interior tariff lines in France. In Germany, the customs union of 1833 reduced the number of tariff lines, and the foundation of the Empire in 1870 completed the process.

Much was done to promote the security of economic activity. In 1836, Sir Robert Peel established the first disciplined police force. Business law was developed to provide adequately for the new economic relations (e.g., the Fourteenth Amendment to the Constitution of the United States, and the *Code de Commerce* of Napoleon I); rapid judicial machinery for business purposes was established (the commerce courts of France and Germany). Effective protection was provided for patent and trade-mark property. In all European countries, rational money systems, unitary, gold standard, with thoroughly organized subsidiary money, paper money, and banknote systems were established. The Bank of England was founded in 1694, the Bank of France in 1800, the Prussian Bank in 1846, the Reichsbank in 1875. In every country but the United States and England, a rational system of weights and measures was introduced, and definite scientific standards maintained for extension, weight, and time. The monumental act was the adoption of the metric system by the French National Convention in 1794.

In many ways the liberal state positively promoted capitalistic development, especially by undertaking the duty of instruction, both general and technical, by advertising devices like expositions, by the granting of privileges for socially (capitalistically) useful enterprises. The ideal in the matter of education—"universal, free, and obligatory"—was attained by all the leading capitalistic countries except England before 1914. In the field of technical education, Germany was in advance of the other countries: the first technical higher school was established in Brunswick in 1745. The Crystal Palace exposition in 1851 was the first of the "world's fairs" which have become so frequent since that time. In the United States, the whole transcontinental railroad development was promoted by enormous grants of land by the Federal government. States and communities bought stock and loaned money to support more local lines.

The significance of legislation may easily be exaggerated. Certainly in large part, capitalism developed outside the law in quasi-revolutionary fashion, and the conformity of the nineteenth century liberal legislation to capitalistic norms is merely a symptom of the victory which capitalism had won before it was enacted. Some of the legislation swept away obsolete vestiges that were of no great positive importance, such as the gild organization; some was necessary for any radical reform, as in the case of agricultural organization and of internal tariff systems.

International Trade Relations

In external economic relations, for a moment, capitalistic Europe seemed to adopt the liberalism which was the common character of its internal organization. In the middle of the century, it seemed that economic freedom was to be established not only within the several states, but even over the whole of the European economic system. Europe was to become an economic cosmos in which the individual was to act as freely as he was accustomed to acting within his own state. "Free Trade" was the symbol of this movement. England abandoned the protectionist system in 1840, and in the first half of the 1850's most of the countries of Europe and the United States (1846) revised their tariffs in the liberal sense, that is to say, reduced them to tariffs mainly for revenue. In 1860, the English and the French organized a policy of free trade by the Cobden Treaty, which was extended to other important parts of Europe by the French through similar treaties with Belgium, Italy, the Zollverein (German Customs Union), Austria, Switzerland, Sweden-Norway.

The free-trade movement, however, proved to be only an incident, and before long the traditional handling of commercial relations as a phase of power politics reestablished itself, as strong as it had been in the palmiest days of mercantilism. Indeed the successes of the free-trade movement were more apparent than real. In England, free trade happened to coincide with national economic interest. The immense advantage which England held as a result of her specially rapid advance in productive power during the early part of the century, put English industry beyond fear of competition and in need of external markets. Cobden, the great apostle of free trade in England, found himself completely without a following when he attempted to create a movement for the surrender of the colonies. In France, he estimated, nine out of ten Frenchmen were opposed to the liberal commercial treaty of 1860. Russia never had been drawn into the liberal movement and went her own way. At any rate, in different ways in different countries, the mid-century economic liberalism gave way to a renewed management of external economic relations in terms of power, to a new mercantilism. In contrast to the old, the new mercantilism was determined by the interests of capitalism, or rather of the several national capitalisms.

In all the countries of continental Europe and the United States, the protective tariffs were reestablished. In France, the protectionist reaction began before the fall of the Second Empire, and after a ten-year battle over the Cobden treaty, attained victory in the tariff of 1881. In the German Empire (originally and by inheritance from the Zollverein liberal), Bismarck turned at last in 1879 to protectionism. In the United States, the Civil War compelled the establishment of high tariffs by way of compensating for the very high internal revenue taxes, and since then, in spite of slight reactions in 1892 and 1913, protectionism has persisted.

The New Colonialism

The leading powers also adopted a new expansionist policy aimed especially at the extension of the national economic controls beyond their own boundaries. In part what was sought was a loose form of purely financial control, as in the case of the South American countries (to be discussed in connection with the export of capital). Another characteristic form was the establishment of limited political control (protectorate, advice, etc.) as in Egypt, Persia, and China. In addition, there was a remarkable extension of the more direct colonial enterprise in which the "sovereignty" of the colonizing power is extended over a foreign area. The following table indicates the importance of this movement in the last quarter of the century:

Region	Percentage Controlled by European Powers and the U.S.		
	1876	*1900*	*Increase*
Africa	10.8%	90.4	79.6
Polynesia	56.8	98.9	42.1
Asia	51.5	56.5	5.0
America	27.5	27.2	—.3
Australia	100.	100.	

The percentage of the world area controlled by the European powers and the United States rose from 28.4 in 1862 to 62.3 in 1912. As a standard of comparison, the economic unity embodied in the Roman Empire under Augustus extended over 1,200,000 square miles. In 1912, the European capitalistic powers politically controlled in various ways 32,360,000 square miles.

Along with this extension of political control went an increase in military expenditure, which only in part followed the lines of capitalistic development (cf. German efforts to control African territories with German capitalistic interests in South America).

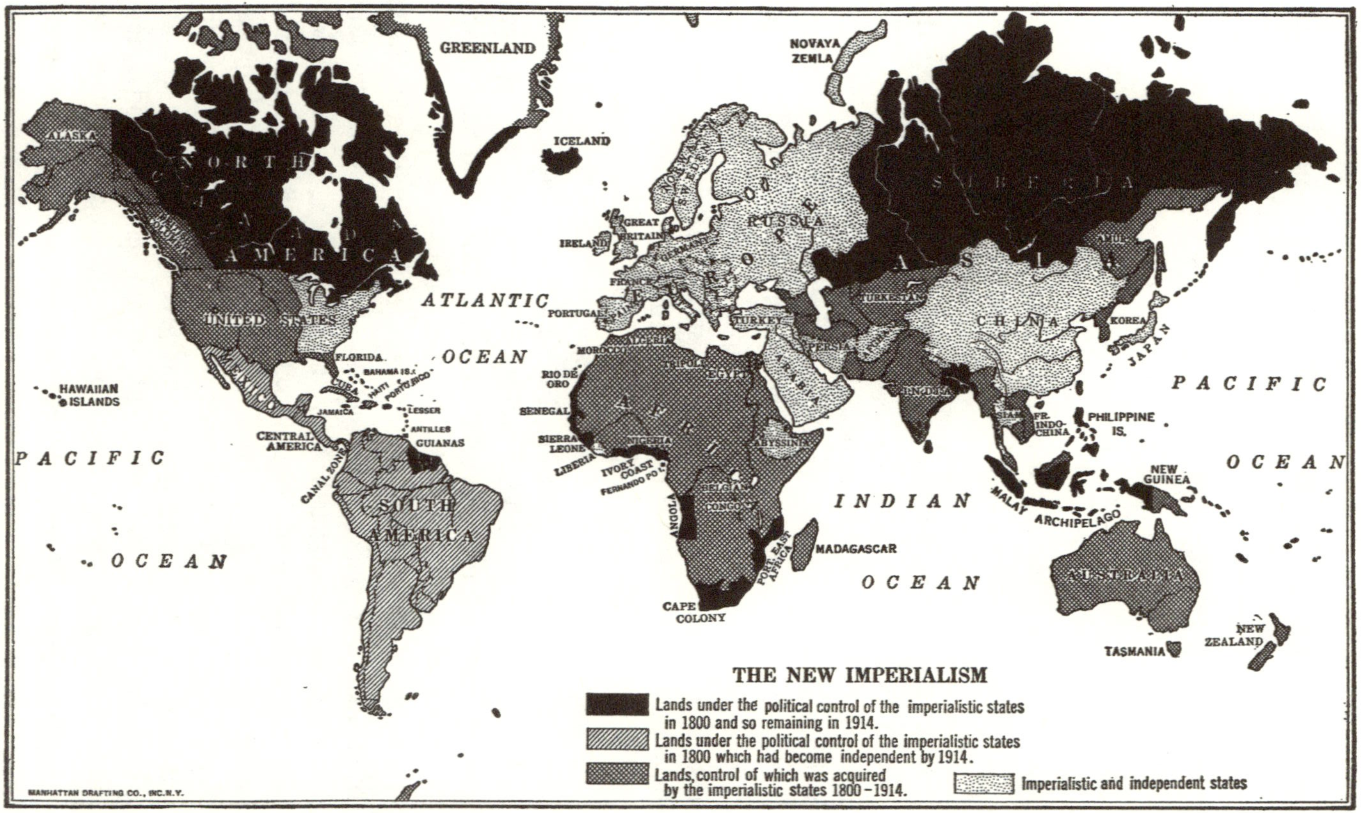

THE NEW IMPERIALISM
Lands under the political control of the imperialistic states in 1800 and so remaining in 1914.
Lands under the political control of the imperialistic states in 1800 which had become independent by 1914.
Lands, control of which was acquired by the imperialistic states 1800-1914.
Imperialistic and independent states
GREENLAND
ICELAND
NOVAYA ZEMLA
ALASKA
NORTH AMERICA
UNITED STATES
FLORIDA
BAHAMA IS.
CUBA
HAITI
PORTO RICO
JAMAICA
LESSER ANTILLES
GUIANAS
CENTRAL AMERICA
CANAL ZONE
SOUTH AMERICA
HAWAIIAN ISLANDS
PACIFIC OCEAN
ATLANTIC OCEAN
IRELAND
GREAT BRITAIN
FRANCE
PORTUGAL
EUROPE
RUSSIA
TURKEY
MOROCCO
RIO DE ORO
SENEGAL
SIERRA LEONE
LIBERIA
IVORY COAST
FERNANDO PO
TRIPOLI
EGYPT
NIGERIA
ABYSSINIA
BELGIAN CONGO
ANGOLA
PORT. EAST AFRICA
MADAGASCAR
CAPE COLONY
ARABIA
PERSIA
TURKESTAN
SIBERIA
ASIA
CHINA
KOREA
JAPAN
INDIA
SIAM
FR. INDO-CHINA
PHILIPPINE IS.
MALAY ARCHIPELAGO
NEW GUINEA
AUSTRALIA
TASMANIA
NEW ZEALAND
INDIAN OCEAN
PACIFIC OCEAN
MANHATTAN DRAFTING CO., INC. N.Y.

The expenditures of the three leading European States for army and navy grew as follows (in millions of dollars):

Great Britain, 1875, 133.2; 1907–1908, 291.8; 1913–1914, 385.0.
France, 1873, 137.4; 1908, 243.7; 1913–1914, 277.2.
Germany, 1881–1882, 106.5; 1908, 290.5; 1913–1914, 352.7.

The expenditure per capita rose in Great Britain from $4.00 to about $8.50; in France, from $3.80 to $7.10; in Germany, from $2.36 to $5.87.

It is then not without reason that the period preceding the World War is commonly called the Age of Imperialism. The relation of capitalism to imperialism is not easy to define. The Bolshevists and Marxists (not Marx) generally have a definite dogma: Imperialism is the dominance of financial capitalism. This is untenable. Neither Russia nor Japan before the war had an expressly organized financial capitalism: in England, it did not have the importance that it did in Germany or the United States, and it was not the financiers but the exporting industries whose interests were served by English expansion; Switzerland had a most highly organized financial capitalism without, apparently, any imperialistic urge. The motivation of imperialism has many aspects—political, military, religious, sentimental, and finally (and by no means in smallest degree) capitalistic.

It is the significance of imperialism for the final development of capitalism to which the attention of the student of economic history should be directed. As we have already seen, the development of capitalism was closely connected with the development of strong absolute states, both as cause and as effect. Imperialism is in a way an incidental symptom of the power which modern economic organization has given to the state. The expansionist impulse did not result in any particular advantage under nineteenth century conditions for the imperial power considered simply as an economic entity. All over the British Empire, for example, foreign trade relations with other powers grew more rapidly than with England; between 1899 and 1913, the imports of the several parts of the Empire from England rose 73 per cent, from other countries, 140 per cent; exports to England rose 122 per cent, to other countries, 170 per cent. The figures for the French colonies show a more favorable position for France.

It is also to be noted in the case of the English figures, that the earlier English ascendancy in industrial methods, which might be regarded as abnormal, made percentile and absolute increase normal for her competitors as they also learned to use the same or equivalent tools and organization. The figures would be more nearly valid if it could be known what the growth of English trade would have been in the same areas without political control. The fact remains, however, that the market opportunities created by imperialistic expansion do not compare in significance with the market opportunities in nondependent areas or even in areas dependent upon other imperialisms.

It is rather in a special kind of export, capital export, that we find a feature of colonial control of the highest significance for high capitalism; political control undoubtedly facilitated the export of capital from the controlling country to the country controlled. The export of capital will be more fully discussed in Chapter VI.

Finally, the advancing militarization common among all the world powers, incidental to their imperialism, has involved a great demand for war materials and thereby has strongly reinforced the development of the "heavy industries," and their fully capitalistic organization as trusts and cartels.

The nineteenth century states were subservient to the needs of capitalism, but they did not in the long run prove adequate. Economic life showed a marked tendency to coincide with the general limits of the culture, rather than to limit itself within the bounds of the several national states into which the culture was divided. Governmental instrumentalities and political organization of a wider range were required. Thus in the several decades before 1914, international and even supernational institutions came to be established in considerable numbers. We are not here concerned with the religious and humanitarian international movements against war, but with organizations specifically created in response to the demands of modern business. Commercial treaties, for example, have increased enormously in number and in range, and have displaced the purely political combinations and settlements as the main body of international agreements. Up to 1786, it was quite normal that the two nations economically most advanced in Europe, France and England, should have no commercial treaty between them. By 1914, it was only under exceptional circumstances that such powers did not have at least one commercial treaty with each other nation, not to speak of the numerous treaties with lesser powers, such as chiefs of tribes.

Even more significant of this international or supernational character of capitalistic economic life are the general treaties which included all states, or at least all concerned and took an almost constitutional character in that they frequently established quasi-governmental organs, international bureaus, for their administration. Such were the international river commissions which controlled the Danube and the Rhine, the Latin Monetary Union, the International Postal Union, and the International Bureau of Weights and Measures. The number of such organizations in operation at different periods shows a rapid increase:

Before 1857	7	Before 1890	31
1870	17	1900	61
1880	20	1910	108

The thoughtful student will recognize that this development, itself a product of the otherwise state-bound capitalism, is an important qualification of the fundamental principle of the modern state—its "sovereignty" and self-sufficiency.

REFERENCES FOR FURTHER READING

General

Sombart, W. Der moderne Kapitalismus, vol. III, pp. 42–73.

Knight, Barnes, and Flügel. The Economic History of Europe in Modern Times (1928).

Ogg and Sharp. The Economic Development of Modern Europe (1926).

The Modern State

Laski, Harold. Authority in the Modern State (1919).

Meinecke, Fr. Die Idee der Staatsräson in der neueren Geschichte (1924).

Tonnies, F. Gemeinschaft und Gesellschaft (1887).

Weber, Alfred. Die Krise des modernen Staatsgedanken in Europa (1925).

Domestic Policy

Cunningham, W. The Growth of English Industry and Commerce in Modern Times (1903).

Fisher, Irving. The Purchasing Power of Money (1913).

Leist, A. Privatrecht und Kapitalismus im XIX Jahrhundert (1911).

Levasseur, E. Histoire des classes ouvrières et de l'industrie en France de 1789 à 1870 (2nd ed., 1903).

Myers, G. History of the Great American Fortunes (3 vols., 1911).

Rogers, Thorold. The Industrial and Commercial History of England (2 vols., 1895).

De Ruggiero, Guido. Storia del liberalismo Europeo (1925).

Sée, Henri. Esquisse d'une histoire du régime agraire en Europe aux XVIIIe et XIXe siècles (1921).

Sombart, W. Deutsche Volkswirtschaft im XIX Jahrhundert (6th ed., 1925).

Sugar, Otto. Die Industrialisierung Ungarns unter Beihilfe des Staats und der Kommune (1908).

Haney, L. T. A Congressional History of Railroads in the United States, 1850 to 1887 (1910).

External Economic Policy

Ashley, P. Modern Tariff History (2nd ed., 1910).

Bastable, C. F. The Commerce of Nations (9th ed. rev. by T. E. Gregory, 1923).

Bonn, M. J. Der moderne Imperialismus (1913).
Bowman, I. The New World (1922). Several later editions.
Cunningham, W. Rise and Decline of the Free Trade Movement (1904).
Dilke, C. Problems of Greater Britain (1890).
Fried, A. H. Das internationale Leben der Gegenwart (1908).
Fullerton, W. M. Problems of Power (1913).
Hobson, J. A. Imperialism: A Study (1902).
Hughan, Jessie W. A Study of International Government (1925).
Lenz, Friedrich. Macht und Wirtschaft (1916).
Madelin, L. L'Expansion française (1918).
Meredith, H. O. Protection in France (1904).
Nearing, S., and Freeman, J. Dollar Diplomacy: A Study in American Imperialism (1925).
Reinsch, Paul S. Public International Unions (1916).
Seeley, J. R. The Expansion of England (1883).
Taussig, F. W. The Tariff History of the United States (7th ed., 1923; 8th ed., 1931).
Veblen, Thorstein. Imperial Germany and the Industrial Revolution (1915).
Wallace, W. K. Greater Italy (1917).
Weber, Max. Der Nationalstaat und die Volkswirtschaftspolitik (1895).
Zimmermann, A. Die Handelspolitik des Deutschen Reichs vom Frankfurter Frieden bis zur Gegenwart (1899).

CHAPTER III

MODERN TECHNIQUE AND ITS APPLICATION TO INDUSTRY AND COMMERCE

Nineteenth Century Invention

Modern industrial technique in contrast to sixteenth and seventeenth century technique became scientific. Theory and practice are no longer two separate worlds: the radio is an example of the way in which the most abstruse scientific principles are worked out into a product of common use. The basic developments of industry are therefore closely connected with the great scientific discoveries. Modern mechanics rests upon the foundations laid by Galileo and Newton, the development of analytic mechanics by Euler, Maclaurin, and Lagrange, and the founding of the study of dynamics by Poinsot and R. Mayer. Modern chemical industry is the creation of men like Lavoisier and Priestley, the founders of modern chemistry, Wöhler and Von Liebig, who laid the foundations of organic chemistry, and Kekule and Van't Hoff, who opened the great field of stereochemistry. Electrical industry is the application of the results of Faraday and Ampère, of Gauss and Weber (conduction), of Maxwell and Hertz (wave theory).

The processes of industry have become like the scientific processes upon which they depend. The empirical standards of the early handicraft processes have been displaced by scientific standards. When blast furnaces were introduced, they were supposed to be a failure, because they turned out cast iron. The reason was very simple by modern standards: the new process left behind more than two per cent of carbon in the iron; the old process left less than two per cent. Men had empirically hit upon a workable contrivance without knowing what the condition of workability (the control of the amount of carbon) was. The transmission of technical knowledge has become impersonal. While the master is still useful for psychological reasons to the budding engineer or chemist, everything about industrial processes is put down in mathematical or chemical terms, so that it could be reconstituted if all the "masters" died tomorrow. The tendency has been to use the scientifically developed machine in the place of all human effort. Thus, automatic power devices have largely replaced human muscle power in lifting and transporting materials. Thus, physical controls, such as thermostats and automatic measuring, weighing, and timing devices, have replaced human watchfulness.

What is the explanation of the extraordinary outburst of technical invention in our time? Really it is possible only to go back one step or so, and the problem of essential cause remains insoluble. Some conditions were obviously favorable. The advance and organization of scientific knowledge is certainly one of those conditions. The favorable reception of new mechanical ideas is not only effect but cause: Pascal in the early eighteenth century noted that the inventor was regarded with a certain hostility by those who did not invent. Every new invention creates a demand for others. After the invention of the "flying shuttle" (1738), the English Royal Society offered a prize for the invention of a machine that would spin several threads at the same time. The new standards of economic activity, especially the normalization of competition, which were a phase of developing capitalism, assured a welcome to new devices of production.

Many of the great inventors were men who had no professional training in the industries in which their inventions were made. Edmund Cartwright, who invented the power loom, was a clergyman; Eli Whitney, inventor of the cotton gin, was a school teacher. Ernest Solvay was "neither engineer nor chemist," and

Bessemer, who made modern steel development possible, was a manufacturer of bronze gilding-powder. Some were workmen: James Hargreaves, the inventor of the spinning jenny, was a weaver, as was also Samuel Crompton, the inventor of the "mule."

Most inventions, however, have resulted from the systematic efforts of trained men, either scientific researchers, such as Baeyer, the inventor of the artificial indigo, and Lewis the inventor of lewisite, or active engineers and industrialists, such as Werner Siemens. Inventing has finally been organized in great research establishments which are a part of all great industries and even of great single firms. Mr. Edison, perhaps, was the outstanding example of a man who made an industry of invention itself.

The general trend of technical development has been toward the economic emancipation of men from the limits of organic nature. Above all, wood has been displaced by various kinds of iron and other minerals for all major forms of building, heating, and machinery. Animal and vegetable oils have been displaced by petroleum products for lighting and lubrication. Vegetable and animal dyes have been replaced by coal-tar products. Organic potash and ammonia have been replaced by synthetic products.

Generally speaking, the whole enormous expansion of modern economic life is due to this substitution of the more rapidly available mineral materials for the slowly growing animal and vegetable material. The central fact, which brought capitalistic society past the crisis of the late eighteenth century, was the substitution of coal for wood.

Processes of production were, of course, profoundly modified by the new technique. Only the organic processes such as growth and fermentation remained substantially unaltered. Chemical processes became more purely chemical by eliminating mechanical elements, as, for example, when the press process was displaced by the diffusion process in the beet sugar industry (1865). They also became more independent of organic materials and instruments by the elimination of wood and charcoal for heating, by the elimination of men by mechanical controls (thermostatic, etc.), and by the direct utilization of the air (nitrogen production).

The changes brought about by machines were of the same general sort. A machine is a series of movable elements connected in such a way that simple power of any kind applied at one particular element of the series moves another element or elements of the series through a uniformly repeated line or pattern, and by the contact of this element or elements with other material (or materials) modifies it (or them) or combines them in conformity to a preestablished pattern. The whole of a machine falls into three parts: the motor (power machine), the transmission, and the working (producing) element or elements. A machine is complete only when all three factors are completely automatic, a condition that is only approached, since back of most automatic machines is some miner digging coal. Machines driven by water power (mills, electrical generators), approach more closely the fully automatic standard.

New motors or power machines permitted the utilization of a new series of powers. Up to the development of the steam engine, men, animals, wind, and falling water were available as industrial power.[1] Modern technique has utilized three new forms: steam, electricity, and internal combustion.

The steam engine was developed during the eighteenth century. Denis Papin, a professor at the University of Marburg, was the first man in modern times to use steam to drive a piston (about 1681), but his boiler was only a kitchen pot. The rapid condensation of steam in a cylinder by a jet of cold water was utilized by Thomas Savery (1698) and Newcomen (1705) to produce a vacuum, working against which atmospheric pressure gave enough power to operate a mine pump. In 1763, James Watt, a Scotch instrument maker, began working on an improvement of the Newcomen engine which proved to be revolutionary: abandoning

[1] See part II, chap. II.

SURVEY OF CURRENT BUSINESS

PUBLISHED BY

UNITED STATES DEPARTMENT OF COMMERCE

Subscription price of the SURVEY OF CURRENT BUSINESS is $1.50 a year; single copies (monthly), 10 cents, semiannual issues, 25 cents. Foreign subscriptions, $2.25; single copies (monthly issues), including postage, 14 cents; semiannual issues, 36 cents. Subscription price of COMMERCE REPORTS is $4 a year; with the SURVEY, $5.50 a year. Make remittances only to Superintendent of Documents, Washington, D. C., by postal money order, express order, or New York draft. Currency at sender's risk. Postage stamps or foreign money not accepted

No. 91 WASHINGTON March, 1929

CONTENTS

PRELIMINARY SUMMARY FOR FEBRUARY

The volume of money turnover during the early weeks of February, as indicated by check payments, was greater than in the corresponding period of the previous year. Industrial activity, as reflected by steel-plant operations, was greater than in either the previous month or January, 1928. Activity in automobile factories, as indicated by Detroit employment, showed expansion over both the preceding month and the same month of last year. The volume of new building contracts awarded during February was lower than in either the preceding month or February, 1928. Bituminous coal output was higher in February than in either the previous month or the same month of last year. The production of lumber showed declines from both periods.

Loans and discounts of Federal reserve member banks at the end of February were somewhat higher than at the end of the preceding month, showing a gain also over a year ago. Interest rates on call money showed practically no change from the previous month, but were higher than a year ago. Time-money rates averaged lower than in January, but were higher than in February, 1928. Stock prices reached a new high point during the month and on the whole averaged higher than in the previous month or February of last year. Prices for bonds averaged lower than in either prior period, reflecting higher interest rates. Brokers' loans reached a new high point during February but declined toward the close of the month. On the whole, brokers' loans were higher, however, than in the preceding month or February of last year. The Federal reserve ratio at the end of the month was higher than at the end of the preceding month but showed a decline from a year ago.

The primary distribution of goods, as indicated by carloadings, was greater than in either the previous month or the corresponding period a year ago. The general index of wholesale prices showed practically no change from the previous month but was higher than a year ago. Prices for wheat averaged higher than in January but were lower than a year ago. Prices for cotton and iron and steel showed practically no change from the level which prevailed in January but reflected gains over a year ago.

A MODERN GOVERNMENT SERVES BUSINESS

Table of Contents of *United States Commerce Reports,* March, 1929

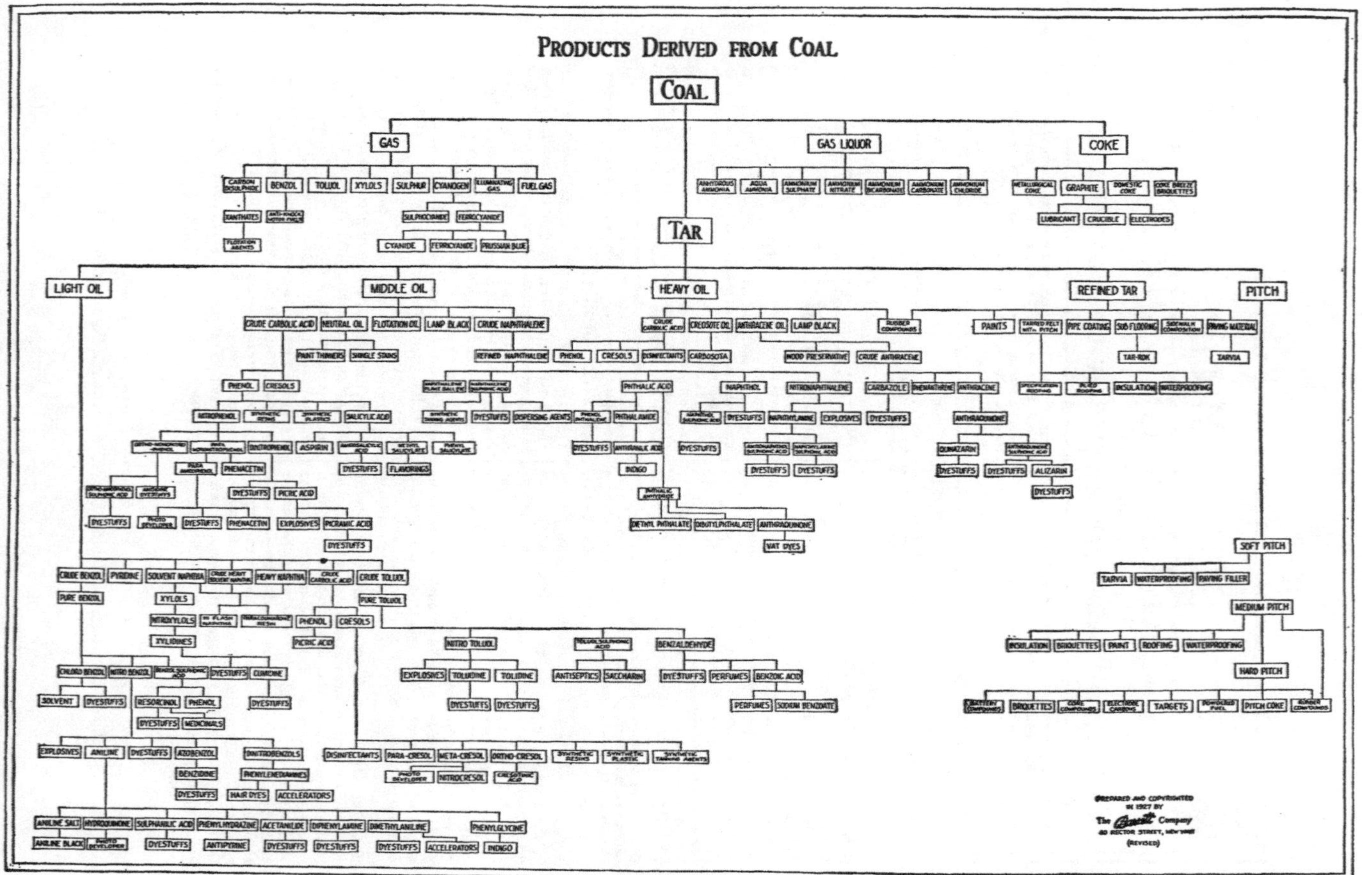

Chart of Industrial Products Derived from Coal by Chemical Processes

the vacuum device, he closed both ends of the cylinder and provided for the propulsion of the piston in both directions alternately. Later improvements by Watt, the crank, the flywheel, coordinated valves and the steam governor, made the steam engine what it was to remain, except for refinement of details, for another century, until the steam turbine was developed.

The application of this newly devised power machine to industry is a long story, and only its high points can be indicated here. It was less rapid than one would expect. Only after 1815 did steam power became predominant in machine industries. Watt made his improvement in connection with a mine pumping machine, and after 1790 it rather rapidly displaced the Newcomen engine in English mines. In the iron industry, it soon followed with the introduction of the cylinder blower for use in coke smelting (1760), and was used by Smeaton after 1790. In 1785, steam was first used for power in a cotton mill. In 1856, it was an essential feature of Bessemer's new steel-making process. Through the labors of John Fitch and especially of Robert Fulton, it was successfully applied to transportation on interior waterways (1807) and later on the ocean (*Sirius* and *Great Western,* 1838). Steam transportation on land was first achieved in an economically useful way in 1825 with George Stephenson's *Rocket,* which operated between Stockton and Darlington at the then unheard-of speed of twenty-nine miles per hour.

The utilization of electric power came much later, and the internal combustion engine, in spite of men's comparative familiarity with explosive forces, such as gunpowder, still later. The first practically useful dynamo was invented in 1866 by Werner Siemens. In 1881, long-distance transmission was achieved between Lauffen on the Bodensee and Frankfurt-am-Main. Electric railway transportation began with the experiments of Werner Siemens in Berlin (1879). A very important application of electricity was in the field of the transmission of news—the telegraph (Gauss and Weber, 1833, and Morse, 1844); the telephone (Bell,

Reis, and Edison, 1866, 1876). The use of electricity had a great influence on the development of metallurgy and chemistry: aluminium was made practicable by the discovery of the electrolytic process by Charles M. Hall in 1886; the Haber process made possible the fixation of the nitrogen in the air by electrolysis. An incidental result of electrolytic process has been to reinforce the world's gold supply from the tailings (waste) of the earlier methods.

The internal combustion engine (Otto and Langen, 1860–1870) achieved its greatest significance in the field of land and air transportation, beginning with the automobiles of Daimler and Benz (1886), the Zeppelin (1900), and the airplane (Wright brothers, 1903). The Diesel motor, using heavier oils, was invented by a German scientist about 1900 and has become of great significance especially for "tramp" ships, that is, ships that have not regular routes and schedules. The gas engine is technically important because it affords a supply of power greater in proportion to its weight than any other form of power machine.

The development of the producing machine—more exactly, the machine producing goods consisting of materials (animal, vegetable, or mineral)—is a large subject, and space is available only for a summary indication of typical lines of development. In the first place, the machine principle took over one part of a producing process after another. The best example is the much used illustration of the development of spinning machinery. The twirling of the spindle, a simple tool, was mechanized by the spinning wheel; the pulling out of the wool, by the roller machines of Paul (1740) and of Arkwright (1769); the foot propulsion of a single wheel, by the jenny of Hargreaves (1767); then the roller and the spindle were combined in Crompton's mule (1779). Another general feature was the gradual extension of the machine principle over the whole production process, as in the shoe industry, and over whole branches of production, e.g., the cotton industry, where the use of improved looms (Kay's flying shuttle, 1745) led to improved spinning devices, and in consequence to mechanical ginning of cotton (Whitney's cotton gin, 1793). It is this insistent extension of the machine principle rather than the mere use of machines in particular cases that is characteristic of the modern economic process.

The machines themselves have undergone a characteristic series of changes in the direction of completeness. They have been made more efficient: a smaller or simpler machine does the same work in less time or with less power. The machines have been specialized: a typical shoe factory has thirty-four distinct types of machines; even so simple a product as a match goes to sixteen machines. Some processes like nail making, which were highly divided, have been reduced to the work of one complex machine, but the general tendency is unmistakably toward specialization. Finally, rotary motion has been widely substituted for back-and-forth motion, with significant results in power economy and continuity of process. The reciprocating engine is being displaced by the turbine. The power lathe, the cylinder press, the rolling of metals (instead of hammering), are a few of innumerable possible examples.

The Economic Significance of Modern Technique

What is the economic significance of technique? Industrial technique is not itself economics, and it has been the aim of this brief book to tell the story of modern economic institutions in economic terms, not political, industrial, or technical terms. From the economic point of view, the essence of technique is the power of production. Power is knowledge, to reverse the proverb. It has already been noted that technical (and scientific) knowledge has been assured a high degree of permanence as a possession of society by its statement and registration in objective form (books, mathematical formulas) and its consequent spread among numerous individuals. It is only a part of this diffusion that technical knowledge of machine processes has been greatly extended, as is indicated by the rapid increase of invention in the last three centuries, greatest of all in the present. The number of patents granted by the United States Patent Office in the decade 1911–1920 was 383,885!

The power of technically developed modern society is illustrated by the comparatively high control it exercises over health. We have already seen that modern economic society could not have developed without an increase in population impossible under the limiting hygienic conditions of 1800. Antisepsis, the reduction of child mortality, the control (even extermination) of contagious disease, objective diagnosis (blood count), objective treatment (inoculating serums), and preventive sanitation, have meant a great increase in the population of all European countries. How intimately bound up this development is with the development of technique is obvious: microscopic and chemical technique is essential in much modern diagnosis; high production technique alone could produce antitoxins, disinfecting materials, etc., for modern purposes; transport and news technique alone made possible the control of epidemics.

Modern technique has enormously increased productivity of the individual. His senses have been supplemented by scales that register to one four-millionth of a milligram, by thermometers that register one-millionth of a degree centigrade, by telephones and radio, by telescopes and microscopes, by loud speakers, and by searchlights, by electric coherers, by X-rays. (Smell and taste remain unaided.) His muscular effort has been supplemented by great concentrations of power, as much as 60,000 horse power in single units of steam power. His production has been speeded up. Steel which it took three weeks to produce in the eighteenth century, a Bessemer converter turns out in twenty minutes. In 1800, he might travel 35 miles in a coach in twelve hours, in 1900, 500 miles by railroad, in 1928, 1,000 miles by airplane.

Of the greatest economic significance has been the increase in precision. Smeaton himself, an inventor, supposed that Watt's steam engine would not be practicable because of the "difficulty of getting its parts manufactured with precision." Emil Rathenau, the German electrical magnate, said of his earlier days: "Precision to one-tenth millimeter was regarded as a fantastic notion, to one one-hundredth millimeter, as a lunacy."

Production became independent of place and season. Steam power, oil fuel, mechanical transportation make it possible to set up a factory without regard to wind or water, to send a ship to Japan and back without refueling, to work ore from northern Minnesota in Pittsburgh and rubber from the East Indies in Akron.

All this has meant an increase in the supply of goods and of power available to society. The development of processes has meant economy of materials and power. Natural forces (water, wind) have been exploited more successfully by means of modern technical devices than they ever were when they alone were available. The soil has been made to produce more generously by drainage, irrigation, artificial fertilizers, new implements. Salts, ores, oils, chalks, coal, have replaced dozens of materials that had to be slowly produced by growth. Humanity, says Professor Sombart, is in the position of a man who has been living on a hard-earned income, and suddenly finds himself heir to a great fortune, the capital of which seems inexhaustible during his lifetime. The substitution of coal for wood, with its incidental consequences, has freed mankind from the limitations of the annual income provided by the sun and given him access to the apparently inexhaustible resources of the bowels of the earth for his enjoyment.

Expansion of technical productive power has become a necessity of modern capitalism—as indeed expansion is a "necessary" feature of every "high" culture: when it ceases to expand, it ages and dies. Technique has made possible expansion on limited territory. For example, it is estimated that motors supplying 200 million horse power were used in industry, transportation, etc., before the war. If we depended upon living horses for this power, this would mean 600 million horses, almost seven times as many as there were in the world. It would mean seven times as much land devoted to forage crops as now and correspondingly less for human food supply and other purposes. The example is artificial, but it indicates well enough how modern technique makes possible expansion that is out of question without it.

This impulse toward expansion manifests itself in the organization of constantly larger production units and the increasing share of production instruments in the total production, both of which will be discussed elsewhere. We can only note the relative increase in the amount of machine capital per worker in a typical German textile factory:

1868	1,308 marks	1889–1899	3,948 marks
1879–1889	2,672	1899–1909	5,541

The transference of the center of gravity of economic life from agricultural and forest products to the mechanical-inorganic products is reflected in the shifting of population elements, generally from country to city, and more specifically, from agriculture to mechanical industry.

REFERENCES FOR FURTHER READING

General

Sombart, W. Der moderne Kapitalismus, vol. III, pp. 74–124.

Byrn, E. W. The Progress of Invention in the Nineteenth Century (1900).

Chase, Stuart. Men and Machines (1929).

Du Bois-Reymond, A. Erfindung und Erfinder (1907).

Hammond, J. L., and Barbara. The Rise of Modern Industry (3rd ed., 1927).

Pacoret, Etienne. La Machinisme universelle ancienne, moderne et contemporaine (1925).

Rossman, J. The Psychology of the Inventor (1931).

Scheler, Max. Die Wissensformen und die Gesellschaft (1926).

Spengler, Oswald. Man and Technics (1932).
Taussig, F. W. Inventors and Money-Makers (1925).
Ure, Andrew. The Philosophy of Manufactures (1835).
Usher, A. P. A History of Mechanical Inventions (1929).
Veblen, Thorstein. The Instinct of Workmanship (1914).

Particular Lines of Invention and Technical Development

Binz, A. Ursprung und Entwicklung der chemischen Industrie (1910).
Diesel, R. Die Entstehung der Dieselmotors (1912).
Mach, Ernst. Die Mechanik in der Entwicklung (8th ed., 1921).
Muirhead, James. The Origin and Progress of the Mechanical Invention of James Watt (3 vols., 1854).
Slosson, E. Creative Chemistry (1920).
Thruston, R. H. History of the Steam Engine (1894).
Stieglitz, Julius. Chemistry in Medicine (1929).

Biographies of Inventors

Bessemer, Sir H. An Autobiography (1905).
Pinner, F. Emil Rathenau und das elektrische Zeitalter (1918).
Siemens, W. Lebenserinnerungen (12th ed., 1922).
Smiles, Samuel. Lives of the Engineers (1884).
Jeans, W. T. The Creators of the Age of Steel (1884).

CHAPTER IV

THE ORGANIZATION OF CAPITAL IN RELATION TO ENTERPRISE

Money and Credit

That an enormous amount of wealth has been invested in the various forms of capitalistic enterprise is of course a truism that hardly needs statistical support. The historical question that remains is double: where did this wealth come from, and how was it made available for enterprise?

The definition of capital, like the definition of money, is a theoretical problem in the solution of which there have been many differences among economists. Because our interest is centered on the evolution of the economic institutions of modern Europe, we may restrict ourselves to a definition that arises from our question: Capital is the sum of exchangeable values which serves as the basis for capitalistic enterprise. It may be money or credit; it may be commodities.

The gathering of potential money capital in the hands of particular individuals then is our first question. First of all, of course, it is the result of saving, of not spending money for consumption goods. Some saving is capitalistically important, some is not. Saving during the year to spend during vacation is not, directly, of importance in the formation of capital—unless the saver changes his mind and decides to invest his savings in some enterprise. If he deposits the money in a bank, it becomes available under modern credit arrangements for enterprise. It is necessary, however, to divest ourselves of the notion that the sparing use of wages or salary and the resulting savings were important for the development of enterprise before our own time. It was rather the "savings" out of large incomes alone, for a long time, that were significant. Unspent wealth was gathered in large quantities in the hands of economically energetic men. This concentration was the result, as D'Avenel shows for France, of accumulations made possible by the collection of ground rents, profits from speculation, and the excess profits of capitalistic enterprises. Of these, the second and third were far more important than the first, and the third was most important of all.

Some great American fortunes are excellent examples of the accumulation of ground rents; the Astor fortune was founded on the purchase of Manhattan real estate and its subsequent rise in value. Speculation, not itself creative of capital, made possible concentration in the hands of the successful speculators. Excess profits—that is to say, profits that exceed the ordinary, average returns of trade—are necessary to the accumulation of significant quantities of capital. Such excess profits arise from the introduction of technical improvements. For example, England's superiority in technical devices in the cotton industry was so great in 1851 that English mill owners had obtained three times as large a share of world markets as their two nearest national groups of competitors, and were receiving excess profits to correspond. Sometimes excess profits come from an exclusive control of the market, as in the case of the American trusts down to 1900. The Standard Oil Company from 1882 to 1906 averaged 24 per cent a year in dividends paid, from 1897 to 1906, 39.9 per cent. Mining also offered considerable excess profits in case of success: American copper mines ranged up to 38 per cent a year. In South Africa and Australia in 1900 there were 33 gold mines that paid more than 25 per cent a year.

Much of this potential capital was expended for consumption goods or converted into landed property or government bonds; nevertheless, in the course of the nineteenth century a constantly increasing portion of it was converted to actual capital. Between 1913 and 1921, for example, earnings of American corporations not distributed to stockholders, but converted into capital, ranged from \$624,000,000 to \$6,327,000,000.[1] Henry Ford, who is so often typical of modern capitalistic thought, declares that "above a very low percentage, the earnings of a business belong to the business rather than to the stockholders." Capital building in this way has become easier because of the great development of the stock company. The stock company has also made it easier to gather the small units of saving into significant sums by the wide distribution of stocks.

The increase of capital in the great capitalistic areas was steady through the nineteenth century. English wealth increased about 1.5 per cent a year until the middle of the century, after that at an average rate of 3.3 per cent a year. German wealth rose about 5.5 per cent a year from 1886 to 1910. The colonial character of the United States and the large immigration make comparisons difficult, but it is apparent that just before the war the rate of increase of the wealth of the United States was approaching the rate of increase in England and Germany: colonial expansiveness was ending.

An indication of the expansion of wealth which confirms the statistical conclusion comes from the application of a principle worked out by Gustav Cassel: when gold production does not affect prices, it is indicated that the supply of other goods has increased in the same proportion. Now the fact is that five times as much gold was in use as money in 1910 as in 1850, while the general price index remained stable: 76 and 76.25. Therefore, the supply of goods has about quintupled. This figure, however, is the minimum, as the effectiveness of gold has been greatly increased by the development of the credit system, which has also been the great instrumentality through which capital has been made available for enterprise.

In ordinary usage, credit is purchasing power without money. One has credit or gives credit or receives credit. For the purposes

[1] King, *The National Income and Its Purchasing Power*, pp. 278, 280, 285.

of economic theory, however, a more technical definition is necessary. In all credit, it is obvious, the delivery of values on the part of the creditor is separated from the counter-delivery of values on the part of the credit receiver. In part, the considerations that lead to the acceptance of this postponement are objective. In modern credit, however, confidence or trust, the subjective expectation that the reciprocal service or commodity, the agreed-on consideration, will be given after a specified interval, is certainly of the essence and not merely an accident of credit. Something of the relation between the subjective and objective aspects may be observed by examining the prospectus of a bond issue by a corporation or by a municipality. It will contain a great deal about the assets and actual or prospective earning power of the corporation, or about the taxable property in the municipality, but at the end there will be a statement as to the character and ability of the management or to the effect that the municipality has never defaulted in any payment—that is, an appeal to the subjective judgment of the potential buyer of the bond.

Credit may be consumption credit (with which we are not here concerned) or productive credit, used for business purposes.

The credit system of high capitalism developed three characteristic institutions: banks, negotiable paper, and money substitution. The bank, as a credit institution, supplies credit upon the basis of a collective loaning fund. The deposits of a bank consist typically of parts of incomes, of money-capital, rents, and profits, arising largely out of what we may call passive business. The banker uses them to finance the credit-seeking active enterprises—in short-time or long-time loans, for facilitating operations or for establishing equipment, in the form of acceptances or in the form of mortgages. The bank obviously serves to facilitate contact between lender and borrower, by its collection of deposits from many lenders obviating the disproportion between the large demands of the entrepreneur-borrower and the limited supply of the individual lender.

Negotiable paper in a broad sense includes all the various acknowledgments of debt that pass from hand to hand. Gold notes of governments (paper money), indorsed drafts, stocks, and bonds are the forms of negotiable paper that are most important for the development of capital. The gold notes serve as a substitute for money and supplement its effectiveness. The draft lessens the burden of settlement by obviating the use of money. Stocks and bonds are means of combining supplies of capital and enabling the credit-giver (stockholder, bondholder) to terminate his relation as creditor without waiting for any given date of payment.

By money substitution is meant the substitution of bookkeeping methods for the actual exchange of money (or goods). It is principally organized in the checking system and the clearing house. It will be remembered that its history goes back to the fairs of early modern times, at the close of which merchants buying and selling "cleared" their mutual obligations. The bank, primarily an intermediary between the credit seeker and the sources of supply, has tended to gather into itself the other two institutions. A complete modern bank (itself a stock company) accepts money on deposit, lends it out, clears checks between its own depositors and, through the clearing house, with other banks, and finances enterprises by underwriting stocks, that is, by undertaking to induce investors to participate in the ownership of the company. This last feature is hardly legitimated as a bank function in England and the United States. In the latter, it is carried on in an indirect way. The owners of the bank stock are also owners of the stock of another company, which underwrites corporate financing (National City Bank of New York, National City Company).

Historically, the development of credit economy is marked, in the first place, by a great change in the attitude of the business world. In the eighteenth century, even in the great centers of trade, the reputable business man did business with his own capital. The Scotch seem to have been the first people to turn generally to credit devices of the modern type: "The Scotch hate gold," runs an English saying. William Paterson and John Law, both Scotch, were the effective ancestors of modern banking in England and France. In 1860, Walter Bagehot, the English economist, distinguished between the "new trader" and the "old-fashioned trader, the man who trades on his own capital." In modern English business, owing to the certainty of obtaining loans on discount of bills or otherwise at a moderate rate of interest, there is a steady bounty on trading with borrowed capital. Today, the entrepreneur not only permits himself to use other people's capital, he *must*. The democratization of enterprise has meant that large numbers of men who have no considerable wealth have become entrepreneurs. On the other hand, enterprises have grown so large that even the largest stockholders hold only a small proportion of the stock. Then, too, as long as interest rates are lower than the percentage of profit on a given capital, the entrepreneur has a great inducement to extend his enterprise by borrowing. Capital organization has also become less difficult, in part as a result of the security provided by the development of adequate legal control, but especially as a result of the increase of gold production. Since credit is a function of the money supply, and money supply is a function of gold supply, it is obvious that the increasing gold supply after 1848 was of great significance for the extension of credit economy. We shall treat of the "crisis" in another connection, but in all crises the "scarcity of money," more exactly, a scarcity of credit, was the obvious feature. Finally, the internal development of the credit system led to competition between banks to furnish credit—see the advertisements in the financial section of the New York *Times,* January 1, of any recent year.

This internal development was completed somewhat as follows. The issue banks were the first to be established. The Bank of England (founded 1694) stood almost alone for another century, and through most of that period its note issue was only £2,000,000.

In the latter part of the eighteenth century, however, the number of banks in England rose to 350. The prejudice against banks left in France by the Law episode faded out sufficiently to permit the establishment of the Caisse d'Escompte and finally in 1800, the Banque de France. This note-issuing function rose in importance everywhere, except in the United States, where a rational organization was lacking after 1836. The note circulation of the Bank of England rose to some £25,000,000 by 1810, remained there until 1890 and then rose again to about £30,000,000; that of the Banque de France from 23,000,000 francs in 1800 to 504,000,000 in 1850, 4,147,000,000 in 1900, and 5,714,000,000 in 1913. The political and economic backwardness of the German states in the early part of the century is reflected in their banking history, but the Reichsbank, founded in 1876, had a circulation of 1,958,000,000 marks in 1913.

The deposit feature, which was even more significant, as we have seen, for capital formation, grew rapidly, especially in the last thirty years before the World War. Before 1900, the deposit banks had surpassed the issue banks. In England, deposits doubled between 1890 and 1912; in Germany, they were more than seven times as great in 1912 as in 1890; in France between 1872 and 1909, deposits of the three great deposit banks grew from 427,000,000 francs to 4,363,000,000; in the United States, between 1880 and 1914, from $1,315,000,000 to $13,901,000,000. Savings accounts show a similar curve except in England. Savings deposits per capita in Germany grew from 44 marks per capita in 1875 to 259 marks in 1910; in Austria, from 29 crowns in 1870 to 211 crowns in 1910; in France, from 18 francs to 98 francs in the same period. Insurance companies, which as credit institutions are essentially mortgage banks, rose to a capital of $1,300,000,000 in Germany and about $3,900,000,000 in the United States.

The emission of negotiable securities in all parts of the world in the decades before the World War is shown in the following table:

1871–1880	74.0 billion francs	1891–1900	100.4 billion francs
1881–1890	64.5	1901–1910	114.1

The total value of securities traded in on the stock exchanges in 1910 was nearly $120,000,000,000. The great significance of securities is shown by the proportion of national wealth that was thus owned before the war:

Germany	20%	England	42
United States	30	France	51

The bearer type had become predominant. The small share had contributed to the increase in the number of persons available as sources of capital supply.

Money substitution was already reflected in the development of exchange.The story of drafts of £10 with 120 indorsements circulating in Manchester, which has been noted, reflects a maximum development of the exchange draft as a substitute for money. The draft has almost disappeared as a form of payment in commerce. Its place has been taken by the "giro-banks," that is to say, the check system, which with the clearing house provides in the United States, where it has reached its highest development, an almost complete substitute for money in ordinary business relations. Clearing-house figures give a convenient index:

London	1868	£3,400,000,000	1912	£16,000,000,000
German Reichsbank	1883	43,800,000,000 marks	1913	379,000,000,000 marks
New York	1880	$37,200,000,000	1913	$ 98,100,000,000
United States	1890	$58,800,000,000	1913	$173,200,000,000

These numerous and enormous figures are by no means a complete picture of the development of money capital in the modern world. They are intended merely to convey the historical notion of a substantial change in the availability of money capital for the expansion of enterprise.

GOODS AS CAPITAL

It is obvious that the modern European world not only is better supplied with capital in the form of money, but also has larger quantities of material, raw, half finished, and fully manufactured, available for its needs and its uses, than had any earlier civilization. This change has two aspects: increasing production, and increasing availability of goods from a distance through the improvements in transportation.

The increase in production is in part an increase in the productivity of labor. Frequently too much has been ascribed to this element. It is obvious, of course, that in a modern cotton spinnery nearly three times as much yarn is now produced per worker as in 1865; but much of that is due to other forms of labor directly or indirectly applied to the production ascribed to him in this way—e.g., the labor put into making the machine which he operates or into providing electric power for it—which would have to be computed to get an accurate result. It is obvious that, if he produced only a small amount of yarn with the machine, it would be much more costly than yarn produced by spindle or spinning wheel and his economic productivity would be a minus quantity. Labor under modern conditions does not become productive until the cost of production of the machines (factory, etc.) has been financially met. It is dependent upon successful organization of conditions of supply and of market. The disappearance of hundreds of automobile companies in the United States in the last twenty years was due mostly to their failure to make the labor which they used productive. These considerations indicate how complex the problem of the productivity of labor really is. Professor Sombart estimates that the increase in productivity, generally speaking, has been from seventy-five to one hundred per cent since 1800. Certainly it has been very large, and certainly it has not been as great as the thousandfold increase claimed by Friedrich Engels. For the development of capitalism, the significance of the simple increase in the amount of goods that a worker with a machine can turn out is of secondary order—less, for example, than that of the advance in the transportability of goods or that of the increase in the economic productivity of the soil.

The economic productivity of the soil was increased in several ways. In the first place, costly food plants were displaced by cheaper ones: thus rye was displaced by potatoes and maize. Easily raised vegetable products displaced slowly growing animal products: cotton displaced wool and silk, celluloid displaced horn, ivory, tortoise shell, and coral; cellulose displaced natural silk, and so on.

The physical productivity of the soil was greatly increased, particularly in European countries. Average soil in Germany produced about 932.9 hundredweight of grain per hundred hectares in 1800, about 2,440.8 hundredweight in 1875. The increases (in values produced per hectare) since that time range from 24 per cent for beet sugar to 68.6 per cent for rye. French wheat production rose from 10.2 hectoliters per hectare in 1820 to 15.6 in 1895. The average grain production for all Western Europe rose from 11.52 hectoliters in the decade 1871–1880 to 13.47 in the half-decade 1900–1905. With the introduction of artificial manures and cultivated fodder crops, stock raising developed with similar rapidity.

Had Western Europe had to depend upon itself for food supplies, economic expansion would soon have found a limit. As it was, in the earlier part of the nineteenth century, the increasing production lagged behind the increasing demand, and prices rose sharply. Between 1725 and 1825 the price of wheat in England had nearly tripled. Economists like Ricardo supposed that this tendency meant the end of "progress": rising prices of food, higher cost of labor, lowering of profits, end of successful enterprise. Such would have been the fact if there had not been a definite building up of agricultural areas. Waste land disappeared in countries like France and Prussia. Eastern Europe, especially Russia, expanded its grain-growing areas to meet the growing demand. Rumania more than doubled its cultivated area between 1860 and 1901. The Mississippi valley, the Argentine, and the Canadian Northwest were so many major additions to

THE ORGANIZATION THROUGH WHICH AMERICAN COTTON IS MADE AVAILABLE AS GOODS CAPITAL IN EUROPE

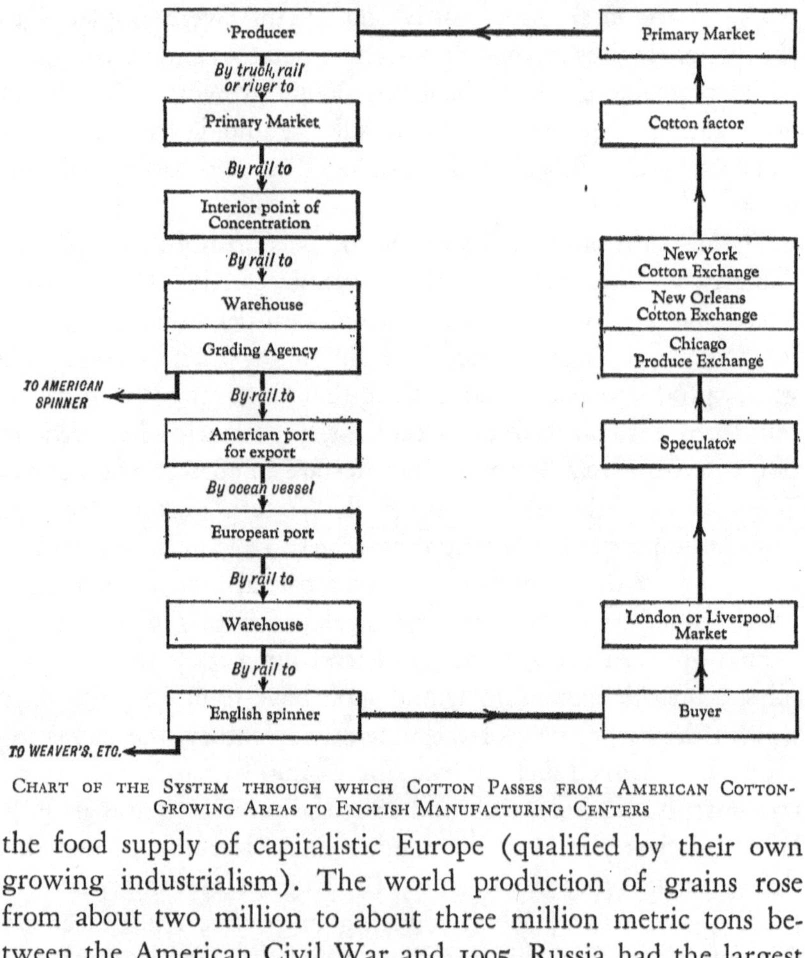

Chart of the System through which Cotton Passes from American Cotton-Growing Areas to English Manufacturing Centers

the food supply of capitalistic Europe (qualified by their own growing industrialism). The world production of grains rose from about two million to about three million metric tons between the American Civil War and 1905. Russia had the largest place as agricultural producer with 22 per cent of the wheat, 68 per cent of the rye, 40 per cent of the barley, and 23 per cent of the oats.

These new lands had the advantage of low production costs. Land was very cheap. Until recently, fertile, productive land could be bought in large areas of the United States for from $10 to $50 an acre. Even in Ohio $100 to $125 an acre was regarded as a favorable "top" price for improved farms. On the other hand, in the 1870's, bare land sold in Saxony for 2,400 to 2,800 marks a hectare, or about twice the American price. In small-farming regions like the Rhineland, the cost was from 4,000 to 8,000 marks (due in part to perennial crops like vines). This meant intensive agriculture in Europe, extensive agriculture in the colonial lands. Even in the years just before the World War the average production per hectare in the United States, Russia, and Argentina was from one-third to one-half that in Sweden, the least productive soil in Western Europe. In Europe, dear soil, cheap labor; in the colonial lands, cheap soil, dear labor!

Despite the pressing need for food, in none of the food-growing areas did the farmer prosper very greatly; he has not yet been fully adjusted to high capitalism. Prices tended on the whole to decline, especially between the American Civil War and 1900. Low prices for raw materials and foodstuffs meant cheap goods capital for European capitalism.

To a large extent, the increased production of soil materials to satisfy the growing demands of capitalistic society has meant the destruction of natural resources. Farming in the United States, as long as practically free land was available, was mainly a process of exhausting the soil's natural fertility. The average production of maize per acre declined steadily from 1866 to 1893. The same story of "utterly unscientific and wasteful methods of agriculture" appears in the Canadian Northwest, in the Argentine wheat fields, in New Zealand, in Australia, and in Russia. The German consumption of artificial fertilizer before the World War was 28 times as great per given area as the Russian, 56 times as great as the Canadian, 360 times as great as the Argentine consumption.

Another aspect of this exhaustion economy is the destruction of forests. The crisis of the eighteenth century taught European countries to guard the forests. The huge forests of America, so long rather an inconvenience than a source of wealth, encouraged a reckless use and waste until the growing industrialization made the basis for a reaction. Americans still use eight times as much wood per capita per annum as Europeans. The extraction of minerals is also an exhaustion economy: in the case of most of them, world exhaustion is nowhere in sight. In the case of petroleum, the demand seems to be pressing very hard upon the visible supply. Altogether this form of exhaustion economy (mineral extraction and exploitation) absorbs a good third of the industrial workers in a modern state like Germany. All great industries rest upon these inorganic materials dug out of the earth. All transportation tends to become "metallized." Except in domestic building in some of the forest lands, stone, clay, cement, and steel have displaced wood in building.

Goods from all over the world have become available in any part of the European economic world: potential goods capital becomes actual goods capital. This result was achieved especially through the development of technique and of organization in transportation.

The particular contribution by technique has been methods of preserving perishable goods. Most notable is mechanical refrigeration, resting upon the alternate compression and release of ammonia. Refrigerating plants, ships, cars, make it perfectly practicable to transport Argentine meat to Paris or London. The steamship and the turbine, the improved roads and railways and the increase in number and capacity of transport devices have all added to the ease of transportation. When Benjamin Franklin voyaged to Europe, he took from four to six weeks; the *Savannah* (part steam, part sail) took twenty-six days; a present-day liner takes from five to ten days. Vasco da Gama took three hundred and fourteen days to reach India; a modern steamer takes eighteen days. The physical conditions of transportation have been greatly improved.

The cost of transportation has radically declined. The cost of modern railroad transport is one-thirtieth to one-fortieth of that of ox transport. From 1866 to 1905, the cost of transporting a bushel of grain from Chicago to New York declined from 23.40 cents to 5.21 cents; the cost from New York to Liverpool, from 5.92 cents to 1.38 cents. Fresh butter is transported from Australia to England for one cent a pound. Before the World War an English laborer could pay for the freight of a barrel of flour from Minneapolis with one day's wages. This decline in transport costs is reflected in a general leveling and lowering of the cost of foodstuffs: the price which the American farmer receives for his wheat is determined ultimately by the price on the Liverpool market.

Shipping tonnage in the world increased from 21,000,000 tons in 1890 to 50,000,000 tons in 1913. Much of this growth came in these first years of the twentieth century. Gigantic growth also took place in world railway mileage—in 1890, 386,178, in 1913, 690,130 miles in operation. The world's average annual investment in railroads was $207,000,000 in the years 1841–1850; $618,000,000 in 1881–1890; $796,000,000 in 1900–1913. This gigantic investment reflects the truth of the saying that "the railroads built themselves," by virtue of the stimulus which they gave to other economic enterprise.

The speeding up of transport was essential to the development of high capitalism and gave to modern commercial ways their distinguishing characteristics. Substantially, all commerce became world commerce. Localism (village economy, gild organization, etc.) is gradually disappearing. Population distributed and redistributed itself at will (witness the "ghost towns" in American mining and lumber regions). Production was centralized with reference to a dozen considerations besides distance from the market or source of supply. Modern transport alone has spared

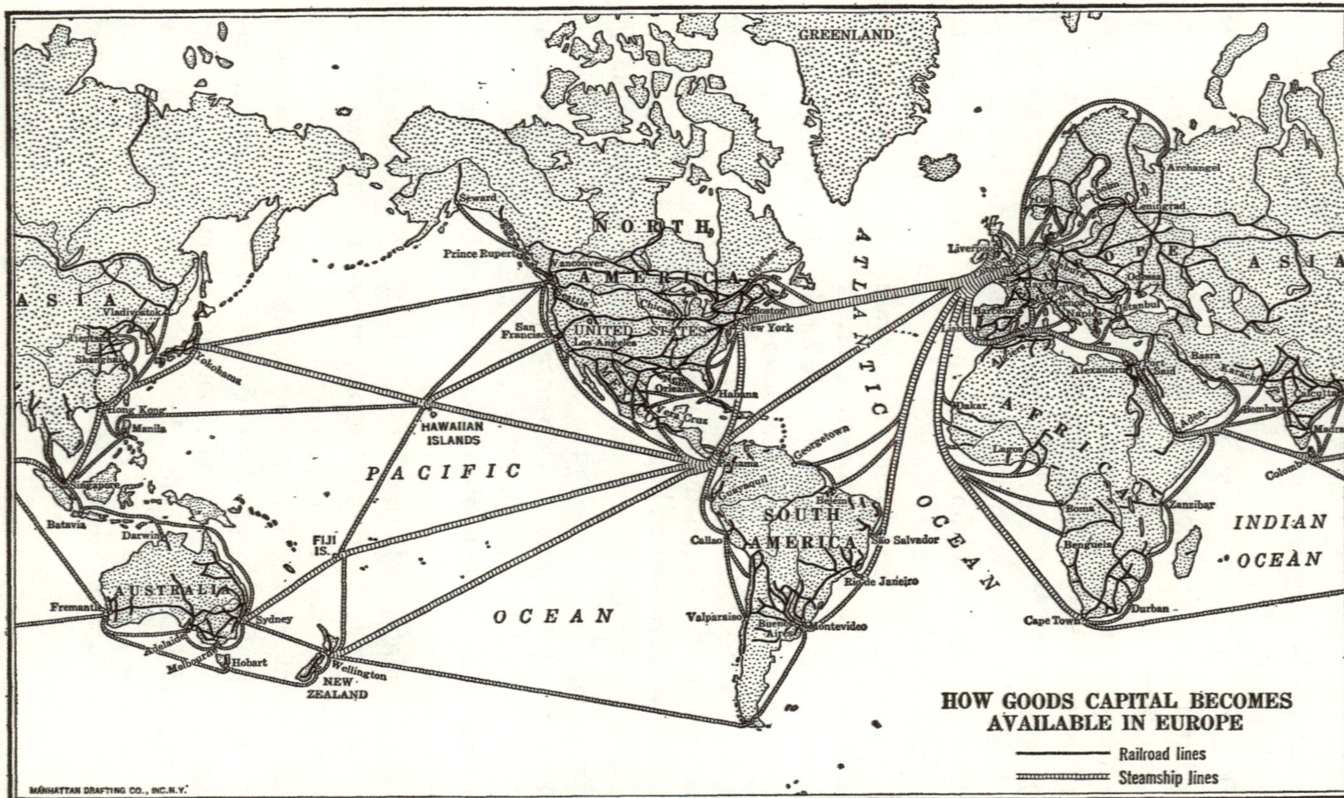

WORLD RAILROAD AND STEAMSHIP LINES

capitalism a general contact with limiting conditions by providing it with the necessary goods capital from the ends of the earth. It has made possible the division of labor into the most highly differentiated production forms: Egypt can grow cotton; it can get grain elsewhere. Cheap transportation of immigrants effectively added great colonial areas to the support of capitalism. Old culture areas like Russia, the East Indies, and the Balkan States were "unlocked" by the railroads and the steamships, and their otherwise unavailable bulk products were enabled to reach the markets of Western Europe.

REFERENCES FOR FURTHER READING

General

Sombart, W. Der moderne Kapitalismus, vol. III, pp. 127–303.

The Concept, "Capital"

Fisher, Irving. "Precedents for Defining Capital," Quarterly Journal of Economics, May, 1904.
Marx, Karl. Das Kapital (1867). Tr. as Capital: A Critical Analysis (1887).
Bober, M. M. Karl Marx's Interpretation of History (1927).
Hawley, F. B. Enterprise and the Productive Process (1907).
Passow, R. Kapitalismus (1918).
Veblen, Thorstein. The Theory of Business Enterprise (1904).

I. Money and Credit

The Growth and Concentration of Money Capital

Corti, Egon. The Rise of the House of Rothschild (1928); The Reign of the House of Rothschild (1928).
Ehrenberg, R. Grosse Vermögen: Ihre Entstehung und ihre Bedeutung (1905).
Giffen, Robert. The Growth of Capital (1890).
Helfferich, Karl. Deutschlands Volkswohlstand, 1888–1913 (1913).
Hendrick, B. J. The Age of Big Business (1920).
King, Wilford I. The Wealth and Income of the People of the United States (1923).

Money, L. C. Riches and Poverty (1910).
Myers, G. History of the Great American Fortunes (3 vols., 1911).
Robertson, J. M. The Fallacy of Saving (1892).
Taussig, F. W. Inventors and Moneymakers (1913).

Credit

Bagehot, Walter. Lombard Street (1873; new ed., 1917).
Conant, C. A. A History of Modern Banks of Issue (6th ed., 1927).
Crane, W. R. Gold and Silver (1908).
Fisher, Irving. The Purchasing Power of Money (1913).
Hilferding, R. Das Finanzkapital (1910).
Minty, L. LeM. English Banking Methods (1925).
Sumner, W. G., et al. A History of Banking in All the Leading Nations (4 vols., 1896).
Taylor, W. G. L. The Credit System (1913).

II. Goods as Capital

General

Levy, Hermann. Die Grundlagen der Weltwirtschaft (1924).
Barker, J. E. Modern Germany, Her Political and Economic Problems (5th ed., 1915).
Ogg and Sharp. The Economic Development of Modern Europe (1926).

The Increased Production of Goods

Clapham, J. H. The Economic Development of France and Germany, 1815–1914 (1921).
Knowles, L. C. The Industrial and Commercial Revolutions in Great Britain During the Nineteenth Century (2nd ed., 1922).
Marshall, Alfred. Industry and Trade (1919).
McVey, F. L. Modern Industrialism (1914).

The Increased Availability of Goods

Kirkaldy, A. W., and Evans, A. D. The History and Economics of Transport (1915).
Critchell, J. T., and Raymond, J. The History of the Frozen Meat Trade (1912).
Day, Clive. History of Commerce (rev. ed., 1922).

Howard, E. D. Cause and Extent of the Recent Industrial Progress of Germany (1907).
Levasseur, E. Histoire du commerce de la France de 1789 à nos jours (1912).
Jackman, W. T. The Development of Transportation in Modern England (2 vols., 1916).
Lotz, W. Verkehrsentwicklung in Deutschland seit 1800 (4th ed., 1920).
Pogson, G. A. Germany and Its Trade (1903).
Smith J. Russell. The World's Food Resources (1919).
Whelpley, J. D. The Trade of the World (1913).

Sources

Statistisches Jahrbuch (Germany).
Annuaire statistique (France).
Statistical Abstract (United Kingdom).
Statistical Abstract (British Empire).
Statistical Abstract (United States).
Rand, B., ed. Selections Illustrating Economic History Since the Seven Years' War (2nd ed., 1902).

CHAPTER V

POPULATION AND LABOR SUPPLY

The Sources of Labor Supply

Without labor supply, no capitalism. How difficult this problem was during the early capitalistic period has already been shown—how lacking in persistence, in discipline, in capitalistic motive, was such labor as the entrepreneurs could get, and what drastic, often inhumane measures were applied in order to secure some sort of labor force.

In 1927, a small item appeared in a distant city paper to the effect that one hundred carpenters were needed in the small college town in which this is being written. The statement was false, but for weeks thereafter carpenters appeared from all points of the compass, each seeking one of these hundred supposed "jobs." The contrast with David Dale's troubles in finding laborers when he was establishing New Lanark embraces nearly the whole of the history of labor in relation to high capitalism. It has freed itself from localism, from communal activity in village or gild, from family dependency. It has increased itself, so that there are always plenty of people to do anything that (capitalistically speaking) needs to be done. They have made themselves ready to go where the money of the entrepreneur tells them to go, they have learned to handle his machines and to punch his time clocks, they have adopted his gain motive and they battle with him and with each other for the highest possible gains in the form of wages.

A great amount of labor power was furnished to capitalism by legal slavery, especially Negro slavery, although, as we shall see, it was capitalism that destroyed slavery. The most important aspect of the use of slavery to capitalism was the cotton production of the United States. When Eli Whitney invented the cotton gin in 1793, the industry and the labor institution were insignificant in the economic sense. Within a few years (1800) the Southern States were producing thousands of bales of cotton, importing legally or (after the prohibition of importation in 1807) smuggling and breeding Negroes, and seizing new lands for exhaustion in cotton culture, until in 1860 there were in the United States about four and a half million Negroes (not all slaves) producing about four million bales of cotton. The Southern flaunt, "Cotton is King," rings strangely to our ears, who watch the monthly report of unfilled orders of the United States Steel Corporation as our economic pulse. It reflects the past glory of the textile industry as the leading industry of the world, to which American slavery gave an essential, if temporary, support.

Other slavery meant little to high capitalism: perhaps the total number of slaves in the slave colonies of the several European states, in Brazil, and at the Cape of Good Hope in 1840 nearly equaled the slave population in the United States.

Slavery was abolished in the English colonies in 1833, in the French colonies in 1848, in the United States in 1865. In other lands it remained still longer: in Cuba until 1880, in Brazil until 1888, in Egypt until 1895; and it is still a problem in the interior of Africa.

The economic significance of slavery is well stated by Wakefield (*A View of the Art of Colonization,* 1849):

> Colonial slavery in its various forms has been the principal means of raising that great produce for exportation, for which prosperous colonies are remarkable. Until lately, nearly the whole of the exported produce of the United States, consisting of sugar, rice, tobacco, and cotton, was raised by the combined and constant labor of slaves; and it could not have been raised under the circumstances by any other means. The like cases of West India and Brazil would have occurred to you without being mentioned.

Slave labor built the Suez Canal and developed the Egyptian cotton growing industry. Forced labor if not chattel slavery still seems indispensable in the tropical domains of European powers.

The legal abolition of slavery by no means ended unfree labor in European colonies. "Contract labor," a system by which natives are bound to long terms of labor by contracts that prove to be unbreakable, at least for the native, and put him in his employer's power, was much used in British dependencies—in all of them, according to Del Mar. In South Africa, the Kafirs thus employed in the diamond mines are penned up in concentration camps for the period of their contract. Up to 1906, an attempt was made to import labor from China and India into South Africa, but this was given up on account of political difficulties. The Dutch in their East Indies colonies used another system, forced production: the obligation to produce a certain amount of goods and to deliver them to the administration at a certain price was imposed on each village. The rulers of the Congo Free State applied the same system with much more brutality.

In general, however, capitalism has been unfavorable to forced labor. The importance of technique alone explains how the capitalistic labor supply has to be built upon the basis of free labor. This repugnance to unfree labor has been put into humanitarian terms and has become a real part of modern capitalistic religion. In the various states, and in international organizations like the League of Nations, this humanitarian opposition to unfree labor is constantly voicing itself and is often successful in removing legal sanctions from the practice. An interesting illustration of the psychology of the capitalistic opponent of forced labor is furnished by William Wilberforce, the English leader of the antislavery movement around 1800, who bitterly opposed any legislation aimed at controlling the conditions of English labor—so much worse, actually, than the conditions of the agricultural slavery against which he fought.

But we are primarily concerned, after all, with the ultimate labor force of capitalism: the proletariat. Of what previously existing elements of the population was it composed, and how were these elements changed into a proletariat?

The breakdown of the old economic forms, the village community and the gild, the estate (as a working community) and the home (as a producing entity) detached a large part of the population, rendered it transferable, available for the entrepreneur.

In this situation, agrarian reform, which in the several countries of Europe meant the substitution of clear-cut individual ownership for the village community, terminated the miscellaneous rights of the individual member of the community, the woods and the waste, the common where he pastured his cow or his pig, and reduced him to the ownership—complete, it is true—of a very incomplete agricultural unit, or even deprived him of all property in land.

The general result was that the "depressed husbandmen" constituted a considerable reservoir of labor available and responsive to the call of the entrepreneur. In England, industrial wages offered an attractive escape. Dr. Price in his famous *Essay on the Population of England* declared that the increase in the population of the industrial centers was "derived from the population of country parishes and villages." A Bolton cotton spinner who testified before the Factories Inquiry Commission in 1834, declared that he recollected craftsmen of several sorts leaving their occupation to spin in the factories, "but a great many more husbandmen left their employ to spin." The progress of enclosures, of large-scale farming and commercialized marketing disrupted the old customs of granting food, drink, and minor articles and of selling wheat and other commodities directly to the laborer, and made him increasingly dependent upon his money wage. This was low (eightpence to tenpence a day) and was kept from rising by social considerations like those of Arthur Young, who believed that workers were generally receiving an income larger than was necessary to support themselves with frugality appropriate to their station in life, and that their wages should be kept as low as possible. His model budget was made on the basis "that wheaten bread, beef, mutton, tea, sugar, and butter, were not to be confused with the necessaries of life." The agricultural laborer's hovel was commonly a damp unsanitary hole, with one room, and an iron pot for the principal furniture. Even at this low level of subsistence he ordinarily had to turn to the rates for aid under the antiquated system of the Elizabethan poor law. "The poor rate is now [1787] in part a substitute for wages." It is obvious that the English farm worker had lost whatever independence and competence of income he had earlier had.

The employers of farm labor made frequent and long continued complaints that wages were rising and that their laborers were being enticed from the farms. Wedgwood boasted that the potteries and other manufactures had transformed a crude, poverty-stricken and isolated region into a populous and prosperous district, with "the workmen earning near double their former wages —their houses mostly new and comfortable."

The general transformation of property in land in France during the Revolution made less change in the personnel of this landowning class than has been supposed and almost no considerable change in the concentration of property in single hands. An estimate published in 1834 gave 21,456 families holding an average of 880 hectares, or a total of about 19,000,000 out of a total computed area of 44,750,000 hectares. Nevertheless, the agricultural population clung more closely to the land in France than in any other of the Western European lands: 58 per cent of the population was still rural in 1906. That, however, the agricultural population had furnished much of industrial labor is shown by the fact that this 58 per cent represented a steady relative and absolute decline since 1846.

In Germany, contemporary observers about the middle of the nineteenth century reflect the ending of conditions similar to those earlier existing, but already destroyed, in England. In Westphalia, "many wage earners lived almost wholly from the common (the mark), . . . got their fuel and fertilizer and fed their swine and cattle," in the common woods. All these advantages were now lost to them, complains the writer, because of the ending of common rights. The same conditions appear in Rhenish and East Prussia. The Prussian law of 1811, while it provided fairly well for the peasant with sufficient holdings to continue as an independent farmer, worked much hardship on the lesser tenants and left them practically at the mercy of the landlord.

In Russia, the abolition of the mir, the communal village, in which even those who had emigrated had the right to participate, did not occur until just before the World War, when every peasant was authorized by law to claim his part in the village as private property in a single piece, if a simple majority consented. It has been estimated that from five to six million emigrants from the villages were thus proletarized: became propertyless workers.

The old forms of agricultural life continued to exist in various parts of Europe well into the high capitalistic period. The form was there, but its continuance had been made possible by the industrial employment provided by the putting-out system and by seasonal wage labor on the capitalistic farms: the sustenance economy of which the farms were the outward expression no longer sufficed to sustain its members.

The village farmer had everywhere depended to a large extent upon some industrial activity for a part of his subsistence: this came to an end. The disappearance of cottage spinning and weaving in England was regarded by many observers as "the first step towards the abolition of the small freeholders or yeomen in many districts" (Gaskell), and as "withdrawing the crofter's mainstay" (Harry Stuart). By 1830 the process was complete, and putting out in the weaving and spinning industries, at least, had disappeared from England.

In Germany, the same process began about the middle of the century. Between 1837 and 1861 the number of linen looms in

Silesia declined from 11,620 to 7,936; in Saxony, from 13,503 to 9,022; in Westphalia, from 26,900 to 18,369. The German census gives definite statistics only for the end of the period (1882 to 1895) but by the latter date only 67,244 people were carrying on industrial processes in connection with agriculture. The elimination of the small, semi-agricultural producer is reflected also in the local concentration of the iron industry: 69 per cent in 1857 in the provinces of Silesia, Westphalia, and the Rhineland, 95 per cent in 1895. The number of distilleries in Prussia declined from about 23,000 in 1831 to 7,700 in 1865; again, concentration.

So too, the conditions of simple day labor in agriculture grew more difficult with centralized control. The patriarchal leadership of the squire, the junker, was displaced by a brief contractual relation with the casual laborer. The intensification of agricultural life in England led to the annual immigration of casuals from Ireland, Wales, Scotland, and from one part to another of each of these countries.

The Movement of Population

While the break-up of the old communal agriculture and industry was making available for the capitalistic wage relation constantly larger fractions of the population, the population itself was increasing at a very rapid rate. The population of Europe grew from 180,000,000 in 1800 to 452,000,000 in 1914, and these figures tell only part of the story. European populations of great size developed in the United States, Canada, South America, South Africa, Australia, and Siberia. The total population of these areas, which in 1800 was about 5,675,000, had grown in 1910 to 131,754,512, so that the European population in the various parts of the world had more than tripled. In the three leading capitalistic countries, England (including Wales), Germany, and the United States, the figures are even more remarkable: taking the population of 1800 as 100, that of 1910 is 495, an increase in a little over a century to nearly five times the original number.

The general increase seems to have resulted almost wholly from a decline in the death rate: at any rate, as far back as our statistics take us (1840), they reflect larger death rates at the earlier period. For all Europe, the figures are 31.0 at the earlier date, 25.9 in 1900; for Western Europe 26.6 in 1840 and 14.9 in 1912–1913. The birth rate also declined, but not so rapidly as the death rate. The advance of theoretical and practical medicine, hospitals, hygienic regulation, has meant the practical extermination of large causes of mortality: smallpox, cholera, typhoid fever, tuberculosis (in many areas). The increase in wealth has meant better nourishment, and consequent increased resistance to disease. Capitalism, in a sense far removed from Marx's, creates its own proletariat.

New fractions of the population and a greater number of potential proletariat, through the total increase of population, became available for the capitalistic wage relation. We are now concerned with the processes by which this available proletariat was organized.

In the first place, in large numbers they moved: left their homes in the villages and went to the factories, or left their native lands and went to the more highly organized countries of Europe—or went across the sea to found or to serve the new extensions of capitalism.

Emigration seems to be characteristic of the first stages of full capitalism. When England was undergoing the transition to full capitalism (up to 1850), the English (or the British) furnished the bulk of immigration into the United States; from 1850 to 1880, it came from Germany; after that, from the peripheral lands of capitalism, Southern and Eastern Europe. On the other hand, since England and Germany have been thoroughly capitalized, their relative and absolute emigration has radically declined, and immigration to these areas has become more important than emigration from them. The phenomenon of emigration for Europe as a whole during the century is reflected in the following table:

Years	Emigrants from Europe per Thousand Population per Year
1801–1820	0.08
1841–1850	.96
1871–1880	1.10
1881–1890	2.06
1901–1905	2.72
1905	4.02

Altogether from thirty to thirty-five million persons are reckoned to have emigrated oversea from Europe before 1914.

Migration within the European states was almost as great and of almost equal economic significance. The agricultural areas have lost to the industrial areas. In 1907, eastern Germany, exclusive of Berlin and Brandenburg, was estimated to have lost to western Germany over 2,000,000 inhabitants. The country has lost to the city: Great Britain was 50.8 per cent urban as early as 1851; now it is 78.1 per cent urban. France still is half agricultural, but in 1851, three-quarters of the population was rural. Urban population in Germany was 36.1 per cent of the whole in 1871, and 60 per cent in 1910; in the United States, 36.1 per cent in 1890, and 51.4 per cent in 1920.

The high development of transportation has produced a thoroughly modern form of local adjustment to the demands of economic life: periodical migration. We are familiar in this country with the immigrant who undergoes patiently the most burdensome toil in the hope of returning to his native home and there enjoying a restricted financial independence. Then there are the seasonal laborers who move about not only within their own country, but from Poland to Germany and to France, from Italy to France and to Switzerland, and even to the Argentine. This periodic movement from Italy averaged some 3,000,000 persons a year before the World War.

For capitalism these vast migrations and shifts of population were significant. The emigration from Europe to the colonial lands was obviously in first intention a limitation of capitalism, a loss of some of the necessary labor power at the centers of capitalism. In so far as he attempted to live from the soil he had won for himself, the emigrant was quite withdrawn from the capitalistic nexus. Before the end of the free-land period in the United States, five-sixths of the immigrants were transformed into free settlers (or displaced other people who became settlers—which for our purpose amounts to the same thing). This loss, however, was more than counterbalanced by the contribution of these settlers to the formation of the goods capital in the form of food supply and raw materials, which was discussed in the preceding chapter. But the end of the free land brought about a great change. As late as the last decade of the nineteenth century, the increase in the number of farms was so great that it was statistically possible for 926 in each thousand immigrants to become settlers on the soil or substitute for Americans who became settlers. Two decades later (1911–1920) the increase in the number of farms had become so small and the number of immigrants so large that only 45 in a thousand could become settlers. Only 1.8 per cent of the "old immigration" (that is, the immigrants from Northwestern Europe and Germany) and only 0.9 per cent of the "new immigration" (Romance, Slavic, and Jewish immigrants from Southern and Eastern Europe) between 1899 and 1909 became farmers. The immigrants had turned from the farms to industry. Immigration was becoming a reinforcement for the labor supply of American capitalism. That is to say, it was becoming interior migration within the lands of capitalism.

Within Europe the drift of population has been to the most advanced centers of capitalism, in a general way, to England, Germany, and France. There the immigrants have served as reinforcements for the labor force of capitalism and made possible the rapid development of capitalism in those areas during the last fifty years. The immigration of alien laborers is an old story in England: Flemish weavers were brought to England by Edward III in the fourteenth century. Certainly the large proportions of foreigners in the mining industries, in the garment industries (Jews and Slavs in the East End of London), in mercantile houses, and in the hotel and restaurant business, reflect a large reinforcement of the English labor supply. Even in the merchant marine, the proportion of foreigners employed rose from 14.6 to 22.5 per cent between 1890 and 1904, while the number of British subjects employed declined both relatively and absolutely. In Switzerland, between 146 and 556 in every thousand employed in the various industries in 1905 were foreigners; of the more than a million foreigners living in France in 1911, 60 per cent were employed in industry. In Germany, the total of alien residents in 1910 was about 1,250,000; to these are to be added about 750,000 seasonal workers from Poland, Russia, and Ruthenia.

The Urban Movement

The most characteristic product of the shifting of population in the last century is the town: the city, the big town, the metropolis. It has repeatedly been necessary to note the increasing proportions of population that dwell in towns. In a wider sense all of modern economic life has been urbanized.

The modern town has not lost the character of its medieval forerunner. It is still made up of people who live from the surplus created in other economic units. The modern great town, however, reaches that surplus in more complex ways and by means of a more elaborate technique. There are still consumers' towns. Much of the greatness of such a metropolis as Paris is due to the presence of governmental bureaus and the large number of employees, and to the flood of tourists and temporary residents. The kings and their courts, however, have been replaced as town makers by the entrepreneurs and their furnishers of capital. These bring the town fillers, their amusement venders, their food venders, their doctors and lawyers and teachers and newspaper men, and a whole long list of employees and servants. They may even bring with them a factory and its employees, but that is not characteristic of the larger forms of capitalistic enterprise. The Krupps lived in Essen and the Duponts in and around Wilmington, but the modern entrepreneur or capitalist town makers characteristically derive incomes from enterprises remote from the places of their residence. They may operate mines in Mexico and live in London, or a South American electrical concession and live in Berlin. Like the medieval baron, bishop, or king, the modern town maker lives from the surplus produced by other economic units; but, unlike the earlier town makers, he uses the power of money rather than the power of the sword to obtain it.

More common and more significant of capitalistic evolution and especially of our present concern, the geographical adaptation of population to capitalism, are the producers' towns. Some of them, Hamburg and Liverpool, for example, are still principally commercial towns. It is, however, the industrial town and the metropolis which appear in the high capitalistic period as the most distinctive features of modern urban development.

When capitalistic industry appeared, it was of little significance for town building. As has been shown, it sought the countryside (domestic system), or, on account of problems of raw material or of power, the woods, the mines, and the streams. The transition to steam power and the increase of production and of the size of producing units were creative factors that made large towns out of small handicraft towns, like Chemnitz, Dortmund, Birmingham, Lyons, or made new towns out of countryside: Zwickau, Bayonne (New Jersey), Roubaix, Lodz. Some examples illustrate how large this town producing force was:

Germany	*1816*	*1910*
Chemnitz	14,000 (1800)	287,807
Dortmund	4,465	214,226
England	*1760*	*1910*
Manchester	30,000–45,000	710,000
Birmingham	28,000–30,000	840,000
United States	*1840*	*1920*
Youngstown	(did not exist)	132,358
Milwaukee	1,712	457,147
Detroit	9,102	993,678
France	*1800*	*1910*
Lyons	109,500	524,000
Lille	54,756	218,000
Roubaix	8,000	123,000
Poland	*1800*	*1910*
Lodz	200	404,000

These towns owe part of their growth, of course, to other factors than industry. That especially is true among American towns (Cleveland, Denver, Minneapolis, and many others), which, while primarily industrial, serve largely also as commercial and financial centers or subcenters for sections of the country. On the other hand, how industrial such towns can be is illustrated by some German towns: Bochum, a mining town, used 70 per cent of its population in industry; Essen, the same percentage; Plauen, a textile center, 77 per cent. Similar proportions exist in the incomplete towns (such as automobile centers in Michigan) where the entrepreneurs and directors live elsewhere and only so much direction remains on the ground as is necessary to carry on the actual production.

The economic concept, the metropolis, does not primarily depend on size, but upon function. "A village is what a village does, a metropolis is what a metropolis does." The metropolis does everything a town (of any kind) can do. It is an industrial and commercial center for a large area, its financial life is organized in such a way as to dominate or at any rate to exert influence on a national and international scale, it is a consumers' city where the recipients of surplus from elsewhere are domiciled. It is not necessarily a political capital. Paris, Berlin, London are metropolitan; Washington and The Hague are not. Many large towns are not metropolitan: Pittsburgh is less metropolitan than San Francisco, although it is larger. England and France have but one metropolis each. Germany and the United States have several each. Besides Berlin, there are Munich, Leipzig, Cologne, and Dresden. Besides New York, there are Chicago, Philadelphia, and San Francisco.

The existence of the metropolitan town is, of course, dependent upon the increased production of goods and their increased availability from a wider area (transportation) and the development of rapid transit within the urban area.[1] The omnibus, the horse car, the underground, the elevated, the taxicab, and the motor bus mark its stages. In Berlin, the average number of "rides" taken by the "average inhabitant" per year rose from 20.2 in 1866 to 516.7 in 1913; in London, from 22.7 in 1876 to 221.2 in 1911.

The great towns depend for their growth upon their attrac-

[1] The limits of this last development have apparently been reached in New York and London, and their problem daily grows more pressing: its solution probably awaits some new geographical or industrial organization. The difficulty of the problem throws much light upon the essential character of capitalism. Because more people come to the shops and offices in New York City, more shops and offices are provided, more people come, more rent is charged and earned, more buildings rise—and so the vicious circle continues, despite all personal considerations, ease and comfort of life, space, personal dignity, net income in the sense of personal enjoyment. It is too much to say that capitalistic society cannot find a solution of the problem of traffic congestion in New York City, but the difficulty of the problem shows how useless it is to say, "Here are light, air, food, shelter, room, all the simple human wants: come out and enjoy them." The solution will doubtless be found, but it will probably be as regardless of personal taste as the existing conditions.

tiveness to nonurban groups. People come to the towns, apparently, to change their occupation, in their youth. In Austria, the average number per thousand between 15 and 60 in the cities varied from 638 to 700 as against 588 in the kingdom as a whole. In Germany (1907), the percentage of persons between 20 and 40 was 36.7 in the large towns, 28.7 outside of the large towns. They came because of economic inducements, especially the hope of higher wages, and also for non-economic reasons—what Bismarck called the "tingle-tangle" of the town.

The tradition of freedom still clings to the town—but now it does not take "a year and a day" to attain the town's freedom from the claims of personality.

The town has afforded a peculiar theater for the unfolding of the capitalist spirit, its intellectualism, its rationality, its calculating habit. It has been a field for the extension of production, as has been shown: to the development of the city is due the evolution of the greatest of capitalistic industries, building. As labor market, the town has furnished recruits for capitalistic industry, as, when, and where wanted.

The Technical Adaptation of Population

The technical adaptation of population to the needs of capitalism has not been less than the geographical. Capitalism had to have a new race of men ready "to identify themselves with the unvarying regularity of the automotor." The records of early enterprises are full of evidence that men of this kind did not exist in great numbers; more common were the "refractory tempers of work people accustomed to irregular paroxysms of diligence." Andrew Ure, from whose *Philosophy of Manufactures* (1861) these expressions come, felt that it was nearly impossible "to convert persons past the age of puberty . . . into useful factory hands." The "natural man" had no impulses to conform to discipline: specially cultivated men were required. Graduated wages and premiums on the one hand "introduced a wholly new life," as Werner Siemens put it, and the strict factory discipline—so strict that obeying it literally became a favored form of sabotage—introduced by Arkwright developed into a fairly effective technique of handling men in masses. Max Weber insists upon the importance of the general puritanism of religion, the emphasis upon industry and "respectability," as an aid in developing the disciplined worker. The prohibition laws of the United States are generally regarded as the result of the alliance of the religious organizations and the employers of labor.

The development of workmen able to carry on the technical processes of production has been simplified by the division of labor, which has reduced the standard of training necessary in most industrial processes to a very low point. This has been accompanied by a rather elaborate classification of labor: workers are no longer simply masters, journeymen, or apprentices, but range through various grades, according to the degree of their skill (and various other conditions). Instead of shoemakers, the modern shoe factory has sole cutters, stitchers, polishers, etc. The entrepreneur naturally seeks to get each process done by as low a grade of labor as possible. It is characteristic of the labor thus trained that it is highly transferable. A steel-worker can hardly become a spinner overnight, but the technique of, say, making optical instruments can be transferred to making taximeters much more readily than the skill of the shoemaker can be used in bookbinding.

Technical adaptation of labor has been carried to such a point that it has become a profession and almost a branch of learning in itself. The personnel officers of modern factories have a whole series of tests, physical and psychological, to measure the potential adaptation of men to their jobs.

The interchangeability of technique has favored a remarkable instability of labor. In 1913–1914 in eighty-four American factories with 244,814 employees at the beginning of the year, there were

470,715 changes in the personnel, an average of 1.92 per worker. In European countries, the turnover was a little lower, about 0.5 for the German glass industry in 1912, 1.72 in the metallurgical industries, 1.76 in the metal-working industries, 1.10 in the textile industries, but 2.06 in machine industry and 3.64 in the chemical industries (1907). Turnover was highest in industries specifically injurious to health, and in industries which used the largest proportion of unskilled labor. On the other hand, social welfare work, such as was carried on by Krupp's, had a distinct stabilizing effect on the labor force. In 1906, for example, Krupp's had a labor turnover of 4.64 per cent a month, while the general average of the Düsseldorf district was 7.68 per cent.

The economic adjustment of labor to capitalism is expressed through the nexus of wages. In the earlier decades, the steam and machine technique had an apparent depressing effect upon wages. Women and children were used extensively in the place of adult male labor. In 1875, 117,994 children under thirteen were employed in the English textile industry. From that time on, however, the number steadily declined, and in all civilized countries it was reduced to very small proportions by 1914. Women's place in economic aspects of life, as in most others except the domestic, grew steadily larger. In Germany, the percentage of women gainfully employed grew from 18.5 in 1882 to 26.4 in 1907; in the United States, from 14.9 in 1890 to 21.1 in 1910. The wages of women for the same work were from three-fifths to three-fourths those of men.

Another feature of the depressing effect of capitalistic organization upon wages is the use of backward races and immigrants accustomed to lower wages than the laboring men of the same race and birth as the entrepreneur. In the South African mines, where the wages of the colored laborers are about one-eighth those of the white, it is not surprising to find the mine operators seeking to have as much as possible of the work performed by natives. Bryce states: "The dream of the manager is to cut down the cost of native labor by getting a larger and more regular supply as well as by obtaining cheaper maize to feed the workman. . . . So white labor might be much cheapened." In the United States, where the effect of immigration has been exhaustively studied, the Italian immigrant without family has been shown to be capable of saving four-fifths of his wages. The greater availability of immigrant and Negro labor is probably an important cause of the depressed condition of the Pennsylvania coal miners as compared to the western miners.

Capitalistic society has a persistent if varying surplus of labor. Aside from the enormous problems of unemployment developed in various countries since the war, English unemployment in the decade before the war varied from 3 per cent to 7.8, in Germany from 1.6 per cent to 4.4. Unemployment is due to personal reasons, to technical and organizational changes, and to the crisis, which, as we shall see, is a normal feature of capitalistic economy. Such a crisis produced 20.8 per cent unemployment in New York State in 1913, 22.7 per cent in the English shipbuilding industry in 1908.

In general, however, this depressing tendency of capitalistic organization has not prevented real wages from rising substantially during the century, although they rose less than profits and although labor costs have actually declined in nearly every kind of industry except domestic and personal service. If we take total wages and total profits in 1850 as 100, the index figure of total real wages rose generally to 1,446 in 1910, while profits had risen to 2,248. That is to say, in spite of the depressive operation of capitalistic labor organization, labor has on the whole effectively adjusted itself to the economic development of high capitalism. The increased demand for labor, minus the increased supply, plus the decreasing labor cost, plus the increased profits of industry (all properly integrated) might account for this adjustment.

REFERENCES FOR FURTHER READING

General

Sombart, W. Der moderne Kapitalismus, vol. III, pp. 304–469.

Theories of Population

Wright, Harold. Population (1923).

Leroy-Beaulieu, P. La Question de la population (1913).

Kautsky, Karl. Vermehrung und Entwicklung in Natur und Gesellschaft (1910).

Gonnard, René. Histoire des doctrines de la population (1923).

The Increase and Movement of Population

Bodenstein, N., and von Stojentin, M. Der Arbeitsmarkt in Industrie und Landwirtschaft (1909).

Cunningham, W. Growth of English Industry and Commerce in Modern Times (1903).

Dawson, W. H. The Evolution of Modern Germany (1908).

Daudet, E. Histoire de l'émigration (3 vols.; new ed., 1904–1905).

Fairchild, H. P. Immigration, a World Movement, and Its American Significance (1925).

Foerster, R. F. The Italian Emigration of Our Times (1924).

Gonnard, R. L'Emigration européene au XIXe siècle (1906).

Hainisch, M. Die Landflucht (1924).

Hourwich, I. A. Immigration and Labor (1912).

Howe, F. C. The Modern City and Its Problems (1915).

Johnson, S. C. A History of Emigration from the United Kingdom to North America, 1763–1912 (1914).

Knowles, L. C. The Industrial and Commercial Revolutions in England in the Nineteenth Century (2nd ed., 1922).

Levasseur, E. La Population française (1889).

Lewinski, Jan. L'Evolution industrielle de Belgique (1911).

Monckmeier, W. Die deutsche uberseeische Auswanderung (1912).

Nitti, F. Population and the Social Problem (1894).

Ogg and Sharp. The Economic Development of Modern Europe (1926).

Paterson, J. W. Rural Depopulation in Scotland (1896).

Roxby, P. M. "Rural Depopulation in England During the XIX Century," Nineteenth Century, 71 (1912): 174–190.

Smith, R. M. Emigration and Immigration (1890).
Souchon, A. La Crise de main d'œuvre agricole en France (1914).
Weber, A. F. The Growth of Cities in the Nineteenth Century (1899).
Willcox, W. F. "The Expansion of Europe in Population," American Economic Review, Dec., 1915.

The Technical Adaptation of Population

Ure, Andrew. Philosophy of Manufactures (1849).
Weber, Max. Die protestantische Ethik und der Geist des Kapitalismus.
Babbage, Charles. On the Economy of Machinery and Manufactures (1837).
Bücher, Karl. Industrial Evolution (1901).
Munsterberg, Hugo. Psychology and Industrial Efficiency (1913).
Tawney, R. H. The Acquisitive Society (1920).
Veblen, Thorstein. The Instinct of Workmanship (1914).

Wages

Clark, J. B. The Distribution of Wealth (1902).
Brassey, T. Work and Wages (2 vols., 1904–1908).
Schoenhoff, J. The Economy of High Wages (1893).
Hobson, J. A. The Evolution of Capitalism (1926).
Van Vorst, Bessie and Marie. The Woman Who Toils (1903).
Willbrandt, R. Die Frauenfrage, ein Problem der Kapitalismus (1906).
Drage, Geoffrey. The Unemployed (1894).
Beveridge, Albert. Unemployment, a Problem of Industry (3rd ed., 1912).
Rubinow, J. M. "The Recent Trend of Real Wages," American Economic Review, Dec., 1914.
Douglas, P., and Lamberson, F. "The Movement of Real Wages, 1890–1918," American Economic Review, Sept., 1921.

Freedom and Unfreedom

Wakefield, E. G. A View of the Art of Colonization (1849).
Leroy-Beaulieu, P. De la colonisation chez les peuples modernes (6th ed., 1908).
Bryce, James. Impressions of South Africa (1897).
Day, Clive. The Dutch in Java (1904).
Del Mar, Alexander. History of the Precious Metals (1902).

Wendel, H. C. M. The Evolution of Industrial Freedom in Prussia, 1845–1849 (1921).

Hammond, J. L., and Barbara. The Village Laborer from 1760 to 1832 (1919).

Bowden, Witt. Industrial Society in England Towards the End of the Eighteenth Century (1925).

CHAPTER VI

THE RATIONALIZATION OF THE MARKET

The Problem of Outlet

Who bought the products which fully developed capitalism, with its steam and iron technique and multiplied labor supply, was able to produce in such great quantities?

The theories of distribution have been various. The classicists held that overproduction was impossible, because every producer would demand as much goods as he produced. The pessimists, whose theory received its most interesting development at the hands of Marx, hold that the possibilities of expansion are limited by the persistent lowering of the proportion of circulating capital to fixed capital. More and more labor is required merely to reproduce used-up portions of fixed capital, leaving less and less for the purchase of new production.

Whatever the validity or invalidity of the theories, it is obvious that capitalism as a producing system has found a steadily increasing outlet for its products, limited by certain developments more or less accidental in character. The products of capitalism are sold to noncapitalistic income receivers (i.e., landlords); to wage earners; to "peripheral lands" (i.e., in terms of the modern world, the fully capitalistic centers, Europe, the United States, Japan, sell to the partly capitalistic periphery, South America, Africa, India); to itself when a new line of production demands a whole series of new production materials.

Certainly capitalism has striven with all its might to expand its external markets. It has sold its excess production of consumption goods: the English cotton industry sold to the farmers and small bourgeois all over the earth. It has sold production goods, railroads in colonial lands, German indigo in China, Japan, and India. At the same time, it has developed its internal market in much greater degree. It has solved (heretofore) its problem of marketing by developing both external and internal markets to the highest possible degree.

The internal market developed among the older noncapitalistic receivers of revenue. Even in so capitalistic a country as England ground rents in 1913–1914 constituted 18 per cent of the total national income. To them must be added those incomes which result from the profits of stock speculation, etc., and therefore lie outside the capitalist production system. The demands of public organs, which secure their purchasing power from taxes and loans, have greatly increased on account of the extension of governmental activities. The expenditures of the French governmental organs increased 386 per cent while the population increased 31 per cent (1816–1913); those of the whole group of European States from 15 francs to 79 francs per capita, or more than five times as rapidly as the population, between 1786 and 1908.

It is, however, with expansion of the extra-European trade that we are here principally concerned. In spite of the development of humanitarianism, the methods of expansion remained brutal, where such methods would serve. When the English cotton goods production required a new market, the Indian cotton industry was destroyed by customs and tax regulations. "The bones of the cotton weavers whitened the plains of India," but cotton exports from England to India rose to 25 per cent of the (increasing) total export. So the various European nations and Japan forced the market in China until they found that the process too greatly increased their mutual difficulties. In other cases, the right of introducing the blessings of civilization in the form of opium, brandy, or gun powder was obtained by force or fraud. The necessity for this kind of foreign outlet still prevents the master minds of the great powers from devising adequate means to prevent the international trade in opium.

An important phase of the development of the foreign markets is the export of capital. A loan in a foreign land, for the construction of a railroad or the building of an electrical power system, does not necessarily mean that the rails or the dynamos will be bought in the countries from which the money was borrowed, but in practice that is what happens when money is thus lent to the industries or governments of undeveloped countries.

In 1914, the three most important creditor countries had the following sums invested in foreign countries:

Great Britain	$17,500,000,000
France	9,000,000,000
Germany	6,000,000,000

The average annual investment in foreign countries and colonies was reckoned at the following sums:

Great Britain	$500,000,000	to	$1,000,000,000
France	400,000,000	to	500,000,000
Germany	200,000,000	to	300,000,000

In England in 1914 the annual foreign investment surpassed the domestic investment by over 4 to 1. On January 1, 1917, all securities quoted on the London Exchange had a face value of £9,324,400,000: over half was in foreign securities. About the same proportions existed between foreign and domestic securities on the Paris Bourse. In Germany, however, the proportion of foreign issues to the total issues had pretty steadily declined from 1886 down to the World War.

A very large proportion of this export of capital was in the form of loans to governments—almost one-half of the British foreign investments, about four-fifths of French foreign investments. Railroads came next, far behind the government securities, but far ahead of any other form of investments. C. K. Hobson (*The Export of Capital*) has shown in an interesting way how the export of railroad building materials followed the export of railroad building capital. In Indian railway enterprises, for example, 33 per cent of the (largely British) loans went back for the purchase of materials in England, 4 per cent to other countries.

The exports from the world-trading countries (Germany, England, France, and the United States) into the other countries multiplied from two and one-half times (South America, 1901–1913) to eight times (China, 1888–1913) in the quarter-century before the War. This trade with less developed countries, however, was not so important as the trade with more developed neighbors. Even in the case of England, the whole trade with Latin America, Asia, and Africa was only 31.6 per cent of its whole export trade in 1904.

New buying classes were added to the markets by the general breakdown of the self-sustenance economy. Even food became a commodity that was obtained market-wise. Western ranchmen who raise thousands of cattle depend upon canned milk. Farmers' wives buy the family supply of bread. In urban communities this commercialization of life has gone even farther. In building and in clothing, capitalistic production has become the rule. This modernizing process operates significantly in debtor countries, where the obligation to pay taxes operates as a compulsion to produce for the market, and thus opens new classes to the capitalistic sales force. Every movement of settlers into new lands adds another group.

Within its own active constitution, capitalism has repeatedly speeded up its metabolism. The increase in the demand for cotton goods led to an increase in the demand for looms, then in the demand for yarn, then in the demand for fast spinning devices, satisfied by Hargreaves, Arkwright, and Compton; then for more cotton (Eli Whitney), then for power to drive machines, steam engines, iron to make the machines, ore, limestone, and coal (coke) to make the iron, etc. Sometimes this effect was incidental. The need for artificial light produced gas lighting; the wastes from gas lighting, the aniline dye industry. This sort of illustration could be repeated indefinitely without clarifying the essential phenomenon—that every advance of technique constituted a new line of demand for new ranges and quantities of goods. The development of transportation has not only opened up new areas and organized more demanding populations, it has itself required enormous quantities of steel, iron, and wood. The development of electricity to a major form of power has created new kinds of demands unheard of before: what was the value of tungsten in 1800?

The increase in the demand for consumption goods within the capitalist structure is indicated by the increase in real wages, the purchasing power of the proletariat. In index terms, the rise in France was from 55.5 in 1820 to 100 in 1900; in Great Britain, from 37 in 1790 to 100 in 1913; in the United States, from 48 in 1830 to 100 in 1913. This general doubling corresponds to the doubling of the productivity of labor that we have assumed: if the assumption is correct, the working classes are receiving just about the same portion of the total economic production as they did a hundred years ago.

Market Technique and Market Control

The outlet for goods was also increased by the development of marketing technique, which underwent changes only less radical and striking than the changes in industrial technique. Slight reflection in regard to the conditions we see about us will aid the student to realize, first, that demand itself (the potential market) has been strikingly modified in directions that facilitate marketing: since we have all learned to demand straw hats on a particular date, it is much more practicable, convenient, and profitable for a larger number of people to make and sell straw hats. This rather illogical habit illustrates quite widespread features of high capitalistic demand.

It is obvious that the effective demand comes from a very different class from that for which a hat factory was established in the early capitalistic period: "persons of high estates, officials of the state, and rich and well-to-do people," [1] unless, indeed, it may be said that the "rich and well-to-do" now include much wider social groups than in the eighteenth century. In the early part of the nineteenth century occurred a certain divorce between art and industry which, combined with this extension of effective demand among wider groups of society, resulted in the obvious debasement of style, called Victorian in England and America, of which the cast-iron dogs, still visible in many older gardens, are the typical monuments. This divorce between art and capitalistic industry was not, however, permanent: the widespread democratic demand of the late nineteenth and early twentieth century has proved or is proving itself capable of eliciting highly styled production. The advance in automobile design since its beginnings (and from year to year) is an example that serves as well as any. The same phenomenon and the same general curve of development may be observed in other lines of production: furniture, fabrics, buildings, food, and many others, even though the American straw hat may remain unconformable to any known standard of beauty.

This democratization of demand is arithmetically expressed by the statistics of income: in the United States the people with incomes between $2,000 and $5,000 have more than four times as great combined purchasing power as those with incomes between $25,000 and $100,000. It is interesting to note that before 1914 the lower purchasing power of money in the United States (from two-fifths to one-half less than in Germany, for example), especially

[1] See page 227.

low in the necessities of life, left a smaller balance of the average income for the purchase of luxury goods than in Europe.

The producers and sellers have taken a new place in modern demand: from mere docile servants of demand, they became creators of demand. The speculative demand for certain products led not only to increase but to change in character; e.g., graded wheat. The financing of new inventions determined the consumer's demand, e.g., for electric light. The entrepreneur's direct control of production and sale enabled him to limit the consumer's demand; a number of other influences enter here, but the point is illustrated by an imaginary case: if the consumer desires an electric light bulb of 36.5 watts, it is (economically) impossible for him to secure it. He can secure a 25-watt or a 40-watt bulb, but not a 36.5-watt bulb. If he happened to wish to buy a book *broché,* to apply his own binding, he could not do so until recently on the American book market. In most cases the psychological discomfort is eased by convincing the consumer by advertising that he wishes the type of goods which is being sold.

This enables the producer to change the mode and to change it frequently. The obvious illustration is clothes. One year, it is easy to buy a straw hat with a narrow brim and a tall crown, the next year the consumer must buy a hat with a wide brim and a low crown. Somewhat more rationally, the producer also discards a machine when some new invention promises more economical results. For the capitalistic market, the significance of the two cases is the same, a new extension.

In general, this speeding up of the change of fashion has been extended to all classes of the population. The French farmer's daughter in the early nineteenth century wore her provincial costume as a matter of course, whereas now she wears modern clothes and wears the old costume only as masquerade. It has been extended to all sorts of goods. Originally a matter of clothes only, the fashions change in furniture, houses, automobiles, from year to year. It has been extended in geographical range. Russians, French, and Americans dress alike and change together from season to season as though in lock step. The extremely modernistic forms of furniture were unknown before the Exposition des Arts Décoratifs in 1925: in 1927 they were produced in Grand Rapids. Occasionally, the demand is unmanageable. Several attempts before 1930 to bring about a demand among women for long skirts failed. Nevertheless, the creation and imposition of modes in rapid succession is a definite method of increasing the capitalist market, generally used with a definite expectation of results. In a sense, the individual entrepreneur (producer or merchant) is bound by the same compulsions that he imposes upon his customers.

A corollary of the changing mode is the speeding up of the act of consumption: a suit of clothes is used only a few months. The speeding up of production intensifies this character of demand: the large metropolitan newspaper, which contains a quantity of reading sufficient for a week, is disposed of in the course of a short city journey. Again, Goethe had "time" to spend three hours at the table, the office clerk in New York has time only for ten minutes.

Collective demand has increased. The construction and operation of schools, libraries, museums, hospitals, theaters, hotels, central water supply plants, central heating and lighting systems, public means of communication, the increased activities of government and public organs, all involve this concentration of demand into large units.

The demand for goods has changed somewhat in the character of the goods demanded. Here is rather a change of balance than a substitution of new for old. There has been an increasing demand for tools and machines, an increase in the proportion of fixed capital to wages.[2] Demand has shifted from the heavy and durable to the light and less durable. Clothes, food, houses,

[2] See page 292.

vehicles are all calculated to outlast only a changing taste, and to prepare new customers for the producer at the end of a short period. Substitute goods (*Ersatz*) have taken the place of older materials: rubber for leather, celluloids and cellulose for rubber and leather, chicory for coffee, margarine for butter, cotton and shoddy for wool, stamped iron for wrought iron. Substitution has been a deadly weapon of capitalism in the struggle with the handicraft system. Standardization of demand has come partly as a result of the common absorption into similar conditions of work and life, partly as a result of controls exercised by capitalistic organization. Mr. Hoover's Bureau of Specifications and the Bureau of Standards have deliberately undertaken to reduce the variations of product among American manufacturers. The types of files and rasps have been reduced from 2,351 to 496, of hospital beds from 40 to 1, to mention only two out of many such changes that have been accomplished in American industry.

To meet the changing extent and character of demand, the markets have been greatly increased in range, and in effectiveness as devices for establishing exchange values.

The capital market has become world-wide. The Napoleonic Wars completed a victory which London had been winning over Amsterdam, and from that time to the World War, London's metropolitan relation to the whole money market remained unchallenged by any near competition. Its supremacy as a center of world trade, the supremacy of the pound as sound money, and the great flow of money to and through London, made it the unquestioned center of the financial world, and even after the great financial revolution of the World War, gave it an ascendancy over New York as a center. One may say that even the postwar ascendancy of the United States in international finance was expressed in terms of the London market. It is not impossible that, when the export of capital becomes again a normal part of capitalistic economy, the misfortunes of American foreign bondholders between 1929 and 1932, a symptom and consequence of the immature and undeveloped organization in the United States of foreign financing, will again create an unfavorable atmosphere there for foreign loans and lead to the resumption by London of its traditional ascendancy in that field. This possibility, of course, is conceivable only if England returns to the gold standard, either by way of simple resumption of specie payments or by way of revalorization of the pound. Just before the War, £422,000,000 sterling of foreign loans were made in London, £78,000,000 in the United States; just after the War (1920), £40,000,000 in England, £464,000,000 in the United States. London had the one great advantage, however, that rates of interest were generally lower there and the South American countries especially showed a tendency to return to London. Paris and Berlin up to the War were important in the world market.

The labor market remained essentially local in character, the subject of particular local contracts. Labor exchanges, as established in Germany and in England before 1914, served in a marginal way to give the labor market a national extension in those countries.

Good markets have been developed on a world scale for some of the larger items of production, such as wheat, cotton, copper, wool, coffee. Retail commerce has only begun to take on the aspect of a widely organized market with the chain-store development in the United States and the "cooperatives" in England.

The effectiveness of the market as a means of price comparison and price determination has been increased by the vigorous extension of devices of information—traveling salesmen, news transmission, especially the newspaper, and advertising. Statistics of advertising are not complete, but in the United States, national advertising, as distinguished from local advertising, cost $600,000,000 in 1922. From our present point of view, such evidence and the evidence of the advertising section of any American journal indicates that market organization is very largely converted into the form of paper and printer's ink. This is almost a truism in regard to the national market. It is also a fact of the international market. A refrigerator company informed the New York *Times* that an advertisement in its rotogravure section brought four inquiries from several South American countries.

Commercial news is published in many forms. Credit rating publication began in England about 1830. In 1841, the first interlocal organization was developed in New York in connection with the southern trade. The oldest French credit bureau dates back to 1857, the oldest German bureau to 1860. In 1872, Schimmelpfeng organized a really national bureau in Berlin and about the same time, the American credit bureaus, Dun's and Bradstreet's, took on their national character.

Banks, universities, governmental organs, separate semipublic institutions, began to publish market news for customers and the public. The labor market was highly organized by means of private and official publications, especially in Europe. In Germany, such organs in 1911 effected the placing of about three and a half million men. In no other country did such organs fill as many as a million places. Of course, the help wanted and work wanted columns of the newspapers performed a considerable function of this type which is important but not statistically measurable. Numberless specialized journals developed, some of them official, like the consular bulletins, some of them almost academic, like the English *Economist* and the Harvard Committee's *Review of Economic Statistics.* The business and financial page of the daily newspaper is perhaps one of the most important forms of this phase of market organization. Not only the business man and the financier but the most remote farmers and villagers are kept in touch with the market. Before the World War, the Berlin prices for wheat were posted daily in Siberian villages.

All this "illumination" of the market has been made possible by a change in the psychology of business men, the disappearance of that secretiveness which we noted as part of the early capitalistic style, by a change in the character of the values handled on the market, and by a great advance in the mechanical instruments of travel and communication.

The change in the character of values handled on the market which is to be noted, can be summed up in one word: depersonalization. We have already noted this process in the capital market.[3] It is illustrated in the labor market by the development of wage scales resulting from collective agreements with unions or adopted by employers of their own motion. The individually negotiated wage has almost disappeared as a feature of industrial life. In the goods market, the change from face-to-face trading with immediate delivery of the goods, to delivery-commerce by means of sample and specification has been completed. On the Chicago Board of Trade, for example, a specified quantity of wheat of a given standard with delivery at a given date fully assured is sold and bought dozens of times over, and not one purchaser ever sees his wheat, or even a sample. The student will do well to attempt a summary of the conditions that make this possible.

One of the incidental consequences of the high organization of the market system was the stabilization of prices. In the twenty years before the World War, the discount rate of the Bank of France ranged only between 2 per cent and 4½ per cent; that of the Reichsbank between an annual average of 3.12 per cent and 6.03 per cent (1907). Nearly all corporations by 1914 had adopted a policy of steady dividends, even when occasional favorable years provided earnings for exceptionally large dividends. In the labor market, the increasing fluidity of labor and the development of the impersonal wage scale linked the variations of wages closely to the general economic situation, and operated to retard sharp rise or decline. In the commodity markets, the development of exchange operated somewhat in the same way and at any rate gave a quasi-mechanical result at any given time. Prices are fixed and

[3] See page 297.

published. Every traveler in less capitalistic countries is confronted with the unfamiliar problem of haggling. The amusement with which the practice is regarded by travelers is a reflection of the degree to which the fixed price has become a part of our economic practice. A French observer in 1835 noted fixed prices as a peculiar feature of English retailing. Prices are also to a large extent controlled in advance of the transaction between buyer and seller, partly by price-fixing arrangements between producer and retailer (automobiles), partly by the tariffs for goods like gas, electricity, water, imposed both by the character of the producing organization and by governmental regulation. The range of prices from place to place and time to time has also been reduced. The average differences in the price of wheat between the province of Rhenish Prussia and the province of Westphalia have declined as follows:

1816–1820	59.0 per cent
1821–1830	23.4
1896–1900	12.5
1901–1905	4.7

In England, the ratio between the lowest and the highest prices of wheat at different periods was:

1401–1500	100:2,000
1501–1600	100: 800
1601–1700	100: 350
1701–1800	100: 450
1801–1810	100: 214
1816–1825	100: 237

Iron prices at Hamburg varied as 100:258.8 between 1871 and 1880, and as 100:150.6 between 1895 and 1904.

The development of well organized world trade, the incorporation of all sources of supply in a single market organization, and the development of transportation technique and organization are the factors that have made this steadiness possible. How these factors operate is illustrated by a description of the changing conditions in Argentina: "Formerly the practice of Argentina was to ship practically the whole surplus in the first seven months of the Argentine cereal year; for instance, in 1908, out of a total of 17,400,000 quarters, 15,200,000 were exported by the end of July. However, now that futures markets are in existence in Buenos Ayres and Rosario, the grower is no longer solely dependent on the export market; if he thinks well of the future, he can hold his actual produce and hedge, if necessary, with futures."

The rationalizing of the market has extended to the qualification in several important aspects of free activity on the part of individuals by "restraints" of trade. Banks generally aimed at a centralized control of the money and credit market through legislation. The general purpose was to effect such an organization as would provide a quasi-governmental control of the money market without putting the government into the banking business. Such centralized control was early attained in Scotland, England, France, Germany, Japan, and other countries; only late (and partially) in the United States, by the Federal Reserve Act of 1913.

By 1914, the skilled labor market had come to be controlled very generally by the labor unions. Commonly prohibited by law in the early part of the nineteenth century, they secured a limited legal toleration in England in 1824, but it was only in the decade 1865–1875 that effective recognition of the unions as proper organizations to secure betterment of wages and other conditions of labor was effectively established. In 1868, a ministerial declaration extended "toleration" to the French unions, but it was not until 1884 that they received full legal character. The English law of 1871 declared that trade unions were no longer to be considered illegal simply because they were in restraint of trade, and gave them legal protection for their funds. The German proletariat showed more interest in politics than in labor conditions, and split

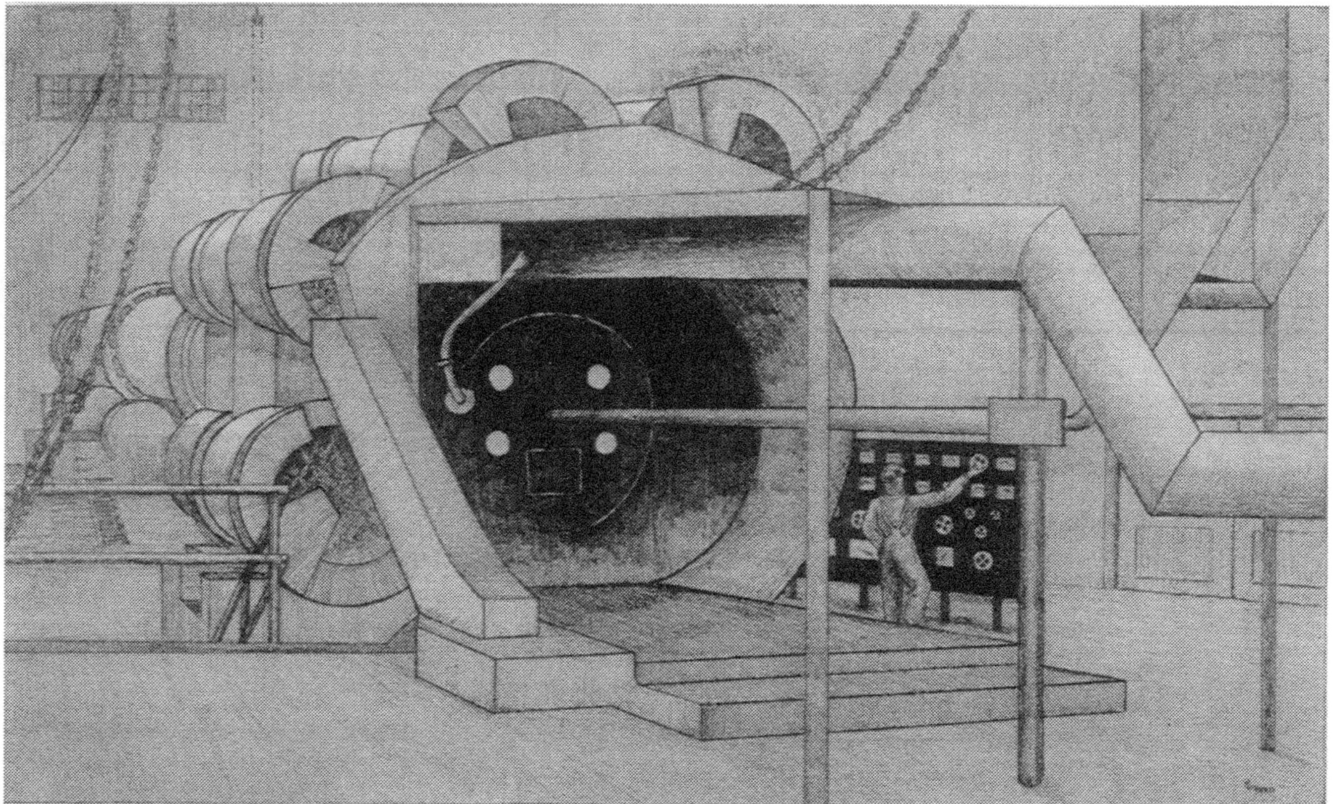

Courtesy of the Monolith Portland Cement Company.

Automatism, Concentration and Control in a Modern Technical Development

A cement kiln, 340 feet in length, the whole operation of which is controlled by one man

into three general groups, the Socialist unions, the Hirsch-Dunker unions (radical-liberal), and the Christian trade unions. Nevertheless, in Germany as well as in the other countries during the period 1870 to 1912, the unions developed a large membership—over 3,000,000 each in England and Germany and 13,892,434 in the whole world—with corresponding increases in income and especially in economic power. Their effectiveness in controlling wages, however, is difficult to measure. It is apparent that on a rising market they secure some considerable advantage for their members; in a badly organized or declining industry, on the other hand, they suffer a great deal of disorganization; compare the railroad brotherhoods of the United States with the miners' federations in England and the eastern United States.

TRADE-UNION MEMBERSHIP

	England	*Germany*	*France*	*United States*
1870	142,530			
1880	251,453			
1890	456,373	277,659	402,125	
1897		412,359		444,500
1900	1,955,704	580,427	492,647	865,400
1905		1,344,803	781,344	1,945,000
1910	2,446,342	2,017,298 *	977,000	2,003,100
1912	3,281,005 †	3,753,807	1,027,059	2,526,112

* This and the preceding figures for Germany above include only the free unions.
† Great Britain.

The commodity market was increasingly dominated by concentrations of control, which will be discussed in the next chapter.

CONJUNCTURE, CYCLES, AND CRISES

Konjunktur is a name which German economists have given to the totality of uncontrollable and variable market conditions.

While capitalism as it developed succeeded in largely obviating the economic consequences of natural disasters such as crop failures, famines, and plagues, which in the earlier centuries of our story were the principal causes of crisis, it has become subject to persistent changes and fluctuations which are not exactly facts of nature or "acts of God," but seem to have the same inevitability and unpredictability. Periods of expansion are followed by periods of depression, and these again by periods of expansion. These alternating successions are called business cycles. They are of several different orders. Comparatively minor changes, to which the name "cycle" is not ordinarily applied, occur every two or three months. Certain wider movements, to which the name is specially applied, vary in duration from eighteen months to seven years. Finally, there have been clearly four great movements of economic life through the nineteenth century: decline, 1822 to 1842; expansion, 1843 to 1873; decline, 1874 to 1893; expansion, 1894 to 1913.

At the turn from a period of expansion to a period of decline, whether in this larger periodic movement or in the smaller intermediate swings, occurs that peculiarly unpleasant phenomenon known as the crisis, varying in character, in severity, and in extent somewhat according to the expansion that preceded it. Some of the symptomatic characters of these movements can almost be measured statistically. As an example of the cyclic process, we may take the minor German movement between 1895 and 1901—expansion, 1895 to 1900, crisis in 1900, then decline during 1901:

1. Rapid rise in prices: coal from 12.6 marks to 17.1; raw iron, from 65 to 107 marks.

2. Rapid rise in profits: average dividends of German industrial companies from 7.34 to 10.96 per cent.

3. Rapid increase in the number of new establishments: 1894, 92 with 88.3 million marks capital; 1899, 364 with 544.4 million marks capital.

4. Rapid expansion of production: mine products, 45.3 million tons to 174.7 million tons.

5. Rapid rise in stock-market values: stamp duty rose from 9 million marks to 21 million marks.

6. Rapid increase of stock sales: transfer stamps brought 8 million marks in 1894, 13 million marks in 1900.

The beginning of the decline manifested itself in the reversal of all these movements:

1. Falling prices: steam coal, from 22.4 marks in 1900 to 17.4 in 1901; index for mineral products, 108 to 89.

2. Limitation of dividends: of 5,500 listed companies in 1901, 1,869 passed their dividends, and 1,003 had deficits.

3. Lowering of production: raw iron, from 8.5 million tons in 1900 to 7.9 million tons in 1901.

4. Decline in number of new enterprises: 261 in 1900; 158 in 1901; 87 in 1902.

5. Decline of stock prices: the stamp tax produced 21 million marks in 1900, 14.5 million marks in 1901.

6. Decline in stock sales: the transfer tax brought 13 million marks in 1900, 12.4 million marks in 1901.

The peculiar and distinctive feature of the capitalistic depression is that it is characterized by falling prices and oversupply (from the market point of view) while earlier depressions were characterized by shortage and high prices.

The first capitalistic crisis was probably that of 1788, which was so keenly felt in the more capitalistic countries of Western Europe, England, France, and Holland. A special committee of the English East India Company appointed to make a study of it reported in words that, with some little expansion and change of terminology, might have been used by a twentieth century economist speaking of the crisis of 1929: "The distress which the manufacturers had complained of in 1788 had arisen from the manufacturers themselves having pushed their enterprizes beyond all bounds upon fictitious capitals." In both France and England, the years following the American war of independence had been marked by a radical expansion in business. The value of goods manufactured in England had risen from £3,200,000 in 1783 to £7,500,000 in 1787. The foreign commerce of France rose from 683,000,000 livres in 1783 to 1,072,000,000 in 1789. Money was plentiful, new enterprises, such as the French India Company, water companies, insurance companies, land companies, were formed in considerable numbers. Prices rose radically on the stock exchanges. In 1788, the crisis came. Foreign trade fell off; prices dropped; thousands of workers in France and in England were thrown out of work; money, that is to say, credit, suddenly became "tight." Then as now, people were disposed to put the responsibility for their troubles on the government. The English alleged that their troubles came because the East India Company imported more cotton cloths than usual from India in 1788. The French alleged that their troubles came because the government had permitted foreigners to trade in the colonies, had established a new monopoly in the India trade and had made a commercial treaty with England in 1786. The crisis was comparatively short, and in 1790 trade was again expanding rapidly in both countries.

Aside from the special disturbances due to war conditions between 1793 and 1815, the next crisis came in 1815–1816 when the inability of the continental peoples to buy as freely as the English had anticipated resulted in the bankruptcy of many merchants and banks. In 1825, another crisis, especially severe in England, followed upon a period of notorious overtrading and crazy speculation of which the story is told that cargoes of skates and warming pans were exported to Rio de Janeiro and loans were subscribed on behalf of a nonexistent South American republic. The crisis of 1837 began in the United States, apparently in connection with the overextension of credit by the state banks which were supplanting the second Bank of the United States. It spread quickly to the European centers that were involved in American trade, London, Liverpool, Antwerp, Le Havre, and Hamburg. The Bank of Belgium had to suspend payments in 1838. The

Bank of England had to get help from the Bank of France. There was trouble in Hamburg, and even in France, which was comparatively little affected, a major firm, Hottinguer et Cie., had to suspend. The railway building of the forties, accentuated by the general European failure of the potato crop, led to another crisis in 1847. The "gold fever" induced by the very great additions to the stock of gold from California led to another period of intense speculative development and to the crisis of 1857, most severe in England and France, less so in Holland and Belgium, and very drastic in the United States. In 1873, a financial and industrial collapse began almost simultaneously in New York and Vienna which was felt throughout the world. Germany, just beginning her modern industrial development, was seriously affected. The crisis of 1893 was peculiarly severe in the United States on account of the irrational character of the American financial system. In 1907, a "bankers' crisis" also peculiarly affected the United States.

Then followed in all civilized countries a period of prosperity without precedent in the history of the world. Increased production, rising prices for commodities and for stocks, a vast expansion in the flotation of new enterprises coincided with apparently inexhaustible supplies of credit at low rates of interest. This prosperity, however, culminated like the earlier periods of expansion in the world-wide crisis of 1913, the full development of which was covered by the beginning of the World War in 1914. It was a particularly mild crisis. Although industry was hard hit and long breadlines were common in the great cities, no great epidemic of bankruptcies occurred. Nevertheless, it was so widespread as to be practically universal over the whole area of capitalism.

In a general way, it seems that the severity of recessions was somewhat lessened during the nineteenth century. Most of the capitalistic countries learned to use their banking systems in such a way as to check overdevelopment of business in periods of expansion and thus to reduce the severity of the consequent crisis. This was especially true of France, where the Bank of France combined an extremely rational and flexible organization with a discreet and intelligent management. Discount rates were raised, not merely for the purpose of protecting the Bank's balances, but to prevent the overdevelopment of business on credit. When crises came, the Bank mitigated the "tightening" of credit by free issue of bank notes. This general line of practice was followed in all the countries with strong central banks. The crisis of 1857 was the last unrestrained crisis in England; that of 1873, the last in Germany and Austria. In the United States, expansion and recession remained uncontrolled until the establishment of the Federal Reserve System provided an instrumentality which was expected to operate in the same way.

The mere increase in the economic structure has reduced the disturbing effect of particular expansions: the building of one thousand miles of railway would be a far less significant factor now than in 1840. The concentration of business into larger units has favored a more conservative and foresighted policy. Well managed corporations build up considerable funds in the form of surplus and undivided profits. Legal controls and exchange rules have imposed severe restrictions on expansion in the form of new enterprises. England learned that lesson as early as 1865, Germany in the crisis of 1872–1873, and the United States not until after the crisis of 1907–1908. Finally, the entrepreneur has learned also to accept the crisis and the recession as a certain prospect, to be taken into account in organizing the policy of his enterprise.

REFERENCES FOR FURTHER READING

General

Sombart, W. Der moderne Kapitalismus, vol. III, pp. 470–711.

The Development of the Market Theory

Taussig, F. W. Principles of Economics (1914).
Marshall, Alfred. Principles of Economics (8th ed., 1920).

Kyrk, Hazel. The Theory of Consumption (1923). Survey and bibliography.
Carver, T. N. Principles of Political Economy (1919).

The Rationalization of Demand

Bernays, E. L. Crystallizing Public Opinion (1925).
Mataja, V. Die Reklame (4th ed., 1927).
Neuberger, O. Die Mode: Wesen, Entstehen und Wirkung (1913).
Presbrey, Frank. The History and Development of Advertising (1929).

Trusts and Combinations

Jenks, J. W. The Trust Problem (6th ed., 1925).
Jones, Eliot. The Trust Problem in the United States (1922).
Stevens, W. S. Industrial Combinations and Trusts (1913).

The Export of Capital

Becque, E. L'Internationalisation des capitaux (1912).
Hobson, C. K. The Export of Capital (1914).
Hobson, J. A. The Economic Interpretation of Investment (1911).
Jenks, L. H. The Migration of British Capital to 1875 (1927).
Sartorius von Waltershausen, A. Das volkswirtschaftliche System der Kapitalanlage im Ausland (1907).
Veblen, Thorstein. Theory of Business Enterprise (1905).
Wilson, Charles. De l'influence des capitaux anglais sur l'industrie européenne depuis la révolution de 1688 jusqu'à 1846 (1847).

The Management of the Labor Market

Webb, S. and B., eds. History of Trade Unionism (1920); The Public Organization of the Labor Market (1909).

The Crisis and Its Control

Aftalion, A. Les Crises périodiques de surproduction (1913).
Anderson, B. M. The Value of Money (1917).
Clark, J. M. Social Control of Business (1926).
Edie, L. D. The Stabilization of Business (1923).
Ely, R. T. Evolution of Industrial Society (1905).
Fisher, Irving. The Purchasing Power of Money (1911).
Foster, W. T., and Catchings, W. Profits (1925).

Hansen, A. H. Cycles of Prosperity and Depression in the United States, Great Britain, and Germany (1921).

Hardy, C. O. Risk and Risk Bearing (1923).

Juglar, C. Des crises commerciales et de leur retour périodique en France, en Angletarre, et aux Etats-Unis (2nd ed., 1889).

Lightner, O. History of Business Depressions (1922).

Mitchell, W. C. Business Cycles: The Problem and Its Setting (1927).

Mombert, P. Einführung in das Studium der Konjunktur (2nd ed., 1925). Bibliography.

National Industrial Conference-Board. Public Regulation of Competitive Practices (1925).

Patterson, R. H. The New Golden Age (2 vols., 1882).

Robertson, D. H. A Study of Industrial Fluctuation (1915).

Sprague, O. M. W. A History of Crises Under the National Banking System (1910).

CHAPTER VII

THE RATIONALIZATION OF BUSINESS ORGANIZATION

It is in the organization of business enterprise that the process of rationalization has been most complete in principle and most thorough in practice. The process is most obvious in industrial enterprise, and therefore the illustrations used in this chapter will be drawn mostly from the industrial (producing) part of economic life. It is equally to be remembered, however, that the same process is going on in the organization of commercial enterprises. It is frequently asserted in economics textbooks that during the nineteenth century commerce yielded a predominance, which it had held before that time, to industry. The statement has a not very obvious truth, although a casual glance reveals that it must be imperfect. Selling and manufacturing must always be balanced: the merchant cannot sell more goods than are produced, and the manufacturer dare not produce more goods than the merchant can sell. The not too obvious truth in the statement is simply this, that the changes of method (and hence the opportunities for enterprise) were less in commerce than in industry. Concretely put, such devices as chain stores and corporate organization came later into mercantile practice than trusts and combinations into industry.

Rationalization in this sense is comparatively new in the European economic world. Cost accounting applied to the elements of industrial process (e.g., the cost per pound of steam pressure, the cost of transportation per unit of raw material, the cost of operating an old machine as against the cost of buying a new one) is almost wholly new within the past generation. The process of rationalization is far from complete. In the United States, where it is most advanced, the Hoover committee found in 1921 (*Waste in Industry*) a considerable margin of waste in the best organized industries, and from one and one-half to four and one-half times as much in the average establishment.

WASTE IN VARIOUS INDUSTRIES IN THE UNITED STATES

Industry	*Waste in best organized concern*	*Waste in average concern*	*Proportion of best to average*
Men's clothing	26.73	63.78	1:2½
Building	30.15	53.00	1:1¾
Printing	30.50	57.61	1:2
Shoes	12.50	40.83	1:3½
Metals	6.00	28.66	1:4⅔
Textiles	28.00	49.20	1:1¾

The process of rationalization involved, first of all, the utilization and development of a new form of business association, the incorporated stock company, which made possible the aggregation of capital in units far transcending the possibilities of personal credit and in relationships that in principle obviated all personal involvement. In the second place, mostly by means of the stock company, combination and concentrations of control have facilitated the development of organization at higher levels and the extension of the entrepreneurs' potential range of action. To use a military analogy, the organization of command has come to include not merely generals and captains who command thousands of men but also marshals and generals who command millions. In the third place, the inner working of enterprises has been brought under the control of objective and accurate measurement of all activities with reference to their return of profit. All this is rationalization, not necessarily with reference to social or ethical interests, but with reference to the dominant principle of capitalistic enterprise, the winning of profits.

The Incorporated Stock Company

The principal manifestation of this rationalizing of organization is the vast development of associative forms of enterprise in the form of stock companies. Adam Smith in *The Wealth of Nations* (1776) considered the stock company suitable only for banking, insurance, canal and road building, and water supply for cities. Now it is a matter for remark when any considerable business remains an individual or even a partnership enterprise.

The joint-stock company or negotiable share company, to give it a name which goes more nearly to the root of its function in economic life, was by no means unfamiliar in the days of Adam Smith; but that its development was very limited is indicated by his comment. Even within his own lifetime, however, the theoretical limitation which he thought he recognized was proved to be incorrect. An outburst of company formation occurred in France and in the United States between the American Revolution and the French. The French Revolution, especially the period of the Convention, was marked by a decided reaction against the newer ways of doing business, and all the stock companies were abolished in 1793. Under the aegis of Alexander Hamilton, this method of aggregating capital continued to prosper in the United States, although the companies formed had a rather dismal record.

The Napoleonic code of commerce in 1807 provided the first general law for the organization of stock companies. It provided for two kinds. The *société anonyme* was like a modern stock company, except that the liability of stockholders might be either limited or unlimited according to the company's own constitution. Companies of this type were subject to a close official oversight. The *société en commandite sur actions* was the traditional silent partnership, with the capital of the silent partners split up into shares. Companies of this type were not treated as corporations, nor were they so subject to official regulation as the *sociétés anonymes.* The active managers alone were fully liable for the debts of the enterprise. These provisions of the code became the basis for the company law of Belgium, Holland, Switzerland, Italy, Spain, Prussia, and the Hanse cities.

The true joint-stock company developed rather slowly in France, where it was confined to the traditional fields of banking, insurance, and public utilities. Only a dozen were created during the Napoleonic period, and 122 during the whole period of the Restoration (1815–1830). The *sociétés en commandite* were much more numerous, and were the instrumentality used in most of the scandalous company promotions of the late thirties and forties. Between 1840 and 1848, 177 *sociétés anonymes* were floated and 1,400 *sociétés en commandite sur actions.* Not until 1867, when the government relaxed the strict control over the *sociétés anonymes,* did they become the prevailing type.

During the thirties, most of the principal mining and metallurgical enterprises of Belgium came into existence as *sociétés anonymes.* About 120 Belgian companies, fewer than were formed in each of several of the boom years, survived the crises of 1838 and 1848. In Germany, no state except Prussia had a general company law before 1850. In England, the Bubble Act of 1720 forbade the formation of companies with transferable shares without a charter from king or Parliament, which was very difficult and expensive to obtain. This restriction was relaxed only in 1825, but even then the English Parliament refused to admit the principle of limited liability until 1855.

The stock company organized as a corporation is perhaps the prime symbol of the elimination of personality from business. Its basic idea is abstraction of a segment of property and the endowment, by legal fiction, of this property with the various business functions. The company buys and sells, contracts debts, hires and discharges workers. The officers and employees are merely functionaries of the property, the shareholders merely creditors. If it becomes bankrupt, for example, neither legal nor social responsibility attaches to officers or shareholders. They may immediately form another company, buy the property at bankruptcy sale, ignore the debts of the original company and have perfectly good standing and credit.

The company—or corporation, as it is somewhat inaccurately called in the American language—is prevalent in every branch of enterprise and in every geographical area. In the United States, where the development has gone farthest, five-sixths of all goods manufactured in 1914 were produced by enterprises thus organized. Between 1885 and 1913, the number of stock companies in Great Britain rose from 8,692 to 60,754, with an average capital in the latter year of about $200,000. The German companies numbered only 5,222 in 1909, but the average capital was about $700,000. In France, 25,451 companies were organized between 1889 and 1913. Nevertheless, it is to be borne in mind that enterprises of the individual form still prevail in number. Even in the United States it was only in 1919 that the stock companies became more numerous than the individual enterprises.

The stock company was originally based on the issuance of a single series of "shares" of stock corresponding exactly to the amount of money capital contributed by the "subscriber." During the nineteenth century, however, this simplicity became exceptional rather than typical. Besides the "common shares," representing the residual ownership and an unlimited share in the profits, the typical stock company also issues—

(a) preferred shares, with preferred but limited rights to the assets and to the earnings;

(b) debentures, or unsecured acknowledgments of indebtedness, with a fixed rate of interest;

(c) bonds, or acknowledgments of indebtedness bearing a fixed rate of interest secured by a mortgage, held by a trustee, upon the assets.

Common stocks are sometimes divided into voting and non-voting classes; preferred shares are often issued in several series, with different rights and rates of return; there are often several series of bonds. The simple structure, with common stocks only, appears typically in two cases: a new enterprise of such uncertain character as not to offer security for bonds or preferred stock, such as a mining venture or an automobile factory, and an organization which has so prospered as to be able to retire its bonds and preferred stocks.

The control of the company nominally lies in the holders of the common shares, in proportion to the number of shares held. Most of them, however, do not vote even by proxy, and the actual control usually lies in the hands of a small group, the real entrepreneurs of the concern. Occasionally, they formalize this oligarchical position by confining the voting privilege to a special class of common shares (Class B stocks) which is issued to them alone and shares in the profits only after a certain dividend has been paid to the ordinary common (Class A). Whatever the form, the actual control of stock companies is effectively in the hands of the leading entrepreneurs, so long as they are successful in producing profits.[1] It is the form in which the entrepreneur finds his most complete opportunity for enterprise.

A great advantage which the stock company affords the entrepreneur is the possibility of linking up a series of individual enterprises under his centralized control. In Germany before the war, the Deutsche Bank held directorships in 186 other corporations; twenty-five members of the Allgemeine Electrizitätsgesellschaft (German General Electric Co.) held 481 directorships; Walther Rathenau, the great economist, held thirty-five. In the United

[1] An interesting commentary on this general condition was the conflict early in 1929 over the removal of the successful manager of the Standard Oil Company of Indiana. A majority of the stock happened to be in the hands of the minority of the stockholders who disapproved of certain moral aspects of his conduct. Otherwise it is apparent that he would have been retained, as a majority of the stockholders voted or let their votes be cast for him.

States in 1912, eighteen banking concerns, through 180 members, held 746 directorships in 134 corporations with over $25,000,000,000 capital. In Holland, nine great banks had representatives in the directorates of 300 companies. This linkage is accomplished also by more formal devices, the subsidiary company, much used in the public utility field, and the holding company, especially favored in railroad enterprises. These developed first in the United States and thence spread to other countries. They imply a certain subordination of one organization to another: the exchange of stock is still another form of combination which serves to bind competing organizations together upon an equal basis.

This linking of enterprises serves to give the entrepreneur a wider range for his activities and affords an opportunity (in expectation if not always in reality) to apply to the larger combined concern the highest forms of rational organization, both in external relations (finance, markets) and in internal relations (the organization of production). It is commonly said that from three to four hundred men manage the whole European-American economic life: it is only through the network of stock-company control that this is possible.

In a broad sense, that fact may be a sign of the transition to old age of the capitalist system. It marks how far capitalism has come from the stage when the capitalist business ideal was marked by that thoroughly capitalistic proverb, "Competition is the life of trade." It is not without significance that one of the great representatives of this linking-up process, Walther Rathenau, proposed complete organization of Germany as a single great corporation. It was at least a logical proposal. If such an organization were completed, the result would be quite different from capitalism.

For all this linking up of enterprises under concentrated control, the art of the financier is as necessary as the art of the manufacturer or that of the merchant. The modern entrepreneur must have all three. The managing group, for example, of such an organization as the General Motors Corporation must not only embody the technique necessary to keep a production line moving and to dispose of the product as rapidly as it is produced, but must also be able to marshal the financial equipment of the various subsidiary companies in just as orderly fashion.

The Displacement of Small Units of Economic Enterprise by Larger Units

One of the most obvious developments of the four or five decades preceding 1914 was that of large enterprises which occupied increasingly large fractions of the growing fields with which they were concerned, thus narrowing the field for other, smaller economic units, crowding out varying numbers of existing units, and preventing the development of others that might have come into being.

This concentration has two aspects. In the first place, from a purely economic point of view, it has proved to be more profitable in many fields to carry on business in larger units; as a result, small units have been displaced by large units. For instance, there were hundreds of small manufacturers of automobiles in the United States in 1910: now there are perhaps fifty separate concerns. The manufacture of automobiles has been concentrated in a smaller number of concerns although many more automobiles are manufactured. From a more political point of view, combinations of previously existing concerns have been effected, sometimes on a nationwide and even an international scale, for the purpose of eliminating competition by nonmembers. The American "trusts," the German cartels and syndicates, the French *comptoirs,* the English associations and unions (of manufacturers), the American mergers, and various combinations of an international character, such as the Royal Dutch and (British) Shell oil interests, the Turkish Petroleum Company, the Continental Steel Cartel, formed by the producers of Germany, France, Belgium, and Luxemburg, are outstanding examples of this phenomenon.

Concentration of this first sort is easily recognized (if not always easily measured), by the statistical indications given by the various census reports and year books.

In the largest field of economic enterprise, agriculture, concentration remains almost entirely excluded in the territory of Western Europe, and was only slightly visible in the United States and in Russia before 1914. In all other fields of enterprise, industry, transportation, commerce, and banking, it is already of great importance and is apparently destined to an indefinite increase of importance.

In industry, the progress of concentration is partly reflected by the distribution of laborers among the establishments of different sizes. In Germany, the general average number of workmen in mining and manufacturing establishments rose between 1882 and 1907 from 2.7 to 5.2, that is, nearly doubled. Still more significant is the increase in the proportion of wage earners employed in the larger establishments as compared with the smaller ones. In 1882, the percentage of industrial wage earners employed in establishments with more than fifty employees was 26.3; in 1907, it was 45.5. The majority of industrial wage earners still worked in the smaller establishments; but in mining, the smaller establishments had practically disappeared, and in machine making, the chemical industry, and the textile industry, they had declined to nearly 30 per cent. In the United States, the concentration in mining and manufacturing was even greater than in Germany. The average number of wage earners in an industrial enterprise in 1899 was 10.4, just twice the figure for Germany in 1907. This particular phase of industrial concentration seems, however, to have reached a maximum about 1919 and to be declining. In England and in France, the process of concentration was much slower. In France, the small establishments with from one to five workers employed 27.7 per cent of all workers in 1896 and 24.6 per cent in 1906.

In transportation in its more modern forms, concentration and combination seem to be dictated by the nature of the functions performed as well as by the gain impulse. The postal system has been from its beginning a governmentally controlled monopoly. In most countries, so also are the telegraph and telephone systems, but in the United States, where they are privately owned, there remain only two telegraph companies, while in the telephone field, the American Telephone and Telegraph Co. stands alone except for occasional local companies. All three are combinations of previously existing smaller enterprises. Where railroads are privately owned, the development has been in the same direction. In England, before the World War, there were seven companies; now there are four. In France, there are six. In the United States, the 13 largest systems in 1877 operated 25.5 per cent of the then existing mileage, in 1909, 53 of the 1,320 railway companies operated 66 per cent of the total mileage. "Control" was still more definitely concentrated in eight groups covering about 70 per cent of the mileage. Similar processes are observable in street-railway transportation. Road and river transportation retained the small-concern character until more recently. Ocean transport has been a favorite field for combinations.

Commerce, buying and selling, has been characterized by the remarkably large (and increasing) proportion of the population engaged in it: 18.6 per cent in Australia, 14.4 per cent in England and Wales, 12.2 per cent in the United States, 10 per cent in France, 6.2 per cent in Germany. It has been characterized also by some interesting concentrations, the great department stores in the metropolises, the mail-order houses, chain stores, etc. Nevertheless, the smaller establishments maintained their relative position up to 1914. The French statistics, which most adequately discriminate at this particular point, show a slight decline among the very smallest establishments (one to five employees): 55.6 per cent of all persons receiving salaries for commercial functions in 1896, 54.4 per cent in 1906. The general proportion between independent merchants (in the broadest sense) and salaried workers in commerce was only a small decimal less than 1:2. The average personnel of establishments employing assistance was: 1896, 2.6; 1901, 3.0; 1906, 2.8. Even in wholesale trade, in spite of the natural opening for large establishments (size of field, necessity for credit, etc.), various factors have contributed to the preservation and development of the smaller enterprise. The removal of certain functions, especially warehousing, which has become a wholly separate function, reduced by that much the burden of providing capital, with the result that in many cases, a typewriter was all that was necessary in the way of equipment, while the actual materials traded in were handled on a commission basis. Nearly 95 per cent of the wholesale business in Germany in 1907 was handled by establishments employing up to five persons. Retail trade possibly showed more concentration than wholesale trade. At any rate, great concentrations in the form of department stores, mail-order houses, and chain stores appeared, not only in the United States, but also in England, France, and Germany. Nevertheless, they were far from dominant in 1914. Statistics are wanting, but a careful estimate indicates that in 1924 these three forms of concentrated retail trade had about one-seventh of the total retail trade of the United States, where they are most fully developed. The quick applicability of credit in commercial business, the greater flexibility of the small specialty shop, the tendency of overhead costs to increase relatively faster than the size of the business, have given the small trade an excellent chance of survival.

In banking, the same tendency appears, a development of large concentrations, together with a remarkable development of smaller establishments. The great banks in England, France, and Germany tripled or more than tripled their resources (capital plus deposits) between 1890 and 1914. Bank mergers were the order of the day in all Western Europe and the United States. In England the number of banking companies radically declined from 104 in 1890 to 37 in 1915. In Germany, the proportion of persons employed in the large banking enterprises rose from 11.9 per cent in 1882 to 33 per cent in 1907; but during the same period the number of smaller enterprises more than doubled.

Business Combinations

Concentration of economic enterprise by combination appears in so many different characters that it does not yield to statistical representation. The difficulty is well stated by Willard L. Thorp in his *Integration of Industrial Operation:* "It is impossible to ascertain the many combinations and alliances among industrial combinations. . . . The lines of control converge and diverge among economic enterprises in a most intricate pattern. The ties which bind establishments together are often quite imperceptible to the outside inquirer and too elusive to permit definite statement. . . . Of the less apparent combinations those resulting from interlocking directorates and interlocking shareholdings are the subject of frequent discussion. The gentleman's agreement and dinner party methods of combination have likewise achieved unpleasant publicity. Such relationships, however, are impossible of accurate determination. . . . [Hence] financial combination, interlocking directorates, bank control: all such obscure forms of relationship are disregarded. This is a study of operating combinations." Further reference to Mr. Thorp's book will illustrate for the student the great complexity, the very indistinct character, of the boundaries between one sort of combination and another.

A rather misleading distinction has crept into economic language—between the "vertical" combination and the "horizontal" combination. The vertical combination is the combination of enterprises that are normally in the relation of buyer and seller to each other. The Ford Motor Company is a favorite illustration of this type. In the expansion of his business, Mr. Ford acquired or created a whole series of enterprises supplementary to his main

Courtesy of the Link-Belt Company.

Concentrated Control of Scattered Industrial Units: the Plants of the Link-Belt Company

business: ore mines, smelters, railroads, agencies, etc., so that as much as possible of the whole chain of manufacturing and selling was under his own management. It is to be noted, in the first place, that, comparatively thorough as this vertical trust was, it did not include such obvious elements of its production as tires, and, in the second place, it was not exactly new for an enterprise to own other enterprises closely connected with its own business. Railroads have owned coal mines and hotels, manufacturing concerns have run their own retail selling organizations (Singer Sewing Machine Co., the National Cash Register Co., the Manufacture française d'armes et de cycles de St. Étienne). Retail merchants have owned their own factories, producing what they sold. Félix Potin, the great Paris grocery firm, founded in 1845, owns bakeries, distilleries, wine cellars, preserving plants, and many other such establishments. Sears, Roebuck and Co. controls various industrial enterprises and owns outright fifteen factories. Electrical industries in all parts of the world own their greatest "customers," the street-railway companies (or the reverse). The United Fruit Company owns its own steamship lines; the milk trust of Paris, its own tank cars. The German A.E.G. owns its own financing institutions. The great department stores in Berlin, Paris, and Philadelphia operate banks as part of their business. The Krupp firm in Germany owns mines, smelters, steel works, railroads, steamship lines, housing projects, schools, and churches.

One reason why the vertical trust has recently attracted such notice is the very illogical combination of enterprises made by Stinnes, the German financier, on the basis of opportunities created by the great decline of the mark after the war. It included mining enterprises, electrical power companies, newspapers, textile factories, and various other enterprises. It was an accidental combination and collapsed with the recovery of the mark. If it had had any logic in it, it would have meant the combination of all German enterprise.

The so-called vertical trust has, however, in its more logical forms, a considerable economic-historical significance as a reaction against the great specialization which took place in the latter half of the nineteenth century, and has by no means disappeared. A manifestation of this sort is familiar to every one, the "specialty shops" in retail trade, necktie shops, orangeade shops, silk shops. It is rather recently that banks developed the function of commercial information; they had specialized as loaning institutions. In industry, more than 56 per cent of the shoe factories in the United States were specialized in 1905 ("made one kind of product exclusively"). As independent enterprises, such establishments were in a weak position, subject to all sorts of misfortunes from the accidents of crisis and changes of fashion. They offered a function and an opportunity to the founders of vertical trusts but also to the founders of horizontal trusts. A packing-box factory is a useful institution. It can make packing boxes cheaper and better than they can be made in the shipping room of a wholesale firm. As an enterprise, however, it is in a much stronger position if it owns a wholesale house that will take a substantial portion of its product (not a likely case), or if it is owned or controlled by a wholesale house (which is more likely). It is also in a stronger position if the possibility that some other packing-box firm will drive it out of business by ruinous competition is provided against by understandings, agreements, or combination in the form of a "trust."

The vertical combination, however, has no such importance as the horizontal combination, either with reference to this particular question of concentration or with reference to economic life in general. The character of the horizontal combination is the same in all countries, even when it becomes international. A number of competing enterprises, usually industrial, find that they are losing money or making less money than they might, because they compete with each other for the same market-outlets or for raw materials. They form an agreement either to produce certain amounts and sell at certain prices or to sell through a common agency and divide the net receipts according to a previously established rate for each member. Each enterprise commonly retains its individuality as an economic and legal entity. The antitrust laws of the United States necessitated a variant that is peculiarly prevalent here, the merger, in which either one competing unit nominally buys another "by exchange of stocks"—so many shares in the (enlarged) purchasing company for so many shares in the (disappearing) purchased enterprise—or else a new company is formed which buys both the competitors by means of a similar exchange of stocks.

The objective is nominally twofold: to effect economies of production, and to eliminate the costs of competition. The former is significant in the lower forms of concentration. For example, the American Steel Hoop Co. divided the eighty-five to ninety distinct models in such a way that each separate establishment produced a single group of products, with a saving of from $1.00 to $1.50 per ton of product. In general, however, the elimination of competition is the more prominent objective—not only between the units combined, but also with other units not in the combination. This aspect was brutally manifested in the early days of the American trusts when many small entrepreneurs who commanded only a local market were forced out of business by local cutting of prices by the "combine," which recouped itself in other areas or by its later monopolistic position. The development, however, has taken on a larger significance than the personal economic fate of individual small competitors. Competition itself is being eliminated from capitalism. The reader will recall that the handicraft system had no place in its ethics for competition, and that the development of competitive practice was one of the characteristics of early capitalism. During the nineteenth century, when the world seemed to afford adequate space for the indefinite extension of capitalistic enterprises, "competition was the life of trade"; now that they have filled it, as the handicraftsmen filled the economic areas available to them, capitalism is turning to analogous standards of controlled competition. The allotment of production in the Continental Steel Cartel is not in principle very different from the allotment of production in a fourteenth century gild.

In Germany, "pools," or price-fixing agreements between producers, appeared in the steel industry early in the period of railway construction. They were informal, temporary, and very specifically limited. After the Franco-Prussian War, appeared the cartel, which, generally speaking, was an agreement as to prices, amount of production, division of the market, etc. As in the American trust, the constituent enterprises remained legally separate, and separate as units of management. The syndicate was a modification of this separateness, in that it was a selling organization through which all the members were bound to sell their products. The period of most rapid development was the decade or so just before the World War. In 1905, a government commission reported that there were three hundred eighty-five syndicates. Those in the coal and iron industries outweighed "in importance all the rest put together." The consortium is a still higher order of combination, partly vertical in character: some of the great mining companies and steel companies that produce raw materials for the Siemens electrical concerns are associated with them in a consortium. The imperial government took a decided part in the formation of the Rhenish-Westphalian coal syndicate, and the Prussian government in the formation of the potash syndicate. Their republican successors have continued and extended their policy.

In Great Britain, combinations of this kind appear in somewhat the same industries as in Germany, especially coal and iron, but also in salt, 90 per cent of the production of which is in the hands of the Salt Manufacturers' Association; soap, 70 per cent of which is produced by Lever Brothers, who also control the association; and thread, 90 per cent produced by J. and P. Coats.

In France, the combination is, generally speaking, rather informal and voluntary in character. There are committees of various industries, syndicates, chambers, all of which seem to operate in the first place as bureaus of information for the industry with which they are concerned, and in the second place as policy forming centers. The comparative immaturity of mass production in France seems to justify our regarding them as institutions as yet undeveloped to their essential form.

In the United States, the rapid and unimpeded development of capitalism involved, naturally enough, an early and intensive practice of combination. The harshness and questionableness of the activity of many of the trusts and combinations produced a political reaction between 1887 and the World War, especially in the last decade of that period, that expressed itself in a determined effort to maintain by the most drastic legislation the principle of free and unrestricted competition. Such measures as the Interstate Commerce Act (1887), the Hepburn Railroad Act (1906), the Clayton Antitrust Act (1913), the prosecution of the Standard Oil Company, the dissolution of the Northern Securities Company, and the dissolution of the American Tobacco Company breathe the purest spirit of nineteenth century individualism. Signs were not wanting at the time, nor did they go unrecognized, that the combination of enterprises was essential and desirable in the modern world. President Roosevelt made his famous distinction between "good and bad trusts"; the Supreme Court of the United States enunciated its "rule of reason"—that only combinations exercising an "unreasonable" restraint of trade could be reached by the law; and American business men continued to pursue the essential aim, the combination of enterprises, under forms that avoided the application of the successive legislative enactments. When the packers of meat were forbidden to operate retail outlets, chains of retail stores grew up that bought and operated packing establishments.

The experience of the country during the World War with the centralized control and management of industries produced a decided reaction which at this date (1932) cannot be given a final evaluation but seems to indicate a tendency to make a place in the social structure for combinations in the widest and fullest sense. The special misfortunes of the railroads, as regulated monopolies challenged by the competition of the newer forms of transportation, led to the development of a positive policy of consolidating the railroads of the eastern part of the country into four or five great systems. Agreements between the Interstate Commerce Commission and the greater railroads about which the systems were to be built were completed in 1932. The Federal Trade Commission Act of 1921 removed some of the barriers to combinations of other enterprises by entrusting the Commission with broad discretionary powers. Aside from completed governmental action, it is necessary to take into account the widespread approval of plans to establish centralized control of business in general, such as the plans to restrict certain branches of agricultural production and the plan of Mr. Gerard Swope to organize all industry on a national scale with planned objectives. It is apparent from what has happened and from what is proposed that the swing away from the older ideal of unrestricted competition is well under way; but the whole development is too rudimentary to be more than guessed at in a perspective as long as that of this book. When the historian approaches his own time, his material pushes him over the line between present and past and tempts him to assume the irrelevant function of prophecy.

The Depersonalization of Business

Business has become scientific. The expression "scientific management" has, rather unfortunately, become attached to what might be called the last or at least most recent link in a long chain of efforts to introduce into the management of enterprise the methods and the results of the natural sciences. The first book on "scientific management" (in the broad sense) which this modern European world with which we have been dealing produced was naturally a manual of agriculture and goes back almost to the earliest of the incunabula, namely, Petrus Crescentius, *ruralium commodorum libri XII,* printed in Augsburg in 1471 or 1474. It was followed by a long series of works with similar purposes through the sixteenth century, especially in Italy and Spain, culminating in the great output of the late eighteenth and early nineteenth centuries, for which the names of Arthur Young in England, Parmentier in France, and Thaer in Germany must suffice as representatives. Scientific management in the mining and metal industries was the aim of Agricola (*De re metallica,* 1556) and of Biringuccio (*Della pirotecnica libri X,* 1540). The eighteenth century was the heyday of books aiming to define and promote scientific management in commercial enterprise. Savary's *Le Parfait Négociant* (1675), Defoe's *The Compleat English Tradesman* (1710), the dictionaries of the younger Savary and of Postlethwayt, the statistical work of Gregory King (1696), of Arnauld (1780–1800), and of Peuchet (about 1800) are only casual selections from a great list. During the nineteenth century, quite a series of publications about bank management appeared, such as Bagehot's *Lombard Street* and Jevons' *Money and Banking.*

The study of scientific management in industry began comparatively late. The *Allgemeine Gewerkslehre* (General Shop Principles) of A. Emminghaus (1868) and the books of Andrew Ure (*The Philosophy of Manufactures,* 1835) and Charles Babbage (*On the Economy of Machinery and Manufactures,* 1832), which were concerned only with the cotton industry, are as early monuments of this type as can be found.

The development of problems of natural science in industry gave a new turn to the development of scientific management. In mining and metal industries, in manufacturing and in agricultural production, a whole series of problems fell away from business management into the hands of the technicians, the chemists, the electrical engineers, the mechanical engineers. With them and their functions as such, we are not here concerned, because their very technical character has removed them from the management of business itself. The head of the chemical laboratory of a rubber company, for instance, is readily distinguished from the general manager.

The problem of business management as such was thus reduced to two elements, the problem of organization and the problem of personnel management. It is to the application to these problems in particular of a technology as definite as that of the natural sciences that the modern expression "scientific management" applies.

From another point of view, the penetration of economic life by scientific methods and processes has favored their extension to these last remaining fields. In a sense, every capitalistic enterprise, from a time long before it was the case with the natural sciences, used exact measurement, in the form of double entry bookkeeping. It was for a long time the only scientific character that enterprise had. The "model farms" of eighteenth century England served in empirical fashion to introduce elements of chemistry and biology into English farming and breeding. The trained chemist, appearing early in the nineteenth century in German chemical industry, gave Germany a lead in that field which was not lost until the World War, while the indifference and hostility of English, French, and American manufacturers to the scientific side of their business put them far behind. On the other hand, England and France were in advance of Germany in the creation and utilization of trained engineers. It was not until the last quarter of the nineteenth century that the trained engineer came to dominate in German machine industry.

The expression "scientific management" in its current sense, was coined and popularized by the American engineer Frederick W. Taylor, whose books, beginning with *Shop Management*

(1903), were the beginning of a large body of literature not only in the United States, but especially in Europe. "Industrial engineers," "efficiency experts," concerned not with the handling of materials but with the organization of enterprise in the most rational forms and with the handling of the personnel of the enterprise, are to be found in every large establishment and extend their services even to small establishments through publications of one sort and another. Their functions include the reduction of labor turnover, the dovetailing of jobs, the training of employees, the training of foremen, the selection, promotion, and transfer of employees, the spreading out of overhead expense, the cultivation of willingness, the improved morale of steady workers.

The problem of morale underwent radical transformations in the later evolution of enterprise, and like nearly every other feature of capitalism became mechanical, depersonalized.

On small farms and in small business establishments, it is still possible to see the older phenomenon, a *personal* morale. Not only are the farmers and their employees likely to live together and either like or dislike each other, but the very processes themselves require individual thought, judgment, and decision from each worker. Even in large enterprises, exceptional personalities are able to survive and function as personalities.

In general, however, a complete transformation has dissociated economic occupation from personality. "A great business is really too big to be human. . . . In a big business, the employer, like the employee, is lost in the mass" (Ford). The old system said to the craftsmen: "You are an honorable workman. Produce the kind of goods that it is in you to produce, and we will take it." The modern system says to the wage earner: "Produce so many units of such and such measurements. It is none of your concern what their use is to be, nor whether some modification might suit an individual purchaser better or worse. Produce them and we will pay you such and such sums at the end of the day, which terminates the relationship." Mr. Ford sums it up in a sentence of *My Life and Work:* "To work together, it is not necessary that men should love each other"; or again, "There is not much personal contact—a factory is not a drawing-room. . . . Paternalism has no place in industry. . . . [The development of industry] has since led to an impersonal system wherein the workman has become something less than a person—a mere part of the system."

The "system" which displaced the personal relationships of an earlier day consisted in general in an elaborate division of labor, an intense application and extension of the principle of Adam Smith's famous chapter on the division of labor, from the top to the bottom of the enterprise. In every large enterprise and in a surprisingly large number of smaller ones, appear three semi-independent systems: a system of standards (management), a system of figures (accounting), and a system of instruments. Each of these is divided into subsystems, also semi-independent, with elaborate differentiation. As an example, an actual organization (a machine and bridge building company in Germany) has two main divisions of the management, commercial direction and technical direction. Each of these has five subdivisions, with a total of thirty different offices. This means a radical division of labor not only horizontally—that is, among workers of the same grade—but also vertically, what a German commentator has called "the subalternizing of intellectual work."

This subdivision of control was compensated by a general application of standards of measurement. The extreme development of this process is perhaps the Taylor system of studies of production. The analysis of "lifting a steel roller one meter long, fifty millimeters thick, from the floor to the table of a machine ninety centimeters from the floor" shows eleven distinct movements: the man (1) bends over, (2) with the right hand grasps the roller from above, (3) lifts it, (4) grasps it underneath with the left hand, etc. And the standard time of the operation is established as nineteen seconds. Such procedures are actually used, and they sometimes produce extraordinary economies in operation. They are applied in the industrial process by quite specific directions formulated in advance by an engineering personnel. Thus the whole production line, human and material elements combined, operates in conformity to a rigid standard, and the time, the costs, and the results of the process can be calculated beforehand with a minimum of error.

They are measured in a very elaborate fashion, often automatically, and the measurements constitute the basis of cost accounting, upon which price, selling policy, and general plans are based in turn. Machines in factories are grouped according to their character, and often, when some new modification of a machine appears, a whole group will be scrapped, in order to make way for a more economical type.

The system of instruments, the machines, has reduced substantially the personal element in enterprise, not only in production but also in commerce and transportation. From the earliest beginnings of the human race, the relation of man to his tools has been one of supreme interest. In our own day his development of tools and machines has been enormous. In full capitalism, man was largely displaced in the process of production by the tools he had created. Single machines performed processes that hitherto had required his hand. In the shoe industry, for example, ninety-six distinct actions were taken over by fifty-five different machines which required far fewer hands to control and direct them for a given production of shoes. Apparatus evolved which relieved him even of the function of bringing his work to the machine: the conveyer-belt. In the (extreme) type-organization, he has even been relieved of the responsibility for the care of his machine. If it "goes wrong," it is turned over to the "emergency repair column," for whom it certainly has no personal associations. Repair work seems to be an area, however, where automatization has only limited possibilities, where the human intervention of thought, judgment, decision is necessarily involved.

The effects and significance of this depersonalization are somewhat difficult to define because the process is far from complete. Accounting, through which much of this depersonalization comes about, has been so thoroughly extended and systematized that it may be regarded as complete. Automatization has been completed in many fields, such as the iron and steel industry, the chemical industries, the cement industry; but in many industries the general run of establishments is still far behind the possible standard of automatization as represented by the Ford establishments, which in their most characteristic features are themselves a development of the period since 1914. The full application of production norms represented by Taylorism was hardly more than begun before 1914. Rationalization in these ultimate forms not only is in itself difficult and expensive, but also evokes considerable resistance among the living objects of the process, the laboring classes. In many industries, it is wholly or partly impracticable, as in the porcelain industry, where the craftsman persists, and the mining industry, where "the skilled, thinking, deliberating miner" is still necessary. In general, depersonalization is limited by the possibilities of uniformity in the conditions of production, and especially of uniformity in product.

The general results that are visible at present can be briefly stated. There has been a general decrease in the whole number of workers in proportion to the amount of goods produced and to the amount of capital in the form of producing instruments.[1] In proportion to the total number of employed persons, the number of persons engaged in superintendence has grown larger. In Germany, for example, the proportion of salaried employees in industry rose from 20 per thousand in 1883 to 57 in 1907; in commerce, from 65 to 113; in the most automatized industry

[1] See page 202.

(chemical industry), from 92 to 168. The development in the last decades has been even more rapid in the United States, where the number of salaried employees per thousand of all employed rose from 63 in 1899 to 103 in 1909 and 161 in 1919. Automatization has, on the other hand, reduced the proportionate place of the skilled worker. In the Ford factory at Detroit, 95 per cent of the labor is unskilled. Of the different processes, 43 per cent require only from one to eight days' training, and only 15 per cent, more than one month. A German machine works reports that after rationalization, 75 per cent of its pay roll was unskilled labor.

These processes have brought about, or at least contributed to bringing about, a general reduction of costs of production, a more effective control of enterprise by the entrepreneur, and a greater independence from the limitations of organic labor on the part of the entrepreneur.

The whole process is summed up from the standpoint of the entrepreneur in a classical form by an utterance of Alfred Krupp, the great German steel manufacturer: "What I shall attempt to bring about is, that nothing shall be dependent on the life or existence of any particular person; that nothing of importance shall happen or be caused to happen without the foreknowledge and approval of the management; that the past and the determinable future of the establishment can be learned in the files of the management without asking a question of any mortal."

The ultimate aim of these processes, of course, was the intensification of enterprise, the increase of the application of energy in a business of given size. It appeared in three forms: the economy of space, the economy of materials, and the economy of time.

The saving of space has already been noted as a feature of Western European agriculture.[2] In transportation, it is illustrated by the double-tracking, four-tracking of railroads, use of particular roadbeds by several lines, manipulation of schedules and train

[2] See page 303.

combinations, etc., sufficiently obvious not to need statistical demonstration.

In industry, the economy of space meant the closer crowding of machines and workers into a given space. In some industries, such as flour milling, brewing, cement manufacture, this process seems to have reached its limit. A German observer notes that "a characteristic of the Ford factory is the close placing of the machines." In part, this economy of space is just another aspect of the increase of machines and apparatus in proportion to human labor which has already been discussed.

The economy of materials also can be passed over without specific discussion, although one aspect of it, the development of by-products, constitutes a very important factor of modern economic life and affords many interesting specific instances of the application of technique.

The economy of time raises more complex problems. The use of all the time there is as labor-time—that is, twenty-four hours a day every day in the year—has been attained, largely by superior organization that has overcome most of the objections to it. In the early years of factory industry this tendency pressed very hard upon the human material, as children were often compelled to labor fifteen or sixteen hours a day. Legislation and labor organization, however, and common sense put an end to this rather crude and socially costly form of economy. More characteristic of high capitalism has been what may be called intensive economy of time. It is certainly characteristic of all capitalistic enterprise to attempt to shorten the time between the beginning of a profit process and the reaping of the profits, whether it be in farming, in industry or in commerce. Ford reduced the cycle of production in his factory from twenty-two to fourteen days. As a result, in 1925 he had in his warehouses only about twenty million dollars' worth of capital tied up, about eight days' production. The German iron industry doubled its tempo between 1895 and 1905. The German beet-sugar industry underwent a similar development:

in 1900–1901, 395 factories in 74 days worked 335,500 tons of beets; in 1913–1914, 341 factories in 70 days worked 496,800 tons of beets.

Such results were achieved by various methods. One of the most important was the shortening of the labor period. Marx recognized that an eleven-hour day had been proved in England to be as productive and more economical than a longer day. That a shorter working day may be more profitable for the employer has been rediscovered more than once since his day, in the last instance by Mr. Ford and the late Judge Gary of the United States Steel Corporation. What the limits of this development are has never been adequately tested.

The shortening of the day, however, merely created the subjective condition necessary to an intensification of work, the capacity of the worker to exert more force in a given time. This potentiality was actualized first by the control of the worker through the personal influence of superintendents and foremen and through devices and arrangements which registered his presence and his productivity. These last became purely mechanical: time clocks, weighing and counting machines.

Wage methods were also used to stimulate the worker to the highest productivity. The first step in this direction was the shift from time wages to piece wages. The direct effect was a substantial increase in the productivity of workers. In theory, it should be possible to increase labor productivity up to the physical limits of the laborer, by reducing the wage per piece; experience shows, however, that the stimulating effect is lost as soon as this is done. Some instinctive or conscious opposition leads the worker to reduce his productivity when he knows that an increase will merely be taken as an occasion to reduce the wage. More recently, modifications of the piece system have avoided this anomaly. Premiums or bonuses are given to workers who attain or rise above a certain standard of production. The other costs remain the same (machinery, management, rent, etc.); hence the total cost of the more productive worker's unit-product is less, though his wage is a larger proportion of it. Piecework, however, has made relatively little encroachment on the hour-wage system in industry as a whole. In England, a Board of Trade investigation in 1906 showed it predominant only in one general division, the textile industries (51 per cent; cotton industry, 66 per cent), while it ranged from 17 to 37 per cent in the others.

It would have developed further, had it not been that the development of machinery and of machine systems afforded an even more effective way of calling out the utmost in effort from the laborer. Again, the Ford factory offers the extreme typical case: the movement of the conveyer-belt along the production line determines the rate of production to which all the workers must conform. By paying time wages above the market, Mr. Ford gets an uninterrupted supply of laborers who are willing and able to conform to that very high rate of speed.

From the standpoint of the capitalist investor and entrepreneur, this intensification of production creates an opportunity for the investment of his capital, or, in other words, an opportunity to take over a larger share of the process (and of the rewards) of production as against the laborer. It makes possible cheaper production with larger wages. An example is given by Taylor: In a given case under the customary piece system, $10 per day is paid for wages and $14 for other costs per machine, with a production of five units. The cost per unit is $4.80. Productivity is stimulated by the introduction of the differential system. The more capable worker produces ten units per day and is paid $14.50. The machine cost remains the same, but the cost per unit is only $2.85.

The great advantage, however, lies in the shortening of the capital turnover period, which, at least from the standpoint of the individual capitalist, is the central problem of enterprise. It is a curious anomaly of capitalistic development, which Böhm-Bawerk formulated in his *Positive Theory of Capital*

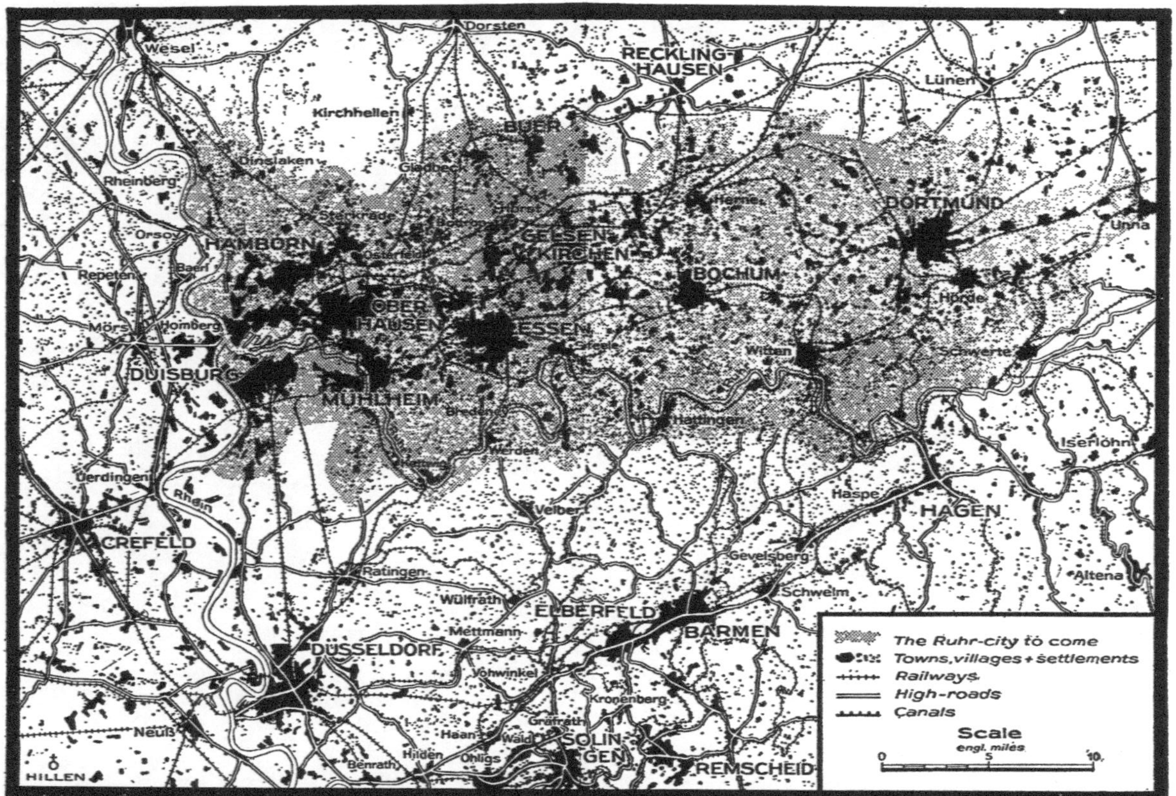

A Territorial Concentration of Industry: the Ruhr Valley in Germany

(1889), that as a whole it has tended to a lengthening of the production cycle. To illustrate in summary fashion: In the handicraft system, if you wished a lock you went to a locksmith and ordered it made; he bought (or you bought) the iron, and in about fourteen days the lock was finished and in your hands. In the capitalist system, you go to the hardware store and buy a lock without waiting, but it was made from three months to a year before you bought it. The primary fact is obvious: Capitalism does tend to lengthen the interval between the production of raw material and the entry into enjoyment (consumption) of the finished product. On the other hand, the desire and the need of the capitalist leads him to shorten that period as much as possible. If Mr. Ford had $100,000 of capital and sold $100,000 worth of automobiles in one year at an average profit of 5 per cent he would make a profit of $5,000 a year. If with the same capital, he sold $100,000 of automobiles each month he would make a profit of $60,000 a year. By means of production and transportation technique, by the speeding up of commercial processes and of money transmission, the latter standard rather than the first is approached. Still another antinomy develops in this connection. The more the capitalist tries to shorten the turnover period by buying new machines, or by setting up new organizations, the greater becomes the amount of "fixed" capital to be turned, and therefore the longer becomes the process.

REFERENCES FOR FURTHER READING

General

Sombart, W. Der moderne Kapitalismus, vol. III, pp. 712–948.

The Financing of Capitalistic Enterprise

Edwards, G. W. International Trade Finance (1924).

Joseph, L. Industrial Finance: A Comparison Between Home [British] and Foreign Development (1911).

Meade, E. S. Corporation Finance (1912).
Passow, R. Die A. G. [Allgemeine Gesellschaft] (2nd ed., 1922).
Riesser, J. The German Great Banks and Their Concentration (1911).
Strasser, Karl. Die deutschen Banken im Auslande (2nd ed., 1925).
Thorp, W. L. The Integration of Industrial Operations (U. S. Census Monographs, III, 1924).
Veblen, Thorstein. Absentee Ownership (1917).

Trusts and Cartels

British Ministry of Reconstruction. Report of Committee on Trusts (1919).
Cushing, A. Voting Trusts (1915).
Jenks, J. W. The Trust Problem (5th ed., 1929).
Jones, Eliot. The Trust Problem in the United States (1924).
Lawson, Thomas. Frenzied Finance (1911).
Macrosty, H. W. The Trust Movement in British Industry (1907).
Myers, G. History of the Great American Fortunes (3 vols., 1911).
Wiedenfeld, K. Cartels and Combines (1927).
Williams, D. J. Capitalist Combination in the Coal Industry (1924).

The Intellectualization of Business Management

Ashley, William (Sir). Business Economics (1926).
Brassey, T. Work and Wages (1872).
Clark, J. M. Studies in the Economics of Overhead Costs (1923).
Comstock, L. M. Modern Retail Methods, Records and Accounting (1925).
Duclos, Léon. Les Transformations du commerce de detail en France au XIXe siècle (1902).
Dutton, H. P. Business Organization and Management (1926).
Ford, Henry. My Life and Work (1922).
Jones, E. D. The Administration of Industrial Enterprises (1925).
Kimball, D. S. Principles of Industrial Organization (3rd ed., 1925).
Lincoln, E. E. Applied Business Finance (2nd ed., 1923).
Slosson, E. E. Creative Chemistry (1920).
Taylor, F. W. Principles of Scientific Management (1911).
Wegleben, Fritz. Die Rationalisierung im deutschen Werkzeugmaschinenbau (1924).

CHAPTER VIII

THE RATIONALIZATION OF ECONOMIC LIFE AS A WHOLE

The Physiocrats

The problem of rationalization which has been the subject of the last chapters has been relatively simple because it has been a problem of rationalization with reference to a very simple principle, the principle of unrestricted profits. This chapter, however, is concerned with the rationalization, in a slightly difference sense, of the economic life as a whole with reference to principles which, far from being generally assumed or agreed upon, are on the contrary the subject of laborious search and of violent disagreements. The rationalization here in question has had a history almost coeval with high capitalism: it is tempting to regard it as a function of capitalism itself. At any rate, since Adam Smith published *The Wealth of Nations* in 1776, there has been an increasing and intensifying attempt on the part of the intellectuals of capitalistic society to reduce to systematic form the vast complexities of economic life.

As a phenomenon of intellectual history, Smith's *Wealth of Nations* needs to be related to the work of his predecessors—not so much those who like Turgot were working in the same direction, as those who, like the mercantilists and the physiocrats, conceived and formulated economic life in a wholly different fashion—the body of thought with reference to which *The Wealth of Nations* was revolutionary. Mercantilism has already been discussed: it must suffice here to say that, as a system, it was the elaboration of the idea that economic life functioned for the whole society, conceived as the state, and should be directed by the state for its interest. The actual method of serving that interest was the encouragement and promotion of capitalistic industry and commerce.

The physiocrats and Adam Smith represent two aspects of a rebellion against this principle and especially against this method. Despite the large development of industry and commerce which has been described, in all of the countries in which capitalism developed, agriculture retained an effective predominance in the economic sense. As a natural consequence of that predominance, thinkers were not lacking to advocate a corresponding preponderance in the political sense. It was necessary to criticize the current dogmas of mercantilism. This criticism, in the highly intellectualized atmosphere of the eighteenth century, took the form of the system which one of its exponents called *physiocratic,* but which Adam Smith appropriately called the Agricultural System. Generally, the physiocrats called themselves "the economists."

The dogmas of physiocracy in brief summary were as follows: First, as to method, they rested upon the prevalent eighteenth century concept of "natural law," a natural order which, it was presumed, was better than the "positive order," and which therefore should control it. It was apparent that all wealth came from the earth and that the surplus or net product after the needs of those who extracted it were provided for, was the whole support of the rest of society. Merchants and manufacturers did not increase the wealth of the nation because what they added, much as it was worth, did not constitute a net product. Hence, the physiocrats demanded that the government should devote itself to the development of the extractive industries, especially agriculture, and abandon all efforts to regulate, direct, or promote manufacturing and commerce. What they brought to the nation, money or a favorable balance of trade, was not wealth; surplus wheat, surplus fish, surplus almost anything, was wealth but money was not. This, perhaps, was their most radical advance upon the mercantilists as economic thinkers. They also had distinct glimmerings of the function of capital and the necessity of some return to it in an economic scheme, but these glimmerings were not clear, full light until the physiocratic fashion of thinking was displaced by a more powerful one.

The home of physiocracy was France, and the principal physiocrats were Frenchmen. Quesnay (1694–1774) was the greatest and most original among them. How radical his thought was with reference to his times is illustrated by the maxim attributed to him: "Poor peasant, poor kingdom; poor kingdom, poor king." It will be noticed that like the mercantilists, the physiocrat found the justification of economic organization in what it did for the king, as the embodiment of the state. Gournay (1712–1759) was a great official of the French monarchy, whose ideas were worked out in administrative proposals rather than in systematic writing. He labored to have the government adopt the policy of restricting its activity to the removal of all regulation from commerce and industry. Turgot (1727–1781), who for a hectic eighteen months was Comptroller-General, a finance minister, is important as an economic thinker, less for his connections with the physiocratic group than because of his divergence from them in a direction which they scarcely realized. In his *Réflexions sur la formation et distribution des richesses* (1766–1769), Turgot recognized more clearly than any predecessor the central element of the economic system that was developing; namely, the separation of ownership of the tools of production from the use of them, capital and labor.

Adam Smith and the Classical School

In 1776, Adam Smith published *The Wealth of Nations,* which was the starting point of a new line of thought about economic affairs that is still viable. What was the revolutionary or differential character of his teaching? Like the physiocrats, he was antimercantilist. For him, wealth was not money, regulation and restriction was conspicuously a failure, natural law and natural order was the final norm, the best economic policy was the removal of impediments and obstructions to "natural" economic life. Like Josiah Child, he regarded menial servants, public officials, and professional men as "unproductive."

The new, revolutionary, different element in Smith's work was its envisagement of the economic aspects of life from the standpoint of the entrepreneur. Like the mercantilists and the physiocrats before him, he sought the nature and causes of the wealth of nations, but that wealth, for him, came from the unrestricted activities of the entrepreneur. Economic life in his day had already taken on a definite and fairly uniform pattern, with the industrialist and the merchant emerging quite clearly as the agents of very considerable additions to the wealth of England. It was obvious to the physiocrats that mercantilism had broken down; it was obvious to Smith that wealth did not come only from land. His conception required a deliberate approach to the question what value is, as a criticism of the rather casual assumption of Quesnay and his followers that value came only from the earth or was attached only to materials which came out of the earth. Like them, he distinguished between value in use and exchange value; but he was concerned only with exchange value, the power which a commodity possesses of purchasing other goods. The "first price" was labor, "the toil and trouble" that a man went to to acquire something. It is even the measure of value; the value in exchange of any commodity "is equal to the quantity of labor which it enables him [the owner] to purchase or command. Labor, therefore, is the real measure of the exchangeable value of all commodities."

What Smith saw clearly, and where he made his revolutionary contribution, was that wealth somehow came from labor and that more might come if it were properly organized. Hence the major and early place which he gives to "the division of labor," the subject of his most famous chapter. Here was the function of the entrepreneur plainly indicated as a leading part in the economic activity of the nation. The self-interest of the economic agent, the entrepreneur, would suffice, according to Smith, to bring about all desired economic advance. "The sovereign is completely discharged from . . . the duty of superintending the industry of private people." No feature of Smith's teaching was more fully appropriated by his generation than this doctrine of *laisser faire*.

Smith's teaching was in its essence the rationalization of what he saw and felt developing in his own time. It had deficiencies that are now obvious. His definition of value was tentative and undeveloped. He was so far from recognizing the actualities of even his own time that he supposed that the interests of the landlords (those who live by rent) might safely be taken as the index of the interests of the nation and as a guide for legislation; while the entrepreneurs (men who live by profit) have interests quite at variance with those of society as a whole. Wage earners, on the other hand, he held, were too ignorant to understand either their own interest or that of society. In the field of industry, his theories referred to the putting-out system rather than to the factory system.

Space is lacking to demonstrate fairly the deficiencies of *The Wealth of Nations*. Enough has been abstracted, however, to demonstrate that the book has shortcomings as an explanation of how economic society works, or as a proposal for its betterment. Yet, like mercantilism, Smith's system was sufficient in its day because it brought into the social consciousness the predominance of the function actually destined to do the creative work of the next generation, the function of the entrepreneur. Smith, more than any other man of his century, set the example of creating systems that accounted for the whole of economic life, and by so doing, gave economic thought a rationalistic deductive habit which has never been shaken off, even by his critics and opponents.

Thomas Robert Malthus (1766–1834) reinforced the systematic

character of Smith's thought by enunciating a "natural" law of population. He started from two assumptions that were based on imperfect observation and were quite false: (1) that the minimum rate of population increase was by a geometric ratio—that is, that each individual would have at least two children (each couple four); and (2) that subsistence could increase only by an arithmetical ratio. More concretely, he held that population, *when unchecked,* goes on doubling itself every twenty-five years, while "*considering the present average state of the earth,* the means of subsistence could not possibly be made to increase faster than in an arithmetical ratio." These principles were enunciated in a world in which large progenies, legitimate and illegitimate, were the rule rather than the exception, but also a world in which the turnip and the clover were increasing cows and sheep as rapidly as the human race that subsisted on them, in which technical advances in agriculture were doubling and tripling the food production of grains, in which the potato and the sugar beet were adding immense resources of sustenance, in which the Mississippi valley was being rapidly added to Europe's potential food areas. These were data which were easily available to him; a very little historical imagination might also have led him to the conclusion that large families were not always the rule even in prosperous periods and areas. A little biology and a little arithmetic might have reminded him that only a part of the age groups at any given time were reproducing themselves in geometric ratios.

The functional relation of Malthus' theory to his time, of course, was in the conclusion which he or others drew from his principles, that attempts at social betterment were vain. Even so acute a mind and so generous a spirit as John Stuart Mill drew back from the advocacy of governmental interference to better the conditions of labor, a logical conclusion of his own thought, because of his belief in Malthusianism.

Nevertheless, Malthus raised the question of propulation to a major place in economic thought. Since his time, it has been necessary to take the question into consideration in all economic thinking.

Malthus was an important supplement to Smith; David Ricardo (1772–1823) started economic thought in a new direction. What we would today call a "millionaire radical," he described economic life, not in terms of a common purpose embodied in the state, but as a conflict between classes. The Napoleonic wars, and especially the critical economic situation following 1815, had led to a bitter struggle between the agricultural landlords and the industrialists over the question of the corn laws (laws maintaining the price of grain at certain levels). The manufacturers of course wished the corn laws abolished in order that their employees might have food without having wages that increased the costs of manufacturing above competitive limits. The landlords wished high prices for grain in order to keep rents at a high level. The question was, whether it was desirable that the landlords or the manufacturers should have the advantage of favorable state action.

In these circumstances, Ricardo published his *Principles of Political Economy* (1817), which was destined to dominate orthodox economic thought until the emergence of the "psychological" school in 1871. With many ideas derived and even simplified from the work of Smith and Malthus, Ricardo made several contributions of the highest order (in the historical sense) to the course of economic thought. Although his Malthusianism led him to lay down the "iron" law of wages, profits were left to the flexible margin between costs and production. This was the idea that Marx later was to develop as the conflict of labor and capital over their respective shares of the surplus value (*Mehrwert*). Rent, according to Ricardo, was the competitive estimate by farmers bidding for a piece of land, of the value of the produce it yields over and above what a similar area of the poorest land in cultivation would yield to a like outlay of capital and labor. Profits tend to fall, because the quantity of labor required to provide necessities for the laborers on marginal land increases as the powers of the soil decline more rapidly than agricultural improvements counteract the decline. Wages go down because laborers grow too plentiful. Only rent rises, because the declining margin of cultivation means larger rents in produce, and each unit of produce means larger purchasing power over manufactured goods. "The interest of the landlord is always opposed to that of the consumer and manufacturer." "There is no way of keeping profits up but by keeping wages down." "Nothing contributes so much to the prosperity and happiness of a country as high profits"—but prosperity stimulates the accumulation of capital, reduces profits, and thus destroys itself.

Most of Ricardo's conclusions also have proved untenable, but he did introduce human elements, if only elements of conflict, into the almost exclusively material concepts of his predecessors. For thirty years, the *Principles* of Ricardo remained alone, the sacred text of the now dominant industrialists. Even John Stuart Mill, whose *Principles* appeared in 1848, only added hopefulness and social sympathy to Ricardo's "dismal science."

By this time, economics began to split into several divergent branches. Besides the "orthodox" successors of Smith and Malthus, nationalism, socialism, and institutionalism were clearly emergent by Ricardo's time. For convenience, however, we shall trace the development of the orthodox school and return later to the others. In 1871, Stanley Jevons in his *Theory of Political Economy* laid down the principle that pleasures and pains, not values, wealth, or profits, were the ultimate quantities in economics. From this and similar ideas developed the idea of marginal utility—the idea that one can have too much of a good thing—that a man will pay a great deal to obtain one meal, but not to obtain a second one at the same time. This concept of margins in relation to economic concepts seems to have descended rather slowly from Malthus, who used it to explain the bringing into cultivation of the poorer lands. Ricardo used a similar idea for the basis of his theory of rent. The psychological school applied the marginal analysis to the concept of value and defined exchange value as equivalent to the utility of the last or next possible addition to a stock. Walras in France, Menger in Austria, and John Bates Clark in America, made the psychological approach fairly predominant up to the World War. It is now undergoing radical criticism, both external from the standpoint of the historical school, and internal, on account of its lack of correlation with the advances of modern psychology.

Nevertheless, the psychological school marked an important departure from the trend of the earlier economists. It discovered that the economic system was made for man, not man for the system. By emphasizing the subjective character of value, it put men, as individuals rather than as groups, at the center of their structure. The "iron laws" of the earlier economists, which were being attacked from other points of view, were thoroughly corroded by this criticism from within the orthodox succession.

The Divergent Schools of Economic Thought

Meanwhile, the orthodox economy had not been free from radical criticism, destructive in intention if not in effect. Two eccentric Scotchmen, Lord Lauderdale (1759–1839) and John Rae, a Scotch-Canadian-American, who wrote about the same time, exposed a serious weakness of Smith and his followers by pointing out that social wealth was not identical with the wealth of individuals. Sismondi (1773–1842), a Swiss, although he began, one might almost say, as a devout follower of Adam Smith, turned Smith's ideas around. Where Smith had derived "the wealth of nations" from production, Sismondi's central fact, once his thought was fully developed, was that national revenue, the profits on land and capital plus the annual labor power, was the true test of wealth. He had begun to see the evil to large groups of population which the intensified production consequent upon capitalistic organization and dear to the orthodox economists had involved. Although he radically criticized Malthus, that economist's influence is visible in Sismondi's opinion that the end of political economy was the discovery of that proportion between population and wealth ("the national revenue") which should assure the highest well-being. Sismondi is interesting also because of his marked historicism, which was exceptional among economists in his time.

The orthodox economists, beginning with Smith, with their strong derivation from eighteenth century rationalism, were cosmopolitan, universalist in their aims. Their principles were conceived as universals, always and everywhere true. Their subject was really the wealth of individuals and how the state might promote it. On the other hand, the strong nationalism, essentially noneconomic in character, which was to rival and limit the capitalism equally characteristic of the nineteenth century, dictated a rationalization of economic society in its terms. Such was the aim of the "nationalists," of whom Müller, List, and Carey are only early and prominent examples. Adam Müller (1779–1829), a reactionary romanticist, criticized Smith somewhat as Lauderdale and Rae had done, and, more significantly, elevated the assumption of the mercantilists into a dogma. National power is the fundamental concern, since all individual values are gained in and through it. Müller was a true romanticist; he imagined that the economic life of the Middle Ages was the normal condition of economic life for all times.

Henry C. Carey (1793–1879) was a philanthropic American who attempted without significant success the overthrow of Ricardo and Malthus, but who is of importance as an example of the nationalist school. He also exercised a surprisingly large influence, not only on German, French, and English thinkers who accepted more or less of his ideas, but even upon his most drastic opponents. He compelled a restatement of the Ricardian theory of rent. Herbert Spencer adopted his idea that there is an antagonism between the intellectual and generative functions, and that, in consequence, as the level of general education rises, the rate of growth of population tends to decrease, so that population is really self-checked.

It is as a nationalist, however, and especially as a protectionist, that Carey is most significant. The development of civilization in America (where he was writing) involved the development of a diversified economic life, as the basis of higher forms of association. Following the English policy of free trade would mean that America would become merely a great farm for a city called England. Even for England, free trade and the dependence on foreign trade is bad. Already, in his time, England was obliged to seek new markets in place of those she had exhausted. Any change in policy or interruption of trade by war or natural calamity must bring misery to the English people. One of his arguments wakes curious echoes of mercantilism and of physiocracy: "The consumer must take his place beside the producer in order to enable man to comply with the condition on which he obtains loans from the great bank of mother earth—the simple condition that when he shall have done with the capital furnished him, he shall return it to the place whence it has been taken." [1]

Friedrich List (1789–1846) was a German professor who in 1820 was exiled to America, where he became a successful editor and speculator in coal mines and railways. His American experience profoundly influenced him. "There only," he wrote, "have I obtained a clear idea of the gradual development of the economy of a people." His first years in the United States were those when Henry Clay was enunciating his "American System" and John Quincy Adams was formulating the magnificent program of national development which is so attractive even in retrospect and had so little realization. To a German liberal, whose fatherland was still shackled in a medieval localism, all this ap-

[1] See pp. 235, 386. See also Fairchild, "The Fallacy of Profits," Harper's Magazine, Feb., 1932.

pealed very powerfully. He went back to Germany as American consul at Leipzig. As an economic writer, he rationalized his American experience, and combined some ideas that he picked up from American economists, notably Daniel Reymond, with the emphasis upon the state as a cultural form which Müller represented, and which was common to nearly all German thinkers of the time. Like Carey, he held that no high state of civilization could be attained without manufactures, that an agricultural people were necessarily rude and barbarous.

As became a romanticist and a nationalist, List was markedly historical in his approach to the general problem. Just as arbitrarily as the rationalists whom he criticized, he postulated a series of five stages through which the economic life of nations passes, beginning with the hunting and fishing stage and culminating in a stage that was characterized by a complex economic life including agriculture, commerce, and manufacturing. The function of the government varied according to the stage of development. When the final stage of complex economic life arrived, it was time for the government to introduce measures of encouragement to manufacturers, particularly protective tariffs. It will be observed that List's stages have relatively little relation to actual historical fact, and that they serve principally to bolster up his argument for protection. Nevertheless, good history or bad history, recourse to historical support was an element of his thought that grew constantly more important. It was a criticism of the rational absolutism of the classical school that was ultimately to make its apparently irrefragable systems yield to more organic conceptions.

Perhaps the most original and valuable feature of his work was the more rational, less mystic turn which he gave to Müller's dogma that immaterial things also had value. Value is produced, List taught, not only by labor, not even principally by labor; most value depends upon the proper organization of society, good laws and good policy, good education and good economic organization. Hence, all that contributes to such ends—the work of teachers or of governmental officials, for example—is truly productive of value.

The nationalists, especially Carey and List, had a political influence all out of proportion to the purely scientific import of their teaching. They fell in with the powerful nationalistic sentiment of their day, and at the same time their doctrine served the interests of the dominant entrepreneurs dynamically and positively, as those of Malthus and Ricardo did negatively. The measure of their influence is the vast development of protectionist systems throughout the European world.

Under the influence of List, the German economists have maintained a distinct branch of study which they call *Nationalökonomie,* the study of national policies, in distinction to *Volkswirtschaft,* which may be translated natural economy, social economy, or simply economics.

The Institutionalists and the Historical School

When Adam Smith wrote *The Wealth of Nations,* historical thinking was very much out of fashion. Before Karl Marx wrote *Das Kapital,* the nineteenth century renaissance of history was well under way. It was quite in keeping with the times that the interval should see the development of a historical approach to an understanding of economic organization as well as a radical criticism from the historical point of view of the limited assumptions and the deductive method of the classical economists.

Richard Jones (1790–1855), in his *Essay on the Distribution of Wealth and on the Sources of Taxation* (1831), assailed the abstract assumptions of Ricardo's teaching by showing that, in actual rent systems of the past and in other lands, they were simply not true. This created the antinomy over which historians and economists have been quarreling ever since. The Ricardians could correctly reply that they were not talking about what happened to actual rents in any limited period of time, but about the long-run tendency inherent in the nature of the relation defined—as defined.

Walter Bagehot (1826–1877), an English banker, pointed out the historical limitation of political economy. "The science of Political Economy as we have it in England may be defined as the science of business, *such as business is in large productive and trading communities*"—that is to say, as it was after the Industrial Revolution. He presents economic society from an evolutionary point of view in his *Physics and Politics* (1872). Thomas Edward Cliffe Leslie (1825?–1882), another historian of land systems, pointed out that the Ricardians assumed society to be stationary, whereas it was generally progressive. Like the German historical school, he insisted that man was not an abstraction but "the actual human being such as history and surrounding circumstances have made him." The English historical school represented by men like Toynbee, Thorold Rogers, Ashley, Cunningham, in hundreds of concrete historical monographs, spread out the factual bases of economic thought over wide ranges of English and medieval history.

The historical school developed with special significance in Germany. Roscher (1817–1894), Hildebrand (1812–1878), and Karl Knies (1821–1898) were the chief early representatives. Like their English fellows, they were strongly influenced by the historical jurisprudence developing under the leadership of Sir Henry Maine and Savigny. They denied the finality of economic "laws." Roscher was disposed to substitute the concrete historical data for the assumptions of the rationalists, but Knies insisted that history could not furnish identities as bases of "laws," but only analogies. The German historical school later turned more to theory. Gustav von Schmoller (1838–1917) and Karl Bücher attempted a combination of the historical-inductive and rational-deductive methods. Bücher in his *Entstehung der Volkswirtschaft*

(1893; translated as *Industrial Evolution,* 1896) undertook to formulate the laws of economic evolution.

Another tendency, of which Othmar Spann and Sombart are representatives, relegates the theory to a subordinate rôle, making the object of historical study understanding rather than explanation—in short, what history is in the minds of its highest representatives.

A radical criticism of the industrial order and its classical exponents came from the exponents of the good life, as opposed to goods. As Tawney, Weber, and Sombart in different terms have shown, Protestantism never felt any serious incompatibility with the capitalist orientation. The Catholic Church, however, with its tradition of poverty as the highest form of religious life, with its long identification with an agricultural society and its Augustinian interpretation of the universe as the City of God, could not and did not identify itself with "progress." The Syllabus of Errors which Pope Pius IX issued in 1864 listed as one of the principal errors the doctrine that "the Roman pontiff can and ought to reconcile himself to, and make terms with, progress, liberalism and civilization as lately conceived." To the nineteenth century liberals this seemed like blasphemy. To them progress, business, fortune making, technology had become a fairly defined religion, the very manifestation of God. It seemed to them that the Catholic Church had taken the last step in alienating itself from the modern world. In 1930, the encyclical of Pius XI, which was in direct sequence with Pius IX's *De novis rebus,* was given a wholly different reception, acclaimed everywhere as an important utterance.

The essentially Protestant voices of Thomas Carlyle and John Ruskin were raised to the same effect. In his *Past and Present,* Carlyle evoked an idealized picture of feudalism in which there was no place for the black misery which he saw about him in industrial England. Not even Marx used harsher epithets for the basic ideas of capitalism. John Ruskin attacked the whole classical economy as a science of "illth" instead of a science of wealth, and challenged the economists with a definition of value: "*There is no wealth but life.* Life, including all its powers of love, of joy, and of admiration. That country is the richest which nourishes the greatest number of noble and happy human beings; that man is richest, who having perfected the functions of his own life to the utmost, has also the widest influence both personal and by means of his possessions, over the lives of others." Ruskin's point of departure was his esthetic interpretation of life. His economic teaching was a protest against the ugliness that was so prominent a feature of industrialism, extending to homes and clothes as well as to the factories and public architecture.

The Socialists

The fundamental idea of the nationalists, that economic activity and organization should be subservient to the general interest of society, was also the starting point of the socialist criticism. Socialism, although that particular connotation of the word has become subordinate, was originally a term set in opposition to the individualism which was characteristic of Smith and his successors. In broad summary, that school said, "Make way for the entrepreneur." The socialists argued that society was made up predominantly of the poor and the miserable, and on one ground or another that economic life should be reorganized in their interest rather than that of the rich and the powerful. In particular, they criticized the ideas of private property and free competition.

The early socialists of the nineteenth century are called utopians. The utopians sought to improve the lot of the poor (and ultimately to regenerate mankind) by bringing down aid to the poor from above. Saint-Simon (1760–1825) advocated the reorganization of government as an association for industrial purposes. His followers went beyond him and demanded the abolition of private property and the socialization through the reorganized state of the instruments of labor. The associationists proceeded by ignoring the question of political organization. Two of the most prominent, the Englishman, Robert Owen (1771–1858), and the Frenchman, Charles Fourier (1772–1837), established communities in which life in common was practiced with some success. Some Fourieristic communities, indeed, still exist in France, notably the one at Guise. Both were much imitated in America. Brook Farm was Fourierist. New Harmony, Indiana, was founded by Robert Owen himself.

Utopianism, however, made rather heavy calls upon the moral as well as the intellectual character of its practicing adherents. It became apparent that, in society as it existed, the mere example of a few "come-outers" living a happy and harmonious, simple life in a Fourierist phalanstery or an Owenite community, was not sufficient to induce any general imitation, especially since the expected harmony did not always prevail. In a society that every day was becoming more industrial and more competitive, the utopians showed a strong disposition to agricultural self-sufficiency. Louis Blanc (1811–1882), a French journalist and historian of the Revolution, attempted to meet that difficulty by proposing the application of the communal idea to industrial establishments under the auspices of the State. In *L'Organisation du travail* (1841) he proposed that the state should set up workshops under the control and direction of workmen, to compete with the private, capitalistically organized shops. In that competition, he assumed, the private workshops would be beaten and in time, the social workshops would multiply until private enterprise would be eliminated.

The Revolution of 1848 in France seemed to offer Blanc a great opportunity, as it was achieved mainly by the revolutionary ardor of the Paris proletariat, and Blanc became a member of the new government. He forced the recognition of the right to work and secured the appointment of a labor commission to study the problem and make recommendations. Meanwhile, under the direction of a hostile politician, Emile Thomas, a system of labor called "national workshops," but only faintly resembling Blanc's idea, was established to keep the large unemployed population of Paris quiet, and out of the control of Blanc and his commission. When the national government got organized and considered itself strong enough to act, it swept away the whole arrangement, Blanc himself, his commission, and the "national workshops." A serious insurrection of the working-class adherents of Blanc was savagely repressed after four days of terrible street fighting.

With the repression of the Paris workingmen, utopian socialism was practically dead. It was the function of Karl Marx (1818-1883) to transform socialism from a program of pious intentions for philanthropically minded people into a movement destined to shake thrones and governments, and into an intellectual system destined to affect increasingly all social thought since his day. Marx's system was in a way a synthesis of most of the divergent movements of economic thought from the time of Smith to his own day. He was as historical as Roscher; as programmatic as any of the utopians; as insistent on the predominance of social interest over individual interest as any nationalist. He was even a good classical economist—his analysis was as close as John Stuart Mill's to that of Ricardo. Like other geniuses, he took what he wanted where he found it and made it his own.

Marx knew so much and had so many ideas, always clever ones, but generally disconnected and often contradictory, that summary statement is more than ordinarily apt to be misleading. Even his followers disagree violently about what he taught. The man who in some sense was his heir and literary executor, another one who was the ablest socialist writer of his time, and the founder of the greatest socialist state (Bernstein, Kautsky, Lenin) represent three radically divergent interpretations of his thought. Certainly a central element of his teaching was his interpretation of history. Here his point of departure was the philosophy of

Hegel, who conceived history as the unfolding of the Idea, a process of inexorable change. Marx revised the Hegelian concept, reducing the Idea as the embodiment of reality to the mere reflection of reality in the human mind, but kept the concept of history as a process of inexorable change and kept also the Hegelian dialectic, which was a method of arriving at truth by means of oppositions.

The inexorable process, then, according to Marx, was the evolution of mankind through a series of stages, somewhat like those of Sismondi and List. The character of each stage and of all its various aspects was determined by the mode of production. In each stage, society was broadly divided into two groups, the exploiters and the exploited, between which there was a constant class struggle, which was the essential mode of progress from one stage to another. Each successive exploiting class, however, destroyed itself—note the Hegelian contradiction—and went down at last when it had become unbearable to the exploited class.

The stage which had been reached was that of capitalism. The capitalists were the exploiters; the proletariat, the exploited. Capitalism was destroying itself by concentration. The condition of the wage earners becomes more and more miserable. When, at last, the process is complete, when all the means of production have been concentrated in a few hands, when the condition of the proletariat has become unbearable, the capitalist expropriators will themselves be expropriated by a class war between the bourgoisie and the proletariat, and the new proletarian state will take over the whole machinery of wealth production.

For his analysis of the existing economic system, Marx hardly went beyond Ricardo. With somewhat less qualification than Ricardo, he declared that the value of all commodities is measured and determined by the labor required to produce them. He proceeded in very roundabout fashion to prove that the laborer produces more than he receives. The iron law of wages keeps his commodity, *labor power,* down in the scale of value to the amount of *labor* necessary to produce the food, clothing, housing, and other things which are necessary to maintain the labor power. If that amount is five hours a day, the workman in another five hours is producing *surplus value* (*Mehrwert*), which the capitalist keeps for himself, under the sanction of the existing morality. Even the workman does not know he is being robbed, because he receives the fair equivalent of his labor power according to the Ricardian theory of value.

All this structure has gone into the limbo of discarded theories along with the Ricardian theory of which it was only an elaboration and along with the particular forecast of the future evolution of European society which Marx thought his formulation of history permitted him to make. Values are produced, values disappear at times and in quantities that have no relation to the amount of labor expended. The proletariat has not become more miserable. Concentration has been limited both by economic and by political considerations. The Hegelian dialectic, even the Darwinianism of which Marx shows some signs, have been displaced by more organic thought. The errors of Marx might make a book as substantial as *Das Kapital* itself.

What then is the persisting significance of Marx, especially in reference to the problem of this chapter, the effort to rationalize economic society as a whole. More than any other man of the nineteenth century, Marx fixed the attention of students on the historical aspects of this problem. As Professor W. C. Mitchell puts it, "Marx saw the central problem of economics in the cumulative change of economic institutions; . . . he showed how vital economic theory becomes when it is attacked from this side, especially if the current processes of change are projected into the future." In another sense, he has been important because of the questions he raised. His work was the discovery of capitalism as a system of economic life, as a phenomenon in history, and this discovery raised hundreds of new questions which are still *the* problems of economics. His conclusions were so startling to his contemporaries that they ignored the importance of his method; but by the last decade of the century Sidney Webb in England, Werner Sombart in Germany, and Thorstein Veblen in America were effecting the combination of historical method and scientific intention that Marx exemplified.

The followers of Marx showed a marked historical tendency, indeed almost absorbed, or were absorbed by, the historical school. With the revival of intellectualism in history marked by the appearance of the historical philosophies of Croce and Spengler, they are tending to become indistinguishable, except by a deeper concern with the consistency of their thought, from the historians as such, who themselves have been drawn toward the orbit of Marx. The socialism of Marx was promptly hardened into a dogma by the development of national and international parties based on his program. Both his intellectual followers and his party were split by the question of "revisionism," formally raised by Eduard Bernstein in 1899, but actually implicit in the development of socialistic legislation by Bismarck after 1880, and in the development of Fabianism (the policy of piecemeal advance) in England. Bernstein's book took into account the flaws in Marx's reasoning which had put his scientific adherents into a false position, and proposed that the theory should be reconstructed. He challenged especially two doctrines of Marx, that capitalism would naturally destroy itself and that the process of concentration was inevitable.

Anarchism had troubled the socialists from the beginning. At the very starting point there is something in common, a sense of the injustice of existing institutions. The drift of the socialists toward state socialism created a breach that was marked by the expulsion of the anarchists in 1872. The anarchist hostility to the state later received considerable organization under the influence of Georges Sorel, whose *Réflexions sur la violence* (1909) spread the ideal of revolution by doing nothing. The state, the organ of bourgeois control, was to be done away with by means of the general strike. Then the unions were to take over their respective industries, with no further organization but a kind of federation among the unions. Gild socialism in England is essentially syndicalism with the consumers included, and without the proposals of violence. The Industrial Workers of the World (the I.W.W., the "wobblies") is syndicalist in its origins, but has latterly been much influenced by bolshevism.

The Bolshevists claim to be pure Marxists. Only recently a Bolshevist professor was disciplined for saying that Lenin thought certain revisions of Marx were needed. Kautsky, the German socialist, who led the opposition to the revisionists of 1899, claimed that the Bolshevists were not orthodox because they maintained the capitalist state and through it established "the dictatorship of the proletariat." Although Marx was generally a believer in the nineteenth century liberal doctrine of the rule of the majority, there is no doubt that in 1875 he did say that the transition from capitalism to the socialist régime would be marked by a dictatorship.

In spite of its close intellectual relations to the nationalism of Müller and List, and in spite of a marked tendency to use the national state, socialism has always professed internationalism. In 1864, this aspect was organized in "The International Workingmen's Association"—the International, the First International—which lasted until the conservative reaction after 1870 and the quarrel over anarchism weakened it to the extent of causing its dissolution in 1876. In another fifteen years, socialism had grown sufficiently to justify the formation of the Second International, which between 1891 and 1914 held regular congresses at which orthodoxy was defined and redefined, and some—not many—common policies determined upon. The outbreak of the World War was as fatal to the socialist International as it was to the supposed internationalism of the capitalists. Although the Socialist parties of France and Germany were pledged not to vote war credits, in each country they supported the War at the beginning on the ground that it was defensive, or more accurately, because they were swept away by war hysteria.

A few feeble attempts were made by the Second International to stop the war. In 1917, at the behest of the more radical socialists led by Lenin, the Second International summoned a conference at Stockholm which, partly because of the refusal of the English and French governments to give passports to delegates, failed to bring any pressure to bear on the belligerent governments.

The failure at Stockholm and the success of the Bolshevist Revolution in Russia led to the formation of the Third International. In 1919 and 1920, successive meetings at Moscow of the more revolutionary elements laid down the tenets of a new orthodoxy, and declared war on the whole capitalist system and the old "yellow" Social Democratic parties, on imperialism, and on militarism. Only socialists innocent of any compromise, intellectual or practical, with capitalism were to be admitted. The organization was highly centralized under the domination of a small committee at Moscow and became in fact an agency of the groups that controlled the Soviet government.

Meanwhile, the Second International reorganized at Bern. The withdrawal of the more radical elements fixed the essentially liberal character which had already been manifested. The dictatorship of the proletariat was condemned and the use of democratic methods of revolution prescribed. A program of action adjusted to these principles was laid down. Some attempt was made to come to an understanding with Moscow, but in vain. Thus the Second and Third Internationals exist simultaneously and in most emphatic hostility to each other.

Two terms used in connection with economic thought require definition, "orthodox" and "scientific." Orthodox, as originally used in connection with religious thought, implied correspondence in dogma and doctrine with that body or party which had succeeded in getting possession of authority or at least the approval and backing of authority. In economics, the connotation is analogous. An orthodox economy is one which is not negative in relation to the dogmas or doctrines of the economic system as it is, or to the measures of law and policy by which governments support it. The parallel is somewhat confusing because in religious history, the concept of orthodoxy is a comparatively late phenomenon (e.g., in the case of Christianity, practically beginning only with the Council of Nicæa in 325 A.D.), whereas, in the history of economic thought, in modern Europe, orthodoxy is early. Adam Smith, Ricardo, Jevons, Marshall are orthodox. The socialists, of course, are not orthodox. We can scarcely call them heretics or heterodox, because those words were not used. The ethical critics were also not orthodox because they denied the *ends* of the existing system. The historical school as such had no quarrel with the orthodox economists as to the ends, but only as to method, and especially on account of their linkage with socialist thought are generally not classed with the orthodox.

"Scientific" is more difficult to define. It does not mean "correct" or even "correct as far as it goes." Nor does it refer clearly to method. The prevalence of inductive methods in the natural sciences led to a decided movement to promote similar methods in economics. Nevertheless, like physics, economics has advanced principally by deduction from a small series of rather simple assumptions. Most of the inductive work, that is, historical and statistical, has resulted either in no formulated conclusions or else in an ethically or politically motivated conclusion, that is to say, in something that is not purely objective and therefore within the limits of the concept "scientific." Actually, economic theorizing is much closer even than modern scholasticism to the medieval scholasticism of Anselm, Aquinas, and Duns Scotus, closer than almost any other intellectual activity in the modern world. In comparison with the natural sciences, the practical applications of "scientific" economics have been relatively few and incidental. The division of labor, the organization of money systems, the (war-time) control of prices, the regulation of international trade, have all in various countries at various times been variously affected, most often advantageously, by the intervention of economists. These interventions, however, are of the order of technique rather than of theory, of economics as an art rather than as a science.

In the general problem of understanding our society as a whole, the development of economics has been radically stimulating. The most unorthodox, the most unscientific, the most institutional of social students derive historically and intellectually (by affirmation or negation) from this vast direct effort to solve the problem of man's effort to get what he wants and why he fails.

REFERENCES FOR FURTHER READING

General

Gide, C., and Rist, C. History of Economic Doctrines from the Time of the Physiocrats to the Present Day (1915).

Boucke, O. F. The Development of Economics (1921).

Haney, L. H. History of Economic Thought (1911).

Encyclopædia of the Social Sciences. Article "Economics," by several authors.

Birnie, Arthur. An Economic History of Europe (1930), chap. VII, "Socialism and the Social Problem."

Knight, M. M., Barnes, H. E., and Fluegel, F. Economic History of Europe in Modern Times (1928), pp. 410–433.

Economics as a Science

Böhm-Bawerk, E. von. Capital and Interest: A Critical History of Economic Theory (Eng. tr., 1890).

Keynes, J. N. The Scope and Method of Political Economy (1890).

Marriott, J. A. R. Economics and Ethics (1923).

Patten, S. N. The Premises of Political Economy (1885).

Tugwell, R. G., ed. The Trend of Economics (1924).

Young, A. A. "Some Limitations of the Value Concept," Quarterly Journal of Economics, 25:409–428 (1911).

Socialism

Böhm-Bawerk, E. von. Karl Marx and the Close of His System (Eng. tr., 1898).

Carpenter, Niles. Guild Socialism (1922).
Cole, G. D. H. Guild Socialism (1920).
Laidler, H. W. A History of Socialist Thought (1927).
Loria, Achille. Karl Marx (Eng. tr., 1920).
Nicholson, J. S. The Revival of Marxism (1920).
Ruehle, O. Karl Marx (1929).
Seligman, E. R. A. The Economic Interpretation of History (1902).
Skelton, O. D. Socialism: A Critical Analysis (1911).

CHAPTER IX

THE VARIANT FORMS OF ECONOMIC LIFE

The Persistence of Uncapitalistic Forms of Economic Life

To what degree has capitalism fallen short of becoming the exclusive form of economic life, of engrossing not only all the economically active persons but also all their economic activities? To one living in the most capitalistic of all areas, the United States, from one point of view, at least, it would seem that the answer is substantially negative. All men everywhere seem to be bound in to the will of men everywhere else through the nexus of the market; South Sea islanders drying copra destined to serve the toilet uses of Europeans as soap; trappers in the Siberian and Canadian wilds prospering or the opposite according to the fluctuations of fashion; American farmers depending upon the price of wheat on the Liverpool grain exchange. From that point of view, indeed, either as victims or as beneficiaries, all the world is involved in the conveniences and complications of capitalism.

From another point of view, capitalism is hardly even predominant as a form of economic life. Excluding the small farmers, the small tradesmen, the employees of the states, such as railroad and postal employees, as not exactly either managers or employees of capitalistic enterprises, Sombart concluded that in the United States about 38 per cent, in Europe outside Russia 25 to 33 per cent, in Russia, about 10 per cent represent the share of capitalism in the whole economic life before 1914. This point of view is most tenable if for capitalism as a category we substitute "high capitalism." Certainly, it is easy to recognize that the small merchant or manufacturer who works with the few men he employs, and the farmer who tills his soil with only occasional employed assistance, are noncapitalistic in a degree that sets them off in decided contrast to the entrepreneur whose relationship to his concern is entirely and exclusively management, and, on the other hand, to the worker (proletarian) whose only relationship to the concern is the wage relation.

With this distinction in mind, an examination of the German statistics (which alone make the convenient distinctions) shows that even in that highly capitalistic land, 94.2 per cent of the establishments and 66.1 per cent of the persons employed in commerce still retained a "handicraft" character, the employer still was not completely differentiated from his employees, but worked with them. Although the railroads, telegraphs, sea transportation, etc., exist only as concerns of the largest class, in the transportation of persons and in river and canal transportation the small enterprise retained a similar preponderance. In industry (inclusive of mining and building) the preponderance had passed to the great enterprise, but even here the smallest establishments (one to five persons) included nearly 30 per cent of all employed. In localized occupations, such as personal services (barbers, etc.) and repair shops, the small establishment retained an overwhelming predominance. On the whole, at the end of the high capitalistic period, in one of the most capitalistic countries, nearly half the economically active persons aside from the agricultural population were still employed in a quasi-handicraft fashion. The actual "hand worker," however, has largely thrown off his limitation to his own products; he sells ready-made products of all sorts connected with his own; and he has modernized himself by introducing various technical devices (see any shoe repair shop in any American town) and rationalizing devices like bookkeeping. His predecessor of one hundred fifty years ago would not be at home in his shop today.

Agriculture, of course, has remained almost wholly small enterprise, to a large degree noncapitalistic in character. Aside from the uncivilized tribes, there are from seven hundred fifty million to nine hundred million individuals (including the families of owners, tenants, and workers) occupied with agriculture in one way or another. The East, including Russia, has about three-fourths of the total number, Europe about one hundred fifty million, and the "West," America and Australia, the rest.

Although the farmer everywhere persists strongly in his own standards of economic life, there is a wide diversity from area to area. The American farmer and the Egyptian fellah, the French *fermier* and the Russian muzhik show little of that uniformity that is so noticeable among more highly "capitalized" elements of the race. They differ widely in economic orientation, from pure need-satisfying to the highest economic rationalism, from pure communism (in the literal sense of that word) to a hard individualism. In the most modernized areas, Denmark, the United States, Australia, the farmer has taken on almost all the characters of the capitalistic spirit. In Russia, certainly up to the Revolution of 1917, and in a sense even up to the present, he has remained peasant. In social position, the agricultural populations vary from half-serfdom to full freedom. Their technique varies through the widest ranges of degree and through great diversities even within the same degree of advancement.

While agricultural workers also vary widely in their standards of economic life, everywhere in a century of great advance in almost every other field, the agricultural life of every culture area has remained comparatively depressed.

In Western and Central Europe, the dissolution of the old agrarian economy, combined with the inadequate credit systems and the decline of the real prices of agricultural products since 1870, gave agriculture a depressed aspect which dozens of remedial laws in various countries have not been sufficient to remedy.

In Prussia, Stein undertook in 1807 the elimination of the peculiarly oppressive system of serfdom which had been established after the Reformation; but the strong influence of the great landlords of East Prussia compromised and delayed the reform and made it burdensome to the peasants. A law of 1811 established two classes of peasants—those who had and those who had not heritable rights in their land; of these, the first had to cede one-third, the latter, one-half of their holdings to the landlord in order to secure title to the remainder, while a still larger class did not receive any benefits under the law and had to remain in a legally dependent position until 1850. In more advanced parts of Germany, the servile status had never been established, as in the northwest, or had disappeared in fact before it was abolished by law, as in Bavaria (1808). The usurious rates of interest charged by the prevalent money lender seem to have been especially burdensome to the German peasants until the imperial usury law of 1850.

In France, the Revolution had destroyed the vestiges of dependent tenure that had remained down to that time, but the essential structure of French agriculture was left substantially unchanged. While the Napoleonic Wars gave a temporary stimulus to production and even to new technique (sugar beets, potatoes), the infinite division of tenures which the Napoleonic Code encouraged prevented the successful application of capital, especially in the form of machines, so that the French peasant got and continues to get a small return in proportion to the effort he expends. Nevertheless, from the national point of view, French agriculture is almost unique in Western Europe in that it has been able to maintain an export balance.

In England, the decline of the old agricultural system has already been sufficiently noted. The growth of the population around 1800 and thereafter supplied a rapidly widening market for the farmer, while the Napoleonic Wars intensified this effect. The end of the wars, however, the increasing political strength of the industrial elements, which were able to bring about the repeal of the Corn Laws, the growing absorption of capital in industry, and the competition of the colonial lands after 1870, which resulted in steadily declining prices, combined to depress the farming industry steadily through the century.

In the lands of Eastern culture dire poverty was the normal lot of the agricultural producer. In Russia, a very low technique led to a very low productivity, and the czarist state took an extraordinarily large share in taxes, while, nevertheless, prices remained very low. The cheaper grain was, the more the peasant was compelled to sell, so that famine scourged the land from which much of the cheap grain of Western Europe came. In British India, the average income was reckoned at about $15.00 per capita, the agricultural land at 1.28 acres in 1901–1902, at .9 acre in 1917–1918. In Java, the steady increase in population from 19,800,000 in 1880 to 28,800,000 in 1900 was accompanied by a decline of about one-quarter in the supply of rice per family.

In the "colonial West," the story is the same, with, it must be remembered, different standards of misery. In the South of the United States, "the Negroes skin the land and the stock, the whites skin the Negroes, but the merchants skin both the whites and the blacks." After the abolition of slavery, the share system was established, the owner advancing the use of the ground, the cabin, the live stock, the implements and half the seed against half the crop. For the other half, the share farmer got credit with the "storekeeper" for what he needed, at rather high prices. The result was that the Negro was habitually in debt. The owner used the same vicious credit system and fell into the same chronic state of debt. Among the wheat growers of the Mississippi valley and Canada, the burden of debt which the farmers carried was high (50.2 per cent in North Dakota, 51.2 per cent in Iowa in 1910), but much of their difficulties seem to have come from the extraordinarily high profits of middlemen: of the consumer's dollar spent in Chicago for potatoes from Minnesota, only 20.6 cents went to the farmer.

Underlying the world-wide depression of the farmer seems to be some lack of adjustment to capitalism. While he is involved with its technical developments and market systems, the mechanism of world price determination is so directed that his increased productivity has resulted in the advantage of the industrial and trading groups of the population rather than his own. Like other capitalistic groups, he has become dependent on credit and, on account of his relatively slow turnover and the slow responsiveness of his markets, has perhaps suffered more than other groups from the fluctuating values of money. Combining in himself the elsewhere separated functions of capitalist, entrepreneur, and laborer, he has been liable to the misfortunes of each.

Cooperation

Cooperation is a large and growing variation from the nineteenth century organization of capitalism. In the abstract economic sense, it is indistinguishable from the process described in a preceding chapter as "concentration." That is to say, a cooperative is essentially an organization of individuals combining their purchasing power or their selling power in order to buy more cheaply or to sell more dearly than they otherwise could. The distinction between cooperation and concentration, as that term was used in the preceding chapter, is rather sociological than purely economic. As it is used here and generally, it applies to combinations of persons, as distinguished from combinations of capital, and of persons who are in a passive relation rather than an active one, consumers in the broadest possible sense of the word rather than producers or sellers. The users of credit, of middlemen's services (as buyers or sellers), of warehouses and machinery combine to secure them on more favorable terms than they could as individuals.

Three principal forms of cooperation developed before 1914: the credit association, the production (and selling) cooperative, and the consumer's (in the more limited sense of the word) cooperative.

The credit association developed largely in Germany. Friedrich Raiffeisen started the movement in 1864 as a way of escape from the oppressive usurer, so prominent in the German agricultural situation. Since that time, the Raiffeisen banks have grown very large: in 1913, their loans (including the Haas-Darmstadt associations) exceeded 2,500,000,000 marks. They were founded on the principle of the unlimited liability of the members, severally and collectively, for each of the loans made, and are limited to the field of agricultural credit. The Schulze-Delitzsch banks applied the same methods to the towns and later also became somewhat active in the field of agricultural credit. The credit associations have received substantial assistance from the State Central Cooperative Societies in Prussia and several other German states, which extend credit to the general associations rather than to the local societies. From Germany, the credit associations spread over most of Western Europe. In England, where cooperative stores have been so successful, they have been difficult to maintain. In France, the credit cooperative developed first as a function of the *syndicats agricoles* (producers' associations) but the *caisses Durands* exist solely for the purpose of supplying agricultural credit. The French government also supplies financial support to the associations. In the Balkans, especially in Bulgaria and Serbia, the cooperative credit societies (along with other forms of cooperation) have appeared rather as a mode of transition from the primitive Slavic commune with its kinship ties, than as a defense against the machinery of capitalism. It was estimated in 1896 that $750,000,000 was "well within" the total amount lent through money cooperatives on the continent of Europe, and eight years later that the amount was about $1,250,000,000.

A form of cooperative credit association which has developed very extensively in England and in the United States is the building and loan association. From its beginnings in Scotland in 1815, it was developed with some difficulty in England on account of the withholding of legal recognition until the first Benefit Building Societies Act of 1836 and even until the second Act of 1874. Meanwhile, the idea was reproduced in a half-derivative way by English manufacturers who had migrated to Frankfort, then a suburb of Philadelphia, where in 1831 the Oxford Provident Association was founded. Adequate statistics are lacking until 1893, when the membership of such associations was between 1,500,000 and 1,800,000 and the assets were about $550,000,000. At these figures they remained until about 1905; the assets began to rise then and the membership shortly after. In 1913, the membership had risen to about 2,000,000, and the assets had approximately doubled. In England, the associations have grown so popular that they find difficulty in lending out the capital which they attract.

The building and loan association differs from the continental credit association, first, in that its members themselves furnish the money to be loaned by paying monthly dues instead of seeking outside money (although some building and loan associations do supplement their own funds by borrowing from trust companies). In the second place, it is more strictly confined than any of the credit associations to one type of property, improved urban real estate, as security for loans. The residence sections of some cities, notably Philadelphia, Minneapolis, and St. Paul, are said to have been almost entirely built with building and loan association money. On the whole, the building and loan associations have lost the philanthopic and even semireligious character that other cooperative schemes retain, and they offer an interesting study of the dividing line, if there is any, between cooperation and capitalism. The performance of the same functions by specialized banks has limited the development of the building and loan association on the Continent. In France, for example, the Crédit Foncier has arrangements for the repayment of mortagages in monthly installments according to definite plans without a cooperative feature.

Consumer cooperatives have spread over the whole earth. They are most highly developed in Great Britain, where the first one was founded in 1828 by Robert Owen. In 1844, Owen's first society succeeded in establishing a small shop, open two days a week, the weekly sales of which amounted to $10.00. In 1914, the number of "co-ops" had risen to 1,390, the number of members to more than three million, the yearly sales to about $440,-000,000, in addition to the wholesale cooperatives with sales of about $221,500,000. The retail cooperatives owned factories with a yearly production of about $145,000,000. In France, Germany, Switzerland, and elsewhere, very important cooperative distributive movements developed which looked to the English movement as their prototype. In the United States, there have been continual but not very successful attempts to spread this type of cooperation.

The outstanding development of the producers' and sellers' cooperative appeared in the agricultural life of Denmark. Like the rest of the Western European farmers, the Danish peasant had gone through the cooperative conduct of agriculture itself in the form of the medieval manorial system, and when, like the rest, he had won his freedom from that system in the early nineteenth century, he clung to his individuality as a producer. Neither in Denmark nor anywhere else in Europe, is agricultural cooperation in any sense cooperative agriculture. It is rather cooperative manufacture and sale, cooperative purchase of materials and tools, cooperative insurance and standardizing. It is a comparatively new movement which has spread with amazing rapidity. In 1882, the first Danish cooperative dairy was started; in 1892, there were a thousand such dairies, and before the World War, they were handling four-fifths of all the milk produced. The first cooperative bacon-curing plant was started in 1887; by 1894, there were twenty, handling half the production of the country. The cooperative collection, grading, and exporting of eggs began in 1895; by 1903, 65,000 farmers were thus organized. In 1921, "250,000 farmers, 40 per cent of the population, were organized into 4,000 cooperative agencies which ramified into every activity. An average farmer belongs to about ten. The Danish farmers perform for themselves almost all the functions that in other countries are performed by capitalistic agencies."

Cooperation has developed in Italy in more varied form than in any other country in the world. There is scarcely a branch of human activity which is not represented in one or another of the one hundred and one different types of cooperative societies that are to be found in Italy. A particularly interesting form of production cooperation is the *società de lavoro* (Labor Association), which deals not at all in materials or credit, but only in labor. It is found among all sorts of laborers, navvies, builders, masons, carriers, stevedores, agricultural laborers. One società will build you a steamship, another will see to the carving of the head of your cane; one drained large areas of the Campagna, another built a railroad in Greece.

In France, the *syndicats agricoles* furnish their members with expert services and buy for them, but are legally disqualified from selling for them except through separate societies specially registered for the purpose. Cooperative butter factories, distilleries, threshing associations, societies for wine making, oil pressing, etc., run into the hundreds.

In Germany, this type of cooperation developed largely in connection with the Raiffeisen banks. In the United States, except for the citrus fruit growers of California, it is a postwar development. In the south and east of Europe, the cooperative movement was complicated by the injection of racial, religious, and political considerations.

The significance of cooperation with reference to capitalism is at the same time conservative and revolutionary. On the one hand, it is an adjustment by which the farmer, the craftsman, and the consumer can make themselves comfortable in a capitalistic world; on the other hand, especially in the form of the consumer cooperatives which undertake to produce their own consumption goods, it constitutes an actually existing way of transforming capitalism into something quite different.

Quantitatively, of course, cooperation includes only a small fraction of the whole economic life. Nevertheless, in certain areas and in certain fields, it has attained major importance. The German credit associations in 1910 held from one-ninth to one-eighth as much "outside" money as the German credit banks. The ascendancy of the agricultural production cooperatives in Denmark has already been indicated. Consumer cooperatives in England do about seven per cent of the total retail business; in Germany, between three and four per cent.

On the whole, the potential significance of cooperation is great, although up to the present it can be said only to have attained a distinct place alongside other economic forms.

Public Ownership

The student will recall that in the beginnings and early history of capitalism, the state, the king, the lords played a major part in the development of capitalistic enterprise. This part was very greatly reduced by a revolution that no one has yet effectively named, but which may tentatively be called the individualistic revolution. The great exponents of its fundamental ideas were Adam Smith and John Stuart Mill. Its events were the successive elimination during the eighteenth and early nineteenth century of the whole system of social and legal regulation which we know generally as mercantilism. Its mottoes were *laisser faire,* "liberty." Its general result was the development of capitalistic enterprise almost entirely by individuals with a minimum of social considerations.

This period, however, was comparatively short. From the fourth decade of the nineteenth century, the states and communities of Western Europe and the Europeanized areas have at an increasing rate intervened in economic life. This intervention has taken several different forms: (1) the regulation of private enterprise through labor laws, social insurance laws, and discriminating taxation; (2) the establishment of enterprises directed and carried on by the states, or by specially organized public bodies; (3) the participation of the state, municipality, or special organ in private capitalistic enterprises; and (4) the exercise of control by agencies *ad hoc,* such as the American Interstate Commerce Commission.

The history of legal regulation of labor relations and of social insurance is too long to be recounted here in any but the briefest summary.[1] In England, after a series of ineffective attempts, industrial regulation was effectively begun by the Factory Act of 1833, which prohibited the employment of children under nine years of age and regulated the employment of others up to eighteen years. From this beginning, as the consequences of unlimited capitalistic activity for the human element became apparent, a vast series of labor protection and social insurance measures were taken by the various European governments as their areas successively became capitalistic. Disregarding the intervening steps of this development, we may briefly indicate its results by a summary list of the typical measures as they had developed before 1914. In England, the Act of 1901 prohibited the employment of children under twelve, and controlled not only the total number of hours, but the distribution of the hours of employment of older children through the day and week. Other measures forbade the employment of women and girls in mines and applied general regulations similar to the factory regulations to the mines. An Act of 1908 stipulated that no workman, adult or otherwise, should be required to work underground more than eight hours in any consecutive twenty-four. The Trade Boards Act of 1909 regulated the conditions of labor in domestic industry, even establishing machinery for the determination of wages. In France and Germany, similar and even higher standards of labor legislation were attained.

In social insurance, the German Empire under Bismarck set the

[1] An excellent account is to be found in Ogg and Sharp, *Economic Development of Modern Europe,* part IV, pp. 355–615.

standard which the other nations of Europe have emulated. By 1914, social insurance systems, more or less elaborate, had been established in Great Britain, France, Holland, Belgium, Denmark, Norway, Sweden, Italy, Switzerland, and Austria. Even in Russia and the Balkan States, such systems had been at least begun. The typical system included various kinds of compulsory insurance to the cost of which the worker, the employer, and the state contributed; compensation for accidents, old-age pensions, sickness insurance, unemployment insurance are only the main features of the whole system as it has developed in most European societies.

The ownership and direction of enterprises by the community as state, municipality, or special organ seems, from the protest against it, to be a more fundamental criticism of the capitalistic system. "Keep the government out of business," is a slogan familiar to American ears. The vigorous propaganda against the retention of the American railroads by the government after the World War, the resistance to government operation of the Muscle Shoals and the proposed Boulder Dam, the widespread disparagement by the public utility interests of the Ontario power and light system, all point to the same conclusion, that public ownership is regarded as a serious threat to capitalistic institutions. It may well be doubted whether this is correct, or, at any rate, whether in principle or in possibilities, public ownership of public utilities is so significant of radical change in the character of economic society as the cooperative idea.

What does government ownership amount to? In every country, in 1914, the postal system was a monopoly of government; in most countries, so also were the telegraph and telephone systems; in many, the railroads. Roads and bridges, schools, libraries, museums represent a class of government properties that can hardly be called enterprises since they generally return no revenue. In addition to these usual state enterprises, Denmark had 73 others in 1911, employing 7,411 people, and the Danish towns had

126 employing 2,274. In Germany, 1,558,315 persons were employed in the public establishments, or about one-twentieth of all gainfully employed. Several states operated monopolies for profit—the match, tobacco, and powder monopolies in France; the alcohol monopoly in Switzerland; the tobacco and salt monopolies in Austria. Municipalities nearly always operated water supply systems, frequently gas and electric plants, and even undertaking establishments. Some German towns had such extensive enterprises that they were able to dispense with taxation; one was so fortunate as to be able to pay its burghers $75.00 a year as well as to supply them with wood. The United States and New Zealand have conducted great land-selling operations and forest enterprises. Prussia, Holland, Victoria (Australia), New Zealand, North Dakota, and the town of Lethbridge (Alberta) own and operate coal mines. Cincinnati, Ohio, and the State of Georgia own railroads which are important sources of revenue.

Various merits and demerits are aggressively attributed to public ownership by advocates and opponents, respectively, but the question seems to be so controversial as to make it impossible to assign to the system of government ownership any clear general significance. Each case seems to be an individual case.

A variant of public ownership is the participation of states and other public bodies in the control of private concerns. In some cases, the public body only retains a right to participate in the control without furnishing any of the capital, a form frequently used in the case of the great issue banks, notably the Deutsche Bank. In others, part of the capital is contributed by public bodies and the rest by private capitalists. This method is much used in the German and in the American public utility systems. A third form, the participation of public bodies and consumers in the direction along with the furnishers of capital, was not much used before the World War, but has since developed extensively in the milk supply business of the large cities (Mannheim, Germany, and Philadelphia).

Conclusion

Such, in broad outline, has been the evolution of the economic constitution of modern Europe. Along with the other phases of European society, it grew from small beginnings to a gigantic system which enfolds the whole world in its ramifications. Its transcendence over the mere will of individual man is such as to make supererogatory the consideration whether it is curse or blessing, the best or worst of possible systems: it IS.

Capitalism has become mature. No longer must it meet the challenge of older institutions; no longer are its standards and its devices, its ends or its means, subject to the disparagement of comparison with the past. It is challenged only by the future. Once one of the great radicalisms, it has become the great conservatism.

It is mature but still prolific. It is still capable of creating out of itself new forms of action, new organs, new combinations: witness the new international bank of the Young Committee. It contains within itself the germs of new economies that will supplant it. Modern socialism, government ownership, cooperation are conceivable only as variations and criticisms of capitalism.

Part of its strength is its capacity for self-criticism. Since the day of Babeuf, it has been producing Saint-Simons, Louis Blancs, Karl Marxes, Hobsons, Veblens, Rathenaus, Tawneys—prophets to point out dangers and the way of escape. Its devotion to technique extends to the technique of its own existence. Technique tided it over the great crisis of the early nineteenth century; technique will facilitate its adjustment to a secondary place in the scheme of things when its greater destiny is fulfilled.

Men propose to do away with it by revolutionary, catastrophic process. The end of its dominance will more probably come as a gradual, evolutionary process. That is to say, its displacement will be one of the great historic transformations that no man can hasten or delay by taking thought. The exhaustion of the mineral sources of power and material that it has so brilliantly used may mean sometime the transfer of the economic centers of gravity to the sun lands and to the colored races that hold them, or to their successors. At any rate, this economy, like the whole culture of which it is a part, like all previous economies and cultures, must face in the long run the destiny of all mortal things.

REFERENCES FOR FURTHER READING

General

Sombart, W. Der moderne Kapitalismus, vol. III, pp. 950–1000.

Cooperation

Blanc, E. T. Cooperative Movement in Russia (1924).
Cassau, T. O. Consumers' Cooperative Movement in Germany (1925).
Fay, C. R. Cooperation at Home and Abroad (3rd. ed., 1925).
Gide, Charles. Consumers' Cooperative Societies (1922).
Lloyd, E. A. Cooperative Movement in Italy (1926).
Lloyd, H. D. Labour Co-partnership (1898).
Schloss, D. F. Methods of Industrial Remuneration (2nd ed., 1894).
Webb, Sidney, and Webb, Beatrice. The Consumers' Cooperative Movement (1921).
Williams, Aneurin. Twenty-eight Years of Co-partnership at Guise (1908).
Howe, F. C. Denmark: A Cooperative Commonwealth (1921).

Public Ownership

Guizot, Ives. Where and Why Public Ownership Has Failed (Eng. tr., 1914).
Thompson, Carl D. Public Ownership (1925).
Howe, F. C. Socialized Germany.
The Modern City and Its Problems (1915).
Walling, W. E., and Laidler, H. W. State Socialism Pro and Con (1917).
Money, L. C. (Sir). The Triumph of Nationalism.

INDEX

INDEX

F

J

N

T

U

Z

www.ingramcontent.com/pod-product-compliance
Lightning Source LLC
LaVergne TN
LVHW090256210926
848480LV00001B/42
9781587981128